An Anthology of Medieval Love Debate Poetry

Florida A&M University, Tallahassee
Florida Atlantic University, Boca Raton
Florida Gulf Coast University, Ft. Myers
Florida International University, Miami
Florida State University, Tallahassee
New College of Florida, Sarasota
University of Central Florida, Orlando
University of Florida, Gainesville
University of North Florida, Jacksonville
University of South Florida, Tampa
University of West Florida, Pensacola

An Anthology of
Medieval Love Debate Poetry

Translated and Edited
by Barbara K. Altmann and R. Barton Palmer

University Press of Florida
Gainesville · Tallahassee · Tampa · Boca Raton
Pensacola · Orlando · Miami · Jacksonville · Ft. Myers · Sarasota

Copyright 2006 by Barbara K. Altmann and R. Barton Palmer
Printed in the United States of America on acid-free paper
All rights reserved

First cloth printing, 2006
First paperback printing, 2010

A record of cataloging-in-publication data is available
from the Library of Congress.

ISBN 978-0-8130-2907-8 (cloth)
ISBN 978-0-8130-3569-7 (paper)

The University Press of Florida is the scholarly publishing agency
for the State University System of Florida, comprising Florida A&M
University, Florida Atlantic University, Florida Gulf Coast University,
Florida International University, Florida State University, New College of
Florida, University of Central Florida, University of Florida, University of
North Florida, University of South Florida, and University of West Florida.

University Press of Florida
15 Northwest 15th Street
Gainesville, FL 32611-2079
http://www.upf.com

To Maram, long-time partner in love debate.

For Tonya, who is blessed with strong opinions and loves a good argument.

Contents

Acknowledgments ix
Preface xi
The Tradition of Love Debate Poetry: An Introduction 1

Guillaume de Machaut 11

Le Jugement dou roy de Behaingne
(*The Judgment of the King of Bohemia*) 21

Le Jugement dou roy de Navarre
(*The Judgment of the King of Navarre*) 69

Geoffrey Chaucer 177

The Legend of Good Women 183

Christine de Pizan 251

Le Debat de deux amans (*The Debate of Two Lovers*) 257

Alain Chartier 307

Le Livre des quatre dames (*The Book of the Four Ladies*) 312

Bibliography 395

Acknowledgments

I would like to recognize research support from the Camargo Foundation, where my translations were begun, and from the Oregon Humanities Center, where they were revised. This project is the brainchild of R. Barton Palmer, to whom I am truly grateful for his generosity and infinite patience. My deep appreciation to James Laidlaw for his authoritative edition of Alain Chartier's text, but also for his gracious, unstinting, invaluable help with its translation. It goes without saying that all remaining infelicities are my own, but he saved me from many more. And last, my thanks to Bill Calin and Wendy Pfeffer, who offered much help with the design and arrangement of this book. An anonymous reader for the University Press of Florida also made many important suggestions for improvement. And last, my thanks to an extraordinary copy editor, Ann Marlowe, who not only carefully reviewed the manuscript, but whose comments, queries, and deep learning made this a much stronger book.
Barbara K. Altmann

The Calhoun Lemon family has earned my deep and abiding thanks for their generous support, through a research endowment, of all my scholarly endeavors, especially this one. Like Barbara, I am very grateful to the various scholars and editors who helped with this ambitious project, saving us from both error and infelicity. Barbara, though this project was my idea, it would never have seen the light of day without your energy, intelligence, and learning. I agree that working on these delightful texts from a bygone era was stimulating and enjoyable. A lasting debt of gratitude is owed to my wife, Carla, and son, Camden, who have cheerfully (well, mostly cheerfully) tolerated my preoccupation with poetry written more than six centuries ago.
R. Barton Palmer

Preface

With this anthology of debate poems in translation, we hope to address more than one audience. The texts and explanatory material should meet the needs of undergraduate and graduate students of medieval literature and culture, but we have also envisioned as readers specialists in the literature of the late Middle Ages who wish to broaden their knowledge of a tradition that is emblematic of the period in many ways and that took shape in several languages and countries. The love debate poem is a genre, or subgenre perhaps, that has not yet received the attention it deserves. We hope that this collection will provide the interested reader with some understanding and appreciation of its subject matter, poetic structures, and literary interconnections.

The general introduction is aimed at all readers who may be coming to this material for the first time. Here we discuss the development of the genre and its place in the larger field of courtly love literature. Each poem is preceded by a headnote that provides information about the author, the historical moment of the work's composition, and its most important themes.

By choosing for inclusion works in both French and English, we hope to make the point that the late-medieval authors represented here were not addressing only their own countrymen. Even though France and England were engaged in that intermittent but bloody struggle known to modern scholars as the Hundred Years' War, the writers of the two countries shared an intellectual and literary culture. Students of Chaucer and of Middle French will find conveniently collected for them here a number of key works that link vernacular literary production on both sides of the Channel.

We have couched our translations of the French poems in a free-verse, line-for-line rendering rather than attempting to reproduce the rhyme and syllable count of the original medieval language. Because Chaucer's English is more readily adapted into modern English, we have been able to keep fairly strictly to his ten-syllable metrical scheme, though we have not attempted to imitate his rhyming couplets. Readers who consult the original texts will find that we have sometimes rearranged words and phrases for the sake of readability. In our choice of vocabulary, we have endeavored first and foremost to respect the tone and texture of the originals. We felt it was crucial, for example, to distinguish the narrative passages, which are written in a relatively easy, free-flowing style, from the denser rhetoric of the heightened, lyrical passages that express the intense emotion of the first-person speakers. As much as possible, we have tried to preserve the figures of speech as well as the wordplays, repetitions, and puns that are the stock-in-trade of the successful medieval poet. Needless to say, much is lost despite our best efforts. What we hope to have achieved is accurate, reasonably polished versions that render most of the literal sense and some of the beauty and finesse of the original. We encourage interested readers to discover these poems as they were first written six and seven hundred years ago. If our translations can provide a starting point for further study and appreciation of an important and entertaining medieval genre, they will have served their purpose.

The Tradition of Love Debate Poetry

An Introduction

At the end of the Middle Ages the love debate, a literary genre devoted to the examination of questions of love and gender, rose to cultural prominence and then flourished for more than a hundred and fifty years. What became its standard form took shape toward the middle of the fourteenth century in the hands of the French poet Guillaume de Machaut. The model he set stages a debate argued by two or more characters, each of whom speaks to a particular side of an issue concerning love. The discussion often takes place in the presence of a narrator figure in charge of recording the argument for a patron who will decide the matter. The whole case is written up as poetry, providing plenty of scope for lyrical expression of the joy and pain brought on by strong emotion. In the hands of the best poets, language and erudition are on display as much as sentiment. Once Machaut pioneered it, the genre immediately proved popular with aristocratic readers and was taken up by some of the other great English and French poets of the age, who produced love debates of great charm and sophistication that are among the finest literary achievements of the period. These works deserve a wider audience. To date, few have been translated, and they have thus been unavailable to the nonspecialist reader.

The present volume is the first to include, complete and in new modern English translations, five of the acknowledged masterpieces of the love debate tradition: Guillaume de Machaut's *Jugement dou roy de Behaingne* (*Judgment of the King of Bohemia*) and its sequel the *Jugement dou roy de Navarre* (*Judgment of the King of Navarre*); Geoffrey Chaucer's *Legend of Good Women*; Christine de Pizan's *Debat de deux amans* (*Debate of Two Lovers*); and Alain Chartier's *Debat des quatre dames* (*Debate of the Four Ladies*). The reader will find that each selection is preceded by headnotes that set out the relevant facts of literary history, including author biographies, and offer brief discussion of important themes and literary motifs. Endnotes after each selection explain allusions to events, people, or other literary works that might not be familiar to a modern audience. This general introduction will avoid, for the most part, any commentary on the individual works. Instead, it offers some remarks about the larger intellectual and literary traditions in which the genre participates in order to trace its literary pedigree and outline the thematic preoccupations that place it at the heart of medieval sensibilities.

What makes these works entertaining and instructive for the modern reader? The answer lies in the range of issues, amatory as well as literary, that are debated in them. These issues of the heart and of literary etiquette have by no means lost their relevance. For example, who suffers more, a man whose beloved has spurned him in favor of another, or a woman whose lover has been killed? The woman can no longer look upon the face of her dead lover, but the man can still see his lady. And yet when he sees her he is reminded of her betrayal and his loss. Is he therefore worse off than the bereaved woman? Is it true that men love with more intensity and faithfulness than women, who, it is conventionally alleged, forget absent lovers easily and soon form new attachments? What about the male poet who writes of such matters? Despite his declaration that he is devoted to the gentler sex, does he actually prove himself a misogynist when he decides that the man hopelessly bound to a faithless woman suffers more than his female counterpart? If the poet is a misogynist, is there any hope for his eventual reformation? Can he be converted to a proper respect for those he should loyally serve by requiring him to produce a series of tales that testify to the superior virtues of women in love?

There is an even more basic question that demands consideration: How are we to understand what we call love in the first place? Older and more experienced men may view such emotional experience more cynically than their youthful and naive counterparts, but which group defends the more realistic view? No matter how we answer this one question, others immediately arise. If, for example, we subscribe to the female opinion that love may be nothing more than a self-fulfilling and self-deceiving male fantasy, does that mean that such idealized emotion is only so much misplaced energy? If men are presumed inferior to women in their ability to recognize the limitations and disadvantages of love, then what sort of man is rightly judged the best? And what about the unfortunate woman in love with a man who proves a coward on the battlefield and thus a traitor to the chivalric values that should govern his behavior? How is she to view her disappointment in love? By what criteria can we evaluate the different degrees of despair and sorrow to which women fall victim when their lovers are separated from them through the various workings of misfortune? Which sad ending to a relationship is, in fact, the saddest?

These are some of the questions about romance and the range of experiences of men and women in love that are raised in the works anthologized in this volume. These love debates explore the nature and dubious value of gender stereotypes, including the arguably greater perspicacity of women in affairs of the heart, as well as the responsibilities poets bear toward both the women they are meant to praise and the readers they are meant to amuse. With insight and sophistication, they analyze the nature of the romantic experience itself, especially its complex mixture of sexual and psychological yearnings. Not surprisingly, those yearnings prove to be of ambiguous moral value, and they affect men and women in both similar and strikingly different ways. The works collected here treat men and women as quite distinct in nature and depict their mutual attraction with both humor and seriousness, exposing the foibles of the two sexes but also praising their virtues. Written primarily by court poets dependent on the patronage of the nobility, the love debate was meant primarily to entertain, but the better works in the genre also prove enlightening about the human comedy.

Of course, love between the sexes is the predominant subject of medieval secular literature, finding expression in a range of literary genres from brief lyric poems to lengthy romances. The love debate that flourished in the fourteenth and fifteenth centuries drew on a number of other literary forms. We will consider briefly here some of those genres and a few particular examples, presented more or less in chronological order, as a way of tracing the formative influences on the poems in this volume.

Reaching back to the late twelfth and early thirteenth centuries, extended poetic debate on the topic of love existed already in what were called "débats du clerc et du chevalier" (debates of the cleric and the knight) or "jugements d'amour" (judgments about love). We have as examples of this genre half a dozen works, some in Latin and some in Old French, that stage a discussion in which ladies weigh the relative merits of clerics and knights as lovers. From these works the later Middle Ages retained, among other elements, the description of the God of Love and his attendants. One of the most compelling and elaborate is the *Concile de Remiremont*, to which we will return below. A second debate form we can consider a forerunner of the works in this anthology is the "jeu-parti," a shorter and somewhat later form composed in the thirteenth century and associated with the city of Arras. In the two hundred or so preserved examples of this type of poem, two speakers debate in alternating stanzas a predicament concerning love and end by each calling on a judge to pronounce on the matter.

While the "jugements d'amour" and the "jeu-parti" certainly influenced the later debate in its structure and even in its subject matter, the courtly romance also played a significant role in developing the great interest in love as a driving force behind the actions of courtly characters. The romance emerged to prominence in the last half of the twelfth century, at a time when European culture was experiencing a flourishing of both learning and letters that has been designated as a "renaissance" by many modern scholars. Perhaps the most striking of these developments took place in the vernacular literature produced in northern France. The romance took shape dramatically and quickly constituted a new literary form. Its subject par excellence was love—a love that, while not excluding sensual pleasure, was also seen as an ennobling psychological and moral experience. This new narrative form dominated the European scene until the end of the Middle Ages and even beyond. Recounting tales of valiant knights pursuing desirable ladies in settings defined by the unexpected and the marvelous, the courtly romance exemplifies medieval literature for many modern readers. What it brought to the European tradition in particular is an enduring literary "matter" featuring Arthur, the semimythical king of England, and his Round Table. With their finely wrought plots and detailed depiction of the inner, emotional life, courtly romances were produced under the enthusiastic patronage of the powerful and wealthy nobility, especially Henry II of England, his wife, Eleanor of

Aquitaine, and Eleanor's daughter Marie, countess of Champagne. The theme of these works, *fin' amors* (refined, courtly love), proved to be a complex, even mystifying mixture of social attitudes and literary themes that had been recently introduced from the sophisticated courts in the south of France and the troubadour poetry that circulated northward from those courts.[1]

Among the earliest and most notable of the romances are the stories composed about Tristan and Isolde, or "Iseut" as the French render her name. The great Celtic tale of Tristan and his beloved Iseut, wife of his uncle Marc, is one of the most enduring stories of Western literature, as aficionados of Wagnerian opera can attest. There are indications that the material was known to poets well before it was set down in the versions we now know. Paradoxically for a story so often retold and so greatly admired, the early French texts are all fragmentary. There are two major strains in the various forms of the story. One is known as the "common" version and is represented by the work of Béroul (ca. 1190), which is somewhat simpler in its style and psychology. The other is the "courtly" version, of which the earliest manifestation is the romance by Thomas d'Angleterre (ca. 1172–76), which is marked by a more complex rhetoric and manner. The work of both of these French authors was adapted and imitated in other medieval vernacular languages as the legend gained currency throughout Europe. What it leaves to the romance tradition—apart from its characters, who embody the very notion of tragic, abiding devotion—includes what we have come to define as the tenets of courtly love: love and passion that find their fulfillment only outside of marriage; love as inner turmoil and suffering; love as a force that ennobles those who give themselves to it utterly; love as a force more powerful than separation and death.

Chrétien de Troyes, writing between 1160 and 1185, makes references to the Tristan story and mentions a version of his own, which is unfortunately lost. His surviving five romances all engage similar cases of all-consuming passion that dramatize the heights and depths to which love drives the knight and lover.[2] Two of these works, *Erec et Enide* and *Yvain* or *Le Chevalier au lion* (*The Knight of the Lion*), show their heroes torn between the conflicting demands of love and chivalry. When Erec devotes himself to his wife, the lovely Enide, he is accused by his fellow knights of uxoriousness and dereliction of duty. He submits himself and Enide to a harrowing series of adventures in order to prove her love and his valor. In a mirroring of that plot, Yvain neglects a promise to his wife to return at the appointed time because he spends too long on the tournament circuit. Distraught at the loss of his beloved, he goes mad when he realizes his breach of faith. Yvain forfeits his name and identity until he can win her back through his loyalty and courage. The seriousness and solemnity with which love is treated in these two romances is transformed in a third, Chrétien's *Lancelot* or *Le Chevalier de la charrette* (*The Knight of the Cart*), where the author takes an ironic and at times humorous tone. In this tale, written, as the prologue tells us, for Marie de Champagne, Chrétien pokes fun at the obsessive nature of "refined love." Those at

Marie's court likely laughed at the spectacle of the proud and renowned knight Lancelot hesitating, while on a mission to rescue the haughty Guenivere, before stepping into a cart of the kind normally used to transport criminals. Such a vehicle is unbefitting Lancelot's dignity, but it can convey him on part of his journey to find the queen. Deciding to put his purpose above his pride, Lancelot jumps in. Later in the tale, he is severely reprimanded by Guenivere for his hesitation, which in her eyes represents a momentary failure of devotion, even though he eventually succeeds in saving her from a gruesome abductor.

Another work composed, like Chrétien's *Lancelot*, for Marie de Champagne teaches us even more about the elusive nature of *fin' amors*. This work is a witty Latin disquisition composed by her court chaplain, a certain Andreas, surnamed Capellanus. Andreas draws deeply on the sophisticated if apparently tongue-in-cheek treatment of seduction in the *Ars amatoria* (*The Art of Love*) by the Roman poet Ovid. Andreas's *De amore* (usually translated as *The Art of Courtly Love*) offers a series of often contradictory meditations on the joys, tribulations, and "customary" practices of love between men and women outside the bonds of matrimony, laying out difficult rules that should govern the conduct of lover and beloved.[3] Modern critics disagree about the tone of the *De amore*. Is the work an extended joke or an attempt to limn the contours of an emerging—and radically innovative—idealization of the emotional life? Like Chrétien's *Lancelot*, Andreas's work seems to refuse to treat "refined love" in an orthodox, sober fashion. We are perhaps safest in concluding that Andreas is ambivalent about a code of behavior so much at odds with the official sexual morality of his age, based on the harsh strictures of Christian doctrine.

To return to the development of the love debate as a genre, let us consider the *Concile de Remiremont* (*Council of Remiremont*), which dates from more or less the same period as Chrétien's and Andreas's work and was also written in France.[4] In the *Concile*, composed in Latin, romantic love is once again treated in a humorously ironic fashion. It is a complex if brief text, containing in its 234 verses all the basic themes and structures of this new genre. Because it is the first important and most accomplished of the "jugements d'amour" that are the first examples of the love debate, it merits a somewhat detailed look.

The *Concile* recounts the extraordinary events that supposedly took place during an assembly of the nuns at the monastery of Remiremont. The nuns have come together on the Ides of April, we are told, not to hear the reading of the Gospel but to discuss *amoris tractatus*, the "practice of love." Such a topic of discussion, we learn, has never before figured as the sole business of a gathering of nuns, who are, of course, pledged to a life of celibacy that hardly includes romantic attachments, platonic or otherwise. On one level, then, the poem satirizes those devoted to the religious life, who were often famed, justly or unjustly, for a failure to observe that most difficult of vows. No men are permitted to attend this council except for "honest clerks," monks from nearby Toul, whose presence is welcomed and for whose "solace" the company of women has, in fact, been convoked. All the sisters know of love, but they have no physical experience of it. In a kind of mockery of religious service, the meeting begins not with a reading from the Bible but with a passage from the teachings of Ovid, which are declaimed by a certain Eve, who is said to be well skilled at following Love's commandments and offering sagacious advice to others. Eve is hardly attired in the modest garments of a nun. Instead she is dressed like a courtly lady, wearing splendid clothes and adorned with precious jewels and flowers. She has come, so she says, to advise them never to hide the manner of life they have chosen for themselves—which, she says, is characterized by its exclusive devotion to, if not the actual physical practice of, carnal love and desire. Eve must also judge if any among the company needs to be reproached for having violated the rules that should govern their order.

Elizabeth of Granges responds for the company, declaring that they have served Love to the best of their ability. If they have transgressed, it has not been through a failure of good intentions. Most important, the community has observed the rule of refusing to have sex with men (*viri copula*) and not accepting the companionship of anyone who does not belong to their "order." Elizabeth of Faucogney, however, offers a somewhat more expansive view of the sisters' behavior. They have never ceased enjoying, she declares, the grace, the worthiness, and the good memory of clerks—and they intend to continue loving them in this fashion. In fact, amorous relations with men of religion are what they truly revere, not the rule according to which they ostensibly live.

Elizabeth of Faucogney then proceeds to catalogue the virtues of clerks as lovers. The clerk is gracious, kind, and attentive, full of courtesy and generosity. Experienced in love, he knows how to treat a woman well, bringing her appropriate presents and never failing to keep a promise. And he is faithful in his love, never abandoning a woman to whom he has joined himself. A knight, in contrast, is not worth the trouble or affection of a virtuous lady. His brand of loving is detestable, unfortunate, and short-lived. The sisters of the house at first sought out knights for lovers but, realizing that they were deceivers, quickly abandoned them for clerks, who are famed for being blameless in affairs of the heart. And so any attachment to a knight has become forbidden to members of their company, she concludes. Such is the life they will continue to live, if it pleases Eve for them to do so.

One of the other nuns present has a different view, however. Clerks, she declares, are not as able in loving as Elizabeth of Faucogney has maintained. Those who share this opinion also belong to the "family of Love." Knights are worthy of respect because they love both war and pleasure. They fear no pain, whether it comes from love or wounds. In battle they are courageous, with a view toward gaining the ladies' affection and possessing the bodies of women. The pasture at Remiremont is always open to their horses, as is the fountain. This nun and her sisters intend to serve the knights who serve them, paying no attention to the psalter. No life could be sweeter or more profitable, in her view.

Those who prefer clerks then state their case once again before Eve puts an end to debate. She affirms that clerks are able, sweet, and affable, while knights are fickle and given to foolish speech. Henceforth, these women should accept the proffered affection only of clerks, and this is what she ordains as a new rule for the sisterhood. Women who shun this advice should not be admitted to the company until they repent and are granted absolution for their transgression. It is Eve's further wish that all the sisters restrict themselves to a single lover. Those who violate this rule will be expelled, as no easy penance can wash away such a crime.

Knights and those of low degree should always be forbidden from touching the women's bodies, throats, and thighs. Giving such men any pleasure is a terrible crime because it will diminish the glory of women. The wisdom of clerks is to be preferred because, when women act foolishly, clerks will know where their best interest lies and direct them to pursue it. Eve orders that those who do not follow her injunction be excommunicated from the community and become objects of hatred. But pardon will quickly come to anyone who shows proper repentance.

Andreas's treatise concurs with Eve's judgment that clerks make the best lovers, but, enforcing a double standard, he affirms that nuns are to honor absolutely their vows of chastity. The *Concile* thematizes this new "doctrine" in a different fashion, making the question of how women should behave in love the subject of a debate that centers on the qualities to be expected in the men to whom they devote themselves. That the debaters, and the judge who resolves their argument, are ostensibly members of a religious house adds a touch of lighthearted social satire, turning the poem into an evident fantasy, set in a spring season that focuses one and all on love. It is suited to the entertainment of its anticipated educated audience, who were sophisticated enough to understand the joke. More important, perhaps, the *Concile* establishes the basic structure of the genre: a debate about an important aspect of the love experience—here the relative suitability of clerks and knights—which is eventually referred for adjudication to an appropriate authority figure.

Another early text in the love debate tradition is worth a brief look. The French *Jugement d'amours* (*Judgment of Love*), which belongs to the same period, offers a distinctive variation on what was becoming a stock theme.[5] One May morning two maidens, pretty and elegantly dressed, make their way to a pleasant garden, where they intend to entertain themselves. After a walk through a valley filled with blossoms and the pleasant fragrances of the season, they find an olive tree, under which they sit and discuss a question of love. The first maiden, Blancheflor, sings the praises of the man with whom she has fallen in love, a clerk, while Florence, her companion, argues for the superiority of her lover, who happens to be a knight. They can reach no consensus and decide to take their case to the God of Love, who, with his knowledge and power, can resolve the dispute. On the appointed day, they make their way to Love's palace, a beautiful dwelling covered with flowers, but the door is barred and there is no porter to allow them inside. Suddenly two birds appear to conduct them to the divinity, who is taking his rest on a bed of flowers. The god listens with interest and summons his council of "barons," who are all birds of different kinds. They debate the issue among themselves, fail to resolve it, and so determine on a single combat between champions representing the two positions. The champion who supports the knights is soon forced to admit that clerks are valiant and courteous, and that all virtues are more evident in them than in any other men. Feeling her lover dishonored, Florence breaks into tears, moans bitterly, and dies. The poem ends with her burial as a martyr to Love.

The "literature of love" reaches its apotheosis in the thirteenth century with the *Roman de la rose* (*Romance of the Rose*), a work of immense breadth and impact that is preserved in more than 250 manuscripts, a huge number for a medieval vernacular work. Its influence is correspondingly large. Virtually all love literature that follows over the next two centuries—including the work of the four poets included in this volume—shows the impact of this work in some way, reproducing, rewriting, or taking exception to its contents, conceits, and characters.

The *Rose* consists of two parts, the first of approximately 4,000 lines and the second of an additional 18,000. It is conventionally assumed that the two parts were composed by different poets. Guillaume de Lorris is known as the author of the older portion, composed around 1230, which begins the story of a young lover who falls in love with a rosebud he sees in the Garden of Delight. The garden is the domain of the God of Love and his company, a group of allegorical personifications favorable to his powers. The second part of the romance, composed by Jean de Meun around 1270, describes the vicissitudes experienced by the lover but also incorporates long passages of exposition on all manner of topics, making it a compendium of knowledge as well as the resolution of the quest for the Rose.

This story is a dream vision that unfolds in the narrator's unconscious, and it makes room for extensive meditations on love. Here, too, we find debates about what are the (at least conventionally) central issues of the emotional life. Becoming the vassal of Love in the first part of the poem, the dreamer is aided in his pursuit of the Rose by Fair Welcome, who is driven off by Danger and Shame before the lover can attain his goal. At this point, Reason rushes to the lover's rescue, urging him to give up on love, which, she maintains, is both unnatural, because not centered on procreation, and unreliably transient. An opposing view is offered by Friend, who emphasizes the positive aspects of the love experience, persuading the dreamer to disregard what Reason has advocated. In the poem's second part, the dispute over the value of love becomes even more elaborate, as a variety of other personifications appear to offer different perspectives. For example, a character known as the Old Woman, who has, perhaps foolishly, been given charge of the Rose's virtue, offers a disquisition on the rules of love, counseling foolishness, promiscuity, and the blatant manipulation of unfortunate men. Her advocacy of an immoral surrender to impulse is opposed both by Nature, who recognizes that "laws" can be rejected by those who make use of their reason, and by Genius, whose view of love's essential connection to the procreative imperative reflects official Church doctrine. In the end, these points of view are, at best, uneasily reconciled. The lover does finally gain possession of the Rose, although his success is depicted in an extended military metaphor that shows his victory as a siege and assault on the tower protecting the Rose, a violent and overtly sexual ending to a tale that began in the most refined of registers. Most modern readers agree that the debate over the nature of love offered in the poem is never really resolved.

The many possible interpretations of the contents of the *Roman de la rose*, in combination with its enormous influence, led to the first literary "quarrel" in French letters, more than a century after Jean de Meun had brought the sprawling work to a conclusion. Christine de Pizan participated in this epistolary debate and was highly critical of the romance. Other participants included Jean Gerson, the brothers Gontier and Pierre Col, and Jean de Montreuil, all leading figures of Parisian intellectual circles. At issue were the truth value and moral probity of the *Rose*, and more specifically its misogyny and use of explicit language. Their arguments demonstrate that the questions of love raised in the *Rose* and other medieval love literature often have wider cultural or moral relevance, including proper behavior in amorous relationships and the difference between male and female sensibilities.

A second literary quarrel took shape several decades later over a work by Alain Chartier, who wrote several debate poems. That quarrel concerned the ending of his best-known poem, *La Belle Dame sans mercy* (*The Beautiful Lady without Mercy*), in which a beautiful lady will not design to take pity on a deserving admirer. Chartier's poem was extended through a series of textual continuations, all of which comment on the lady's refusal.[6] Some suggest that she is merciless, while others point out that she may be eager only to avoid an experience she regards as utterly foolish and fraught with peril. Some praise Chartier and blame his female protagonist, while others defend her actions and blame him for an unchivalrous depiction of her. It is the inconclusive ending of Chartier's poem, like the equivocal and multiple opinions laid out in the *Rose*, that invited further debate and discussion, marking the later Middle Ages as an era in which the principal literary themes of an earlier age came under greater (and often mockingly playful) scrutiny, furnishing the matter to compose new texts from old. The issues raised in these literary quarrels are similar to those debated—and likewise never given final answers—in the love debates included here.

We can conclude this introduction with some brief comments about how these various literary strands are eventually woven together to give the love debate new life some two centuries after its emergence. In his *Jugement dou roy de Behaingne*, Guillaume de Machaut reopens the debate begun in the *Rose*. The

Behaingne offers, first, a confrontation between human characters (a gentleman and a lady who disagree about a love question in the manner of the disputing sisters in the *Concile de Remiremont*) and, later, the opposition of different views about human life and purpose (an intellectual confrontation in the manner of the *Rose*). In Machaut's poem, Reason makes a reappearance, and this time elicits violent disagreement from both Love and Youth. The dispute between the gentleman and lady is brought to the court of the king of Bohemia, whose courtiers are the personifications made so familiar to medieval readers by the *Rose*. There the question ostensibly to be decided is not whether clerks or knights make the better lovers; rather it is who suffers more, a man betrayed by his disloyal beloved or a woman who has suffered the death of her knight in battle. The discussion at court, however, soon ranges far beyond the rather simple question of comparing degrees of suffering, launching into a disagreement about the nature and value of the love experience.

At the end, the king sides with Reason, agreeing both that the man's suffering is worse and that love is worthless and should be avoided if it cannot offer rewards commensurate with the service and pains it requires. As we will see, the king's (and by extension Machaut's) judgment hardly ends the debate. Machaut, for reasons we will explore, takes up the same issue in a sequel to the first debate, his *Jugement dou roy de Navarre*. And Christine de Pizan, Geoffrey Chaucer, and Alain Chartier all compose works that offer, in one way or another, "answers" to Machaut's text. These answers, of course, like Machaut's own, are never final. For modern readers, as for our medieval counterparts, they remain thought-provoking, subtle, and entertaining, extending an invitation to continued discussion and reasoned disagreement. With finesse, sophistication, humor, and subtle wit, the love debate poems of the later Middle Ages provide a suitable coda to the exploration of refined emotion and the proper behavior of those in love that so dominates the literary history of the era.

Notes

1. A useful discussion of these developments is found in Boase, *Origin and Meaning of Courtly Love*.

2. See Kibler, *Chrétien de Troyes: Arthurian Romances*.

3. An English translation is in Walsh, *Andreas Capellanus on Love*.

4. The Latin text and a modern French paraphrase of the *Concile* are in Oulmont, *Les Débats*, 92–107.

5. The *Jugement d'amours* is in Oulmont, *Les Débats*, 122–42.

6. For further discussion of these two quarrels, see Baird and Kane, *Querelle de la Rose*, and Champion, *Histoire poétique*, 1:60–73. Chartier's *Belle Dame* and its continuations have recently been edited by Hult and McRae as *Le Cycle de "La Belle Dame sans mercy."*

Guillaume de Machaut

Le Jugement dou roy de Behaingne
(*The Judgment of the King of Bohemia*)

Le Jugement dou roy de Navarre
(*The Judgment of the King of Navarre*)

⸙

Guillaume de Machaut (1300?–1377) was one of the most esteemed poets and musicians of fourteenth-century France, and this high regard for his many artistic accomplishments is echoed by modern scholars. Machaut's reputation among his contemporaries rested on the production of an immense and varied corpus of works, many of which were composed for, and in honor of, the several grand nobles with whose courts he was at various times associated, including the kings of Bohemia and Navarre, who figure as characters in the love debates or "judgments" collected here. In addition to a large number of lyrics, Machaut composed ten long and four shorter narrative poems, most of which take *fin' amors* as their theme. A principal influence on his work was the *Roman de la rose* in particular and the tradition of twelfth- and thirteenth-century love literature in general. Unlike earlier writers in this tradition, Machaut was very much concerned with establishing a "poetic identity" for himself, first, by often making a fictional alter ego a character and, second, by ensuring that his works were collected and attractively presented in special manuscripts whose production, it seems, he sometimes personally supervised.

Little is known of his birth or upbringing, but it seems that Machaut was born into neither a noble nor a bourgeois family. Instead, quite evidently a very enterprising and energetic man, he made a career for himself in the church, probably completing a master's degree at the University of Paris after attending a cathedral school at Reims, which was not far from the small village of Machaut where he had been born. In his early twenties he became associated with one of the most colorful nobles of the era, Jean de Luxembourg, king of Bohemia. To the modern historian, Jean appears an extravagant and perhaps unstable figure. To his contemporaries, however, the king's fabled prodigality, the restlessness with which he sought to expand and consolidate the lands under his rule, and his social finesse made him the very type of ideal ruler, perfectly qualified (when reimagined as a literary character) to adjudicate the question of love that arises in the course of the debate recounted in the *Jugement dou roy de Behaingne*.

Sometime after Jean's death on the battlefield at Crécy (1346), Machaut found other patrons, first Jean's daughter Bonne, who died in 1348 of the plague, and then the very young and dashing Charles of Navarre, who had received his crown at Pamplona in 1350. Though ruler of a somewhat distant realm, Charles was largely French by blood and also bore the title of count of Evreux. Because of his largely unsuccessful meddling in French dynastic affairs, early modern historians tagged Charles with the perhaps undeserved title Charles the Bad. In any event, he was a shrewd, charismatic, and handsome man whom ladies evidently found attractive. Much like Jean de Luxembourg, Charles was a paragon of courtly demeanor and thus also suited to the role of presiding authority that Machaut assigns him in the second "judgment" poem, a sequel of sorts to the first, which apparently had proved quite popular with Machaut's aristocratic readers. During the 1350s, Charles made a bid to seize the French throne, and this likely led Machaut to sever the association, for the poet had always entertained cordial relations with the royal house of France, who were now Charles's bitter enemies. Machaut enjoyed the patronage of the great nobles of France for the rest of his life, continuing his career as a poet and musician with great success and productivity into his early seventies, a remarkable and indeed unparalleled achievement among male authors of the Middle Ages.

Le Jugement dou roy de Behaingne

> A ce dous temps, contre le mois de may
> Par un matin cointement m'acesmay,
> Com cils qui trés parfaitement amay,
> D'amour seüre
> (lines 9–12)

Though it was to inspire a new genre, Machaut's first judgment poem begins in a most conventional fashion, with the narrator's reminiscences of the adventures he passed through one late April morning, the time appointed by Nature and God for love. Love, he affirms, is an emotional experience that affects many men and women, bringing them both joy and pain. This narrator confesses to being an experienced and successful lover, so he can give himself over quite happily to the enjoyment of the beautiful sunshine and reawakening nature. Following a nightingale, he enters a lonely glade, there to contemplate in solitude the indescribable beauty of the natural music he hears. This short opening passage (1–40) draws explicitly on the *Roman de la rose*, in which the archetypal Lover similarly falls prey to the enticements of springtime. In the *Rose*, after falling asleep, the lover Amant similarly experiences a vision of the Garden of Love, and there the poem's complex allegorical drama unfolds. In Machaut's reworking of this structure, however, the narrator does not fall asleep, but becomes a witness to a very different kind of drama that takes place nearby (41–124).

The structure of the *Rose* has been invoked, then, but radically transformed. The elaborate interplay between allegorical personages that lends psychological and intellectual depth to the *Rose* has been rejected, if only initially, in favor of a confrontation between two human characters, a man and a woman, unknown to one another, whose experiences in love—which are related in substantial detail—have been, up to a point, similar. Both have known not only the joy that love brings but also the overwhelming and enduring sorrow that comes from its loss. Yet this loss, in their two cases, has intriguingly different sources and the poem takes as one of its main themes the measuring of one loss against the other. Which of these distressed lovers suffers the greater pain? The issue is debated first (and inconclusively) by the protagonists, only later to be submitted as a question of love that is given a definitive answer, at least of sorts, by the king of Bohemia's courtiers, allegorical personages who each represent, in the tradition of the *Rose*, different and to some degree incompatible aspects of the love experience.

Enjoying his springtime walk, the narrator spies an obviously troubled lady and a serving girl approaching down a lonely path. At the same moment, on the other side, he sees a knight walking down the same path. Thinking he may be intruding into a lovers' meeting, the narrator hides in the bushes, becoming an involuntary witness to their encounter. The knight gives the lady a fair greeting, but she ignores him. Puzzled, he seizes her robe and questions her. The lady apologizes for her inadvertent rudeness; it seems she was lost in thought. Like a true gentleman, the knight offers his assistance, but it is declined since, as the lady declares, her difficulties are so severe that no one save God could alleviate them. Though sympathetic, the knight politely disagrees with this statement, responding that his own suffering is more than any human being ever has or indeed ever could endure. Their dispute leads almost immediately to a joint undertaking. The lady and knight will explain their troubles in full in order to determine who bears the greater burden of grief. With this the narrator is displaced from his role as main character of the developing story and becomes, if only for a time, a clerkly witness not himself of noble birth (for his class affiliation has now become evident) to the debate between the two aristocratic figures.

The lady begins her account of emotional distress by describing her dedication as "serf and vassal" to Love, who favored her with the affection of a knight who, in her view, was the best man who ever lived. His death, she maintains, has left her with an irremediable sorrow, the proof of which seems to be the dead faint into which she falls at the end of her speech (125–205). After reviving her, however, the knight refuses to concede, remaining committed to his initial view, and in an even more elaborate response (261–860) recounts his faithful service to the God of Love, which eventually earns him the reward of a young girl's heart. But Love's favor leads in the end only to misery, because his beloved throws him over for another man, betraying his trust. The bereaved lady, though sympathetic to his plight, is not persuaded that the jilted knight's suffering is worse, and she makes a telling point to support her contention (881–928). She argues that since his beloved is still living, it is possible for him to regain her favor through loyal and patient service. In his rebuttal, the knight maintains the contrary: were she dead, he could forget the girl and be released from pain, but, being alive and forever unattainable, she will make him suffer endlessly (929–1167).

Having reached an impasse, the two disputants obviously need a judge to decide the case, but, constrained by the rules of polite intercourse, neither wishes to nominate one. Nearly forgotten during the progress of the debate, the narrator once again assumes a prominent role, if a quite different one (1185–1442). He is no longer free to lose himself in his own thoughts of love, awakened by the spring morning. Instead he must serve his betters in their time of emotional distress. Like the knight and the lady, he finds himself in a difficult position, for, though he wishes to help them find a proper judge, he is embarrassed to reveal his presence. Chance soon intervenes. The lady's dog spots him hiding in the bushes and runs toward him, barking. This provides him with the opportunity to return the animal to its master and then to introduce himself. Confessing that he has heard all of their discussion, the narrator proposes the king of Bohemia as a judge to hear the case. The pair concur, and the narrator quickly leads them to the nearby castle of Durbuy, where the king is in residence. Jean listens graciously to a summary of the disagreement provided by the knight (1509–1608), and he then turns the issue over to his court for further discussion, charging his courtiers, sixteen allegorical personages with such names as Reason, Love, Youth, and Loyalty, to provide the proper explication of the issues involved.

Reason, who holds a position of prominence at court, speaks first, and in a long response (1665–1784) confirms the correctness of the knight's argument, maintaining that, since love is a carnal affection, it cannot survive the death of the body. But the knight sees his unfaithful lady constantly and so cannot forget, even though Reason advises to do so, because Youth and Love urge him on in this mad error. Love then intervenes (1788–1811), agreeing with Reason's solution of the dispute, but challenging her view that the knight should abandon the love he feels for his beloved because she has proved a traitor to him. In an emotional rejoinder (1824–1847), Loyalty condemns the faithless behavior of the knight's beloved. She argues that Love is wrong in demanding that the knight continue to love someone from whom he gets nothing but misery. Loyalty agrees with Reason that the knight suffers more because Love holds him fast in a sorrow from which he cannot recover. Youth finds herself in agreement with Love, asserting that the knight will never give up his love as long as her power can prevent it (1857–1991). Like Love, Youth argues that the experience of love is reward enough, even if its object has proved unworthy, a position at whose foolishness and impracticality the king gently laughs, reproving Youth for wanting to keep a faithful servant of Love in such continual pain that he might die (1900–1914). So be it, says Youth; he will then attain great honor as a martyr (1915–1920). Delivering his judgment, the king endorses the view that the knight suffers more than the lady. They have not assembled, he reminds them, to determine if that man should indeed continue to love the woman who has betrayed him (1923–1956).

And yet the debate does move from a weighing of the sorrows felt by the knight and the lady to a consideration of a much more difficult question, one that is, by royal command, never finally adjudicated: Should reason guide the behavior of those in love, who are under the powerful sway of both the affection itself and the impetuousness of their immature age? In this "digression," we see Machaut coming to grips with a question developed more fully, if never answered decisively, in the *Rose*. The king, a mature man, sides with Reason, not only reproving Youth for overtaxing the knight with misery, but agreeing that the woman, once her grief passes, will find another lover in accordance with natural imperatives. The assembled court assents unanimously to this judgment, though we can imagine that Youth and Love are not happy with the outcome, which endorses Reason's opinion that love does not survive the death of the body (1716–1723) and thus can exert but a limited power over those under its dominion. For eight days the courtiers attempt, with little apparent success, to assuage the suffering of the king's two guests, who are finally allowed to depart after receiving generous gifts.

Beyond the two questions of who suffers more and whether lovers should heed the dictates of the head rather than those of the heart, the debate, if only indirectly, raises a third, which will become the focus of the poem's sequel: Who prove superior in love, men or women? The knight is judged the winner in the debate, an indication, perhaps, of the greater power of male reasoning and discernment—or it may be that the king has simply decided in favor of a fellow male. In any case, it is the knight's continuing devotion to his lady, however undeserving, that occasions the court's discussion of the relative claims of reason and emotion to direct human action. Moreover, the cause of the knight's sorrow is his lady's faithlessness. Of the two women who figure in the poem, one is given to mistaken opinions (overestimating a misery that, it is predicted, will soon pass), while the other is a promiscuous betrayer of male trust, who inspires virtuous devotion only to inflict pointless pain on a man who merits, as all present agree, a quite different reward.

The poem's two men, in contrast, reflect the highest masculine ideals. Both are submissive to love and mindful of the proper service due the women to whom they have pledged themselves. These exemplary men suffer only because of what lies beyond their control: for one, the vagaries of fortune leading to an early death; and for the other, the instability of a woman's heart that mocks the steadiness of the love bestowed upon it. It could be argued, as a female figure of great authority does in *Le Jugement dou roy de Navarre*, that the author who has created a fiction that so obviously favors men over women has insulted the gentler sex. If this was unintentional, then she thinks that the author must be under the sway of that complex of incorrect notions about the "inferiority" of women that we now term *misogyny*. Whether Machaut is guilty of this charge is the question that, with no little humor and irony, is debated in the *Navarre*, where the poet becomes his own main character. And so what was extratextual in the *Behaingne*, namely the author's intentions and his responsibility to advance only "true" opinion, becomes the center of the new work, as Machaut himself—or, more precisely, a humorously inept fictional version of the poet—is called to account.

This transformation, however startling, is by no means unanticipated. An important feature of the *Behaingne* is its reflexivity, that is, its self-conscious presentation of the role the poet plays in court society. There is an unmistakable autobiographical strain in the poem, which gives voice to Machaut's likely uncertainties about his own position—as clerk and commoner, but also as the designated spokesman of emotional idealism. At first, the narrator's solitude indexes both the importance of his subjectivity (which is a potential source of a meditation on the love experience) and his openness to instruction or enlightenment, which should conventionally come, as in the *Rose*, in the dream that follows this figure's falling asleep in the springtime setting. The dramatic interchange between the knight and the lady, however, means that the narrator's solitude comes to indicate his sudden displacement from the debate to follow, as well as his conversion into an unseen and eavesdropping witness. In effect, the narrator becomes a more recognizable figure, the very image of Guillaume de Machaut the courtly poet, who attends to understanding the ideas advanced by the debating pair. Using his artistic powers, he will convert these ideas into poetry, as in the work's coda he confesses he has done (2052–79). Giving way to the concerns of the class he serves, the narrator (and by extension Guillaume himself) is not content to be a simple witness, serving a narrating function that effaces itself behind the story. The role he fulfills is a larger one, for the poet, as Machaut sees it, is also a guide. His fictions are not just entertainments but are also intended to inform and comfort. If his experience in love must be denied the privilege of focus, the poet's duties as teacher and advisor cannot be so easily laid aside. That experience, however, offers no easy truths to be confidently endorsed. The conflict between Reason, on the one hand, and Youth and Love, on the other, does not finally admit of a simple solution in favor of either clear-headed restraint or reckless self-abandon. The debate ends but does not conclude, much in the manner of Machaut's most notable model, the *Roman de la rose*.

Unlike Machaut's other narrative poems, which use the octosyllabic couplet then standard in verse of this kind, the *Behaingne* is written in concatenated quatrains, rhyming *aaab, bbbc, cddd*, etc. The first three lines in each stanza are ten syllables in length, while the fourth and concluding line is four syllables. For the sake of easy reading, these stanzas are not set off by spacing in the translation, nor is the short fourth line indented from the left margin.

Le Jugement dou roy de Navarre

> Guillaume, mervilleusement
> Estes estranges devenus.
> Vous ne fussiez pas ça venus,
> Se ce ne fust par mes messages,
> Je croys que vous estes trop sages
> Devenuz, ou trop alentis . . .
> (lines 760–65)

If Machaut's first judgment poem suggests something of the poet's life, particularly his service to the noble class above him, its sequel is more deeply autobiographical—and also a more complex work of greater scope. In fact, the initial section of the work, instead of evoking the springtime setting that is such a conventional element of love poetry, offers a detailed description of what is arguably the most important historical event of the fourteenth century. Apparently resident in Reims and performing his office of canon in the cathedral chapter, the poet describes his feelings of melancholy on November 9, 1349, and then his reactions to the outbreak of the disease that became known to many of his contemporaries as the Black Death. His detailed account (1–458) is one of the most vivid and evocative of those penned by writers who lived through the epidemic, and it has substantial historical value as a witness to both events and cultural attitudes. Machaut describes the various astrological configurations of the year that were widely interpreted as predicting the subsequent outbreak of the disease, including the appearance of a fiery comet. Also preceding the plague were great wars and killings. A violent anti-Semitism, which the poet cites approvingly, arose after the initial appearance of the disease. Having no apparent cause, the plague can be ascribed to the Jews, who are accused of having poisoned the wells. Machaut connects the phenomenon of wandering companies of flagellants to the disastrous events predicted by the heavens. Because men were so intent on putting an end to themselves, he suggests, Nature decided to assist in this destruction by sending terrible storms to the earth, and many, the poet included, expected that the world would soon end since this strange weather had given rise to a poisonous miasma. The towns and villages were quickly emptied of people, and ditches were dug in churchyards to bury the unnumbered dead. But the poet survives, having locked himself up within his house.

Rich in historical and autobiographical detail, this account only serves as an introduction to the patently fabulized events that constitute the bulk of the poem, where the historical Machaut makes way for his textual counterpart, the bumbling and ungracious Guillaume, who resembles the real-life poet only in some particulars. With the end of the plague, Guillaume takes horse and hounds, heading out for a day of hare hunting in the fields (459–759). There a lady of great nobility meets him, but he is too absorbed to greet her properly or even acknowledge her presence. Summoned by her squire, he rides over to discover that the august personage whom he has unintentionally slighted is his patroness (much later identified as the obviously allegorical figure Happiness), who is insulted not only by the poet's inattentiveness on this sunny afternoon. For some time, it seems, she has been terribly displeased by his previous work, which is unnamed but, as her summary makes clear, is the *Jugement dou roy de Behaingne*. In that poem, Happiness declares, Guillaume promulgated the "incorrect" view that the man betrayed by his beloved suffers more than the woman bereft of her lover; this judgment, she suggests, demeans women (802–1038). The poet, his pride wounded, refuses to admit error and retract his judgment. And so the two enter into a debate that the poet, so he says, intends to win even though this means opposing a grand and noble person whom he should unquestioningly obey (1039–88). The pair ride on, accompanied by the lady's entourage, to a handsome manor house where she holds court and where the poet is introduced to the twelve damsels who comprise the lady's retinue (1089–1356). As at the castle of the king of Bohemia, these damsels are personifications who all represent moral or psychological qualities such as Discretion, Prudence, and Generosity. Their duty is to ensure that the lady does only what is right and avoids all evil. After the lady, despite Guillaume's protest, rehearses the case to the assembled courtiers, the king of Navarre arrives by chance and is immediately recruited by the lady to judge the dispute.

The debate itself occupies most of the remainder of the poem (1629–3751). Its lively give-and-take covers many topics and points of view as Guillaume and his interlocutors attempt to find arguments to support or condemn the opinion the poet made the king of Bohemia render in the earlier poem. These deliberations are much more elaborate—and humorous—than those in the *Behaingne*. Machaut enlivens the sequel by having the debatants recount examples to prove their points; a number of these examples are tales drawn from classical mythology, more specifically from the monumental French adaptation of Ovid's *Metamorphoses* called the *Ovide moralisé* (Ovid Moralized). The dispute eventually shifts to the relative merits of men and women, specifically the supposed greater capacity of women to suffer the pain caused by love. In a long speech (2699–2822), Frankness recounts the stories of Ariadne and Medea, whose experiences, she believes, illustrate the point that women are made to suffer by men, but emerge victorious in the end.

Guillaume rudely attacks this argument, saying that he could easily find a host of examples to prove the opposite, namely that men have a greater capacity for suffering than their female counterparts. In support of his view, he relates one of the strangest examples advanced in the debate. A woman has given her lover a ring on the condition that he never remove it unless she do it for him. One day her husband notices that his wife is missing the ring and demands to see it. She sends a message to her lover asking for its return, and he sends it to her along with his finger in order not to break his word. Needless to say, the poet does not advance his cause much by offering evidence that seems to testify more to the stupidity of men in love than to their emotional perseverance and strength of character.

Guillaume's ineptness in debating, and the opposition he faces from intelligent and crafty interlocutors, soon lead him into a more fatal blunder. Angry, he gives voice to the view that men are indeed far superior to women in love because there is nothing stable or firm about a woman's emotions and beliefs. Such ideas, he goes on to say, are affirmed by everyone, and that is the reason they found a place in his earlier poem. Further wrangling ensues, but the lady soon asks the judge to begin his deliberations, aided by the lady's courtiers, who are, of course, those who have argued the case so strenuously against Guillaume. It is hardly surprising that complete condemnation quickly follows. Moderation rebukes Guillaume for daring to debate such a noble and respected personage, for advancing a mistaken opinion, and for offering insufficient and dubious evidence in support of his position. Reason agrees and, when the court has reassembled with the accused, condemns him on these three counts (3767–3832). Seeing Guillaume saddened by the outcome, Reason reveals to him the identity of the lady and describes her immense powers. She is Happiness, who distributes talent and wisdom to those she favors. Reason's long description particularly emphasizes the different gifts that Happiness accords to clerks and to knights (3839–4006). Now more reconciled to his fate, Guillaume asks to be sentenced, and the judge signifies to him that he owes three amends for his three faults. The judge determines that he must compose three lyric poems, of different types, as his penance. The poem closes with Guillaume's confession that he has composed the *Navarre* in order to recognize his fault better; he intends to present it to the lady along with his promise of continued service.

One of the assigned lyric poems, the "Le Lai dou plour" (The Lay of Weeping), is appended to the *Navarre*. Here the poet adopts the voice of the bereaved woman from the *Behaingne*, lamenting her lost lover, even as Machaut takes seriously the judge's admonition to see the merits in the female point of view. There is no little humor in this finale, as the strident male (and clerical) voice of the *Navarre* narrator ventriloquizes the sorrows of female experience, demonstrating the unwavering grief she feels after the death of her lover. And yet the performance is more authentically poetic than authentically "womanly." The emotions expressed in the lay's outburst must be read within the context of the series as evidence of Guillaume's reformation—or, at least, of his desire to appear reformed—not as the personal product of emotional experience of an obviously fictional woman.

The *Navarre* is unlike all other medieval works in its complex exploration of the poetics of authorship, in its meditations on and comic reduction of the difficulties presented to the court poet by the literary tradition within which he worked. We are meant, like Machaut's original readers, to distinguish between the foolish self-importance and ineptitude of Guillaume the character, who resents the accusations of Happiness and loses his composure as the trial begins to slip away from him, and the audacity of Guillaume de Machaut the poet, who with remarkable finesse and sophistication puts his own poetry on trial, testifying to the power of his confident talent. Here the main character is not a lover but a poet, struggling to remain true to his understanding of men and women even as he must please the patrons upon whom his continuing production of poetry finally depends.

But this does not mean that the debate over the relative merits of men and women has receded into the background. It is simply dramatized in a different and more striking fashion than in the *Behaingne*. Guillaume is called upon to measure his intellectual resourcefulness and rhetorical skills against a formidable band of determined women on their home turf (the earlier debate occurs at the king of Bohemia's residence, the later at that of Happiness, where the king of Navarre is a guest). In that confrontation Guillaume is found wanting and must submit to a penance that, if not humiliating, is at least chastening. And yet, perhaps, the male poet has the last word. For the lyric he pens requires that he adopt a female voice. This transvestite performance indicates his (at least temporary) solidarity with female suffering. But neither Happiness nor the king of Navarre requires that he actually retract the judgment rendered in the *Behaingne*. And that, perhaps, is a victory of sorts for the male side and the power of the pen.

Like all of Machaut's narrative *dits* except the *Behaingne*, the *Navarre* was composed in octosyllabic couplets, the standard form for verse of this kind in the French Middle Ages.

Le Jugement dou roy de Behaingne

At Eastertide, when every creature rejoices,
When the earth with many a gay color
Adorns herself, when Good Love leaves no wound but
Pierces
The breasts of many pretty ladies, 5
Lovers, and young girls
(And this brings them many
New joys and many cares),
At this sweet time, close to the month of May,
One morning I elegantly arrayed myself, 10
In the fashion of a man who loved most perfectly
With a love secure.
And the day was just balmy enough,
Pretty, clear, sunny, crisp and pure, without a chill.
The dew on the greenery 15
Was shimmering
So brightly it completely blinded me
Whenever I looked upon it
Because of the sun shining down from above.
And the birds, 20
For the sake of the sweetness in that joyous new season,
Happily and with such grand celebration
Were all singing, so I moved to the call
Of their sweet song.
Then I spied one among them in flight 25
Who soared above the others crying:
"Oci, oci!"[1] And I followed him until
In a solitary byway
Above a stream, close by a beautiful tower,
Where there were many trees and flowers 30
Of different colors that smelled sweet,
He perched.
Then I simply dropped to the ground
And hid myself as well as I could beneath the trees
So that he could not see me, 35
In order to hear
The full sweet sound of his pleasant song.
It pleased me so to delight in hearing
His sweet singing that I could never
Describe it. 40

But as I was enjoying
His very sweet singing, on which I was intent,
I saw approach by a narrow path
Covered with grass
A lady deep in thought and all alone, 45
Save for a little dog and a serving maid.
But her forthright demeanor showed clearly
She was sorely distressed.
And on the other side, a short distance from me,
A knight of quite noble array 50
Came toward her right down the path
With no companions;
So I thought they might be lover and beloved.
Then I pushed myself into the leaves
And was so hidden they didn't see me at all. 55
Now when that lover,
To whom Nature had granted considerable gifts,
Had approached that worthy lady,
He greeted her like a gentleman gracious,
Wise, and well mannered. 60
And so oppressed by thought was the lady
That she passed him by with no response.
And at once the man retraced his steps,
Took her
By the robe, and said softly: 65
"Sweet lady, do you scorn
My greeting?" And when she saw him,
With a sigh
She answered so that he waited no longer:
"To be sure, sir, I did not hear you at all 70
Because my thoughts prevented me;
But if I've done
Something improper or wrong,
Please pardon me if you would."
The knight, making no further argument, 75
Said softly:
"Lady, no pardon is needed,
For here there is no misdeed or ill will;
But I beg you please tell me
Your thoughts." 80
Then the lady sighed deeply
And said: "For God's sake, leave me in peace, fair sir,
Because I don't need you to increase the grief
Or frustration
That they give me." With this, he began moving 85
Closer to her to draw out her thoughts,

And said to her: "Sweet and noble lady,
I see you are sad.
But I swear to you and promise upon my faith
That if to me you reveal your trouble, 90
I'll do all in my power
To put it right."
And the lady undertook to thank him for this,
Saying: "Sir, no one can help me,
And no one save God could alleviate 95
The terrible grief
That mars and pales my complexion,
Binds my heart in sorrow and weeping,
Keeps me in such bitter misery
That, truth to tell, 100
There is no heart that could have more."
"Lady, what misfortune makes your pain so great?
Tell me, for I think I suffer
A hurt so painful,
So miserable, so strong, so grievous, 105
So bitter that—of this you may be sure—
There's no woman, no human being,
Nor was there ever one
Who endured such pain."
"Surely, sir, I firmly believe you 110
Bear not the same burden in your heart that I do.
For this reason you shall learn
These thoughts that you wish to know.
Yet right away you'll promise
To tell me all your own without any lies." 115
"Agreed, my lady.
Upon my faith and soul, I promise
That the thought that scorches and inflames me,
Often eating at my heart and rending it,
I'll reveal to you 120
Completely, and in nothing will I lie."
"Agreed, sir, and now I'll tell you."
"Speak, then, and I'll listen
Most willingly."

"Sir, altogether now it's seven years or eight[2] 125
That my heart's been serf and vassal
To Good Love, whose ways I've come to know
Since childhood.
For when I encountered Love the first time,
I gladly put heart, body, strength, life, 130
My goods and power, what I had,

At her disposal.
And as her vassal she retained me
And with a very loyal heart gave me
To a man handsome and good, gentle, wise, and gracious, 135
Who was
The very flower of courtesy,
Perfect honor, and pleasant demeanor;
Of the very good indeed he was the best.
And the man had 140
A noble body, elegant too, gracious, well-formed and pleasing;
Young, genteel, graced with charm he was,
Full of all that a true lover requires.
And he was acclaimed
Worthy of being loved above all others, 145
For he was true, loyal, and circumspect,
Discreet in what pertained to loving.
And I loved him
So loyally that I devoted all my heart
To loving him (no other thought was mine); 150
So in him was my hope, joy,
And pleasure,
My heart, love, thoughts, and desire.
In every kind of goodness my heart could rejoice
Simply by seeing and hearing him. 155
All my comfort
Lay in him; he was all that pleased me,
All my solace, delight, and treasure.
He was my wall, my castle, and my refuge.
And he loved me; 160
Above all else he served and respected me.
He called me his heart, his love, his lady;
He was mine completely; my heart knew this well.
Nor could anything
Displease him that should please me. 165
So true a pair were our two hearts
That one never opposed the other;
Rather they were
Always in accord; one thought they shared.
They were the same in will and desire; 170
A single good, one ill, one joy they felt
Together,
And it was never otherwise for these two;
Instead our love was so faithful
It never gave rise to an immoral thought 175
Of any kind.
Alas! What sorrow! Now the opposite is true.

For my sweetness now is painful suffering.
My joys are bitter hurt,
And my thoughts,   180
In which my heart used to delight
And find sweet solace for every hurt,
Are, and will remain, painful, bitter, sad.
My days
Will be dark and filled with misfortune,   185
My hope will lack any certainty,
And my pleasure will become enduring sorrow,
For without fail
I will pale and tremble, startle with a change of mood,
Moan, cry out, sigh, and wail,   190
And in fear of despair
Even shudder;
Nor will my sad heart experience any good;
No comfort, no joy will ever touch it
Until death seizes me,   195
Death who greatly
Wronged me by not bringing herself
To bite me with her painful bite
When of everything she stripped me and killed
My lover sweet,   200
Whom I loved with a pure heart, as he did me.
But alas—sorrow—what pain! I do not wish
To live on after him even a day or half of one
In such terrible grief;
I'd rather die from the pain that grieves me."   205
And I, who lay hidden within the brush,
Saw that at this word the lady with the gracious manner
Fell down as if dead.
Now he who was a type gentle and kind
Many times begged and exhorted her   210
Quite tenderly to take comfort,
But to no avail;
For assaulted by a grievous pain, the lady
Felt such a severe attack for her lover's sake,
Both breath and strength did fail her.   215
And when he saw
How the lady neither heard nor attended to him,
He was as pained as he could be.
Nonetheless the man realized
That she had fainted.   220
In his hand he then gathered up some dew
From the green grass and sprinkled it over
Her tear-stained face

So gently
That the lady who for so long   225
Had lost strength, reason, and understanding
Opened her eyes and began to sigh
Deeply,
Bemoaning the man who made her desire
Death because of his faithful love for her.   230
But the man, whose noble heart lacked bitterness,
Said: "Dear lady,
For the mercy of God, get hold of yourself.
Carrying on like this will be your death,
Since I see well that you pay most dearly   235
For loving him.
Yet let your heart not fail so.
It is neither worthy nor honorable."
"You tell the truth, sir, but it was quite bad luck I saw
The hour and day   240
I ever loved with such a perfect love
Because in no way can I escape it.
Instead, I see a death with no respite."
"Lady, now hear
What I will say, and please don't take it ill.   245
No wonder you are distraught
Since you are saddened.
Yet truly
A person could much sooner find relief
For your troubles than for mine." "Sir, how so?   250
Tell me, and you'll fulfill
Your agreement."
"Quite willingly, but listen to me
And abandon the sadness in your heart
So you can give all your attention   255
To hearing me."
"Surely, sir, I can scarcely cheer up.
Still, I'll do my best, and that's no lie."
"Then I'll reveal to you what pains are mine
With no more delay.   260

Lady, from that time I knew myself[3]
And my heart could feel and understand
What loving is, I've never ceased striving
To be loved;
So for a long time, to have the name of lover,   265
Before my heart was securely placed or given,
Or granted, or even inclined to one lady,
I many times

Devoutly requested that Good Love
Place my heart to the honor 270
Of a woman in whom it would find a home,
And that this would be
So she would receive glory and praise thereby;
And that if my heart could ever do
Anything to be worthy of attention 275
Or earn
Some reward from a lady through serving her,
Love might sometime deign to remember
Me, who would be her vassal, never to depart
For all my life. 280
Finally it happened that among a company
That included many pretty ladies
Who were young, noble, happy, and amusing,
I chanced by Fortune
(Whose custom is to lie to all), 285
And from the others I picked out one
Who, just as the sun surpasses the moon
In brightness,
Conquered all the others
In esteem, honor, grace, and beauty; 290
And she was so modest and unpretentious, to my taste,
That, truth to tell,
No one could in the entire world find
Her equal, nor could the whole world itself
Suffice to describe her beauty 295
Perfectly.[4]
For I saw her dance so debonairly
And then sing so very beautifully,
Laugh and play so graciously
That never yet 300
Was seen a treasure more elegant,
For her hair resembled golden threads,
And these neither too light nor dark.
Her forehead was
White and smooth, no wrinkle there, 305
Without a flaw, of such correct proportion
It was neither too broad nor narrow.
And her brows
Had a very noble shape
Beneath that whiteness and were like black thread, 310
And to be prized among a hundred thousand.
But her two eyes,
Intent on passing the threshold of my heart
By their strength and fair welcome

To give me the pain that grieves me so, 315
Were smiling,
Not really very gray, to be more piercing,
More striking, sweet, humble, and alluring,
All full of traps to snare a lover
In pure affection. 320
And they were modestly lowered,
Just big enough, not opened too wide,
Conquering all by their sweet piercing;
Nor as they opened
Could any man prevent 325
Their going to strike his heart a blow,
If it pleased them, and claim him for their own.
But their glance,
Seeming to grant mercy, to dawdlers
Was not at all unwisely parceled out, 330
For wishing to throw a dart,
So craftily
Could it do so—and so subtly—
No one could ever truly know
Save him upon whom it properly fell. 335
Pretty, dainty,
Long, and straight, of the proper shape
Was her nose, suited to her face,
For it was neither too big nor small;
But her little mouth, 340
Just small enough, rose in hue, somewhat rounded,
Always smiling, delicious, and sweet
Makes me languish whenever my heart sadly recalls her.
For whoever heard it
Speak so well and saw it laugh, 345
Received with pleasure its sweetness,
Would value it above all others and say as much;
For her smile brought
Two dimples to her cheeks,
So white and colored like a rose, 350
Making them prettier and rounder.
And there's even more:
Her teeth were white, small, and even,
Her chin a little cleft,
Arched below and rounded all above. 355
Wondrous indeed
Was her complexion, surpassing all others,
For it was vibrant, fresh, and pink,
More than any May rose before it's picked;
And, in a few words, 360

White as snow, smooth, pleasantly plump
Was her throat, not wrinkled or bony;
Her neck was beautiful, for which I prize and praise her.
It's also fitting
That I speak of her arms long and straight, 365
Which were in every way well fashioned;
For her hands were white, her fingers long.
Just to my taste
Were her breasts—white, firm, and high-seated,
Pointed, round, and small enough, 370
Suiting her body, gracious and well shaped.
Without a flaw,
In proportion was her body,
Noble, well-shaped, pretty, young, genteel, amply fleshed,
Long, straight, pleasing, lovely, agreeable, and svelte. 375
Very well shaped
Were the hips, thighs, and legs—the feet
Arched, plump, and well formed,
Cunningly shod with exquisite shoes.
Of the rest, 380
Which I did not see, lady, I'll tell you this:
All answered the requirements of Nature.
It was well fashioned and elegant in form.
And this remainder,
Of which right now I'll say no more, 385
Must be considered beyond compare,
Sweeter and more beautiful than any other.
Her delicate skin
Was white and soft; more than other women's
It glistened—and one marveled; 390
There was no flaw or fault, only goodness.
Sweet and firm
Was her flesh, tender with moisture,
But she was endowed with a manner humble
And assured—and she was beautifully groomed. 395
And truly
She was so beautiful (I strongly believe)
That if Nature, who makes all things craftly,
Intended to make another woman just like her,
She would fail; 400
And that she'd never know how to do so
Had she not for a model the one
Who surpasses all others in loveliness.
And so I tell you
I have never seen in all my life 405
A woman's body of such perfect shape.

And she was aged fourteen and a half,
Or thereabouts.
So, lady, when I beheld her appearance,
Which was so beautiful, without any flaw, 410
Within my heart the sweet impression
Of her face
Was so imprinted that it still endures,
Nor ever since has departed, and for this I suffer
Many pains and enduring miseries. 415
And beyond all doubt,
Before I left her presence,
Pleasure so fixed itself within my heart
From marveling at her sweet face
That you may be sure 420
If I possessed Octavian's riches⁵
And knew all Galen's science,⁶
If all goods were mine,
I would have thrown over
Everything in order to see her 425
As I wished, or to accomplish something
She might have liked with which to please her.
But Noble Love,
Who saw I was captured by the snare
Of Pleasure, who'd locked me in her tower 430
Because I'd marveled at the lady's gracious presence,
Without threatening
Made a sweet and smiling look go
Straight through my heart to trap me
So that I had to submit to her very sweet dominion 435
Without repenting.
So pleased was I to feel this domination
When her look deigned
To fall upon me that (I do not lie)
I didn't know 440
What was happening to me or where I was
Since senses, strength, and bearing I had lost,
So forcefully through her eyes was I
Brought to love.
And thus the desire to be loved by her 445
Was so hotly inflamed within my heart,
I have since then called myself 'miserable captive' a hundred times
While sighing;
For such misery did I feel in my desiring
That my strength began to fail me, 450
And many thoughts I had marveling at
Her sweet countenance.

Now willingly I'd have gone to tell her
How with my heart I loved her with no hesitation.
Yet the fear of being refused prevented me   455
From doing so;
And on the other hand, Fair Welcome beckoned me;
His Sweet Look, smiling, reassured me,
And Sweet Hope sweetly told me this
In faith,   460
Affirming to me that so great a beauty
Could never exist without pity.
So these three spoke and encouraged me so much
I after all
Agreed to tell her of my affection.   465
Alas! In this fashion I declaimed all alone to myself.
But when I thought to rehearse my pains to her,
So fearful,
Weak, beaten down, so weary and full of anguish,
So troubled, trembling, and shamed   470
Was my heart, and with lovesickness
So grievously infected
It lost all reason, composure, and wit.
In contrast, my heart was transformed and overwhelmed
When clearly, face to face, I could look upon   475
Her pure beauty.
Then my heart was stung
By an amorous sting, pierced with a joyful point,
And nourished with sweet nourishment
By Sweet Thought,   480
Who relieved all my pain
And gave me hope for cure.
Thus often for Love's sake I experienced
Joy and torture.
And I remained a long time in this state,   485
One hour happy, sorrowful the next,
For I never dared seek relief
For my pain.
Nonetheless this great distress from love,
This burning desire, this cruel languor   490
In which I remained for many days,
Her Fair Welcome,
The hope of ending my pain,
Her great beauty, her sweet, smiling gray eyes,
And that no whit of pride was in her—   495
All this gave me
The strength to beg for mercy
Like a coward. And so I said humbly to her,

Flushed and fearful:
'My lady dear, 500
Your beauty so burns, inflames my heart,
I love you above all else without impure thoughts,
With my heart, my body, with true desire and soul.
So I beg you,
Sweet lady, have mercy on me; 505
For truly, I will die of love
If from the heart that has turned mine black
I find no relief.'

And when in this fashion I dared tell her my grief,
I watched her sweet expression slightly change, 510
So I thought; so I feared
Being rejected.
Yet all the time her look assured me,
As well as her sweetness and gracious smile,
So that by these I was emboldened enough 515
To cry 'Alas!
Gentle lady, for God's sake, don't kill
Your faithful lover, who in your snares
Is trapped so tight he is forfeiting all joy
And comfort.' 520
Then she drew toward me, quiet and demure,
The woman on whose account Love tortures and abuses me,
And said: 'Friend, surely I would never want
To do to anyone
What might pain or grieve him; 525
And no one should do to others
What he would not have done to him.
And, sweet friend,
No good deed goes unrewarded,
No evil one unpunished. 530
Thus if Love has urged you to love,
She will reward you
In her time and season
If you love her with no thoughts of trickery.
And if she found you other than good, 535
Don't doubt at all
That she would be your mortal enemy
And that no help or cure
Would ever be granted you by her, or given
For your pains. 540
Therefore, fair sir, present yourself to Love
And to her rehearse your moans and cries,
For your rescue and your death lie in her,

But not in me;
I am not the cause of your discomfort   545
(Or so it seems to me) and should not suffer for it.
In good faith I know not what else to tell you;
I say goodbye.'

At this that beauty took her leave from me,
She who had portioned out to me such pain   550
My heart nearly broke in two
At her leaving.
But the sweetness of her pleasant look
By its agreeable artfulness made me dare look upon her
So that, as she left, (may God protect me!)   555
So sweetly
Did she look my way it truly seemed
Her expression actually said:
'Lover, I love you with great affection.'
Therefore I was   560
All comforted by the noble power
Of the look that since has proved so precious
It has always nourished and sustained me
In good hope.
And had it not been so, I certainly expect   565
I would have fallen into despair,
But nothing on earth could pain me
When her glance
In a smile had so settled on me
That, my lady, in every way   570
Her look consoled me, aided me
In my distress.

There in great turmoil I remained alone,
And in my mind I began to marvel at
Her bearing, her great sweetness, her appearance,   575
Her courage,
Her fair looks, the manner of her comings and goings,
Her noble body, her gracious speech,
Her genteel carriage, her pleasant look,
And her expression,   580
Which was so sweet, so humble and elegant
That she was the paragon of all beauty.
And having marveled at all she did,
I found, to be sure,
Much great delight and perfect joy   585
And considered myself quite fortunate
For no other reason than that I loved her loyally.

Thus since then
I have been so bent and dedicated to her service
That in serving her I find all my delight; 590
Since that moment I have been able to perform no other labor.
And so I served her,
Loved, protected, respected, obeyed her
A very long time, and my reward was nothing.
At the last, however, I loved and cherished her so much 595
She saw well
I intended only honor for her and good,
And also that my heart did love her above all else;
Thus I did enough so that she took me for her own
In such a way 600
That with a good and happy heart, a pleasant face
She told me: 'Lover, see here your own dear love
Who no longer will treat you haughtily,
Since this is the wish of Love,
Who with a good heart has directed me to do this; 605
And, in truth, it cannot be otherwise,
Because this can only be a quite serious matter
Since my love
And heart as well I present you, never to be returned;
And so I beg you to guard my honor well, 610
For I love and honor you above all else.'
And when I saw
That my lady called me her lover
So sweetly, and that she had bestowed upon me
Without reservation the delightful gift of her love, 615
If I was happy then,
Do not marvel, sweet lady;
For until that moment I had been discouraged,
Forlorn, lost, exiled, and wretched,
With no recourse, 620
Lacking her quite sweet comfort,
But now I was recovered, brought back from death,
Enriched beyond belief, filled with great consolation,
And without tribulation
Was I when she told me: 'Lover, I give myself to you 625
Most willingly.' And this quite sweet boon
Made me a hundred thousand times grander than a king,
So that no one
Could describe the joy I felt.
For I was so happy I could not 630
Utter my thanks, was not able to speak.
But in the end,
Like a lover loyal and pure, with a noble heart,

Inflamed to love, without a devious thought,
Very humbly, with lowered head, I told her 635
Without difficulty:
'Lady, whom I love above all others, myself included,
To whom I devote reason, heart, time, life, and affection,
As much as I have power, but not as I should,
I thank you 640
For the noble gift of your sweet mercy
Since you have so greatly enriched,
So elated, so cured, so rewarded me
That truly
If everything beneath the sky 645
Or all that was or will be
Had been given me entirely to do my will,
I would not value it
A hundredth part as I do your mercy.
So I pray God I may never wrong you 650
In anything that might sully our love,
And also that I might fulfill
Your will as much as I intend,
Humbly, not haughtily, not proudly—
For, if I can, much better than has been my wont 655
I will serve you
Quite faithfully from my heart and love you;
And in all things I will guard your honor well.
Not in word, deed, or thought
Will I do anything 660
Against you or anyone that will make you angry.
Instead you will be my lady and my sweetheart,
My divinity on earth, adored above all others;
And without a doubt,
If I do something against your pleasure, 665
Whatever might anger or torment your heart,
Know truly it would be through oversight alone.'
My lady, in this manner
I thanked her, just as you have heard,
For the noble gift of her sweet mercy. 670
And she in turn pledged to me and swore
Quite adamantly
She would from this day forward love me loyally,
Without forsaking or deserting me.
And so for a long time I was crowned with joy; 675
Nothing
Contrary to joy did I experience;
Instead I was happy and full of celebration,
Much more jolly and gay than I had ever been.

And it was proper
That I did my best to be kind and thoughtful,
Since it seemed in all ways that I was
The best loved of lovers and their king.
But when Fortune,[7]
The betrayer, who does not treat everyone the same,
Had lifted me up so high, in an evil and miserly fashion
She valued my goods and me no more than a fig.
Instead she frowned,
Denied me, turned her face away;
After she had seated me atop her wheel,
She turned it, and I tumbled into the mud.
But she did this,
That traitress who is quick and ready on all occasions
To undo those she puts beneath her wing,
Because God and beautiful Nature,
When they shaped
The woman I love, so greatly delighted
In the incredible beauty they bestowed upon her
That they forgot to give her faithfulness.
And what a loss!
For I know well and clearly see
That my lady, whose body is so lovely,
Whom my heart respects, loves, obeys, and serves,
Has taken a new
Lover without cause, someone other than me.
And so, lady, if I moan and cry
Quite bitterly and often utter 'Oh me!'
It is no wonder
Since her pure beauty without peer,
Her vibrant complexion, fresh and rosy,
And that sweet look that tortures me still
Have abandoned me,
And she has uttered her last goodbye
And, too, has completely dismissed me.
Alas! How could my heart be happy?
And quite wrongfully
She has taken back my joy and comfort,
Putting me in such great distress
That I know well it will be my death.
Nor might anything
Save me from this or provide a single comfort.
But what tears and breaks my heart
Is that I don't know whom to blame
For my suffering,
Since it seems that if I was thrown down

The ladder I once had climbed through Fortune,
Whom I do not trust or depend upon,
Then, to tell the truth,
I should feel no bitterness toward her for this,
Since in the deed she simply did her duty;   730
And she ought to have no other task
But betraying
Those she watches mount up, grow rich,
As well as raising high those of low estate.
Nor can she love any person so dearly   735
That she would issue
A guarantee for him to keep his luck,
Whether it is happiness or disaster,
And would not suddenly bring him up or down.
Such is her nature.   740
Her goods are but lucky happenstance,
Which is merely breeze, deceptive form.
They are a joy that hardly lasts and is worth little.
He's a fool who trusts it!
She deceives and defies all,   745
And if I say that the death destroying me
I can blame on my pretty lady,
By what logic
Would I do so and for what cause?[8]
She has become subject to the rule   750
Of Love, to whom she gives herself
Completely,
And she is eager for Love to govern her
As her sovereign and to be under Love's command.
So she cannot go against   755
The wishes of Love;
Instead she finds it always necessary to obey.
Then if it is my lady's pleasure and desire
To abandon me and cherish some other man,
Love does this,   760
Not my lady, who is completely worthy,
For she did her duty and the honorable thing
In obeying her sovereign lord.
And so, when Love
Inflamed me to love, I think   765
That Love, so doing, wronged me more
Than my lady did,
That is,
If Love indeed could wrong me.
But that I cannot understand at all,   770
Since for a long time like a sweet and tender mother

She nourished me
As best she could with her sweet goods,
Nor have I yet perceived,
For any hurt I might have received, 775
That she has been
Less than a friend by my side,
Serving me with all her meals,
Tears for starters and sighing for a sweet.
Such is my meat; 780
My appetite does not wish or ask for more;
And, by my soul, I am not drawn toward anything
Save what breaks my heart.
And therefore Love
Grows in my heart in proportion to my pain, 785
Nor does she leave by night or day.
Instead she is my companion in my painful weeping
Because of her goodness.
And so I maintain that it is great friendship
To be my mother in prosperity 790
And in adversity the same.
Then I should be
Quite wicked if I complained of her,
For I find her always at my side,
Nor does she destroy me in the least, 795
For she cannot
Alter hearts, since God does not wish it so.
But when God made the lady who was wont to
Call me lover, for whom my heart feels such pain,
If He and Nature, 800
When they created her noble and pure beauty,
More pleasing to all men than that of any other,
Had they then in that sweet form
Put loyalty,
I would yet be called her lover, 805
And her heart, which promised me so much,
Would never have been my foe.
So in this matter I say
That God and Nature did act in ignorance
(Saving their honor and the respect due them) 810
When they fashioned such a pretty shape
Without loyalty.
For if she had been a hundred times less beautiful
And yet faithful, the great virtue
Of loyalty would have done her more honor 815
Than if she had been
A hundred times prettier—and she would then have been more pleasing,

And she should have been more pleasing
Because there would have been nothing to fault.
So I believe 820
That not Good Love, not Fortune, nor my lady
Should be blamed for my sorrows.
Then can I blame myself in any way?
Yes, certainly!
For I took myself from riches to wretchedness, 825
From safety to mortal peril,
From joy to pain through her subtle look,
And from freedom
Into a servitude where no one loves or values
Me, my honor, affection, or service, 830
Or even my precious life as much as a cherry.
Nonetheless
It seems that I did no wrong
By falling in love with her, for in this world
There was no lady living as excellent, 835
So they said.
Thus with good intention I became hers
And never hoped for anything but good
Because of the grandeur of her most impressive fame,
Which has destroyed me. 840
But all that glitters is not gold,
And no one should love his delight so much
That he cannot abandon it when he thinks to.
And had I been
The world's greatest man, I would not have chosen 845
Anyone save her, nor could I have done better
Had I found loyalty in her.
So I do not know
Whom to blame or accuse
For the grievous pain and misfortune I suffer. 850
Were I asked, to all I would answer
That God and Nature
Did this; so it is misadventure and sorrow
That they made her body so beautiful
In every way, so noble, so sweet no one could do better 855
Had it been faithful.
Should I call these two to account for my woes?
I will not, because they are too exalted for me;
Instead I shall endure; that's my best course
From this moment on. 860

Now I have told you how
Love made me a true lover,

The circumstances, the means, and all that was agreed;
What happened to me;
How I was taken, how I was held; 865
How my lady does not think of me;
The joys, the sorrows I have had to endure
Right until this present day;
How I have help from no one;
How I cannot avenge my grievous hurt, 870
Which harms, destroys me so much
That I say
(If you have heard me well and listened)
The pain in which I languish, dying,
Which has made pale and wan my face 875
With its harshness,
Is a hundred thousand times greater than your pain;
For pure joy and perfect sweetness
Are your ills measured against the hurt
That tortures me." 880
"Certainly, sir, I would not deny
You feel much pain and anger
To have lost her whom your heart thus desires;
But nonetheless
It seems to me, and I dare say it, 885
Considering your pain and mine,
You feel less hurt and more joy
Than do I.
And I will tell you the reason why.
You have said to me that you love faithfully 890
The lady who gives you so much distress
And that you'll love her
With a loyal heart as long as you do live.
Since you love her in this way,
I certainly believe you desire her love, 895
For very seldom
Have I seen love to exist without desire,
Or the desire for love to be able to last
Without hope; and memory comes to you
Sometimes, 900
So that whenever desire devastates your heart,
You remember the beauty with the blond hair;
Of whom you have more thoughts than three.
Then it cannot be
You never have a single thought that makes 905
Joy grow within you and relieves
The pain that so tightly binds you;
So in the end

Through memory you have happy thoughts
That shove the sorrow out and make you forget it. 910
But mine multiplies day and night
Without a rest,
And every day the stream of my tears increases,
And I cannot ever think about
Or have hope of recovering my love. 915
But by serving,
By honoring, remaining discreet, respecting,
By happily enduring and suffering,
By loving well from the heart and obeying
Quite humbly, 920
You still might find relief, joy,
And the love of the woman your heart is drawn toward.
So I say I am the one more tormented,
And quite evident
Is the reason, it seems to me, and sound; 925
For it possible to have your lady back,
But to have my lover back, that is impossible
According to Nature's law."
"Lady, there's more honor, wisdom,
And moderation in you than in any one else. 930
Now by your reasoning I should be undone
Quite quickly
Could I not answer your arguments.
Yet truly I cannot accomplish this
With as much wisdom as required. 935
But I intend
Going over your reasons if I can manage it.
You argue that I love without deceit
And will as long as I might live
Without repenting; 940
And since I love, I must experience desire,
Which cannot do without or lack
Hope; and so I have memories
That often
Move me to thinking many thoughts. 945
Lady, I certainly grant all that you say
Save only this: I have no hope at all.
But mark well,
Lady, even though our intentions here are only good,
In this your understanding and my own 950
Do not accord at all, agree in nothing;
Rather they are opposed,
As I think to make clear to you
When the time is right. But I will not pass over

In silence your statement that I can still do so much 955
By honoring,
By serving well, suffering, respecting,
By obeying, by loving loyally
That I can in joy get my lady back.
Now it would be 960
Quite a trick to keep her, whoever could;
For her heart would not remain in one place,
No more than a ball on a roof.
And your lover,
Who was so strong and worthy, 965
You cannot recover in any fashion;
Thus your color is wan and pale.
So you say
That my pains are much less
Than your own; and therefore I have not triumphed, 970
Nor have I earned the judgment by my merits.
For this reason I will answer
Your arguments as best I can,
And I will spend time on each one;
Also I will reveal what I think and know 975
From my point of view.

Lady, it's true I love quite faithfully the woman
Who hates me, that is, my lady of noble form
Who is my death and my destruction
When I witness her 980
Love another man and she thinks no thoughts of me,
Whom she in good faith ought to love;
So I am almost driven mad
By this love.
For if she loved my life or honor, 985
She would not for all the world
Let me languish one hour of a day
In the state where I live and dwell.
But with great force they increase the tide
Of suffering that floods my heart: 990
Love first, and my lady second.
For this reason I feel desire.
But what for? To die swiftly,
For nothing could possibly happen
That would give me hope for cure, 995
And had I
A better love from her than I once had,
I don't know if I would trust it.
Surely I would not! Why? I would not dare.

For nurture, 1000
As they say, conquers and overcomes nature,
And always, if he doesn't go against his kind,
The wolf makes his way to the woods—that's the pure truth.
For this reason
My desire has no hope at all, 1005
But instead a despair so fierce
That I will be destroyed in the sharp corner
Of memory,
Which, you said, gives rise in me
To the thought that makes me rejoice. 1010
Surely I'll not be able ever to find joy in this thought,
Nor have I yet;
And I have not seen, felt, or heard it
Since my lady took a new lover,
For that thought parted from me at that time. 1015
So I intend proving
That this memory is what grieves me
More and makes my heart
Despair more. You know—it's clear,
Everyone sees it— 1020
That if I never thought about
My lady, who binds me so tightly to her,
My pain would be forgotten.
And were she
Forgotten, the forgetting would make 1025
The pain die completely out or cease;
And this could cure me of all my sickness.
But what would happen?
This memory, by its subtle trickery,
Recalls to me the gentle face 1030
And the noble body for whom my heart breaks;
Yet this memory is conceived,
Born and perfected, endures
All in suffering. Why? Because I considered myself
Loved when I was called lover 1035
Quite sweetly.
Alas! Sorrowful! Now it is quite otherwise
When my lady has taken to loving another man.
And could one do worse, lady, unless he hanged himself?
Surely not! 1040
For such a thing sends a lover into ruination,
And not one man in five hundred thousand
Is apt to escape such deadly danger.
And so it happens
Often when I remember this 1045

That the weary heart in my body becomes
So full of pain I have to faint.
And if thought
Takes shape through memory in me,
What is it? It's something with no comfort, 1050
Sad, mournful, filled with sorrow, and despairing.
And by my faith,
I have no thought that is not my foe.
So this makes it worse. Do you know why?
Because I witness my lady change her heart. 1055
And if the joy
I had when in her grace
Had not been greater than I could describe
Or was able to imagine or even conceive,
The grievous pain 1060
That grips me would be rather less.
But as much as I did once possess great joy,
So is my suffering crueler.
And that I could
Get my lady back or have any hope of doing so— 1065
This I cannot imagine or conceive.
And I'll tell you what makes me suffer in this regard:
Lady, it seems
That something which separates and then unites
In several places, and likewise is in motion, 1070
Keeps no more still than an aspen leaf,
And lacks stability,
Instead is always variable and changing,
Now here, now there, at the hearth, at the table,
And then elsewhere, is something to be wary of. 1075
For in no way
Might any man possess it in security.
It must truly be the play of some spell,
For believing to have it for certain,
One does not at all. 1080
So it is, lady, whatever anyone might say,
With my beloved, who changes and varies,
Gives and takes back, now hates, now is a friend,
And all her heart
Is not in one place, and if anyone shares in it, 1085
I certainly believe his portion is a poor one
And will soon vanish from him.⁹
Nor, to judge rightly,
Could a lover hold another man so dear
He would want that one to share 1090
His loving, plain and simple—that's not even in his thoughts.

And because I clearly cannot
Possess her whole heart, I lament;
For a heart that goes this way from hand to hand,
Should some man own it by night, he won't in the morning. 1095
And in any case,
The true lover is a proper bird of prey
Since he, as his joy, wishes nothing
But the whole heart of the woman to whom he is devoted.
And so I say 1100
You will get your lover back as quickly
As her heart will be so transformed
That it will be granted me completely,
Never to be withdrawn.
For no man can remove the wolf's pelt 1105
Without flaying him, nor can anyone turn
An ox into a sparrowhawk or vice versa.
And, sweet lady,
The custom is universal among men and women
That when the soul has departed the body, 1110
And the body is in the ground beneath the tombstone,
It is forgotten
In a brief while, though it is wept over.
For no man or woman I have seen has remained
So long in mourning that they fail to seek out joy again 1115
Before a year
Has passed, however faithful the lover,
And I will not except those of either high or low degree.
And truly I believe this is reasonable.
So you will follow 1120
This custom; you will not violate it at all,
For no one will reproach you;
And you will pray for the soul with a good heart.
But I cannot
Ignore the woman whom I do not forget 1125
Because Memory keeps her very close to me
Without leaving for a day, an hour, not even half an hour;
For I see her
Rather often, and this at once undoes me
Whenever I follow her with my eyes a long time 1130
And find no joy, no good, no guidance there.
Instead, I witness another man
Taking joy in her. This is what destroys me;
For if she would not love either him or me,
I should have complained of my pains to no one; 1135
Instead, I would have borne them
Humbly within my heart and kept them secret,

Enduring in the hope of joy,
And thus I would fear neither misadventure nor pain.
And because I fear desertion 1140
I do not wish to take back my heart,
I who remain too long alive, and—it's no lie—
I do not know how to repent of loving.
And I would be
A faithless lover if I left her, 1145
Because with no 'but' I gave her my love.
And I will love her whatever happens to me;
And, by my faith,
So faithfully do I love her that I feel a hundred times
More pain for her than for myself 1150
Because I see her honor ruined; for with their finger
They will point her out,
Those who learn of this business,
And they will trust her much less in every way,
For they will always consider her false. 1155
Now deception
Is a vice so base and ugly
That the person who indulges in it, however powerful,
Will never be completely rid of it or reformed.
So I conclude, 1160
Lady, that I feel much more pain
And that your ill will come sooner
To a cure than the one that grips me tight.
And I would truly dare
To expect the judgment, 1165
Had we a judge who would decide
Faithfully and according to the truth."
"By my soul, sir,
I intend and dare to say for my part
That with all my heart I wish a judgment. 1170
Let us look now to whom we would choose,
Some man who without foolishness
Could determine which of us is wrong;
For the trouble I bear, it seems to me, is so cruel
That no one this side of death could endure more." 1175
"Lady, I want
The judge to be as you wish."
"I yield to you, fair sir, and so I counsel
That he be chosen by your advice alone,
For you have 1180
First sought him; so you must say."
"Surely, my lady, don't wash your hands of this now;
Please, you say because you know much more

Than I do."
And when I saw they desired[10]   1185
A judgment to be rendered about their painful cases,
Joy came over my heart.
And I did not know
Which of two things I would do:
Move toward them or restrain myself.   1190
For I would have willingly put them on the path
Of finding a judge
Able to undertake ruling on their cases
So skillfully there would be nothing to do but learn from it,
And afterward there should be no cause for dispute.   1195
So I deliberated
Quite a while and decided
I would go to them. Then I rose up
Without delay and made my way toward them,
All unseen   1200
Through the grass so green and thick;
When I had drawn near enough
That I could see them all in the open,
The little dog,
Who did not know me at all, began to bark;   1205
And because of this the lady, who knew much of virtue,
Startled (this I clearly witnessed)
And called him.
But he thought little of her summons
Since, barking, the dog drew nearer   1210
Until he tore with his teeth at my robe.
So I picked him up,
And he stopped barking out of fear.
Now in my heart I enjoyed this very much
Because I returned him to his mistress   1215
In order to have the chance
And excuse to go where I wanted;
And all the time I stroked his fur,
But when I got where I wanted to be,
I was not silent   1220
Or embarrassed at all; instead with a cheerful face
I saluted all the company,
As I knew how to do for my part.
The knight,
Who was wise, courteous, and well-spoken,   1225
Big, tall and straight, handsome, noble and graceful,
Well taught and accustomed to do the honorable thing,
Without further delay
Graciously came forward to return my greeting.

And the lady in whom Nature wished to make clear 1230
How no man could comprehend her great beauty
Drew toward me
Quite softly, quietly, and slowly,
For her appearance was very gracious
And her carriage meek, pleasing, and beyond reproach; 1235
And her hair was blond,
Her eyes smiling, grayer than any falcon's,
And her body noble, well-shaped, pleasing, and long,
Formed better than a hunting bird's.
And attractively spaced 1240
Were her eyes, her manner and bearing pleasant,
Yet while her demeanor and noble dress
Were simple, they were beyond compare.
Whiter she was
Than snow on the bough, 1245
Wise, faithful, courteous, generous at heart,
And in all aspects of her character so perfect
That her loyalty
Was much more attractive than her beauty.
In her was neither haughtiness nor cruelty, 1250
Nothing contrary to friendship.
Yet her face
Was stained by tears, much stained by them;
Nonetheless she was endowed
With a perfect complexion, a pure sweetness. 1255
And so the lady
Beckoned, then questioned me, asked
Very wisely how I had come to that place.
And I, who was eager to hear her,
Related and told 1260
Her the truth from beginning to end
Of how I had come there and where I had been
While they were recounting their misfortunes.
Then the knight spoke
Softly, in a joking way: 1265
"I think he has heard all our debate."
And I said to him: "Sir, do not doubt it,
For truly
I listened to it most attentively
And willingly; but you must not think 1270
My intentions are anything but good; for in truth
I came here
From above the stream by a grassy path
Into these woods, where I found delight
In the birds whose song I listened to. 1275

And after coming
To this spot, I noticed you,
And from the other direction, sir, I saw this lady arrive.
And I will tell you what I did with myself.
I searched out											1280
The leafiest part of the greenery and hid there,
For I greatly feared annoying you two;
And there I listened to your joys and sufferings
From beginning to end.
Now it seems to me you would									1285
Eagerly learn through a judgment which one might be
The more grievous: your mischance or that of the lady
Whose head is bowed.
You did not wish to be the first
To select the judge, and neither did my lady.							1290
So I came forward here advisedly
In order to name for you
A knight who does much to make himself loved,[11]
For on this side of the channel or on the other
No heart is nobler, none more generous, none less cruel.					1295
Because in generosity
He surpasses Alexander[12] and in prowess Hector,[13]
He is the pillar of all nobility,
Nor does he live as a slave to his wealth.
Instead he wishes nothing									1300
Save the honor from every worldly good,
And he is happier when he can say 'It's yours!'
Than the greedy man is to take from his riches.
He loves God,
The Church, loyalty, and justice so much							1305
He is called the Sword of Justice;
He is humble and pleasant, full of generosity
For his friends,
Fierce and cruel toward his enemies;
And to be brief, he always earns, so good men say,						1310
The highest esteem for his intelligence, honor, and worthiness
Wherever he might go.
And if it happens that he gets the upper hand
Of his enemy, Nature teaches him,
As does his own good heart, to pity the man.							1315
He sets a noble example,
For Prowess everywhere carries his sword,
Hardihood accompanies, encourages him,
And for him Generosity opens the door
Of every heart.										1320
To the virtuous (I make no exceptions),

To those of all conditions, the great and small, those in between,
He is like a brother and sister.
Sir, of Love
He knows all the assaults, the skirmishes, 1325
The joys, the pains, the sorrowing and moaning
Better than did Ovid himself, who knew all its intricacies.[14]
And if his name,
So good and of such gentle renown,
You wish to know—or don't—then tell me." 1330
"Certainly, my friend, tell us, we beg you,
For never yet,
So I think, has any man been,
Nor will ever be, as perfect in every way
As is this one in both word and deed." 1335
"Sir, his battle flag
Proclaims Luxembourg, and he is king of Bohemia,[15]
Son to Henry the good king of Germany,
Who by force of arms, no matter who might bemoan it,
Was crowned 1340
Emperor at Rome with his mother.
So if this man is good, it is surely right he appears so,
For this he owes to his mother and father.
And so, fair sir,
To choose such a judge would be wise, 1345
A man who could with skill demonstrate and explain
To you both which one suffers greater pain;
So choose him."
Like a wise man, the knight answered:
"I believe God has led us to this spot." 1350
And he said: "Madam, if you accept him as our judge,
I will agree to it."
Without any foolishness, the lady responded:
"Sir, I have heard so much good spoken of this king,
Who is so wise, so brave, of such magnificence 1355
That I concur."
"Many thanks, lady; now we are in agreement.
So I pray God may comfort the good king
And lead us safely to good harbor
So that we might 1360
Speak to him wherever we must go."
I answered: "I know quite well how to tell you
Where he is, and, if you please, lead you there.
Of that I am certain,
For truly I ate and drank yesterday 1365
With his entourage in Durbuy Castle.
There he yet remains and will not leave today;

Nor is it
Very far from here, not even a league, or half,
Not the quarter of a distance a voice will carry." 1370
The knight then asked the lady to set out
Without further delay.
The lady said: "I have no wish to refuse,
But I do not know which path to take."
I said: "Lady, I am quite willing to show you. 1375
Come on.
I will go ahead and you follow along."
And so I started out, eager to go,
And when they saw Durbuy Castle close at hand,
They stopped 1380
And greatly marveled at the sight of it,
Since never before in their lives had they
Seen any place this beautiful, this noble, so they said.
And, no doubt,
The place is quite secure and extremely pleasant, 1385
Beautiful and attractive, easy to defend,
For if the kings of both Germany and France
Were before it,
Those inside need never give up
Going in and out as they wished, 1390
Anytime they had cause to travel
Into the countryside.
It is on a rise in the middle of a valley
Thoroughly encompassed by a river
That is huge, noisy, deep, rough, and wide; 1395
And the orchards
All around are so pretty that, to give them their due,
None prettier could ever be hoped for.
Within them, moreover, the birds make such a commotion
That night and day 1400
The valley echoes with their song.
And the river too gurgles pleasantly.
As a result, one could find no greater delight.
And then beyond
There are cliffs all around, but not too close, 1405
Instead at such distance from the castle that no weapon,
No siege machine, no arbalest could shoot at it from there.
But the keep
Above the rocks is so ably fashioned
Never was another seen of more beautiful form, 1410
Since it lacks faults of any kind.
And the spring
In the courtyard is by no means unpleasant;

Rather it flows free from clean and healthy rock,
Cold as ice, sweeter than the Seine.   1415
But the fountain
Into which it falls was chiseled
From fine marble, white and gray-brown, so pretty
There has been none its equal since the time of Abel.
Above the riverbank   1420
The meadow is broad, long, and ample,
Where many kinds of grasses are found.
To my story, however, I must return.
After they had looked over
The residence, I advised them,   1425
Saying: "It's time to go.
Let us proceed; for we are accomplishing nothing here."
So we walked along
The length of the path and crossed the bridge,
Halting neither here nor there   1430
Until at last we knocked on the gate.
But the porter
Opened the gate cordially and willingly.
It was I who took the lead and knocked,
Being rather familiar with the place,   1435
And I said:
"This knight and this lady too
Have come to speak with the king if he is here."
And the porter answered me at once
That he was within.   1440
I said: "Friend, please find out if one might
Speak with him." And he said he would go.
Yet just as he was leaving us
To make his way above,
A knight who was handsome, noble, broad-shouldered,   1445
Friendly, and attractive approached us;
His name was Honor, and he knew more about it than anyone.
And in no way did he come
All alone to us; instead a beautiful lady,
Pleasant and friendly, was his companion,   1450
And she was called Lady Courtesy.
And, truly, this she seemed to be,
For as soon as she spied us,
She offered a greeting, then received us graciously.
Honor did the same, just as he should do.   1455
And then the two of them,
Courteously, smiling, without ado,
Each took one of the couple by the hand.
But Courtesy, I should say,

Merrily 1460
Accompanied the knight with no haughtiness,
And Honor intended to escort the lady;
Then they began to converse and in this manner
They set out,
Talking all the while, to where they were leading them, 1465
Climbing some marble stairs
Until they at last entered the good king's hall.
And the good king,
Who was wise in all circumstances,
Loyal, valiant, generous, and well-mannered, 1470
Kind, unassuming, and courteous to all,
Was seated
In very great contentment on a silk rug,
And some clerk whom I cannot name
Was reading to him the battle of Troy. 1475
But Hardihood
Was his companion, and Prowess too, that one's daughter,
And quite gently he was holding the hand of Generosity,
A lady of quite great nobility.
Wealth was present, 1480
Love, Beauty, Loyalty, and Happiness,
Desire, Thought, Will, and Nobility,
Liberality, Honor, Courtesy, Youth.
These sixteen were
With the king and never left his side; 1485
God and Nature had bestowed them upon him
At birth; and so all did him service.
The favor was great.
And if a gentleman or lady ever did
Something that could be called misdeed, 1490
Reason was present to erase the fault.
And in this way
Was the noble king enthroned, and seeing the lady,
He rose and took her by the hand,
For this was what Courtesy had taught him. 1495
Afterward he received
The knight, and esteeming him greatly
In his heart, then asked these two
Quite wisely why they had come,
Inquiring about 1500
How they were, which greatly interested him.
The knight asked the lady
If she would speak to the king, and she said
She would not do so;
Instead, he should explain, it being more fitting for him. 1505

Then he answered that he would tell him
Everything step by step, just how the matter stood
Right to the end.
"Sire," he said, "close by is a garden
Green and flowery, where there is a grand chorus   1510
Of nightingales; I went there this morning
To listen to
Their beautiful service and pleasant singing,
Though my heart could take
Little pleasure because nothing can comfort it.   1515
However,
When I had come to that spot by chance,
Full of the pains Love provides and thinking on them,
I saw arrive by a narrow path,
Green and grassy,   1520
This lady who has accompanied me here.
And I thought her manner distraught;
So at once I made my way
Through the thick grass,
Directing my steps toward her.   1525
And when I was close, I greeted her,
But she said not a word, at which I wondered,
And she took no notice
Of me, not with her eye or manner.
And I, bewildered why this was so,   1530
Said pleasantly: 'So sweet dear lady, why is it
You will not heed my words?'
And at the panel of her skirt I tugged.
And she startled and her pretty face   1535
Changed color.
Without further pause she then responded,
Fervently apologizing to me
For the thoughts that preoccupied her.
And I asked   1540
Why she was so melancholy at heart.
At last I said and did enough
That she told me what I had asked
So truthfully
I swore upon my faith and pledged to her   1545
That when she had finished speaking,
I would tell her my own thoughts.
And so she said
That once she had a faithful lover
Who loved her loyally, as she did him.   1550
But death took the man from the world,
And the valor,

The intelligence, the worthiness, the prowess, the honor
That, she said, had in him their flower—
These had made him the very best among good men. 1555
For this reason she was deep
In thought and never ceased being so,
And, while thinking, cried for and bemoaned him
So that her face was bathed in tears.
Therefore she maintains 1560
That the pain is more grievous that comes to her
On her lover's account than the grief that grips me.
Sire, I maintain (and so I must)
Just the contrary.
I love faithfully from the heart without desisting 1565
The woman most beautiful and with the sweetest face
Nature has ever yet been able to create,
Who once gave me
Her heart completely and abandoned it to me.
She called me her heart, her love, her lover, 1570
And she said she loved me above all others.
But now,
Sire, she no longer cares for me:
Instead she has thrown me over and taken a new lover.
And, by my soul, I have in no way deserved this. 1575
And elsewhere
She bestows and shares out what was my reward,
Nor of this can I have either share or portion.
For this reason, Sire, my heart is breaking.
And so I think, 1580
Considering my reasons, to have it worse
Than the lady, since, although her lover
Has died, he may be with God in paradise!
And, Sire, this clerk,
Who seems friendly and merry and knowledgeable, 1585
Was hidden in the garden and covered up
In the thickest brush, which is all green.
He emerged
After he had clearly heard all our discussion
And advised us to put the right and wrong of it 1590
Before you, and this was our agreement.
For our talk
Had lasted a long time,
And we made many arguments,
Just as it is written more fully 1595
Here above.[16]
Now we have come before you
So that the right might be judged and known

And your sentence be kept by us both.
Therefore you can end   1600
This debate at once if it pleases you;
For we have made you our judge.
Sire, now you have heard all our dispute
In full;
So please render a judgment   1605
Because we have desired one a long time,
And this lady and I earnestly
Beg you for it."

After he had put their cases to him,
This man who knew well how to do so quite wisely,   1610
The noble king, a very worthy man,
Answered him:
"So God keep me, you have chosen in me
A judge who is ignorant and lacks discernment;
And never before have I heard or seen   1615
Such a case.
And I know little about judging it.
Nonetheless I wish to hear the counsel
Of my court; for mine is both noble and good."
Then, smiling,   1620
He summoned Loyalty, who was present,
As well as Love, Youth, and Reason, who was the first
To speak, and the noble king
Then asked them:
"What say you who know all the laws?   1625
This knight who is noble and well-mannered
And also this lady with the blond hair
Have come here
Before me, for which I thank them,
And they wish to hear a judgment from me   1630
As to which suffers greater pain and worry.
The lady had
A faithful lover who loved and served her,
And she him, as much as she was able.
Now it is that death, who receives everyone,   1635
Has taken him from her.
So her heart is sorrowful and troubled,
For in his time he had such great virtue
There was none better, no man more handsome.
The knight,   1640
Not repenting, loves with his whole heart
The most beautiful woman alive in his opinion,
And she pledged him her faith not to alter,

Not to change,
And she accepted him as her lover, 1645
Loved him well—of this he was quite certain.
Now the lady has given another man her heart
And thrown him over
Completely in every regard, showing him no concern.
And with his very eyes he sees this beauty and the man 1650
Who possesses the sweet goods that he himself has deserved.
Now I have told you
Why they have come to hear my sentence.
And, doubtless, a heart that languishes this way
Quite destroys itself and lives on in much pain. 1655
So you are to offer
Me advice in this matter, the best you can;
For each of you is my intimate and friend,
And I place much trust in you, as well you know.
Speak, Reason. 1660
I want to hear your opinion first,
For you have given me much good advice."
Reason, who was beautiful and of good repute,
Answered thus:
"Sire, I say that these two lovers are 1665
Greatly anguished because they have lost
Those they love, and their hearts melt
Just as, before the flame,
The wax wastes away, grows smaller.
But that they are just the same in suffering 1670
And misfortune—this I do not intend to say.
What sways me
I will state since it is necessary:
This lady can never see
Her lover true as she once did. 1675
And so it will happen
That because she sees him no longer,
I will work to make her forget him,
For the heart will never love a thing so much
Not to forget it 1680
As time goes by. Of course, I do not say at all
That for a time she will not feel pain and torment,
But Youth, who is so very gay and happy,
Will not allow
For any reason that he not be forgotten. 1685
For Youth, Sire, no matter what,
Causes one to forget quickly what one does not see.
I state further
That Love does not have the power

To sustain itself without the lover 1690
Neither for a single hour of a day, nor without the beloved either.
And if one of these three
Is missing, the other two will fail;
For Love, lover, and beloved must remain
Together or the affair is worth nothing. 1695
And since the beloved and Love
Have lost the company of the lover,
I certainly would not give
A rotten apple for their love affair,
And here is the reason: 1700
This love is a worldly thing.
For love is quite good at doing its job
So that the soul can feel it.
But there is no soul,
No man alive who loves this way without sin 1705
When struck by the amorous flame,
Loving the body much more than the soul.
And why?
Love arises from fleshly attraction,
And its desire and nature 1710
Are inclined completely toward satisfaction.
So no man
Or woman who intends to love can prevent
Vice or sin from being part of it; it must be so,
And this opposes the soul, which sorrows over it. 1715
Furthermore,
As soon as the soul departs
The body, love leaves and distances itself.
I see exactly this everywhere, may God preserve me!
And so this lady's 1720
Love, which has so much strength,
Diminishes day by day.
And in proportion her suffering does the same.[17]
But this lover,
Who has rashly undertaken to love 1725
Against my advice and embarked upon this course,
This unfortunate man, all weakened by it,
Finds
The pains of love in his heart too bitter
Because Love makes him burn night and day, 1730
And he would not or could not forget
His enemy.
Do you know why? Because Companionship,
Love, Beauty, and joyous Youth,
Loyalty too (whom I will not forget) 1735

Make him languish
In great madness, in rage,
In obliviousness, and in great jealousy,
And in the peril of his soul and life.
For early and late   1740
His sorrowing heart never leaves his lady,
But without departing is everywhere her companion;
And the man closer to the fire gets more burned.
And Loyalty
Prevents him from proving false.   1745
But had he acted on my advice
When his lady took a new lover,
He should not
Have continued the affair; for in such a case,
If the lady sings high or low,   1750
The man must proceed at a trot or walk.
Afterward Beauty
Told him he would do much better languishing
In love for her than in finding joy from some other.
Love did the same. Youth fed him   1755
On madness
In this misery, in this foolish error
So that he lost strength and wit.
Thus the grieving man languished in pain;
But seeing that other man,   1760
With him present, rejoice in his beloved,
In this lady who used to call him her lover,
His heart is so jealous, so distraught
It's a wonder
The man does not kill himself or set out   1765
To kill the one who torments him so.
And Jealousy puts this in his ear.
And if he possessed
Her love as was his wont,
What would he do with it? Surely, nothing.   1770
For never a single day would he trust it.
Therefore he has
No hope of ever having other comfort
Because he cannot cool in his affection
For this lady who hurts him so.   1775
And thus I maintain
That he feels more pain than this lady here,
And that his heart experiences more anguish
For the reasons you have heard.[18]
And, to my satisfaction,   1780
This knight has spoken quite well to them,

As I found all in writing here above,[19]
And with reason he has proved his contention.
Such is my view."
After Reason had stated all her opinion,   1785
Love spoke up, who was very good looking,
Gracious in manner and appearance,
And said: "Reason,
You have quite ably made known your reasoning,
And I agree, save it would be a grievous misdeed   1790
To rescue the lover's heart from its prison
Within the beautiful lady,
For whom he feels love's spark.
So it is my wish that he love and serve her as one
In whom he has found much happy news,   1795
For if he could
Live a thousand years and serve her every day,
Never by service would he merit
The great sweetness she was wont to show him.
And if Pleasure,   1800
Who has brought on many a strange alteration,
Makes him doubt his lady,
Must he then despair?
Surely not at all!
For in my service are a hundred thousand more   1805
Who love almost as strongly as does he
And have for it not the price of a whetstone.
And I have the power
To cure him or worsen his pain,
But he no longer has trust or hope   1810
In me, and that is what makes him suffer most."[20]
"How so, Love?"
Said Reason, "Is it then by your design
That the man will love without experiencing any relief
The lady who has granted her heart elsewhere?   1815
And he who serves you
Receives in no way the reward that he deserves?
Surely, it's a fool who persists in serving
Such a master when he loses his wages."
After this,   1820
Loyalty drew herself up in front of Love
And said that no wrong would have been done
Had he made a sop from such bread.
"And it's not right
If he is true, loyal, and worthy   1825
That he should be one who beats the bushes
From which others take the birds.

For if the lady,
Whom I blame and condemn quite harshly
(And quite rightly since she deserves 1830
Much blame for proving fickle in this serious game),
Had not
First taken back her heart from this lover,
Who was completely under her control,
Love, Love, I would have spoken differently. 1835
But there is no doubt,
Since he loves her with all his might
And she for no cause ignores him,
He ought to dance the same dance that she does;
This wouldn't be 1840
Something that merits the loss of my favor,
But if he abandoned her and looked elsewhere,
I would not consider that he had sinned against me.
So I concur
Completely with all of Reason's conclusion 1845
(For she has offered a good and true accounting):
Namely that the man is right, and this lady is wrong."[21]
And when Youth,
Who was very gay and full of happiness
And pays no mind to gifts or promises, 1850
Only to what appeals to her,
Heard
What Reason had said and stated,
And Loyalty as well—she thought little of it
Because she was quite full of her own willfulness; 1855
And she said loudly:
"Surely, Reason, your wisdom fails you,
And Loyalty, know that nothing is of any use,
For this lover, despite any pain, any assault
Love may inflict upon him, 1860
Will never be parted from that lovely topaz
Who in beauty and sweetness surpasses all others,
In pure color as well: may it never please God
It comes to pass
That he holds back from loving such beauty! 1865
For if at present she does not want, will not bend to him,
At least he loves her and his heart is her companion.
And isn't that enough?
Must he tire of loving her?
Surely not! For no one is loved, 1870
Or treated kindly, or called lover every day;
That's true, beyond a doubt.
Reason, the lover is a fool who listens to you

Or follows your dictates or path.
And whoever does, I say he can see nothing. 1875
And by my faith,
We will do much, Love, my lady, and I,
To so imprison his heart in such straits
That night or day it will not leave of its own accord;
Nor will your efforts 1880
(Don't doubt this) ever be strong enough
To make this lover's pure heart abandon
The quite beautiful lady in whom it finds so little comfort.
Thus Love, my lady,
Who burns, pales, scorches, and inflames his heart, 1885
As well as I, who am still in my prime,
Will hold him fast in this love affair; for by my soul,
So must it be.
And should more painful ills fall to his lot
Than to the lady standing beside him, 1890
His strength's sufficient; he bears and suffers them well."[22]
Then the noble king
Took stock and laughed heartily at
Youth, who had said these things;
Even so he prized her none the less 1895
Since she did
Her duty only by saying what she had,
And he valued her wishes much more dearly
Than he loved ten pounds of his own profit.
So he said: "Youth, 1900
Beautiful lady, you are the great mistress
Who holds this lover fast in such terrible distress,
In poverty, misery, sadness,
You along with Love.
You witness how the weary man has lost all help, 1905
Nor does his heart find refuge or recourse,
Save in death, which quickly comes upon him.
But you would
Torment him too much, estrange him from everything.
Now he has found, if you please, a counselor 1910
Good and true; let that person advise him.
In this way you will do well
For he is caught in so tight a place
He knows no trick or scheme to escape."
"Surely, sire, I will do nothing of the kind. 1915
Instead he will love
The great beauty on whose account he feels such bitterness,
And should he die, everyone will call him
A martyr to Love, and it will do him honor

If he does die for her."

When Youth brought her speech to an end,
The king spoke to them, saying:
"We have not assembled here
To dispute
Whether he should love his lady,[23]
But rather to learn who feels greater unhappiness
And suffers more the cruel pangs of love—
Or so it seems to me.
Now you all agree completely
That this lover feels much more pain
Than the lady; and in no way do I differ
From this conclusion,
But support it firmly in every way and concur
That this lover is further from consolation
Than this lady, may God console her!
So I will judge
This case according to my understanding,
For in these matters I have no experience.
And another man, truly, well I know it,
Would do better.
I say this: in proper consideration
Of the opinion of Reason, here present,
And the arguments of you who are eager for justice,
And of Loyalty,
Who has spoken the pure truth in this matter
And does not resort to ruses or deception,
And also of Love, who has here argued skillfully,
And of Youth—
That this lover suffers more sadness
And love's pains wound him more grievously
Than they do the lady, in whom there is great nobility;
And that he is much further
From the consolation he truly needs.
And so I announce and render my judgment
That he feels more hurt than does she, more worry
And distress."

After the good king offered his decision,
Whose logic had been proposed by Reason,
The knight thanked him there,
In his presence,
And, lost in thought, the lady so forgot herself
She uttered nary a word.
Nonetheless in the end she granted

She would accept
The judgment that the king had rendered 1965
Because he was so wise and loyal that
He would do only right by everyone.
Then the king,
Smiling, took them by the hand
And seated them on the Norwegian rug 1970
Far from the others, just the three of them.
And he urged
And begged both of them to take comfort,
For should the heart bear such a pain a long time,
He might die, and so could she 1975
(May it never happen!);
Instead they should regain their senses,
For the heart destroys and harms itself greatly
That wallows in such weeping and pain;
And often repeated 1980
Is the view that a man should forget
Whatever he cannot better
Or change by weeping and wailing;
And, so doing,
They should not sin against Loyalty, he said; 1985
But crying so for love they did wrong,
Making themselves the murderers of their own souls
And lives.
Afterward the king summoned his court.
So Liberality, Honor, and Courtesy, 1990
Beauty, Desire, mirthful Happiness,
And Hardihood,
Prowess, Love, Loyalty, and Generosity,
Will, Thought, Wealth, along with Youth
And then Reason, mistress over all, came forward. 1995
The king asked
That each strive to honor these two lovers;
And that Love should drive away melancholy
From them; and, afterward, that a meal
Be prepared, 2000
For it was quite close to vespers.
And without delay they carried out his wishes
Like a retinue good and well instructed.
They approached
The lovers, offering no more debate, 2005
And each did to the best of his ability
What he thought would please and suit them.
For with good will
They were eager to do so.

And the lovers asked to go 2010
But were adamantly refused,
For Courtesy,
Liberality, Honor, and Generosity his friend,
The noble king, who did not forget himself at all,
And everyone else quite fervently begged them 2015
To remain
Because it was nearly the dinner hour.
And as they talked, the call to wash sounded with horns
Throughout the castle accompanied by loud trumpeting;
So the company 2020
Rose and entered the hall two by two;
There they politely washed their hands
And sat down. They drank and ate
In moderation,
For there was a great abundance 2025
Of whatever one could request or have that is good.
After the meal, the noble king took them
By the robe
And said to them: "You will not leave us for some time,
Because my intention now is to free you 2030
From those thoughts that do so trouble you."
The knight
Began to thank him quite humbly,
And likewise did the lady, who could delay
No longer, she said, before returning. 2035
Yet in the end
The king lodged them eight days quite happily
And at their departure bestowed generously upon them
Horses, harness, jewels, gold, and silver.
At the end of the eight days, 2040
They parted, taking leave of the king,
In whom they found so much honor, so they said,
That they had never seen a ruler this good or noble,
And Honor
Accompanied them, as did Courtesy, 2045
Youth, Love, contented Wealth,
And many another I cannot name.
For they mounted
Their horses and escorted them far enough
To lead both back to their residences, 2050
Afterward returning to the king at Durbuy.
Here I intend to end
My account; I will rhyme no more,
For I have enough other matters to put in poetry.
But at the end of this book, I will see to it 2055

That anyone
Who would truly like to learn my name and surname
Will be able to recognize them clearly
In the book's last verse, see them there.
Let him simply remove   2060
The first seven letters from the whole
And reassemble them in another fashion,
Forgetting or omitting none.
In this way, whoever
Wants to learn my name will be able to,   2065
Though he will not esteem me more.
Nevertheless, it will never happen
That I will not be
A lover loyal, pleasant, and full of mirth,
For if in this world I possessed nothing   2070
But loved my lady, humble and demure,
Against her will,
Then I have enough, since Love has honored me
And richly rewarded my pain ever since
I bestowed my heart upon my lady   2075
For all time;
What comforts my heart in its suffering
Is that when first I felt the pangs of love,
I expected a humble relief for a noble ill.[24]
Here ends *The Judgment of the King of Bohemia*.

Notes

The edition on which this translation is based is Palmer, *Guillaume de Machaut: The Judgment of the King of Bohemia*.

    1. "Oci" is not a sound that birds were, at least conventionally, thought to make in Middle French. The word, however, is the imperative form of the verb *kill*. Perhaps here the springtime birds sing out "Kill! Kill!" in acknowledgment of Love's proverbial destructiveness, but it is difficult to pin down the precise meaning of the word in this context.

    2. The debate proper begins at this point, with the lady's long account of her experience with love.

    3. Here the lover offers his account of the suffering inflicted by his faithless ladylove.

    4. The long portrait of the lady's appearance that follows is a love poetry convention, as much illustrative of the lover's devotion as of the charms possessed by the object of his desire.

    5. Grandnephew of Julius Caesar, Octavian (63 BCE–14 CE) is better known as Augustus Caesar, the name he took after becoming the first emperor of Rome. His reign was marked by lavish expenditures on public buildings and the road system of the empire. Octavian was also a generous patron of the arts.

    6. Galen, who lived ca. 130–200, was the most noted physician of the ancient world.

Born of Greek parents in Asia Minor, he moved in his early thirties to Rome, where he eventually became court physician to the emperor Marcus Aurelius. A remarkable polymath, Galen was the author of more than five hundred writings, mostly on human physiology, but on other topics as well, including philosophy.

7. The figure of the goddess Fortune (Fortuna) derives from one of the best-known works of the Middle Ages, Boethius's *Consolation of Philosophy* (ca. 525). The ancient Romans worshipped Fortuna, the personification of luck, but Boethius assigns her a more important role in human affairs, making her responsible for the apparently random and capricious distribution of goods to human beings. Those she favors climb up upon the wheel she holds as a symbol of her power, but the wheel, ever turning, eventually throws them off into the mud, depriving them of the benefits that they had previously enjoyed.

8. The lover demonstrates both his virtue and his intellectual finesse in his extended meditation on the cause of his suffering. Should he blame Love or his lady? He decides that neither is actually at fault, thereby showing his loyalty to both the divinity and his beloved.

9. The lover, understandably, here charges his lady with fickleness and instability, two of the conventional "truths" about women in the misogynistic tradition.

10. Long a silent witness to the debate between the two people of higher rank, the narrator now feels summoned to action by the difficulty they are experiencing in finding a judge to decide between them.

11. This laudatory portrait of Jean de Luxembourg, king of Bohemia, is one of several in Machaut's works.

12. Alexander the Great (356–323 BCE) was king of Macedon and conqueror of much of Asia Minor and the Middle East.

13. Hector, the son of Priam, king of Troy, is one of the principal characters of Homer's *Iliad*.

14. Publius Ovidius Naso (43 BCE–18 CE), usually known as Ovid, was one of the most celebrated poets of ancient Rome. His works on love, particularly *The Art of Love*, a guidebook for prospective lovers, exerted a great influence on the writers of the Middle Ages.

15. For further discussion of Jean de Luxembourg, king of Bohemia, see p. 11.

16. The nobleman's playful and, in the context, nonsensical reference to the "written" text of his encounter with the lady calls attention to the poem's fictionality, to the fact that it does not represent "real" experience. Later, Reason makes much the same kind of metafictional reference in line 1782.

17. Reason's argument to this point may be readily summarized: (1) because the lady's lover is beyond recovery, Reason will work to make her forget him, an attachment to the dead being an unreasonable state; (2) Youth, preoccupied with jollity and the pleasures of the present, will also push the lady toward forgetfulness; and (3) there is no love without sexual attraction and, in the absence of a body to love, it will disappear, especially since the soul is always ambivalent about the emotion, which is inherently sinful to some degree.

18. Unlike the lady, so Reason argues, the lover is forced by Youth, Companionship, Beauty, Love, and Loyalty to continue in his affection for his faithless beloved, the constant sight of whom fills him with pain. And there is no relief possible for him, since even if his beloved took him back, he would no longer be able to trust her.

19. See note 16.

20. Love agrees with Reason's assessment of the lover's suffering, but finds nothing extraordinary in the man's inability to find secure happiness, for it is the fate of all lovers to serve without the expectation of meriting the reward of the lady's favor.

21. Offended by the lady's faithlessness, Loyalty sides with the nobleman, accepting Reason's explanation of why his suffering is greater.

22. At this point in the dispute, the question for which the court has been convened has been forgotten completely. Youth addresses instead the issue of the nobleman's situation and finds, much like Love, that it is hardly desperate or regrettable.

23. Though he himself admonishes Youth to allow the nobleman to abandon his attachment to an undeserving woman, the king reminds the court that they have other business to consider.

24. Characteristically, Machaut signs his poems with an anagram to be solved by rearranging the letters of a verse or pair of verses. He thereby makes his authorship part of the text, difficult either to ignore or to delete when copying or reading.

Le Jugement dou roy de Navarre

At the passing of a beautiful summer
That had been pleasant and joyful,
Ornamented with flowers and leaves,
Adorned with shrubbery,
Drenched by sweet dew, 5
Dried by the seasonable heat
That the sun provided it;
A summer in which the birds
Held their assemblies with song and verse
Through meadows, arbors, and glades 10
In the season's service and honor
So that all should linger
Despite the weather that, by its nature,
Changes summer's warmth into cold
A little after autumn comes, 15
When everyone who has vines to pick
Does his harvest and puts it into casks;
When, with little trouble, there are
Peaches, must, pears, and grapes to be had,
Which are shared with neighbors; 20
When the wheat sprouts in the ground
And the leaf falls from the oak
Because of nature or a gusting wind;
In the year thirteen hundred forty-nine,
On the ninth day of November, 25
I was walking about my room.
And had the air been clear and pure,
I'd have been elsewhere; but it was
So dark that the mountains and plains
Were full of haze. 30
And so I sheltered indoors.
For all that ordinarily was green
Had been changed into another hue
Because the north wind had robbed everything of color
And had cut down many a flower 35
With the coldness of his sword.

So there I suffered sadness[1]
All alone in my room and thought
How the world in all its aspects
Was ruled by a drunkard's wisdom: 40

How justice and truth
Have been murdered by the iniquity
Of Greed, which in many realms
Rules as sovereign lady,
As mistress, as queen—   45
For Greed spawns hatred,
While Generosity gives, bestows glory—
Truly that's an irrefutable notion,
Which one can prove and clearly see
Through just and accurate experience;   50
How no one does his duty;
How everyone seeks to deceive
His neighbor, for I see no father
Or son, no daughter, sister, or brother,
No mother, stepmother, or cousin,   55
No aunt, uncle, or neighbor, man or woman,
No husband, wife, lover, or beloved
Such that one does not deceive the other—
And if anyone refrains from this,
Every man looks suspiciously at him   60
And says he's a hypocrite,
Were he even St. John the Hermit;[2]
How the lords pillage their subjects,
Rob, despoil, and mistreat them,
Put them all to death   65
Without pity or compassion
So that great misfortune, I think,
Comes from joining vice and power.
And one indeed often sees just this,
And nothing makes a heart so criminal   70
As great power when it's used for evil.
Now I witness that everyone abuses it
Because I see no powerful man
Without ten, now twenty, now a hundred
Towers, troops, catapults, or arbalests   75
To despoil brave men and cowards.
For avarice captures them
So that no one escapes their grasp
Unless he's one of those who have nothing to lose.
They have no desire to rob such a man.   80
For nothing concerns the man who has nothing.
Such men are never troubled,
But the greedy have a failing, which is that
The more they have, the more they want,
And the more powerfully rich they are,   85
They are that much more greedy and miserly;

For the burning avarice that feeds on them
Grows younger the longer they live.
And from this comes the tempest
That destroys the world and rages on, 90
The strange events and misfortune
That today are so commonplace that
No one hears news from anywhere
That might be agreeable or pleasant;
For there's a greater difference 95
Between the conditions I witnessed in my youth
And those that now are so unpleasant
Than there is between winter and summer.
But what grieves me more
To endure, and troubles me more too, 100
Is that God is accorded little reverence
And that there is no order to anything;
And today everyone ruins himself
With what is called vituperation.
Therefore, more than I dare say, 105
Melancholy had taken hold of me,
But whoever knew the half of it
Would think much less of me.

And because melancholy
Extinguishes every happy thought, 110
And also because I saw well
I could do nothing about this,
And because if anyone had discovered
My state of mind he'd only have mocked it,
I abandoned my sad meditations 115
And tried to concern myself with other matters,
Thinking that he pleases God
Who makes the best of things.
And then another thought occurred
To me because it is proven folly 120
For any man to be saddened
By something he cannot better;
And I determined that if the weather
Were even ten times worse,
Even a hundred times, a hundred thousand, 125
There would be no counsel wiser
Than to let all this be
Since it cannot be changed,
And instead to act like the wise man
Who says and demonstrates in his writing 130
That, when he has considered everything,

Imagined everything, seen all there is,
Tested, examined, observed
The world, that it is all vanity
And there is no other course 135
But to be happy and do good.
And just as I was at the point of
Abandoning the reverie I was in,
A thought occurred to me
That was even more bizarre and frightening, 140
More troubling by half
And much more filled with sadness.

This was of those horrible, uncanny events
That have been unlike the others
That anyone might remember, 145
Since in reading history I have not
Discovered any so unusual,
So hard to bear, or so threatening
By a fourth or even a tenth part
As these of my own time have been; 150
For it has been a rather common occurrence
That the sun and the moon, the stars,
The sky and earth have been seen
Displaying the signs of war,
Misery, and pestilence, 155
Offering tokens and manifestations.
Indeed everyone could see with his own eyes
Eclipses of the moon and sun
Much fuller and darker
Than others had been for many years past, 160
And as a sign of misfortune these two bodies lost
For a long time their color and light.[3]
Furthermore, there was a star with tresses
That seemed to be fire with a tail,
And it prognosticated 165
Murder and conflagration.
The heavens, which saw from their heights
The evil fortune to come
Into the world, wept in many places
And cried tears of blood from pity, 170
And because of the strange rain that issued from them,
The earth trembled with fear
(So said several who saw this),
Because of which villages and cities were destroyed
In Germany and Carinthia, 175
Somewhat more than forty altogether,

Although I cannot tell their exact number.
But the event is well known at Rome
Because an abbey there
Of St. Paul's was brought to ruin by it.⁴   180

But the Lord Who made everything
Through His direct intervention,
Like a sovereign gracious ruler
Over all things, showed us the meaning
Of these marvelous tokens   185
And dispelled our doubts
So directly and properly
That every man saw it clearly.
For the battles and the wars
Were so great throughout every land   190
That no one knew in all the world,
As much as it encompasses,
Any country, kingdom, or region
Where there was no strife;
For this reason five hundred thousand men and women   195
Would have lost their bodies and souls
If He Who is in harmony with all good
Had not taken pity on them;
And many countries were destroyed by it,
And the results endure still.   200
The story would be long to tell
About captures and outrages,
The savage killings as well
Of noblemen and knights,
Of clerks, townspeople, squires,   205
And of poor people of little note
Who died as a result or were brought to ruin,
Of the kings, dukes, lords, and counts,
For so many of them perished in this way,
Some by fire, others in war,   210
That everyone was completely confounded by it.⁵
After this appeared a group of scoundrels
Who were false, traitorous, and heretical:
This was shameful Judea,
The evil, the disloyal,   215
Who hate good and love evil of all kinds,
Who gave and promised so much
Gold and silver to the Christian people,
That they in many places
Poisoned the wells, streams, and fountains   220
That had been clear and healthy;

And so many lost their lives
Because all who used them
Died quite suddenly; and in this way
Ten times a hundred thousand certainly 225
Perished in the countryside and towns as well
Before this deadly affliction
Was taken notice of.⁶

But He Who sits on high and sees far,
Who governs everyone and provides all things, 230
Did not wish for this treason
To be hidden any longer; instead He revealed
And made it known so widely
That they lost their lives and goods.
For all the Jews were put to death: 235
Some hanged, others burned alive,
One drowned, another beheaded
By the axe's blade or sword.
And likewise many Christians
Died a shameful death because of this. 240

At this time a company was formed
At the urging of Hypocrisy, their lady,
And these people beat themselves with whips
And crucified themselves flat on the ground
While singing to instrumental accompaniment 245
Some new song or other;
And according to them, they were worthier
Than any saint in Paradise.
But the Church dealt with them
By forbidding them to whip themselves 250
And condemning their song,
Which little children were singing—
And by excommunicating all of them
Through the power granted it by God
Because their self-abuse 255
And song were heresy.⁷

And when Nature saw what was happening,
That her work was in these ways destroying itself
And that men were killing each other
And were poisoning the waters 260
In order to annihilate the human race
Because of greed and envy,
She, beautiful and noble, was much displeased,
Quite vexed, greatly pained.

So she made her way without delay 265
To Jupiter and had forged
Lightning, thunder, and storms
On working days and feasts.
Because she was so eager for the task,
She paid no mind to either weekday or holiday. 270
Afterward Nature ordered
The four winds over which she had command:
That each should make ready
And prepare to race off
And issue from their caverns 275
To give rise to raging cyclones
So that there should be no king's realm,
Nowhere in heaven, the earth, sea, or clouds
Where the air would not be troubled;
And they should do the worst they could. 280
For when she saw her works destroyed,
She wished the air corrupted as well.
And when the winds had taken their leave
And Jupiter had forged everything,
Lightning, storms, and turbulence, 285
Then one might have seen them
Marvelously disperse in all directions
And thunder quite horribly,
Blow in gusts, let fall hail and rain in torrents,
Disturb the clouds, the sea, 290
Shake the woods, make the rivers flood,
And force all things that live
On the earth to seek shelter
To save themselves because they feared death.
This turn of events was quite remarkable, 295
Terrifying, and filled with peril!
For stones fell from the sky,
Killing whatever they touched,
Men, beasts, women;
And in many places lightning and tempests 300
Descended with great flames
And turned a multitude of villages into dust;
Nor was there anyone in the world so brave
He didn't then have a coward's heart;
For it seemed that the world 305
Was about to fall into ruin and end.

But no one could have survived
Had this weather lasted long,
And so these storms came to an end;

But they gave rise to such haze, 310
Such filth, and such vapors
As were hardly loved;
For the air that had been clear and pure
Was now vile, black, and cloudy,
Horrible and fetid, putrefied and infected; 315
And so it became completely corrupted;
And about this corruption
Men held the view
That it was corrupting them in turn
And they were thus losing their health. 320
For everyone was badly afflicted,
Discolored, and made ill;
People had buboes and large swellings
From which they died, and, to be brief,
Few dared to venture into the open air 325
Or talk at close quarters with one another
Because their infected breath
Corrupted others who were healthy.
And if anyone fell ill,
And some friend visited him, 330
That man faced the same peril.
Five hundred thousand died of this
So that father failed son,
Mother failed daughter,
Son and daughter failed mother 335
From fear of this plague;
And no one was so true a friend
That he was not thereupon ignored,
The recipient of little help
If he fell ill with the disease. 340
And there was no physician or any healer
Who knew enough to name the cause
Of its appearance, or even what it was
(And none of them applied any remedy),
Beyond that this was a disease 345
One called an epidemic.

When from His house God saw
That the corruption in the world
Was this great everywhere,
It is no wonder He was eager 350
To take a cruel revenge
For the great disorder;
And so at once, waiting no longer,
In order to have His justice and vengeance,

From his cage He released Death, 355
Who was full of rage and anger
And lacked any check, bridle, or rein,
Any faith, love, or moderation;
So very proud and arrogant he was,
So gluttonous and famished, 360
He could not be satisfied
By anything he could consume.
And he hastened throughout the world,
Killing and running down one and all,
Whomever he chanced upon; 365
Nor could he be resisted.
And, in short, he undid so many,
Struck down and devoured so great a multitude
That every day could be found
Huge heaps of women, youths, 370
Boys, old people, those of all degrees,
Lying dead inside the churches;
And they were thrown together
In great trenches, all dead from the buboes.
Because the cemeteries were found 375
So full of corpses and biers,
It was necessary to lay out new ones.
These were strange new tidings.
And so there was many a fine town
Where no boy or girl, no man or woman 380
Was seen to come and go,
Nor was anyone found there to talk to
Because all of them had died
This unbelievable death.
And they lay ill no more than three days, 385
Sometimes less; the time was short.
And there were certainly many
Who died of it suddenly;
For those same men who bore them
To the church did not return 390
(This was often witnessed),
But instead were to die right there.
And whoever wished to undertake
Discovering or putting down in writing
The number of those who died, 395
Those who are still here and once were,
And all those to come,
Never would he be able to compass it,
However hard he might labor.
For no one could count them, 400

Imagine, conceive, or tell of them,
Compute, make known, or record them.
And, to be sure, many times
I have heard it said and openly
That in thirteen hundred and forty-nine, 405
Only nine survived of every hundred.[8]
And so one saw that, because people were lacking,
Many a fine, noble estate
Lay idle without those to work it.
No man had his fields plowed, 410
His grain sowed, or his vines tended
Though he'd have paid out triple wages,
No surely, not even for twenty times the rate,
Because so many had died; and thus it happened
The cattle lay about 415
The fields completely abandoned,
Grazing in the corn and among the grapes,
Anywhere at all they liked,
And they had no master, no cowherd,
No man at all to go to them; 420
And there wasn't anyone who might call them back,
No one to claim them as his own.
There were many estates
That remained without owners;
Nor did the living dare to stay 425
Any time at all inside the houses
Where the dead had been
Either in winter or summer.
And if anyone did so,
He himself then risked death. 430
And when I witnessed these events
That were so strange and ominous,
I was not at all so brave
That I did not become quite cowardly.
For all the most courageous trembled 435
From the fear of death that overcame them,
And so I quite thoroughly confessed myself
Of all the sins I had committed,
Putting myself into a state of grace
In order to accept death where I was 440
If it should please our Lord.
Therefore with uncertainty and fear,
I closed myself up inside the house
And determined resolutely
In my mind that I'd not leave 445
Until the time when I should learn

What conclusion this might come to;
And I would leave it for God to decide.
And so for a long time, may God help me,
There I remained, knowing little 450
Of what was happening in the city,
And there more than twenty thousand died,
Though of this I knew nothing
And so felt less sadness;
For I did not wish to know anything 455
So that my sorrows would be fewer,
Even though many of my friends
Had died and had been buried in the ground.

And so I remained long in hiding,
Just like a hawk in moult, 460
Until at last one time I heard
(Which made me greatly rejoice)
Horns, trumpets, drums,
And more than seven pairs of instruments.
Then I went to a window 465
And asked what this might be;
And at once one of my friends
Who had heard me answered
That those who remained were acting
Just as if all of them were getting married, 470
Feasting, and celebrating weddings;
For the deadly plague of the buboes
That was called an epidemic
Had completely ceased everywhere;
And people were no longer dying. 475
And when I saw them celebrating
Joyfully and with good cheer,
And all just as merrily
As if they had lost nothing,
I wasn't troubled in the least, 480
But regained at once my composure;[9]
And I turned my eyes and face
To the air that was so sweet
And clear it encouraged me
Then to leave the prison 485
Where I had passed the season.
At that moment, I was beyond grief and worry,
And I mounted on my palfrey
Grisart, who moved at a pace
Quite calm, as was his nature. 490
And I went quickly to the fields

In order to ride for pleasure,
To entertain and solace myself,
And to claim as my own the sweetness
That comes from the peace and from the enjoyment 495
In which the heart willingly delights
That feels no concern for the pain
That arises from either trouble or strife,
But would instead pursue
Whatever might bestow honor. 500
I was very excited about
The honorable thing I was bent on.
I had the desire and the urge
(If, in my good time, I could manage it)
To catch some hares by surprise 505
And then be able to hunt them down.
Now, someone might ask
If hare hunting is honorable.[10]
My answer to this question would be
That it's an honor, diversion, and delight; 510
It's a sport that the nobility value,
Something of a gracious enterprise
And quite advantageous to undertake
Because it improves one nicely.
Certainly, the activity itself is pleasant enough, 515
And honor comes with perfecting it.
At this time I had so directed
My attention toward that end,
I was thinking of nothing else.
And the good hare hounds I had 520
So multiplied my enjoyment
I could not have felt weary
After releasing them
And watching them run off
Just so in a pack across the fields; 525
And then there were the songs
Of birds, lovely to hear,
As well as the air of the mild weather
That soothed my whole body.
One could easily believe that if 530
Some people were to ride up
So that they might speak to me,
Although I might know well one among them,
I should indeed not notice,
So much had I to this sport devoted my attention. 535
It was then that an adventure befell me
Which frightened me somewhat,

Yet quickly became pleasant enough,
Just as I will relate immediately
Hereafter; I'll not lie about it at all. 540

While I was disporting myself there,
I who had forgotten all
Those other melancholic thoughts,
As much the sad as the pleasant ones,
A lady of great nobility, 545
Nicely decked out with rich clothes,
Appeared with a beautiful company.
Yet I didn't see them at all
Because I was back from the road
And, moreover, because of the manner 550
In which I was attending to
And had concentrated all my attention on
My hunting alone;
But the lady was the first to take notice
Of me before anyone else spied me there 555
Or before anyone made a sign of doing so,
That is, from among the company
That was escorting her noble person.
Then she summoned a squire
And said to him: "Do you see that man there 560
Who is pleasantly disporting and enjoying himself?
Go to him and then report to me
Who he is, and return quickly
Without delaying there at all."
At this the squire did not fail, 565
But came to me in some haste
And loudly said hello.
I didn't stop what I was doing,
And I said to him: "You're welcome, fair sir."
He returned, without saying any more, 570
As fast as he could to the lady:
"Lady," he said, "By the faith I owe my soul,
That's Guillaume de Machaut over there.
Know well that nothing interests him
Save what he is pursuing. 575
He is so involved with his hunting
I believe firmly he has no time for anything but
His hounds and himself."
When the lady heard these words,
She seemed to rejoice at heart, 580
And this was no simple outward show,
But the absolute truth,

Because her heart was joyful, her manner happy,
Like a woman gay and merry,
Not for my sake, I don't mean that at all, 585
But rather for another reason entirely,
Because of a particular matter
In which she took much interest
And which she was eager to bring to my attention
In order to delight and entertain herself 590
And, in turn, to sink me into melancholy.
This I did not fail to do,
For I was mocked by her,
Reproached and contradicted
Just as if I had sinned 595
Quite grievously against the woman.

After the squire had related
All he wished about me,
The lady said in a loud voice:
"Now let's see just how 600
Agreeable and sharp Guillaume is.
As far as I know, he is knowledgeable
About those kinds of merriment
That accord with morality.
By night, he stays awake studying, 605
And then by day he labors his body
With the work the good man seeks out,
Those things that bring and confer honor;
And so he goes around amusing himself
At all times by doing what is proper. 610
Such activities do cultivate the demeanor
To maintain a man in worthiness.
But shortly I will take from him
A large part of his enjoyment
Because I will have some fun at his expense 615
That will puzzle the man a good while.
I have been eager to do that for a long time.
So in this fashion I will fulfill my wish.

Now return to him as fast as possible
Because I am quite anxious 620
That he be brought over here. So tell the man
In as few words as you can manage
To proceed here directly;
And say to him firmly
That it must be with no excuse 625

And no matter what other business he has
And that it is at my command."
"Lady, as you order,"
Said the squire, "Without any 'but'
I will go tell him just what 630
You have said, or as close to it as
I am able; I am quite ready to do this."
Then the squire rode off
In my direction until he approached me,
And as he drew near, 635
He called out to me while still riding,
Galloping at a quick pace
Until he came fairly close;
And as soon as I heard his voice,
I quickly went toward him 640
Because I had known the man a long time.
And as a token of his great joy,
He saluted me by God the Father
And by His sweet dear mother;
And I responded at once, 645
Greeting him courteously.
Then I inquired what news,
Good and pleasing, there might be for me,
If my lady were hale and happy,
At peace, not annoyed by anything. 650
"Guillaume, have no fear at all
Because my lady is in every way
At peace, in good health, happy, and well;
And this is certain,
You will be able to learn rather quickly 655
From what you'll hear me say;
For quite true it is that she summons you,
Not that she really commands you to go to her;
Rather she asks in such a fashion
That it counts the same as an order, 660
Neither begging nor commanding.
Instead it pleases her to request,
Somewhere between 'green' and 'ripe.'
Yet mark this point for certain:
It is her intention beyond any doubt 665
That you come to her willingly
Without making any excuses;
She trusts that you will do so,
And thus, if you please, you will come to her
And there express your pleasure." 670

After these words, I answered him:
"My very dear friend, this much I will tell you,
That not a fourth or even a third
Of what I am, but my entire being
Is completely hers, with nothing held back. 675
And I could not restrain myself
From going to her, nor would wish to,
Inasmuch as I would truly feel
What my lady would think about it.
And so when she sends for me, 680
It would surely be madness to believe
That I would ever think twice about it.
But I do want to ask you about a small point,
Just so there will be nothing to remedy:
How far is my lady from this spot?" 685
"Guillaume, here is my answer:
That it is not quite three days' travel.
And may those days dawn brightly!"[11]
I said: "Let us go on now without delay,
And let us ride night and day 690
To do what is good for my lady.
I cannot better replenish myself
With joy than by doing her pleasure,
And so I will offer no resistance at all."
"Guillaume, I have listened attentively 695
To what you said in response.
And I would like to appease you a little
With something other than a kiss.
Look toward the broad clearing
A bit below that fallow field: 700
That's my lady with a great troop,
And she has drawn herself up there for your sake.
At that spot she attends you; be certain of this.
Now let your heart be not at all troubled
By any fear of having to travel too far, 705
Because you can speak to her over there."
At these words, my face brightened,
And I turned my eyes toward
The place he had indicated.
And when I saw she was waiting there, 710
That my journey was shortened,
I was scarcely annoyed,
But pleased instead; and I began to laugh
And then started to say to him:
"Good friend, you have nearly made me 715
Melancholy with your jokes,

Your trickery, and your true words
When you gave me to believe
Through a clever lie that my lady was far away;
It has pleased me much to realize 720
The truth of what you lied about
Because you afterward spoke the truth,
Namely that my lady was rather close by.
I'm on my way; come along now
Or stay here as you please." 725
"Guillaume, there is still time
For talk; no need to hurry.
You will get there soon enough
If my lady can arrange it.
And if you have some skill in debating, 730
It will be good in this situation
Where you will play the lawyer's role;
For you could be taken by surprise
If you prove unable to defend yourself."
We bandied about these words 735
And with such game amused ourselves;
Thus absorbed in talk we rode on
Until we neared the lady's entourage.
Then I went on ahead, and when I saw
Her noble person replete 740
With honor, grace, and learning,
As a sign of great reverence
I made to get off my horse;
But at once she started to forbid it,
Saying quite politely: 745
"Oh no, Guillaume, this will not do.
You must not dismount.
Speak to me from your horse."
And when I heard this, I obliged
And gave her as fine a greeting 750
As I could and knew how to,
And in the manner I should have,
Just as I had learned
To honor people of such rank.
And without dissembling, she in turn 755
Knew how to take care of the rest,
Responding in friendship,
Guarding her honor and integrity.
Then she spoke to me quite firmly:

THE LADY

"Guillaume, you have acted 760

Too much the stranger.
You would not have come here
Had it not been for my messenger.
You have become, I think,
Too wise or too backward, 765
Inattentive and disagreeable,
Eager for your sport;
Or else you value ladies too little.
When I climbed the ground over there
On that highest rise, 770
I took the path on the right
And looked toward the left;
Quite clearly I saw you riding,
Whistling up and calling your hounds.
I heard you doing this 775
And likewise saw
You and your goings-on.
So I believe quite surely,
Guillaume, that you must have seen us.
And why, then, when you heard 780
Our horses pass by and whinny
Did you not deign to come forward
Until I gave you the order,
Just as if I made it a command?[12]
So I thank you just as much for this 785
As I should and no more."

GUILLAUME

Then I said to her: "For God's sake,
My lady, don't say so.
I will reply to that, saving your honor,
For by the faith I owe our Lord 790
I saw nothing and heard nothing either,
So much was my heart enthralled
By the hunting I was intent on,
By the goal I wanted to attain.
And so I was spellbound. 795
My lady, only involuntarily would I do
Anything against your will.
And how would it profit me
To commit such petty, spiteful acts?
I know well I would be demeaned by them. 800
And so you should well excuse me."[13]

THE LADY

"Guillaume, I don't want to fool with this further.

Because it is so, my heart believes you.
But on the other hand a different matter
Has arisen—and seriously— 805
To your discredit, and it needs explaining.
And I will keep you very busy
And offer much argument against you
If you do not admit your error.
Guillaume, listen and pay attention: 810
You have sinned against women,
And so you have taken on a burden
You will not be able to hold up under
Or put down when you would like."
With these strange words, 815
Perverse in their severity,
She showed me a manner that was
Bitter, cruel, hurtful, and haughty
As a sign of her great anger,
In order to make my heart heavy, 820
And also to make fearful, hesitant,
And full of uncertainty my every thought.
She took pains in doing this
Because she was convinced
That, valuing her so highly, 825
I should fear her anger greatly.
And this I did; I became afraid of her
When I heard these words,
Not because of any misdeed
I myself had committed; 830
Rather because I feared those gossipmongers
Who are at times harmful
Because of their falseness and envy
To good people who lead decent lives.
And so I dreaded this turn of events.[14] 835
Yet I was certain I had done
No harm in my whole life
To any woman whomsoever,
And with this in mind I answered her:

GUILLAUME

"Lady, you have brought up something 840
That heaps great dishonor upon me,
But the trial is not yet arranged
Or begun in proper form.
For a certain judgment to be rendered,
You must tell me how 845
I have erred and also explain in detail

All the facts of the matter.
At present your purpose here
Remains secret and hidden from me.
If it is not divulged to me, 850
I will not be able to respond.
Now please, if you will, expound upon
The matter that troubles you;
And if you agree to do so,
You will be following the proper path 855
Of the law; for otherwise I would not be able
To learn what the issue is and dispute it.
If not, you ought to grant
That I should go free and clear
Of the allegation you have made against me; 860
It is right that I should expect you to do so."

THE LADY

"Guillaume, know right away
That you will hear nothing more from me.
Instead this is how things stand:
If I know about it, you know too, 865
Because the case against you is something
You have written down in one of your books,
Something well laid out and described therein.
So look through your books.
I know well you are not drunk 870
When you compose your love poems.
And so you know well, with regard to your own tales,
When you compose and write them,
If you did right or wrong there,
Because into these works you put your heart 875
As much in a single word as in six.
If you please, go look there,
Because you will get nothing more
From me for the present.
Be sure this is my intention." 880

GUILLAUME

"Madam, what have you said?
As you are very well aware,
You know much more than you admit.
I have all sorts of written texts
In front of me, of various kinds, 885
Devoted to very different themes,
Each of which is quite unlike every other.
Examining all these at the same time,

And each one rather thoroughly,
Section by section and sentence by sentence, 890
From the beginning of the first
To the very end of the last
(If I wished to look through all of them,
And this I should indeed like to avoid),
All this would take too long. 895
And in addition I might not
Come across what you are taking issue with
If you do not tell me more.
For I would never seek to read such a thing,
Madam, except to contradict you. 900
Yet it is hardly to be expected
That I would prove able to decipher
A hidden thought of yours
Except through the proper key
That might unlock your heart; 905
And so that I might be informed about this,
Let your mouth tell it to me.
If I refuse to respond
After you have told me yourself,
Then I would like very much to be condemned 910
And reproved by your own words.
Madam, if you please, now decide
If my view here is mistaken
According to your own opinion."

THE LADY

"Guillaume, since this is how things stand, 915
I agree completely with this point.
At the moment I admit myself defeated;
But this matter of your transgression,
Which is so grave against women,
Would call for a severe punishment 920
Should someone wish to exact it.
So from this point listen carefully
To what I will say from my own mouth
Because the issue touches me right to the heart.
And after I have told you about it, 925
I will reproach you for it in such a place
That there you will be much blamed on this account,
Losing your reputation among ladies.

One time an issue was
Advanced in a very pleasant poem,[15] 930
Prettily embellished and with refinement,

But afterward quite unfortunately developed.
At first it was supposed,
And, in supposing, proposed
That a lady of great worthiness   935
Through a very loving bond
Did love a faithful lover
So that at all times, in loving well,
She was at heart a loyal beloved.
And he, obedient to courtesy,   940
Always loved her with a good heart
And expended his energy
In cherishing and honoring her;
And in order to deepen her love,
He upheld everything noble: 945
Honor, courtesy, and generosity.
He was a handsome man, strikingly so,
Renowned for his limbs, body,
And countenance, perfect in grace,
And as well proven in deeds of arms   950
As any man at all could be
Who had spent his life and energy
In attending to tournaments and jousting,
As well as all other pursuits pertaining to love.
Though they loved each other in this fashion   955
And always closely observed
The courtly rules of faithfulness
In both reason and truth,
Such a chance befell them,
Whether through nature or violence,   960
That the lover did pass away.
And the lady, when she learned this,
Lived on, sorrowful and abandoned,
A true beloved no longer loved.
Because her heart was still aflame   965
And the heart of the worthy lover
Had been undone by nature,
Her heart was the more afflicted
By the fact of his demise.
I will say no more about the matter.   970
Instead I would like to bring up another
In order to set it beside this one,
In order to make my comparison.
Listen now, Guillaume, and learn.
Another lover of high degree,   975
As worthy as the one
I have already mentioned in his deeds,

In grace as much as in virtue,
And in all other respects
Rightly and honorably endowed,   980
Also loved a lady
With no thought of evil or infamy;
And this he made known to her,
And when she had learned the truth,
She received him willingly   985
And granted the man her love
Joyfully, offering no refusal.
I have no intention of drawing this out,
But he loved her faithfully
And trusted her very much,   990
Without any hesitation or doubt
Because he thought he had acquired
All her love for the rest of his life
And would never have to share it.
Yet his path was quite different.   995
When he was the most happily
Joined to her and confident
In the promise of being loved,
She did him wrong,
Outrageously and with no excuse,   1000
And in this he discovered her falseness
Toward him, her disloyalty as well,
And could not explain it away.
If this gave him much pain,
That's hardly much of a surprise.   1005
But it's not the same at all
As the love affair that causes me to sorrow
And was ended by death.
Guillaume, if you have listened to me,
You should very readily   1010
Acknowledge your misdeed
In order to lessen your shame.
You have stated and recounted,
And also decided, advised of these facts,
In a conclusive judgment   1015
That this man experiences much more misfortune,
Grief, torment, ill, and suffering,
The one who found his lady false
To him through her double dealing,
Than does the gracious, dear lady   1020
Whose sweet lover had been joined
Irrevocably to her heart
Through love and not otherwise—

Then she learned he was in the grasp
Of death and will there remain, 1025
So that she will never see him again.
And how did you dare say this
Or write it down in your book?
It's true that you have done so,
And thus you have grievously erred. 1030
Therefore I advise you to do what you can
To void this judgment
And overturn it at once.
If you are truly a worthy man, Guillaume,
You could do so rather easily 1035
By affirming exactly the opposite.
For the opposite view is the correct one
Wherever people esteem proper loving."[16]
"Madam, by the faith I owe Holy Church,
Where all my trust lies, 1040
I would do so for no reason;
Instead, I will pursue the matter
To the very end now that I am involved.
The moment my judgment is made public
By me, I will uphold it 1045
As long as I can uphold it.[17]
Yet whoever might come forward
To defend the other side—
Quite willingly I will submit
To whatever I must submit. 1050
For I am hardly powerful enough,
And my endurance is scarcely so great,
Or my storehouse of knowledge, for that matter,
That I could not be overcome.
But if I can, I will prevail. 1055
Should I prove unable, I will pay the price.
Let's look now to how we should proceed.
I don't want to banter more about the issue.
But nevertheless, my sweet lady,
So that you will not be angry at heart with me, 1060
We will deal with this matter
Openly, not in secret,
In a way that will preserve your peace of mind
And uphold my honor as well.
For it would be to my great shame, 1065
As you yourself have admitted,
If on my own I should reverse myself
About this case I judged,
As was my right, having done so in such a way

That I accomplished it all alone.　　　　　　　　　　　　　　1070
We will find ourselves a powerful judge,
Someone of sufficient renown
Who would be wise and discreet;
And he shall be told from beginning to end
The private details of this affair　　　　　　　　　　　　　　　1075
That involves you and me.
Let it be done as we agree.
Yet you should assume the responsibility
For selecting such a man as you'd prefer.
You will hear me voice no opposition;[18]　　　　　　　　　　　1080
Rather I am in agreement on this point from now on
With whatever pleases you and no 'buts' about it.
Truly, my heart is already in this,
Because it will be a pleasant task
To hear the arguments rehearsed　　　　　　　　　　　　　　1085
And the parties dispute
With subtlety, with impressive reasoning—
And they will merit some kind of judgment."

THE LADY

At these words the lady began to laugh
And at once, while laughing, to speak:　　　　　　　　　　　1090
"Guillaume, I very much agree
With what you've just said;
And I will speak to it, no matter what might happen.
And so, for whatever it's worth,
I nominate and choose the man named　　　　　　　　　　　1095
The king of Navarre.
He is a prince who loves honor
And hates dishonor of every kind;
He is wise, loyal, and truthful,
Reasonable too in all his doings.　　　　　　　　　　　　　　1100
He knows so much, is so worthy
That I could choose no one better, to speak the truth.
The case will appeal to him
Because he is rather romantically inclined,
Wise, courteous, and well taught.　　　　　　　　　　　　　1105
He loves the honor and the glory
Of arms, love, and ladies.
He is the king who would never
Support any kind of infamy.
He is devoid of all uncouthness　　　　　　　　　　　　　　1110
And graced with all the nobility
That belongs to high rank.
I couldn't say enough of his virtues

If I spoke of them the whole day."

In this way we came to an agreement, 1115
Just as it is recorded above;
Then we spoke much about love
And, as we talked, rode on
Until we fell into the righteous bonds
Of repose, joy, and solace, 1120
Which means into a sweet state
Whose conditions were so pleasant
They could be no better, to my taste;
It was of the highest degree,
Full of good sense, so I think, 1125
Delight, and sweet leisure too,
Where a heart that seeks to act accordingly
Might discover peace.
A handsome manor stood at the spot,
And there she wished to halt. 1130

Many there helped her dismount
And attended to the lady;
And, without delay, she was led
Inside a room decorated
So well, so beautifully, so expertly, 1135
And in all things so richly
That never before (which made me marvel)
Had I ever laid eyes on anything similar.
And, quickly, everyone, high and low alike,
Made her welcome and honored her. 1140
And she very much seemed to be mistress there
Because in great nobility she was
Seated on cushions made of silk.
Yet she was very wise and self-contained,
And of such a confident age 1145
That she was quite pleasantly mature,
Being neither "green" nor "ripe."
More than any other, she was meek, friendly, and noble.
Very well attended the lady was
By a virtuous and beautiful entourage. 1150
None was a country girl;
Twelve damsels they were instead
Who attended to her day and night,
Served, and instructed her as well.[19]

The first was Understanding, 1155
Who showed her the difference

Between virtues and vices,
Between good deeds and evil ones as well,
With the help of Discretion, who escorted her
To a mirror that gleamed so brightly 1160
No one could ever grasp
Or gaze at a clearer reflecting glass.

Reason held this in her right hand,
A scales in her left,
And so the lady looked at herself there 1165
More often than anyone could say.
There she saw clearly,
Without obscurity or impediment,
What it is that God and Nature might grant
A truly fortunate person: 1170
And that is to abandon evil and do good,
And not to wish to cross anyone.
For the man is a fool who does something
To another that he does not wish done to him.
And if there might be in her person 1175
Or noble body, of such beautiful shape,
Or in her heart any fault or vice
Or malicious thought of any kind,
It could never be so well hidden
That it could not be seen in the mirror. 1180
And there without doubt she gazed on
The way and manner of all things,
How Reason justly rules
Through fair, good, and loyal precept;
And so there she found an example 1185
Of everything she ought to do.
Moreover the scales of justice
Showed to her this truth:
That she should in every instance live
As correctly as the scales, 1190
To which one in no way can add
Or take anything from and not have it seen.

The third was named Temperance,
Who wore a garland of endurance
On her head as an adornment; 1195
And with this, to increase her worthiness,
She had a confident manner
And was wise in her speech, mature too;
Not in deed, or in her behavior, or her countenance
Was there any vice or impropriety. 1200

The fourth, and well I remember her,
Was Peace, who held Concord
By the finger out of friendship
And spoke to her quite sweetly,
With a laughing heart, a happy face: 1205
"My sweet sister, my dear friend,
If we intend to live in joy,
Peace, leisure, and satisfaction
In regard to all we say and do,
Let us allow no anger at all into our hearts,   1210
And let us not be concerned with the arrogance
That bears the name of revenge,
For whoever intends to avenge the shame done him
Makes it grow larger and further disgraces himself.
Let us hold to good people in friendship,   1215
And let us take pity on evildoers
Because no man ever attained perfection
Who was eager to avenge the wrongs done him."

The fifth among them was called
Faith, who was escorted in grand style   1220
By steady Constancy,
Who so strengthened and strengthens her
That nothing disturbs or worries the lady;
Instead she was like a castle built on rock,
Strong and secure on its foundation,   1225
Free from unpredictable change.

The seventh was Charity,
Who felt such great pity
For those she knew to be in need
That she gave them whatever she possessed.   1230
But she could never give so much
That she did not have much more to share.

Afterward Honesty seated
Herself quietly and with much politeness,
And this lady was adorned in great nobility   1235
With a simple mantle.
For she was proper, beyond reproach
In her heart, body, hand, and speech.

The ninth was Prudence.
In her heart she bore Wisdom   1240
And guarded her so closely

She burned with love for her.
Wisdom knew the reason why heavenly bodies
Are suspended within the firmament;
Why the sun endures 1245
In conflagration and the moon in ice;
All about the stars and the planets,
As well as the limits of the twelve signs;
Why God through Nature did assemble
Wet, dry, cold, and hot together; 1250
And why the four elements
Were ordered in such a fashion
That earth always remains below,
Water clings quite closely to it,
Fire always rises to the heights, 1255
And air remains in the middle.
In short, of celestial movements
And also of earthly matters
She knew so much she was a master
And possessed such a lively and able wit 1260
No one could explain it.
For she could answer
Any question a person might ask,
And no one could improve on what she said.

Right next to Prudence sat 1265
Generosity, who sees nothing
But rather gives with both her hands,
More to one and less to another,
Gold, silver, chargers, hunting birds, estates,
And whatever else she might acquire, 1270
Counties, duchies, and baronetcies
In perpetuity and for life.
She keeps nothing from any of these
Except honor. This she clings to;
Nobility has so instructed her. 1275
And furthermore, which increases her worthiness,
She condemns Avarice
As the worst vice of all.
The next, about whom I'll not be silent,
Was wariness of misdeed, 1280
Who was so afraid of error
That she could hardly attend
To any matter save for being on her guard.
In all her doings, she was a coward,
But Shame and Fear protected her 1285
And were everywhere her companions.

The twelfth was Sufficiency,
Who in quite humble tranquillity
Was richly turned out
And gorged to overflowing, 1290
Full too of all earthly goods.
There was nothing that she needed,
Nor did she lack a thing.
She was beyond the grasp of Fortune
And her most fearsome domination. 1295
She ate little at her meals
Because she was more sated by an egg
Than another might be by a cow.
She was as happy as could be
And perfect in her virtue. 1300
She still is and always will be
As long as the world endures.
For she is, to judge rightly,
The blessing one should most desire.

But just as many rivers 1305
Provide water and many lights
Glow and give off their brightness
To every place they reach,
These twelve noble damsels,
Who were the servants of all good things, 1310
Each one according to her nature,
In customs, manner, and appearance
Embellished this lady's
Heart, body, honor, and soul.
So adorned by them was she, 1315
Nurtured and enlightened,
For each improved the lady
With whatever good flowed from her
And shared with the lady
The virtue she bore within. 1320
And the noble creature, in addition,
Possessed endowments from Nature:
A cultivated manner, loyalty,
Noble bearing, good breeding,
Grace, pleasantness, and courtesy, 1325
And she was much improved by these.
But her sovereign goodness
Surpassed by a great deal her beauty.

When I saw her enthroned
In such exalted fashion and so very nobly   1330
Adorned with great riches,
And, too, served and honored
With such affection by all the men and women,
My heart filled with doubts
That made their way there because of folly   1335
And genuine melancholy.
For I was taken much aback
And also struck completely dumb,
At the same time so tempted by error
That I thought I had been enchanted.   1340
But in this state of bemusement
I did not very long remain,
Because I followed the advice of Discretion,
Who made my presence of mind return
In the proper fashion through Reason,   1345
And she is always ready at the right moment
To bring back to themselves the true hearts
Who have wandered off too far.
Then Reason fixed me with a look
And ever since has maintained in her keeping   1350
My heart, senses, and thoughts.
In this way I could resist and struggle
Against misbegotten notions,
And, too, expel the temptations
That intended to enjoy the victory   1355
Of making me think incorrectly.

By then, I had gotten beyond this thought,
And the lady, her ideas well considered,
Addressed me quite wisely
And, as she talked, inspired me   1360
To respond after she finished talking;
Thus I could speak better and with more flourish.

THE LADY

And she said to me: "Guillaume, fair sir,
What we said out in the fields
Was what should have been spoken first.   1365
So let's repeat our argument
In the presence of these twelve damsels,
Who are wise, good, and beautiful,
And also of the many good people who will be present.
They will listen to us willingly."   1370

GUILLAUME

I did not hesitate long at all,
But fell to my knees straightaway
And answered her humbly:
"My dear lady, I have already said enough.[20]
Would that it please God in Paradise   1375
The man who is to hear our pleadings
Were in this place right now,
That is, the good king who will know how
To listen and pay attention quite intelligently,
To do what is right and then judge   1380
After he has heard
What will be told him.
He will know well how to deliberate
And then, even better, what to decide.
And I believe firmly that he will judge   1385
According to the testimony he will hear.
Yet nevertheless, since it pleases you,
You can certainly speak before the debate,
Making suppositions without any prejudice.[21]
And I, who intend no malice in the matter,   1390
Will listen willingly to you,
And if I think it good, I will respond."

THE LADY

"Guillaume, you answer quite eloquently;
However, listen to me just a little.
Get up now, for it pleases us   1395
That you say no more while kneeling.
And if you have something else to say,
Speak whatever way you please,
Either seated or standing,
For this much is all we require."   1400

GUILLAUME

Then I quickly got up
To carry out her command
Once she had spoken her mind.
And then right opposite her
I proceeded to sit down   1405
In order to face her directly.
For whoever looks a person in the face,
Intending his speech to find favor—
He will hear much better what is said
And the point being made as well.   1410

Then the lady assumed a manner
That was forceful, assured, a way of
Speaking so eloquent
That everyone thought
She was looking at the written text   1415
Of what she said and described.
For no one could speak better
Even if he planned his words in advance.
She organized her discussion,
Starting from the very beginning   1420
When she had sent to have me searched out
And then, the second time, fetched;
Also how I'd made my way to her;
How she had attacked me
With angry words;   1425
And how she'd been cruel,
Reproaching me roughly,
Only to make me squirm
And sink me into melancholy,
Which she knew quite handily how to do.   1430
Shall I go on telling you about it?
She expended so much fine talk
That she brought out the facts
Of the matter fully in a declaration,
Point by point, step by step,   1435
So ably that nothing needed correction.
And in this way all the young ladies
Became quickly, and beyond any doubt,
Knowledgeable and enlightened about this case,
Completely informed as well   1440
Of all that had been discussed
And concluded below in the fields.

After these explanatory words,
Which were ably spoken and competently organized,
My heart suddenly felt joy   1445
Because, while listening, I heard
Horses come up and people talking;
For at that very hour the good and worthy king
Had come, and for pleasure, into our presence,
The man we had chosen for a judge.   1450
And the lady, who had been looking
At the door and had not hesitated to do so,
Saw and recognized him as he entered;
And she rose to her feet at once,
Proceeding to greet him   1455

And waiting for no one to do so.
Seeing her, he stepped forward
And embraced her lightly,
As she did him with much humility,
Welcoming the man courteously, 1460
Joyfully, and with a pleasant look.
And he said to her: "My dear lady,
I am quite unhappy you came forward.
Why did you not remain
Quite demurely on your throne?" 1465
"Dear sir, so God guide me,
I should never have done what
Very much would seem improper to me;
For it is said—something true enough
And rather easy to credit—that in the case of 1470
Those of exalted rank and lesser persons,
All honor should be paid to every great lord.
But let's drop the matter;
It should delay us but little.
Instead, let us take our seats on the throne. 1475
There I would like to see about
Telling you an extraordinary thing
That is quite unlike other marvels.
Go on ahead; I'll follow along,
Keeping quite close to you." 1480
"By God, my lady, I shall not do so.
At the very moment I ascend
You will go up right with me;
Never will you make me agree
That we should not proceed side by side. 1485
I believe I have already been too forward."
On this point they easily concurred
And then ascended together.
And after they had gone up,
Again, in their great humility, 1490
They argued about sitting down.
But in the end they sat,[22]
And once they were seated,
The lady spoke, her thoughts composed:
"Sir, listen to me a little while 1495
And take some pleasure
In attending diligently to
What I would like to tell you.
You see there Guillaume de Machaut.
He's a man who is indifferent 1500

As to whether he upholds wrong or right.
In fact, he would just as soon defend
The wrong as the right,
As you will presently hear.
We have entered into a debate   1505
About an outrageous deed,
And this argument, sir, we should put before you,
But only if you would not be annoyed.
By his wish and my own,
You were chosen to be the judge.   1510
And so for us it is a happy chance,
Fair sir, that you have arrived here.
And this case will please you
If you have any interest in love.
For of necessity our disagreement concerns   1515
Something that pleases the romantically inclined
Since it's about love, the lover, and the beloved,
And of their noble governance.
Guillaume says, maintains, and affirms
As true and unassailable fact   1520
That when a man has given all his heart
To a lady, with the result that he becomes her lover
And she grants him her affection,
And so he thinks the woman a true beloved,
But then he has the experience   1525
Of finding her proven false—
This man, he says, feels more pain
Than a lady who discovers
Faithfulness in her true lover,
And she in turn loves him as much   1530
As any lady can love a man,
Completely and without bitterness,
But then it chances that death,
Which with stealth stings mankind,
Takes the life from her lover.   1535
And when she learns that he has passed away,
Has been completely undone,
Has been married to death,
And that their affair has thus ended,
Would that first man grieve like this woman?   1540
Not at all! It could not happen;
This view is indefensible.
And so I have made, do make, and wish to make
A protest to the contrary.
That is the gist of our dispute.   1545

And we would like you to be its
Judge; thus you would decide
According to the disputation you'd hear."

THE JUDGE

"I will answer you, my dear lady,
By the faith I owe God and my own soul,   1550
From my own perspective:
To occupy the privileged position
Of a judge is a very noble thing,
Especially for someone who risks so much
As to judge questions of Love.   1555
But because the petitions offered here
Have greatly pleased me, I will undertake the office
Without improper thoughts or malice.
If I have but a little sense, I will learn
From the speeches that I will hear;   1560
And if I can be well counseled,
I would be much happier than if someone
Gave me five hundred marks of gold.
And yet I do inform you,
Dear lady, that I will choose   1565
Whatever advisors I desire
From among your splendid entourage,
Which has accompanied you.
Truly, it is fitting for a competent judge
Who is weighing a decision   1570
That he has counsel from all sides.
Let us begin, whether it is correct or not.
So I ask you that this be done,
Either with courtesy or grace.
And on the other hand, no matter what anyone says,   1575
Proper justice most certainly needs help
So that it may at once proceed with grace
To assist the rendering of judgment in every court."

THE LADY

"Fair sir, concerning your request,
I certainly agree that it is proper.   1580
Choose now whomever you wish,
And you will have nothing to complain about."

THE JUDGE

"My lady, I choose Understanding,
Who is the very substance of good counsel.
Discretion will be at her side,   1585

And he will not protest at all,
Because she is his good friend;
Willingly he will accompany her.
And I should also be pleased that Reason
Be present, who deceives no one   1590
But instead is always for her part
Ready with good advice.
So she will listen to the testimony
In order to make it part of the judgment.
She will know how to advise me so well   1595
I will never need to review anything.
Moderation will stand by her;
For whoever does not moderate his judgment
Will not be able to proceed correctly
And come to the proper point   1600
Where he can release the parties
And deliver justice to each."
The lady heartily agreed
And spoke to him enthusiastically:
"Fair sir, you have done well   1605
In obtaining such advisors!"

THE JUDGE

"It will benefit me, my noble lady,
Because I desire quite fervently at heart
That I be well attended.
For the man not so attended is shamed.   1610
By their mutual agreement, I am now the judge
In the particular case of the dispute
That divides these two parties
And awaits a just decision.
Now the court is assembled and ready;   1615
And the way is quite clear, I think,
For us to be able to proceed.
Lady, you will speak first
And formulate your complaint,
Not because I ask that the details   1620
Of the case be recounted to me,
Since I am already adequately informed,
But rather because the parties to this trial
Should explain to me the circumstances
That make you sorrow and complain;   1625
And also in order to charge Guillaume
With his wrongdoing, if he is indeed wrong.
Otherwise, I cannot know the situation."[23]

THE LADY

"Sir, this speech pleases me.
Since we've begun the pleading, 1630
I will formulate my complaint in a rhetorical figure
From the works of Nature,
All for Guillaume, who has turned from
The truth and has in this way erred.
You know about the turtle dove, 1635
Which is pretty, noble, and attractive,
Quiet, happy, sweet, and beautiful
While her mate is alive,
And if it happens that she loses him
Through death, it is readily apparent 1640
That she will never find joy,
For she demonstrates this through signs.
Her heart is so filled with passionate burning
That she will never perch on greenery;
Instead she always seeks out darkness, 1645
Strange places full of misery,
Dead trees, fallow fields, and crossroads.
Her perch is often found in such locations
When she wishes to take her rest.
She will permit her heart nothing 1650
But a sorrowful life,
So grief-stricken she is for her mate.
I say it is just the same for a lady
Who has sworn fealty to Love.
When she lost her lover 1655
Through death, her heart became
So distressed she will never find joy;
Instead she seeks places, times, people, and paths
Where there is always total sadness;
She chooses a simple habit instead of finery, 1660
Shadows instead of sunlight;
And rather than the gaiety that comes
From wearing chaplets of flowers,
Weeping and tears flow from her face.
And if she looks for any relief at all, 1665
She does so modestly;
The lady who remains in mourning for her lover
Conducts herself in this way,
That is, when she is a true beloved.
Now I will speak to a second point. 1670

When the swan is unfaithful
And her mate learns the facts of the matter,

I am convinced that he is greatly upset
And feels much anger in his heart;
But he can find relief   1675
Because he can avenge himself.
And so he immediately begins to search;
Through the bird nests he looks for
Those of his own kind
Until he finds a multitude of them.   1680
Then he assembles these around his own nest,
And when he has them all together,
They hold a great council
And, afterward, make that one suffer
Death who, so they say, has wronged her.   1685
There she is undone and devoured.
The male has lightened the burden of his pain
After taking revenge in this fashion.
Similarly, I maintain that a man
Must be fierce as a lion   1690
In the face of any wrong done him.
And he can imagine many ways
That he might consider
In order to end his trouble,
Many different schemes to try.   1695
But that lady has no recourse at all,
Nothing that will heal her pain
Once she sees her lover die.
And she suffers a hundred times more misery
Than that other lover ever feels.   1700
Guillaume, find an answer now for this.
If you are wrong, then make amends."[24]

GUILLAUME

After these arguments, I drew myself up
And addressed my words
To the judge, who attended closely to   1705
What she said and what I was saying.
And I told him: "Sir, without doubt
My lady, whatever the outcome,
Has stated her case wisely and well,
And with a subtle understanding   1710
Well supplied with lively arguments
So as to establish her comparisons,
Which are nicely developed and ably conceived,
So thoroughly expounded as well
That whoever wished to offer improvements   1715
Would find this impossible, I believe.

And what she has recounted
You have well remarked,
Heard, sensed, and understood.
For from her mouth all this made its way   1720
Into your heart as you listened;
And so there is no need to repeat it.
Furthermore I believe without question
That it comes from genuine feelings,
What she has brought up, that is,   1725
Maintaining her grace and goodness,
And it lacks vain intention of any kind.
And I hold an opinion that is different
From her own; and I will state my reasons why,
If it pleases and interests you,   1730
Not in order to undermine her point of view,
But rather to make my own case.
A man can quite well value his own position
Without belittling the contrary opinion."

THE JUDGE

"Guillaume, I won't contradict you.   1735
Say whatever it pleases you to say,
Either quickly or taking your time.
Work at this as you like.
I would very much like to listen and hear,
And I have enough leisure to wait."   1740

GUILLAUME

"Many thanks, sir. I will speak,
And I believe I'll say nothing false.
I tell you that unfaithfulness on the part of a lady
Is such a bitter and difficult thing
For a lover's heart, so unnatural as well,   1745
That, when the fact of it has taken firm hold,
It will never leave again.
Now the man does not know where to go
In order to seek relief:
If he thinks to avenge himself   1750
Through murder (and well might he do so),
He should be firmly opposed
By the prospect of great madness
And a powerful, encompassing grief,
A fire to afflict every passion,   1755
A water to extinguish sweetness,
Nourishment for every mischance:
For to commit murder would be a sin.

And a sin that tortures the heart
Is one way that death can begin, 1760
The death of what is called mortal life.
For whoever languishes in this way is not alive at all.
In my case, the one I am presenting to you
Now in your presence,
There is more grief and burning torment 1765
Than in the other, and it is much harder to bear.
And so I ask now if
For this reason I might claim victory."[25]

TEMPERANCE

Immediately Temperance arose,
Who was holding Endurance by the hand, 1770
And she spoke in a temperate fashion,
Saying: "Guillaume, how
Dare you ask for the decision on your behalf?
I am amazed that you should consider this
After offering only a brief argument. 1775
Either your intelligence is quite limited
Or you are ruled by overconfidence.
Don't you know who determines
What is the right when parties argue,
Desiring a decision and waiting for it? 1780
I would like very much for you to know
That Reason is in charge,
And along with her, her entourage;
Each of them holds a prominent position
Among us other damsels. 1785
Don't doubt this in the least:
No decision can be rendered
If they all are not a part of its making
In order that things might be done properly
(If the one who made the laws does not lie). 1790
I myself have the responsibility
Of resisting any kind of malice,
Which many times diverts the right;
And by my efforts I put things back on track.
When a proper trial takes shape, 1795
And I see it going awry,
I can very well do what is needed
For it to be put right and return to form.
If there is too much, I can remove something.
And now please note this point well: 1800
If there is too little, I can add something

Whenever I wish to take pains.
And if everything is just right,
I can make certain it remains so.
That is the office of Temperance 1805
Anytime there is some need.
Now I wish to speak of something else
That contradicts your view.

You have defended an opinion
That does you little honor, 1810
And it concerns what my worthy lady
Maintained about the swan:
How she is put to death
After having proved unfaithful to her mate.
Do you believe my lady meant 1815
That the female who did wrong
To the male who loves her
Should be made to suffer death?
Not at all! Truly that would be folly.
And my lady does not maintain in any way 1820
That he should kill her or have her killed.
Instead she advises that he struggle
Against the temptations
Of those false ideas
That might come into his mind. 1825
Furthermore, although it might happen
That she die naturally,
It would be better (justice upholds it)
Had she remained alive.
For as long as the person lives 1830
Who intends to sin in mad error,
One has no pain, no sorrow,
No grief, suffering, or mischance
That one cannot overcome.
When he feels pain of any kind, 1835
He must truly think,
Having served her faithfully,
That he has not deserved this at all.
This is a valid thought,
Useful for comforting the man. 1840
What else should I tell you?
There are as many remedies
In love as painful wounds,
However bitter, painful, or hard to bear.
Each points to its proper remedy, 1845
Teaches the man what is good to seek.

But a lady who witnesses
The death of her very sweet lover,
In whom on no day of his life
Was found anything but courtesy— 1850
She could be so terribly stricken
And so grievously, beaten down so far as well
That she will never prove able to recover.
Instead, she will not fail to die.
Written texts tell us 1855
That this has happened many times.
And so I will relate a short tale
That will bring great shame upon you
And great honor to my lady,
As well as much clarity to my lord, 1860
For he will see more distinctly
How foolishly you err.

Not long ago it happened
That a great lady came to Paris,
And she brought along a daughter of hers 1865
Who, intending neither deception nor trouble,
Did love a noble knight,
A man wise, courteous, happy, and sophisticated,
Skilled at arms, strong and powerful,
Possessing every grace. 1870
This news of him came to her
And greatly afflicted her heart.
He had been killed in a tournament.
'Alas!' she said, 'What grief
This news brings me!' 1875
With this word, the young girl
Fell to the earth in a heap.
Quickly her mother went over,
Running to her with great sorrow;
And she began to cry softly 1880
And had her carried to a bed.
There she found little comfort
Because her heart was so terribly afflicted,
And her face so pale and discolored,
Her body so stricken 1885
And her limbs so withered
That she could hardly stand
Or hold anything in her hands.
And she did not recover enough afterward
To be able to eat or drink. 1890
Physicians were sent for,

And it was asked of them
If she could be saved from death;
And that each should see about
Bringing her back to health, if it could be done; 1895
And that they should boldly demand
A great deal of what these people possessed,
As much as they desired to have.
And they diligently applied themselves,
And quite eagerly and with care 1900
Attempted to devise
A cure for her if they could.
First they examined her urine,
And then they palpated her.
One after the other they touched her 1905
Wherever palpation should be done:
The feet, the wrists, and then the temples.
And after this they discussed examples
Of the various cures they had brought about
And accomplished in many places; 1910
But the more examples they discussed,
The more bewildered they were.
Her urine was judged healthy,
And the examination did not reveal
Any symptoms of coldness or heat 1915
From which they would have gotten indications
About where or what this illness came from,
Or what remedy was called for
In order to soothe her somewhat
Or alleviate her ills altogether; 1920
But in the end one of them took stock
And spoke these words of wisdom:
'Colleagues, I've seen in her urine
A little something of what's causing this,
Namely that she is troubled in spirit. 1925
Now our science casts little light
On this point unless one thinks it over.
For we are aware of a saying
That the good philosopher affirmed:[26]
He states, and I believe what he says, 1930
That illnesses of every kind—
And there are never exceptions—
Are cured by their contraries.
And so we cannot infer at this point
That there is only one contrary 1935
Side in regard to this particular illness.
For these sudden maladies

Can arise for two reasons:
That's to say, so God guide me,
Great sorrow or overwhelming joy. 1940
And as a cause joy requires
That she be made angry and irritated,
And sorrow asks for just the opposite:
One should make merry
In her presence, do what would please her 1945
And whatever she asks for;
And, too, minstrels should be summoned
To entertain her.
Then it will be necessary for her to admit
The cause of the illness 1950
So she can be given certain advice.
This is what I advise and counsel.
So let one of us go very quietly
In order to speak to her privately.'
They were agreed on this point; 1955
And so one went to ask her
What you have already heard.
Her heart was hardly happy about this.
Instead she answered quite unwillingly,
And yet still told him 1960
Face to face the whole truth
So ably that she hesitated not at all.
Then he asked her this,
As ably as he could in all honesty:
'Young lady, answer me one question 1965
That I will now put to you.
Would you want from this moment on
To see him alive,
Even if this were in such a way
That he would never show you the demeanor, 1970
The speech, the look of a lover?'
And she answered: 'Alas!
Sir, may God grant me health,
Such is indeed my wish,
And I would willingly see him alive 1975
Again even if it were
That he has taken another beloved,
Who would be served by me
All my life, even to taking off her shoes.
Please press me no more about this; 1980
For my heart breaks completely with sorrow,
A sorrow so bitter and deep
Every time anyone speaks of him to me.

So I do not want to hear about it anymore.'
After this word, he left
And walked to the place
Where the others were awaiting him,
And they were eager and anxious
To learn what end she might come to.
And he told them that she would die:
'I do not see any recovery from it.
Her heart has been locked within the tower
Of Love by the key of Sadness,
Where she suffers great distress,
And thus she shall die
Soon; she shall never escape.
Because of this we will leave here;
We will remain here no longer.'
Within the hour they left the place,
Saying to the mother:
'My lady, nothing can be done,
But please do your best
To watch over and stay close to her.'
After they left, she cried out
All at once in a loud voice:
'Oh! Sweet mother, I'm dying.
I commend you to God, sweet lady!'
And just at that moment, she gave up the ghost.
She was lamented by the household,
And her mother suffered terribly.
But of this I'll take no account
Because it adds nothing to my theme.

Guillaume, where will you discover
The proof you need to establish
That a man would be compelled to die
As a result of the experience you describe,
Namely the betrayal of his dear beloved,
When it is already well established
That after she sinned so wickedly,
He did in fact remain alive?
The case of the young girl is true,
But it would certainly be too hard to believe
That his misfortune was greater
Than hers. Well you know it!"

GUILLAUME

"Temperance, you speak very prettily
Every time you wish to.

On this occasion especially
You have spoken quite wisely.
And whatever you have said here I affirm,
And I do not shrink from believing any of it.   2030
But this has nothing to do
With my case in any way at all.
When this noble maiden
Granted her devotion to the knight
And he became her true lover   2035
And was afterward delivered to death,
For which reason Love held her so close
That death presently struck her down in turn,
Love showed her great favor in this,
For the blow passed quickly.   2040
In any case, she did have to die;
No one contests this fact
Whom death does not come and take.
No person might avoid it.
When a man is unhappily condemned   2045
To death by the sentence
Of a good judge without impropriety
And that judge puts him in a miserable prison
Enclosed within some horrible place
Where he could be eaten by worms   2050
Or by a host of other vermin,
And he serves a long sentence,
His neck and arms hung with irons
And his legs as well—that's hell for sure.
There he's turned away from faith   2055
In order to renounce his Creator.
Willingly he'd renounce Him
For whoever might deliver him from that place.
But at the time he is arrested,
Condemned to death in a just decision,   2060
It avails him much more to be delivered
By death than to live on in such suffering.
So it is with the true lover
Who has been betrayed in loving a lady
For the same reason as described above.   2065
I affirm and state in my poem
That no misfortune compares to
The suffering his heart endures
As long as he and she live on.
Also I know quite well that Nature   2070
Has established by her proper right
That a person will be forgotten

Who dies and cannot be had back
Either through great trouble or for treasure.
On this point I expect the decision for myself.   2075
I could not wish to be judged on a better issue."

PEACE

After these words, Peace rose up
And said, like one well schooled:
"Guillaume, you have buttressed
Your argument rather sufficiently   2080
According to your lights;
But you have cut it much too short
To gain the judgment for yourself so quickly.
For there is another point that deprives you of it.
You have drawn on Nature   2085
To prove your case, a rather nice ploy
That has been much appreciated.
But I have laid another trap
For this, a quite formidable one
In which you shall be caught,   2090
And it's contained in a certain exemplum, in fact,
One quite useful to recall.
And so I offer it to you
Because it serves my purpose well.

Dido, queen of Carthage,[27]   2095
Felt very great sorrow and anger
Because of the love she bore Aeneas,
Who had pledged her his faith
To take her as his woman and wife.
And the traitor called her his lady,   2100
His heart, his love, and his goddess,
His sovereign mistress as well.
Then he sailed off across the ocean
Like a thief, he and his companions,
So that Dido never saw him again.   2105
Hear now what she did!
When he'd failed her by breaking the promise
He had agreed to make in good faith,
Just as many lovers do
Who pretend to be loyal lovers,   2110
That desperate and crazed woman,
Whom love had shamed, whom love had driven mad,
Found the sword of Aeneas
And tried it out on her own body
And could not spare herself   2115

Until she made it bathe in her blood;
And so she died in pain
Because she loved and was mad.
Yet she did not die alone,
But cut instead the throats of two,   2120
For she was carrying the child of Aeneas;
And afterward she was much mourned and lamented.
But before she killed herself,
She ordered a blazing fire
To be laid in her presence.   2125
And when in her desperation
She killed herself, the woman struck so forcefully
That with the blow she fell into the fire
And was at once roasted and burned up.
In this way Dido ended her life.   2130
This is the truth, I firmly believe,
For so I found it in the written history.

To conclude, Guillaume, truly
My view is just the opposite of yours
In the light of and in view of   2135
The reasons I've laid out above.
For it can be clearly seen
That misery, pain, and torment
Cannot be compared
To what she was intent on paying in return   2140
For the grief brought by her lover.
And if a man found himself among
A great horde of his enemies,
All of whom had promised him
Death and indeed could kill him   2145
As they wished, whenever they liked,
Though living in this fear
(Disregarding the pain and terror)
Still he might find consolation.
Yet there is an even stronger argument: 2150
Whoever might take him to hang on the gibbet
At that very moment with no reprieve,
He would yet be comforted
And sustained and heartened
By the hope of escaping: 2155
And neither evil error nor despair
Might assault him
As long as he holds on to hope;
For hope will accompany him
Right until the moment he dies.   2160

You have also made a point
Against Love that's badly off the mark:
It is that Nature has control
Over the people of Love at her will;
And thus if Nature commands, 2165
No one would disobey that command.
She asks that one forget
The death of both lover and beloved
Because in this instance nothing can be restored
By great treasure or by taking action. 2170
Let her command; indeed we welcome it!
We do not have any worries on this score
Because this doesn't concern the lover at all.
For Good Love keeps for herself
And herself alone a lover's heart 2175
Without any command from Nature.
Whoever does not agree is not forced,
And yet one is so constrained by Love,
He must, feeling that power, obey.
Anyone who resists is a fool. 2180
Guillaume, I advise you therefore
To drop this unpersuasive argument
That maintains Nature has the ability
To enforce her own command,
Whatever its value, in matters of love; 2185
Nature lends a good appearance
To a lover's frivolous thought,
And this makes him foolishly determine
To do something Love hates.
And because of such foolishness, 2190
Much misfortune results,
And this is worth much less than nothing.
I need discuss it no further
Because no point of honor is involved.
I am Peace, who would willingly 2195
Always do what's good and bring down
Evil; Concord would do the same,
For whatever I desire, so does she
At all times, both morning and night.
Thus I hold her by the hand 2200
In order to do what might please her.
Go on with your argument,
Guillaume, in the way you must,
Without being hindered by Nature.
If, by my advice, you follow the principles 2205
Of Discretion, you will do wisely."

GUILLAUME

"Peace, young lady, faith in you
Brings all good things, that is something true.
So I will guard myself from wrongdoing.
But I wish to defend my opinion   2210
As forcefully as I can.
In this regard I will relate an exemplum,
Which here follows, in order to prove my view
And refute your mistaken opinion.

In Orleans there formerly was a clerk   2215
Who was renowned and said to be
A noble cleric, a valiant and powerful man,
And so was neither miserly nor cheap,
A lord of laws, and of decrees
The master, and a man quite discreet   2220
In the demonstration of what he knew
And the valor that was his.
He had been born in Provence,
Though well connected by blood to princes
And counts in France,   2225
If indeed my story is true.
He was attended by noble people,
The competent and the learned in great number,
And had among his company
Many well-born knights   2230
To whom he would give rich robes.
This quality very well became him,
Because in order to merit his good will
They took pains to serve him.
Now, he was very much taken in love   2235
With a worthy damsel
Who lived near Montpellier,
The daughter of a valiant knight,
Descended from a very aristocratic line.
And the relationship had been established   2240
So firmly between these two
That it could not have been better.
Each of them had committed to the other,
He as her loyal lover
And she as a loyal beloved;   2245
And always, moreover, all their life
They upheld truly
The courtly rules of faithfulness.
But the distance between them became quite great

For he went to live in Orleans, 2250
And she remained in Provence.
Even so, quite ably, as it behooved them,
They maintained the secrets of love
With letters they sent to one another
By their special messengers, 2255
Honest men, discreet and wise.
They carried on in this fashion for some time.
But Fortune, who destroys quickly
Much of honor throughout the land,
Saw to it that he had a terrible shock, 2260
Much worse than losing five hundred marks of gold,
Just as I will now relate.

It happened one day,
Which dawned evilly for him,
That a messenger arrived 2265
From Provence, a man noble and adroit
Who was bringing him a sealed letter
Enclosed within a little chest.
This he took and looked over,
Refraining from reading out loud, 2270
For it contained many private things.
And at the very end the letter
Related how his beloved had been married
To the worthiest man of that region
And was at that time big with child. 2275
'Oh no!' he said, 'My heart is breaking.
Oh Death, why don't you take me now?
I'm almost ready to hang myself!'
Then he started pulling out his hair
And, afterward, tearing his robe. 2280
When his people saw him in such a state,
They moved quickly forward,
And each one tried to restrain him.
But he escaped them by force.
Down to the town he fled. 2285
He became deaf and dumb,
And from the time he left that place
He never spoke again with his mouth
A word that any living man
Might hear, however well he knew him. 2290
Nor from the time this happened
Did he ever return home;
Instead he slept on rubbish heaps,
Becoming accustomed to this.

And when his friends would restrain him   2295
And tie him up somewhere,
He would refuse to eat or drink;
Instead, and this is certain, he went mad.
And so they let him go free and clear
To roam where he liked across open country.   2300
But he never did any harm
To any man, other than himself.
Twenty years altogether he remained in this state;
And he was grieved for and lamented
By the people who knew him,   2305
Many of whom wept bitterly.
So from up high he was pulled down low.
A long discussion is hardly needed
To establish a certain truth,
Namely that he felt more misery and pain   2310
Than any hundred ladies ever experienced
Who witnessed the death of their lovers.
When it pleases you, take this into consideration
And refrain from judging incorrectly."

FAITH

Faith immediately got to her feet,   2315
Like someone wise and well schooled
In law, custom, and practical matters;
And she said: "Guillaume, you have certainly
Spent your time here foolishly,
Straying from the path of justice,   2320
At least in some respects.
And I intend to make a discrimination,
That is to say, a division
By way of a distinction
Between things that do not enforce belief   2325
And those that are able to enjoy
The success of being believed
Or considered possible,
Of which I would prize the latter
And put little stock in the former   2330
At the urging of my friend Constancy,
Who argues in all my disputes
And supports my side, giving me strength
To uphold everyone who trusts in me.
That this clerk was of great valor,   2335
A noble man, and very powerful,
Renowned for his great gentility,
And, too, provided quite abundantly

With worldly goods,
Smitten and burning with love, 2340
A friend of the heart, loved by his beloved;
And, further, that in all courtliness
They had formed their liaison
Through a most loving bond
So that they kept the secrets 2345
Of love as long as they did live;
Also that he was living in Orleans,
Well connected by blood to people
In France with such honor
That it could not be greater— 2350
All these things are possible.
Also, in regard to the quite horrible illness
That attacked him so suddenly that
It came upon him as he read the letter
And then lasted quite long, 2355
Enduring twenty years altogether—
Once again I say this could well be.
For God has ordained
So many secret things in this earthly life
That they could not be explained 2360
Through the wisdom of mortal man.
Furthermore, from your own knowledge
You have just now said
By your own admission that this letter
Contained several secret matters. 2365
Now, no one knows whence they came,
And so I have truly found a point
You have not proved in the least:
That this was sent to him by his beloved.
This reason makes it impossible 2370
For anyone in any way to decide
The matter in your favor.
And I certainly know other things
That will be discussed, if I can bring it about,
In order to defeat you utterly, 2375
If someone here is able to address them."

GUILLAUME

"Young lady, kindly stop
Your threatening, if you please,
For it will profit you nothing,
And it grieves my heart."[28] 2380

CHARITY

Charity then reflected
And said: "Faith, listen to this!
I should like to tell you something extraordinary."
And then she whispered in her ear
Secretly what she had in mind. 2385
When she heard it, Faith demurely began
To laugh a little about it
And, smiling, started to say:
"Charity, my dear young lady,
This matter is something for you to bring up 2390
Cheerfully and in a pleasant fashion.
You are better able to recount it,
And this is certain, than am I.
Indeed, you have got a head start
Because it is something you feel, 2395
And thus I beg you to do so."
"Faith, my very sweet and dear friend,
I will not fail you at all in this,
But will make known my view,
For the thoughts of 2400
Two people together are useful
When the pair is trustworthy;
And so I will speak to Guillaume about it,
Demonstrating to him a particular point
That will make him acknowledge defeat 2405
If he is not too foolish or malevolent.

Now, friend Guillaume, listen to this:
The power that has caused me
To be called Charity
Ordains I be proven so through my works, 2410
And the signs of this are seen
In all those closest to me.
They are the noble, faithful hearts
Who enter the royal court
Of Good Love, which has no peer. 2415
Now note where I appear:
I am manifest in fulfilled promises
And reasonable generosity,
Especially in the bestowing of gifts
And the pardoning of any wrongdoing: 2420
For happy are those who give
And also those who forgive.
Let's examine what Love demands

One give her, and more she does not command.
She expressly asks for the hearts   2425
Of good people to be hers completely.
She demands this be granted to her
And desires as well that some deeds
Be pardoned, according to the rule
Whose justifications I here propose.   2430
And I will demonstrate this through a figure
That Good Love embodies in my own person,
Doing so briefly and not drawing it out.

A prominent man owns an orchard
In which there are a great many trees.   2435
Most important, planted in that place
Is a very graceful grafting
That appeals more to the rich man
And pleases him much more
Than do all the rest.   2440
And he has loved her
As long as she has been called grafting.
Now it happens that time passes
Until the youth of the little one ends.
Into the wind her limbs reach   2445
So that she enters into that second age
That is called the middle years,
As her branches extend on all sides
While they enlarge her beauty
And increase her goodness   2450
In order to draw toward the goal
That is termed perfection
So as to delight and amuse him
By bearing flowers, leaves, and fine fruit.
At this moment, it will happen, I suggest,   2455
That the lord will ask
How the grafting is doing
And what condition she is in.
The gardener might then say: 'Sire,
I can truly tell you   2460
What seems to me good news about her;
Ask no longer how she is doing,
But rather how he does,
For your grafting is a perfect tree
And in such estate takes great delight   2465
In bearing flowers, leaves, and fine fruit
And thus has lost the name of grafting
And gained that of tree,

Under which one can find shade
And relax quite pleasantly.' 2470
Now I will sing and respond as well
In order to make my meaning clearer,
And in this regard I will ask the following question:
Should one grieve at heart
For that which improves, 2475
If she has lost an insignificant name
Either through nature or good works
In order to gain a much greater title?
I answer no, not at all:
For this would be terrible foolishness. 2480
But whatever a man loves dearly
Or has bought at a high price—
Were he to see it completely perish,
And it were not possible to save it,
Such grievous misfortune might be the result 2485
That he might well lose his head,
Indeed his whole self too.
I know this for certain
Because some have done so,
True lovers as much as beloveds. 2490
Now I will say something about the issue
That has moved me to speak.
This beautiful maiden
Who was the clerk's beloved—
She was the graceful grafting 2495
Planted like a sweet young girl
Within the magnificent orchard of Love.
There she could grow up so much,
Her branches extended so far,
So finely clad with leaves, 2500
So cunningly adorned with flowers
That she compared to the very best.
Now for a moment I wish to reflect a little
In order to describe these parts:
The branches of good reputation; 2505
The leaves of being well spoken of;
The flowers of having the ability
To conduct proper dealings with others,
In her appearance as much as in her actions.
In this condition, she says: 'Friend, here take this. 2510
I give you for your enjoyment
The favor of bearing the fruit of honor.'
Then come to him many thoughts
That are born of necessity:

To have her be married 2515
According to the advice of her family.
If she does so, it is not something
That he should worry about so much
He then begins to despair.
Instead, he ought to wish and hope 2520
That it profits and honors her
When through a lord's favor
She would rightfully be called a lady.
This reason encourages the virtuous heart
To love far better than before. 2525
So from this point on I maintain
That he did not love her with a good intention.
Surely this is quite apparent
Since Good Love wants him to suffer,
Offering his body to such torment. 2530
Guillaume, fair sir, I will say no more about it.
Say whatever you wish."

GUILLAUME

"Charity, so God give me joy,
You have ably and in a subtle fashion
Brought up several points—and in pretty words. 2535
But I do not see that what you have said
Has done me any harm at all.
I have a brief as consistent
And compelling as before
In its evidence; and so I maintain 2540
I shall never be defeated
Unless I am confronted with other arguments.
One point remains established
That makes it necessary for someone to prove
The opposite of what I say; 2545
If not, I will consider only as inconsequential
All that you have already brought up,
Notwithstanding your great goodness
And that you have done this in a worthy cause:
To lend your opinion authority 2550
And denigrate my own.
So I intend to say a little something
About the clerk who was a true lover
And then plunged into such misfortune
For twenty full years, as I have related. 2555
Now prove to me only the third of these points:
That any lady ever suffered
So terribly she offered her body to death.

Prove this point alone,
But this you will not be able to do." 2560

THE AUTHOR

After this Charity wanted to say something,
And she had her mouth already open
In order to give shape to her speech.
But Honesty was so quick
She was ready even sooner 2565
And said: "Charity, sweet friend,
Let me speak, if you please;
For I will never be satisfied
If I do not speak my mind
In order to trouble his heart." 2570
Charity was in complete agreement,
And then Honesty presented
Her view in an honest fashion,
And this the court warmly welcomed.

HONESTY

And she said: "Guillaume, now listen. 2575
You have laid little foundation
For the point you're trying to establish.
And I will tell you why.
It is true enough that he experienced
A great misfortune that came suddenly on him. 2580
But immediately, that moment past,
His terrible troubles were gone as well.
Even though it may last long,
A grief that pierces right to the heart
Will never endure beyond its time. 2585
And if any sorrow touches his heart,
There can be no emotion
Unless there is consent.
This principle is easy enough to credit.
He had lost his memory, 2590
Reason, bearing, and understanding;
Thus it can be clearly seen
That he had no will at all,
Only a heart eager for
The incredible foolishness he was doing. 2595
When he lay down on a dung heap,
That was his peace, his bed.
In every way, that was his delight,
A place where he slept deeply.
There is yet another matter 2600

You have yourself brought up.
It is certain—and well you know it—
That when his friends restrained him
And in different places locked him up,
He never ate or drank, 2605
But, instead, continually raged at
Whoever held him again his will;
He did nothing for anyone
And lived in the open like an animal.
This was a quite disgraceful life, 2610
Shameful had he taken account of it;
But he felt no shame at all.
So I have proved my point sufficiently
And reproved your wrong opinion
By the single point I have brought up. 2615
And a lady who comes to know
The death of her lover will find more than a hundred times
The suffering in a single day than will that man
In a century through such a blow
As you have described here above. 2620
Guillaume, you will either suffer,
Or you will bring up another point,
Because you are defeated in this one
And it is not worth a penny to you."

GUILLAUME

"Honesty, in truth I will not do so. 2625
I will speak a little more about this issue,
Since I have much with which to defend myself
If you would please hear me out.
When he lost all his senses
Because of the pain that assailed him 2630
And deprived him of all the honor he had,
He lost much more than what little he retained.
You say he did not feel any pain
Because he was disoriented
In his behavior and understanding. 2635
But it is certainly quite otherwise
Because, before a man can lose his mind
Or madness afflict him,
An illness grips and seizes him
That drives him to madness. 2640
Now I will argue this briefly
In order to demonstrate vividly to you
What proof I can offer for my view
In order to gain the judgment for myself.

When two causes are brought together 2645
And manifest themselves within a single body,
The one that arises first
Sets things into motion
Because it has the first effect
And therefore it is the chief cause. 2650
And if someone removes the first cause,
Then the second disappears of its own accord.
Now some might say:
'Guillaume, *verbi gracia*, thanks for the words,
But what is your point?' 2655
Here, right now, is the explanation.
We witness a dog going mad;
But what brings on this madness?
A worm that pierces his tongue.
Afterward the cause spreads so widely 2660
He loses the ability to drink and eat,
And then he must go mad.
This is then the first cause
From which the madness derives.
And when for this reason the dog cannot bark, 2665
That's the time to take care
He does not bite someone.
Now to bring this point home better,
I'll talk about what happened to
A dog that did go mad, 2670
One well loved in a rich man's home.
Listen now, and you will hear the crux of the matter.
The rich man had heard spoken about
The cause of such a malady:
And he wished to see it for himself, 2675
The better to understand.
So he had his dog taken by force,
Tied up, tightly bound, and spread-eagled,
And then its tongue pulled completely out
So that the worm could be plainly seen. 2680
Then the worm was extracted;
And when it had been fully drawn out,
The dog began to lick the hands
Of the man he had felt touch him;
And it was entirely cured. 2685
And so I affirm that this was the obvious
Cause of an obscure malady;
Therefore I maintain that the attack
Of grievous illness the man's body suffered
Kept him in the condition he was in; 2690

And so my point is quite adequately proved
And your grievous error corrected."

THE AUTHOR

After this, Frankness stood up
And was not very timid;
She had good will and a pleasant expression, 2695
And her manner was gracious.
Then she started to speak
And said the following in her remarks:

FRANKNESS

"It has been in most places—and always—
Observed about true loving 2700
That women have conducted themselves better
And have remained more faithful in it
Than men in every way.²⁹
This I think to prove—and it's right to do so—
With some instances I intend to relate 2705
Because they are relevant to my theme.

When those of Athens had put Androgeus³⁰
To death, Minos, the king of Crete,
Felt such bitterness on this account
That by wise and prudent means, 2710
Through the force of arms and war,
He made desolate all their land.
And because of this outrage, Minos
Forced a deadly service upon them:
That every year they were to send him 2715
One man; but they were to cast lots
And for that man upon whom the lot fell,
It was a quite fatal mischance.
For King Minos would have him
Devoured there without delay 2720
By a monster quite strange,
Very malevolent and dangerous too.
But no one ought to wonder
If Minos wished to oversee all this
Or if he were strongly moved to do so, 2725
Because he was the father of Androgeus.
Now it happened that the lot fell
On Theseus, and this dismayed
Many, for he was the son of the king,
A noble man, valiant, and of fair appearance. 2730
But because of the death of Androgeus,

Theseus went to Crete
To have himself killed by the monster
If he should not manifest his prowess
And prove able to defend himself against him. 2735
Otherwise he could expect death.
And if God should grant him victory,
He would acquire honor and glory,
For he would free the Athenians
And acquit them of their servitude. 2740
Yet nothing would have availed him, wood or iron,
Had it not been for beautiful Ariadne,
Who forgot about Minos, her father,
And Androgeus, her dear brother,
Her land, and her blood relations, 2745
For the sake of Theseus, to whom she gave
Her heart, and so she showed him
How to kill the proud monster
In order to deliver himself from bondage;
And she gave him her maidenhood 2750
So that he would make her his wife
And take her off to his own country
Along with Phaedra, her beloved sister,
Whom she would leave behind on no account.
Theseus, perjuring himself, 2755
Swore to her by his gods and law
That he would never prove false
And would always be faithful to her.
He lied when he said this, the traitor.
Why wasn't he drowned in the sea? 2760
After he completed his mission,
He embarked them on his ships.
But he grievously betrayed her
When he left Ariadne asleep
And all alone in a strange land, 2765
Abandoned, sorrowing, and deceived,
And led off the young girl,
Her sister Phaedra, and made her his wife.
This betrayal was quite fatal.
Also, I will talk about Jason,[31] 2770
Who took by force through Medea's arts
The golden fleece of Colchis,
And that trickster overcame
The fiery breath of the bulls,
Put to sleep the guardian dragon, 2775
Which was more dreadful than any other beast,
And defeated the armed knights

In their hundreds and thousands.
But no man could have accomplished all this
Had Medea not done it for him.   2780
She deserted her country and father,
Had her brother dear cut to pieces.
Because of her great foolishness, she killed Pelia.
And all of this was to make Jason king.
Whatever she owned, she gave him freely;   2785
Her honor and love she bestowed upon him.
But Jason abandoned Medea
For Creusa, demeaning himself greatly
And sinning grievously
When he left her and took up with the other woman.   2790
When Medea learned the news,
Which was hardly pleasant or appealing to her,
She was so desperate,
So insane, so crazed
That she killed the two children   2795
That were her own in order to spite Jason
Because they resembled him;
And then she torched her own house!
Afterward the wretched woman fled
Through the air with her serpents.   2800
But later in foreign lands
There were women who were crowned queens.
For Aegeus, the king of Athens,
Was beguiled by Medea;
Bacchus honored Ariadne   2805
Greatly, for he dearly loved her.
These two married the women
In their own countries and crowned them;
And so, Guillaume, that is the gist.
Loyalty as great as that of women   2810
Cannot be found in any man;[32]
Nor would men ever be as deeply
Inflamed by the spark of love
As a worthy lady would.
For when there is less love,   2815
There is that much less suffering
Because it comes from feeling pain.
And I cannot agree
That, enduring the ills of love,
Any man would feel as much as a woman.   2820
And the man has a hundred
Remedies unavailable to women."

GUILLAUME

"Young lady, the treason
Of either Theseus or Jason
Has nothing to do with our issue,   2825
And that was hardly the first
Or last betrayal
That there's been with lovers,
As often with women as with men.
And I wouldn't give two apples   2830
For proving your point
By bringing up such examples.
For if I intended to establish my case
By examples, I would find
More than ten, indeed more than twenty of them.   2835
Everyone knows well what happened
To the lover of the chatelaine
De Vergy; he loved her with a love
So certain he killed himself without hesitation
When he saw her dead for the sake of his love.[33]   2840

Virtuous Lancelot and Tristan[34]
Experienced ten times more pain
Than any woman could suffer,
As much as she could subject herself to it,
And they were a hundred times more loyal   2845
Than Jason was disloyal,
Or Theseus either, who sinned greatly
Against Ariadne when he seduced Phaedra.
Still, I wish to tell of another
If you are willing to listen to me.   2850
A lady was loved
By a knight without any baseness,
And she gave him a ring that was
Quite beautiful (it was neither cheap nor ugly),
On the condition that he always wear it   2855
And never remove it
From his finger unless she did so.
And the knight, who was
Hers completely, promised this in good faith,
And then the lady put it on his finger.   2860
Now it happened that she had a husband
Whose heart was gloomy and vexed
Because he recognized the ring,
Having seen it another time.
So he went at once to ask   2865

The woman and command her
To furnish him with it on the spot
On pain of losing his favor.
The lady said that she had it,
But where, she did not really know. 2870
So she made a show of going to look for it
And, opening a drawer,
Like a cunning and sharp woman
Spoke this secret message to one of her people:
'Go directly to my lover 2875
And tell him I am in for a bad time
If he does not send my ring back;
And do not delay along the way,
For my master wishes to have it
Without hearing any excuses. 2880
Make it clear he shouldn't fail me.
For if he does, I am shamed
And in danger of losing the honor
And the favor of my lord.'
The messenger did not delay at all, 2885
But proceeded faster than at a walk
To the knight and told him everything
That I related earlier in my tale.
When the knight heard this,
His heart nearly broke 2890
Because he feared his lady
Might be dishonored or accused on his account.
So he said: 'Friend, by the faith I owe her,
She will have my finger along with the ring,
For I will not remove it.' 2895
So then he took out a knife,
Cut off his finger, and sent it to her
Along with the ring she had put there.
Could anyone do something more loyal
Than this, or more loving? 2900
Surely, not at all. Such is my view.
For her lover was very trustworthy.
And so I should very much dare expect
A judgment of truth with no more debate,
For men should have more respect 2905
And in every case be counted superior
To women, whose words
You maintain that I consider frivolous,
Because as everyone says—and this you know well—
Virtue should triumph everywhere. 2910

And these men were considered
Virtuous and loyal in every royal court,
However much the ladies did for their lovers
And no matter how much they suffered.
But people say—and true it is— 2915
It's always one extreme or the other,
That is, too much or too little. And so I see the matter thus.
These extremes are not worthy of praise.
However, he who is caught in the snares
Of love and shows moderation, 2920
That man acts wisely and well.
And the sage, a man who does not lie, declares
That the fortunate hold to the middle path
Wherever they go."[35]

PRUDENCE

Prudence responded to this, 2925
And she neither implicated nor involved herself
In the issue at hand;
And this lady said: "Guillaume, now
I see well what your intention is.
But I hold a contrary view, 2930
And it is very different from yours.
It is well known that the chatelaine
Died for the sake of a young man
Because he could not keep her secret.
Instead, he related all their affair 2935
To the duchess of Burgundy.
And the duchess did a terrible thing
When at a feast she let it slip
That she knew all about the business
Of the trickery with the little dog. 2940
And the chatelaine died therefore, saying 'alas'
Because of her lover's error.
And when the lover saw his beloved
Dead and undone because of his gossiping,
If he killed himself, he did what he should, 2945
For he deserved to suffer another kind of death,
And he did nothing less than what was just
When he killed himself to punish his misdeed;
For they should have had wild horses
Tear him to pieces for what he had done. 2950
So it is my view that the chatelaine
Suffered more misfortune and hurt
When she had to die for no reason

Than did the young man who killed himself
And who deserved to hang; 2955
For this reason his torment was less.

And if Tristan and Lancelot
Were valiant, I dare well say
That their valor and prowess
Meant glory, honor, and riches to them; 2960
And no man might acquire
Such goods without suffering some earthly pain.
And so, Guillaume, I dare say
That the ladies in question endured
A hundred times more pain and torment 2965
Than the lovers to whom they were committed,
For they suffered mournful thoughts,
Fears that confounded them,
As well as the words of slanderers.
And if these men had waited around for years, 2970
Never would they have found perfect joy;
For whoever waits is quite annoyed,
And nothing grieves the human heart so much
As slander and nagging thoughts;
And the ladies found no benefit in all this 2975
Except what little joy they received.
And so it is with many ladies
Who surrender their hearts and souls
And whatever they own to their lovers;
And when each woman has given so much 2980
That their men acquire knightly honor,
Which is manifest in word and action,
The women draw no other salary
Save a little glory from what they do.
The men have the kernel; the women get the chaff, 2985
For the honor belongs to the men, whatever might happen.
And if misfortune is sometimes their lot,
The ladies are the first to suffer.
Surely, this is an inadequate reward
When for good they get strife in return. 2990
In regard to the man who cut off his finger,
He struck an unfortunate blow in truth;
For Guillaume, whatever anyone might say,
I consider it a quite foolish thing,
And I intend to argue a little against this view. 2995
For there were three or four
Paths that should have sufficed,
But he chose the worst of all.

And furthermore, I do not believe at all
That the woman who was his beloved, 3000
If the love she felt for him had been faithful,
Would not have preferred the risky business
Of her husband and his anger,
Even if it meant the bond ought to have been
Broken between those two right at that moment, 3005
Rather than depriving her lover of a finger
So that he would always be disfigured,
Less esteemed, and quite impaired."

GUILLAUME

"Frankness, no doubt you have
Spoken well, for you can speak ably. 3010
But I know for certain
That this is against your own conscience
And that you have argued the opposite
Of what really lies in your heart.
But I ask you, please 3015
Let us narrow our debate,
For we have moved too far from the question
That was broached at its beginning.
It is indisputable, and this I affirm,
That there is nothing stable in a woman's heart, 3020
Nothing certain, no constancy of any kind,
Except for complete changeability.[36]
And since she is so fickle
That she is firm about or convinced of nothing
And alters for the slightest reason, 3025
It follows that she laughs or cries over trifles;
And so great joy and immense suffering
Cannot remain with her for very long
Because her nature leads her
To laugh quickly and cry over little things; 3030
She agrees readily and demurs just as fast.
She has her say but then denies it,
And she forgets utterly
And easily what she does not see.
Now since she cannot ever possess 3035
Her lover again, for money,
For tears, moaning, lamentation,
Or for anything she might do;
And also since by her nature
She forgets quite readily 3040
Any person out of her sight,
One could well conclude that if she experienced

Loss and hurt because of her lover,
She would be ready again in such a short time
That 'for the one lost, two recovered' 3045
Would be the reproach made to her.
In contrast, a man's heart is firm, secure,
Wise, experienced, and mature,
Virtuous and strong in endurance,
But humble in suffering adversity. 3050
And when it is all aflame
With amorous burning, it so embraces this
That it would rather die behind its shield than
Be seen beaten down or vanquished.
What I maintain is hardly arguable, 3055
For everyone says and agrees with it,
And since everyone says the same
I have written it in my poem.
So I say in conclusion
That, considering the nature 3060
Of men and women, no woman
Can suffer as much torment,
However much she moans and carries on,
As any man can bear within his heart,
For it is simply not in her nature. 3065
Reason and good custom concur.
In any case, the misfortune that ends
Is less severe than the one that does not,
But rather endures right to death,
Until it has killed the one suffering the ill." 3070

LARGESSE

Largesse, who was sitting nearby,
Then spoke up, for it suited her well to do so,
And she said: "Guillaume, truly,
I am astonished how
You dare to malign women; 3075
For you should not talk this way.
And any blame in what you have said
Falls more on you than on women.
You have said in your poem
(And surely you are wrong) 3080
Everyone considers it the truth
That all women are fickle,
And their word is worth no more
Than a weathercock in the wind.
But this entire company 3085
Believes the opposite and opposes your view.

So for this reason you can certainly say
That you are not endorsed;
And so you must pay the piper.
I don't know what more to say, 3090
For no one can construct a valid
Argument on a faulty premise."

WARINESS

"And I cannot keep silent about this,"
Declared Wariness,
"Rather I will say what is on my mind; 3095
For all my heart shakes and quivers
When for no reason I hear
Ladies maligned and defamed.
Now listen to my question.
Fair Guillaume, I ask you 3100
If that woman alters or changes
Who is all the days of her life
A loyal beloved, never betraying
In deed, desire, or thought?"

GUILLAUME

"Surely, damsel, not at all! 3105
But I believe that not one such would be found
Among five hundred thousand,
For this seed is too thinly sown."

WARINESS

"My fair sir, may God preserve me,
Your point of view is very strange 3110
And your words amaze me!
So you must have been to the school
Of constant change, or so I believe;
And because your own heart is fickle,
You believe that everyone is the same 3115
As you are. But, please God, it is not so!
For I will prove the contrary
In fact, whomever it should displease!"

GUILLAUME

"Damsel, I hope you won't be dismayed
If I look at you in a friendly way, 3120
For I do not dislike you so much
That I would frown at you.
And if my words are unwelcome,
It's a good cart that never overturns.

But I believe I am speaking the truth, 3125
However much you would like to dispute it.
So I am quite badly treated here
If for speaking the truth I am beaten down."

SUFFICIENCY

And then Sufficiency rose to her feet
And said: "Guillaume, without a doubt, 3130
Now you have misspoken.
Look to what you are saying!
For no man who wishes to speak the truth
Would be able to defame women
Or what they are (this is well known) 3135
Since so much good can be said;
And so I advise and counsel you
Not to say, without counsel, anything further,
For you are a very young man
To proffer arguments such as these." 3140

GUILLAUME

Then I heard a murmuring,
For each lady was whispering
About how forcefully I was upholding
What I had said about women;
And I saw that each was giving the impression 3145
That she was displeased.
And when I perceived the manner
Of their talk and the looks on their faces,
And that all were eager
To add fuel to the fire, 3150
I made a request to the judge,
Who seemed fairly honest to me,
And I begged him humbly
And stated in my proposal
That they should speak at once 3155
And thus have done more quickly.
For so they were doing, it seemed to me,
Talking all at once, that is;
And at this the judge started to smile,
For he saw each of them was getting angry. 3160
And, to be sure, I felt quite great joy
When I saw them in such a state.
But the judge, who was intent on
Making a wise judgment,
Immediately imposed silence on them, 3165
With the sole exception of Sufficiency

And Wariness.
And then Wariness began to rehearse
A story that pertained to her viewpoint,
And she began in this fashion.³⁷ 3170

WARINESS
"What did Thisbe do for Pyramus?³⁸
When she saw him naked and dead
Because of her, without any recourse,
She became so grief-stricken
That she ran herself through with a sword, 3175
Right through the body, and there she remained;
For she would not live on after him,
But instead put an end to her love and life
With laments, tears, and wailing.
Surely this was a perfect love. 3180
For there is no pain or suffering
That can be compared to death;
Nor could anyone convince me
That any man's heart could break
So cruelly, or that he could injure himself 3185
As did Thisbe for love.
And whoever would say that a man is strong
In suffering the hardships of loving,
With a heart stronger than adamant
Or any diamond might be, 3190
I would not give for his strength
A bit of putrid peel,
Nor do I value highly his fortitude.
His virtue or maturity either,
Or anything he endures. 3195
But when a woman suffers some pain
That she conceals in her heart,
She acts on it in such a way
That she gives herself to it body and soul.
But, Guillaume, I don't believe at all 3200
That any man has ever been seen
Who died from a lack of reward
Or who was not quickly comforted,
However disconsolate his heart might have been;
Nor is there any pain that compares 3205
To death, however grievous it may seem,
No more than fire fashioned in a painting
Can be compared to fire in nature.
For Nature cannot produce anything,
No matter how contrary to the human body, 3210

That might be compared to death,
Nor can a heart endure anything like it."

SUFFICIENCY

"Wariness, stop your arguing,
For I wish to afford you a little help
To bring your point 3215
To an even truer conclusion,
Although you've developed it quite well
And reasonably, better than anyone else could do."
Sufficiency then began
And said the following for all to hear: 3220

"Leander, that handsome and clever man,[39]
Was friendly with a young girl
Who was named Hero the beautiful;
In all the land there was not
Another damsel so attractive, 3225
None so noble by far or so pretty;
Nor was there in Abydos or Crete
Any love affair this discreet,
For no one knew of their bond
Save a serving woman 3230
Who had raised beautiful Hero.
She alone knew about it.
They loved each other with a quite perfect love.
With great difficulty they saw each other,
For between Hero and Leander 3235
Extended an arm of the sea
That was so wide and deep
No one had ever found its bottom.
And this fact troubled them greatly.
But every night Leander 3240
Passed over that arm of the sea in the open
Completely naked, alone, with no boat or barge.
Beautiful Hero of the noble appearance
Had a house with a tower
Where every night she waited for him, 3245
Keeping a candle burning
Toward which Leander often directed himself
When the sea threw him off course.
Now it happened that the sea, blown by
A strong wind, rose high, 3250
And it became all troubled
Because of the wind that disturbed and roused it.
Leander stayed on the shore,

Struggling mightily against his heart,
For Love enjoined and commanded him, 3255
As did his heart, that he should determine to cross.
And on the other side, summoning him,
He saw the most beautiful woman in the world;
And so the miserable man did not know what to do,
Nor could he see a way out of the fix, 3260
For the sea, he saw, was so threatening
That it was impossible to traverse.
And all the region was in an uproar
With storm and thundering.
But in the end Love so provoked him 3265
That he leaped into the water,
Where he quickly drowned,
For he could not make his way to her.
And, surely, this was a great loss,
For he was a quite valiant and wise man. 3270

Beautiful Hero did not know what to say;
So much anguish and anger did she feel
That she could find consolation in nothing.
She wished very much to be dead
When her lover was so delayed. 3275
From the heart she sighed; from the eyes she cried.
That night she had more than a thousand thoughts,
Multiplied some five hundred thousand times.
All she could do was call upon
Neptune, the god of the sea, 3280
And she promised him calves and heifers,
Oblations and sacrifices
If only he would make the sea be calm
So that Leander might cross it.
She continued all night doing so 3285
And held the burning candle in her hand
Until a new day dawned at last.
But this day brought her ill luck,
For in the waves she spied Leander,
Who was floating aimlessly, 3290
And when she could see him close up,
She threw herself upon his body
Right at the foot of her tower;
And she held him close,
Crazed as she was, and cried out: 'Alas!' 3295
Beautiful Hero met her end in this way,
Drowned in the sea from grief
Along with her lover because of love.

And so there is no pain or misfortune
That might afflict a lover's heart 3300
And bring such grievous pain
As that which spared nothing,
Which made Hero die
For the sake of the lover she saw dead.
Nor could anyone, with reason, 3305
Make a true comparison to anything else,
No more than bitterness set against balm.
And so, Guillaume, I counsel you
That this debate be suspended;
For truly you are mistaken." 3310

GUILLAUME

"Young lady, if I were wrong,
I know well I should be condemned,
But not by you; for the passing
Of this sentence ought not
To come from your mouth 3315
Since you are involved in the matter;
Instead, it must be pronounced by the judge,
Who will decide fittingly and truthfully.
But my heart greatly rejoices
In what I have heard you say; 3320
For truly it all helps my case."

SUFFICIENCY

"Helps yours, fair Guillaume? How so?"

GUILLAUME

"Young lady, now please listen,
And I will tell you without delay.
When Love so tightly snared 3325
Leander, who was swimming across the sea
Naked, without boat or oar,
At midnight or thereabouts,
The fool who erred terribly
To cross the sea for the sake of love, 3330
He did more and suffered worse
Than did Hero, who gave herself to death,
If one considers the great perils
That in the end destroyed him.
For Hero did not do the same out of love for him, 3335
Notwithstanding her death and lamentation.
For he who first does
Something honorable is commonly said

To get the grace from the good deed,
Not the one for whom it is done. 3340
And he is truer to love who bestows
Than he who gives in return.
So it is with all kinds of service,
And likewise with every kind of mistreatment.
For whoever troubles himself to hurt another 3345
Ought surely to bear the punishment for it.
Thus, my dear damsel, you
Who are very keen to honor the beautiful lady,
To speak the truth, you should certainly
Have the honor of this encounter. 3350
For you have discoursed ably,
Skillfully, and wisely; but surely
God made you speak for my sake,
For I am the one who will profit from this.

And so, noble and worthy lady, 3355
I think you understand quite well
The opinions of the two parties,
And if the ladies who have here sided
Against me wish to say something more,
I will offer no protest. 3360
But I have said what I think
In the presence of the ladies here assembled,
And it is sufficient, I do not doubt at all,
To win the debate for me."

THE LADY

And then the sovereign lady, 3365
True leader of the twelve
Who had spoken on her side
(And this pleased the judge greatly),
Said this so all could hear:
"I find nothing that has happened 3370
In our debate displeasing;
Instead I am quite well satisfied
And wish to be done with it now.
Sir judge, render your decision now
So that sentence may be passed. 3375
I have very high hopes
In regard to the judgment I expect from you.
When it pleases you to decide,
You have competent and assured counselors
Who are cool-headed and quite mature. 3380
So proceed, if you please, to deliberate;

I so advise and recommend.
And take this matter under advisement at once.
You could do no better
Than to request in a fitting way 3385
Some good advice and afterward rehearse
The issues that bear on the judgment,
According to our understanding,
Preserving our honor at all times.
This you ought to do, my lord, 3390
For you certainly are so competent
You shall not be found wanting in any way."

THE AUTHOR

The judge, listening closely
To her words, paid such good attention
He did not fail to understand them. 3395
His advisors he assembled at once,
And then they retired.
Now I did not know at the moment
What they said in private.
But quite soon afterward a lover 3400
Who was very fond of me did me the favor
Of telling me about everything,
Not through favoritism on his part,
But because of his good breeding,
So that I would not disagree at all 3405
Or be surprised by anything
And thus could assume a manner
Of complete composure and assurance;
For I was obliged to react the same
To a decision for me as to one against, 3410
And so I set myself upon this course;
Therefore my heart was put more at ease.
When they had disposed themselves in council,
The judge said: "I have been commissioned
To be a competent and trustworthy judge, 3415
Amicable toward the two parties
To the same degree and without bias.
Thus I must examine quite carefully
All the evidence as it was presented
To us while we listened 3420
So that I can judge in a faithful fashion.
This is what good judges should do.
And you all should exert yourselves
To advise me in good faith.

So let everyone say what she wishes 3425
Because we have the time for it."

DISCRETION

And immediately afterward Discretion,
Who was at the side of Understanding, said:
"I am Discretion, who must attend carefully
To how I should advise you, 3430
For someone might be quite unwilling
To judge without good advice.

I advise you to do what is good
And undo what is wrong.
And so it is your task, 3435
In order that nothing may lack perfection,
To attend to four things
That are not so difficult
A man cannot see to them properly
If he wishes to take a little trouble. 3440
When you've a judgment to render,
You must undertake first
To learn what the wrong might be
And against whom it has been done.
And then you must also come to learn 3445
And seek out with great wisdom,
Having already discovered the wrong
And the injured party as well,
In order to understand the matter entirely—
Namely what moved the man to do it. 3450
Now of the four things you have three.
And the fourth is the most difficult
And you must carefully attend to it
In whatever way it can be best seen to:
And that is you should pay attention 3455
To following the principles of nature
Or of custom related to law.
In this way, you will judge on a sound basis.
Now I will say no more. Whoever wishes, let her speak.
For my part, I have said enough." 3460

UNDERSTANDING

Understanding, who paid attention
To the points Discretion had well developed,
Said loudly: "Discretion, my friend,
Has just given voice to several points

That he has ably described, 3465
And these I have noted well
Because I am Understanding,
Who lends Good Discretion the substance
To devise what he devises,
With which he advises this good company. 3470
I make understood the meaning of Discretion,
And he makes Understanding increase
Through the courtly advice he gives
Many a person by his right.
Judge, please make plain 3475
How closely you will hold
To the terms and customs of Discretion.
Do so, and you will act wisely.
And as for me, who am his companion,
Listen to how I instruct you. 3480
This debate has been here conducted,
Proceeding through its different stages
Until the point of hearing a judgment.
Look to who shall be pleased with it.
Judge according to the testimony 3485
That has been offered before you.
In this way you cannot go wrong.
For if anyone wished to fault you,
The pleadings would demonstrate
The rationale that would justify you. 3490
Be bold in your judgment therefore,
And require that with full understanding
The condemned party pay the price.
You have the right to command him.
I, Understanding, am in agreement. 3495
And I accept also the opinion
Of Moderation, who is seated there
At the side of Reason, and this suits her well;
And Reason will also say
Whatever she deems appropriate." 3500

MODERATION

Then Moderation stood up,
Saying: "My highly esteemed friend
Understanding, I wish to say nothing
That might be objectionable to you;
Instead I very much agree 3505
With what you have been saying here.
And in your honor I will speak of it
To the judge, this noble lord

Who is courteous and friendly,
Wise, valiant, and honorable."   3510
Then toward him she turned her face
In such a loving fashion
He could not refrain from laughing.
And Moderation began to say to him:
"Fair sir, you have been fortunate   3515
In the counsel you sought out.
At first you had a quite good
Beginning with Discretion,
For one assuredly should, in a royal court,
Receive advice as trustworthy as this.   3520
I do not say that another company
Would not proffer advice
As proper and as well considered,
Fittingly dressed out with proper speech.
But let us look to the nature   3525
Of Discretion, as he himself understands it.
He provides counsel free and clear,
Expecting no reward at all in return
Except that the judge might do
What would afford him peace, honor, and thanks.   3530
And Understanding, his companion,
Accompanies him for the same salary,
Without demanding anything further;
And so a trustworthy judge rests easy,
One advised by such as these.   3535
Therefore, Sire, you ought to be happy about it.
Although they have spoken ably,
I will say something more about a point
That Discretion has taken notice of—
And yet has not described at length—   3540
And that Understanding has understood.
Now in this case they have been obliged
To exert themselves to honor me;
And so I will offer it to you
Because I have certainly noticed   3545
That they have paid me due heed.
Even so, I will go ahead and say
Some things about my nature.

I am Moderation moderated,
Temperate in all good deeds,   3550
And also I am moderating,
Firm, stable, and strong in endurance
For all who wish without trickery

To make proper use of moderation;
And whoever does not, what will be, will be. 3555
And let him be mindful of his own hurt.
In this regard, a master of great wisdom,
Who had a very virtuous conscience,
Was instructing his disciple
And explaining the teachings about me, 3560
Saying: 'Friend, I admonish you.
If you do not acquire moderation yourself,
She will make herself felt in you regardless.
Remember this saying well:
If she comes to you, you are done for. 3565
But if you welcome her, you will be all right.'
Now I would like to review thoroughly all the points
That Discretion and Understanding raise.
They have served out generously
And courteously their good advice, 3570
Just as one serves at a meal,
Without judging the particulars of the case.
And since they have served well,
They have earned thanks.
I would like to add up the bill 3575
And give everyone his due.
Guillaume, who once was
So well mannered in all his actions,
So honest and courteous as well,
Conforming to the chastisements of love, 3580
Has launched an attack against Frankness
And all those of her high rank
When my lady properly approached him
About the deed she reprimanded him for
And he felt himself upbraided 3585
For just case and reproached as well.
He then proceeded forcefully,
Putting every effort into it,
To defend himself against her.
This fact distresses me a great deal 3590
Because he acted immoderately.
For these reasons, he has abandoned
The rules and principles of Moderation,
And this will trouble him greatly
When I bring him back to me; 3595
For I will turn him away from honor
When Discernment informs him
Of the misdeed he has committed.
He should have properly measured

The station of the gentle, honored person 3600
Of that sovereign lady;
For in all the Christian realm
There is no man who, if he knew
Her—and it is good to believe it would be so—
Would not honor her highly 3605
And would not measure himself
As humble and of lesser courtliness
In regard to her great nobility;
And so Guillaume was deceived
When he did not perceive this. 3610
For he began much too haughtily,
And so has advanced himself but little
In the competent presentation of his case.⁴⁰
And this is quite enough to have him punished.
Now let us look to the issue itself 3615
From its proper commencement
In order to distinguish between the parties,
How they are divided,
In order to learn which one is in error.
I say Guillaume is wrong. 3620
For of all cruel misfortunes,
Death is the absolute worst;
Which is to say, it surpasses all miseries,
And that is because no one recovers from it;
For a person can suffer more easily 3625
What he can recover from.
I do not wish to go on further,
For to condemn him I have enough
Evidence, much more grievous things that are
Simpleminded, foolish, inane, and vainglorious. 3630

Sir Judge, now listen to me;
For the sake of the goal at which you aim,
Namely the rendering of a faithful judgment,
I wish to consider somewhat
How this trial was conducted. 3635
And if you please, look
Into this a little yourself,
So that you can the better refrain
From judging in any but the proper fashion.
For you will recognize the point 3640
On which justice is properly fixed
When a judge directs himself toward true justice.
I want you to be certain
That Guillaume is to be reproached

For the part of his argument 3645
That has been badly presented,
Notwithstanding that in every way
And in everything the law is against him;
And so my lady is completely victorious,
As much in the debate as in the correctness 3650
Of her complaint, which has been completely
Clarified and put out of doubt.[41]
My lady has by her damsels
Alleged quite pertinent reasons
And facts that are all true, 3655
Firm, assured, and unassailable,
All drawn from written tradition
And connected to the law.
But whoever might want to recount all this
Would have too much to consider here. 3660
And, furthermore, this thing is certain:
That the court has been sufficiently provided
With all that anyone wished to say
On my lady's behalf with no infamy;
And so I will be silent about my lady. 3665
And concerning Guillaume, who has been
Intent on arguing his case,
I will say something—for I wish to do so—
But only in regard to his pleading.
And I will pass over this quickly 3670
By the faith you owe all your friends.
Let us see what he has brought up.
Concerning the clerk who went mad,
Has he proved what caused this,
That it was something his lady did? 3675
Sir judge, by the faith I owe my soul,
He has proved nothing of the kind;
And so he ought to be reproved therefor.
And concerning the knight who in his anguish
Not to violate his pledge 3680
Cut off his finger with the ring still on it,
He erected in her honor a monument
Full of shame and madness
When in a fit of great craziness
That man sent it on to his lady. 3685
For I certainly believe he found it troubling,
Or at least it should have troubled him
To send her such a thing as a present.
For when a lady loves her lover,
By the law of Love she claims him as her own 3690

And has the right to claim an injury, so I think.
Now let us consider how in regard
To this principle the knight erred.
The thing that she loved he harmed,
And it was hers by the law of Love; 3695
And so I lodge a complaint
Against Guillaume on this point
Because I think he has accomplished nothing.
For this instance he has presented as evidence
Damages and undermines his case. 3700
And also, in regard to the chatelaine
Of Vergy, I can refute this example
Sufficiently with only a little trouble,
Using the reasons I will here rehearse.
The evidence that Guillaume adduces, 3705
Sire, you know it contends
That the lover, filled with loyalty,
Found falseness in his lady.
And beginning with this assumption,
He makes an allegation 3710
To be proven by a contrary fact.
The respectable chatelaine
Did not wrong her lover in any way.
Instead, he himself did the deed
On account of which she killed herself. 3715
When he learned of it, he felt remorse
And came to the recognition
That vengeance was required;
And so he passed judgment on himself,
Punished and corrected himself for it all; 3720
And thus Guillaume, with all that he has said,
Has said less than nothing to profit him.
I will say no more about it; rather Reason will speak
Here afterward whatever she wishes."

THE AUTHOR

At these words, Reason stood up 3725
In the manner of one well schooled and wise,

REASON

Saying, "Let us go back to the council room.
There we can with truthful speech
Render a truthful judgment, I think,
If there is any man capable of understanding it." 3730
At once they left that place.
And they again sat down in their own seats,

Where they had sat earlier.
With measured words, Reason then said:
"Sir judge, certainly   3735
There is nothing beneath the firmament
That does not seek its proper end:
Some things tend toward perfection
For various reasons pertaining to their own laws;
And there are yet others that descend   3740
From on high where they have been,
Declining from the season of summer
Into the so-called winter of destruction;
Just so, this pleading is tending to arrive at
A speedy conclusion according to the law   3745
Through a definitive sentence,
So as to perfect what has been done well
And remedy what has been done badly.
And the moment has arrived, as well you know,
The point when you must speak of it   3750
Or command that it be spoken of."

THE JUDGE

"Lady Reason, it is not appropriate for me
To speak at this present time.
But I receive well the notion
Of deciding. And concerning my decision,   3755
So that it may be to your liking,
You say and do enough here
That everything wrong may be effaced.
And the right may be restored to the hue
Of every honorable honor,   3760
You who can paint in such colors
As no one else save you can manage."

GUILLAUME

Then Reason halted a little
And leaned toward her right,
While glancing to her left   3765
In order to see better how I was doing,

REASON

And she said to me: "Guillaume, fair sir,
You have just now heard said
That it is madness to take on
More than ability can compass.   3770
And yet when a man undertakes to do
Something that gives offense,

If he repents of it in the middle,
Then he will still make out all right.
But he who persists in his error 3775
And exerts himself to see it through
Until he comes right to the very end,
And at that point he finds nothing
Except his own grief and harm,
If then he acknowledges his own misdeed, 3780
He comes too late to repentance.
Guillaume, be sure—and it's no lie—
That this is how you have carried on,
And so you have merited some misery
That soon will fall upon you, 3785
And this will endure a long time,
Truly, if you do not repent.
But I believe you are the kind of man
Who will not deign to do so,
For you were quite rude in your behavior 3790
When the lady approached you
About the deed for which she reproached you,
One you had done some time ago.
If you had shown in yourself
Any recognition of this at all, 3795
Which would have been a sign of repentance
For having committed this wrong
Against ladies of great worthiness,
You would have acted very much the wise man.
For the custom of Love is such 3800
That when any man vilifies women,
If he does not recant and henceforth refrain
From so doing, he must make great amends
Or pay a very high price.
Now, concerning this initial misdeed, 3805
I tell you on behalf of sovereign
Love, who is master and lord,
The physician for the wounds of love:
Namely that a judgment has been rendered
That condemns you in this matter. 3810
And so it is necessary you make amends.
The time for this quickly approaches.
In addition, I am empowered to order
That you must make amends
For another deed that displeases me, 3815
In that you undertook to debate
A lady of such worthiness
And of such very noble authority

That no highborn person I know of,
So far as the world extends, 3820
No prince or duke, count or king,
Would dare commit such an outrage,
Guillaume, as the one you did
In the dispute you undertook against her—
And you put into this force and vigor 3825
As you proceeded aggressively.
And you've continued in the same vein.
In this way, you have stripped your mind
Of courtesy and respectfulness.
And if she did not have the patience 3830
That she does, you would have lost so much
You would have come to grief."

GUILLAUME

When I heard this, I was distressed;
But I was neither too abashed nor hesitant
To ask her humbly 3835
If she would briefly explain to me
The truth about the lady
And something of her powers.[42]

REASON

Then she said: "Guillaume, willingly.
But today I will not describe even a third, 3840
No, not even a hundredth part of it.
For from the sky down to the pit of hell,
Her powers extend through all things,
And from these powers flow
Quite marvelous results, 3845
Things that are dangerous to utter
And show this through their contraries.
For these reasons, it is well to pass them over in silence
Because of faulty understandings,
And these sometimes are perverse. 3850
The lady's name is Happiness,[43]
And she holds Security by the hand
Among the company of Fortune.
For there is no person at all
Whom Fortune can bring down 3855
If the lady wishes to contest it.
And when she intends to work through Nature
Because of some special concern she has,
She can be seen there readily
In truth by the astrologers 3860

Who recognize the different nations
Among the constellations,
That is to say, in the birth of infants,
To what sign they will belong.
And so when the dear lady is regnant   3865
And an infant is born into his sign,
If Happiness takes charge of him,
Nature does not take him back from her,
But instead very much lets her do her will,
No matter how it is to turn out.   3870
It is true that Nature takes care of
How the infant lives and laughs.
And Happiness leads him
Into the domain of good luck
Until the time has come for it to show   3875
That Happiness is caring for him.

Now these people are all around us,
And in them the lady makes herself manifest
Through the benefits that they receive,
As long as they do not betray her in some way.   3880
Now I want to tell you specifically
In what different ways she manifests herself,
In some, but not in all.
And have no doubt of any kind
About the words I will speak,   3885
For in no way will I lie.
She appears in prosperity
And in the leaving behind of poverty.
She is there in the making of friends
And in the punishment of enemies   3890
With a victory, without any wrongdoing.
She appears in every good deed,
And when she is present in love,
It is that the lover, through his demands,
Through his service and pleadings,   3895
And because of proper deeds of all kinds,
Is able to enjoy his lady in peace,
To take pleasure in the special privilege
That Love grants in her generosity.
There Happiness sits   3900
Between the lover and loyal beloved,
Those who wish for only what is courtly
And who have by an explicit pledge
Placed great trust in one another.
She sustains them in a quite grand style.   3905

All goods are hers to bestow properly.
And for this reason she is much more gay and friendly.
She is the acquaintance of all virtuous folk.
She appears in many pleasurable things,
In jousts as much as in tourneys, 3910
In order to exalt chivalry
And advance the deeds of good men
In the understanding of women.
There honor grows; there infamy falls away.
For the man who has been maligned 3915
Is afterward cherished and loved
By those who spoke ill of him
Because they see openly
That he puts his life at risk;
And so the time comes when he takes his chance 3920
In a trial of arms he embarks upon,
Until in the end he rises to the highest rank.
In this way Happiness advances
Her own through her great power.

If Happiness through Nature, 3925
Or by fortune, or according to custom
Does appear in chivalry,
She also appears in learning.
There she holds honor in her hands.
More to one and less to another 3930
She makes her generous distribution.
And she gives out the greatest shares
To those who obey better the summons
That Happiness issues them.
She is also manifest in knowledge 3935
And encloses herself within the mind
In order to safeguard at times those
In whom are peace and good faith,
Those who have not in any acknowledged fashion
Put their wisdom into a public form, 3940
But rather are wise in secret.
In them she keeps herself hidden;
And in them Faithful Secrets and Good Living
Afford her good companionship.
And there she wishes to rest 3945
And appropriately turn those hearts
Toward the contemplative life.
Then by the active path she returns
To encourage those to speak
Who willingly hold discussion 3950

About the virtues of contemplation.
And therefore many, with good intentions,
Then incline themselves to her teachings,
So they each teach themselves on their own
How to be diligent and eager 3955
To become contemplative.
Why should I go on speaking about this to you?
Happiness possesses so many goods
That I would never have related
The hundredth part of her virtue. 3960
So in the world there is no great lord,
No lady, however much honor they might possess,
For whom it would not be pleasing and noble
If they could be among her company.
Now I will be silent. I will say no more about her, 3965
But deal instead with what remains
Of the two counts on which you have been condemned.
And I have my thoughts in order
For what I intend to tell you about the third count
On which I shall condemn you. 3970

It is certainly an indisputable fact
That if someone opposes a complaint,
Busies himself with producing evidence,
And then comes to the test,
Yet fails to prove his view adequately, 3975
The truth of the law then reproves him
And he must be condemned therefor.
This legal principle arose so long ago
That there is no memory of its contrary.
Now let us see what I wish to recount, 3980
So listen carefully to what I say.
Whatever the lady told you
About her evidence, you opposed,
And you tried to offer proof for your view.
Yet you have so badly failed to prove it 3985
That you ought to be reprimanded
And, as a consequence, condemned,
According to my opinion.
You have said nothing here save
Words that are frivolous. 3990
They are pretty to mouth in private,
But they contain no substance
That might afford you an advantage
In sustaining the proof of your case.
And so we have looked into and 3995

Examined this case as best we could
In order to seek out a faithful judgment.
If it pleases you to know the particulars,
You will be told about the different opinions,
And how they are distributed among those involved,   4000
And also all aspects of your error.
And if you see that it might be time
For your sentence to be pronounced,
Then tell us what you think in your heart.
For whatever pleases you, it will be done   4005
Thoroughly enough to satisfy you."

GUILLAUME

"Lady, I have listened to you quite well
And have waited some time
To be sentenced.
So I beg you to be diligent   4010
About delivering me to it,
That is, about granting me my sentence.
Since what I did is so serious
It requires three compensations,
And since things cannot go otherwise,   4015
I do not wish to discuss the matter further."

REASON

"Guillaume, be completely assured
That you have received justice here.
And we will not be negligent in any way.
But now you should be just as diligent.   4020
So get on your feet at this time
To do what you should do
In the presence of that man who sits as judge.
And then he will do what he thinks right.
From now on the matter rests with him   4025
Since he holds in his hands all the legal power."

GUILLAUME

At this word, I went over to the judge
And got down on one knee.
There I offered my person to him
In as appropriate a speech   4030
As I was able and knew how to say to him.
At this point, he began to smile a little.
Then I took my gloves and tendered them to him.
And then he who paid this close attention
Took and then dropped them.   4035

In a moment, he leaned down again
And took them up a second time,
Then letting them drop, then taking them up once more
As a sign to demonstrate to me how
I owed him three payments for damages. 4040
Quite well he signified this to me,
Assuring me in truth
That I would have to pay them.
Then without hesitation he told me
That I should go back and sit down, 4045
For he wished to look to
What penance he would assign me,
And to this he would shortly deliver me.

Then he drew up close to the lady,
As did Reason, quite demurely, 4050
And he counseled privately with them,
Taking care to speak softly.
But in their whispering
I found some enjoyment,
Because I saw well 4055
That their council was a joyful one,
For from time to time they laughed,
And just at that moment when they were
Most seriously deliberating,
Discretion said to me: "I advise you 4060
To look at this lady
And attend carefully to
The rightful aspects of her estate.
There you will see a great deal
Of her grace and power. 4065
And in this way you will have a much stronger heart
For enduring and for suffering
Whatever justice will render you."
Then I said to him: "Dear sweet friend,
You describe these things to me, 4070
You who know the obvious
And hidden details of so many things.
Often you take on such a task;
That's something I know well."
Discretion said then: "This merits doing. 4075
Now pay quick attention:
As far as describing the parts is concerned,
If this is something you wish to mark well,
She has put on a blouse
That is called Frankness 4080

In order to liberate secret lovers
And enrich them with Seriousness
On behalf of Silence
With Understanding in agreement.
For until she has arrived   4085
Her cause should be kept silent.
And her fur wrap, that is Simplicity,
So soft it does not wound her,
For it comes from Goodwill,
Gilt-edged by Sufficiency,   4090
With the pelts from Sweet Pleasure,
Who moves good hearts toward every good.
And the robe that she wears
In very honorable virtue
Was crafted by Loyal Friendship,   4095
Pleated by Steadfastness
Tipped by Perseverance,
Neatly, without any disorder.
Now this robe is beautiful and flowing,
And by proper right it is called   4100
Because of its special status
Honest Familiarity,
And the belt she has girded herself with
Is no insignificant thing in regard to Love,
For it is properly called Loyal Promise,   4105
Studded with Stable Commitment,
For whoever makes promises,
It is necessary that they be trusted.
And the belt medallion, because it is heavy,
Serves to beat down dissension and discord   4110
And thus it hangs down all the way to her feet.
And her feet prevent many an argument
Between the beloved and her loyal lover
Whenever any lover cries 'Alas!
I have been refused by my lady;   4115
But my right has not been abused,
For I believe that she has done so
To my profit and to her honor.'
And so her feet keep this company in line,
Whomever she holds in her domain;   4120
For they are shod with Relief,
Laced with the cord of Diligence.
And she has put white gloves on her hands,
Which have been equally made
By both Charity and Generosity,   4125

With which she shares out the riches
Of Love, which cannot be exhausted
Nor reduced at any time.
The more that is taken, the more remains
From day to day and hour to hour. 4130
I would like to tell you about the mantle,
Which is so handsome to describe,
And he who wears it finds it better than handsome
In words, demeanor, and deeds.
The wool of Good Reflection 4135
Along with Courtly Speech,
Knowledgeable Introduction,
And Friendly Intention
Were woven there together,
Properly felted by Goodness. 4140
And the cloth of good appearance
Was made by assembling these things,
Dyed a merry color
Of most honorable worthiness
That is called Nobility, 4145
And it was lined with Gentility.
Now Happiness is covered
With the mantle, and it is obvious
That all good things are therein enclosed.
But it reveals, in truth, 4150
No matter what she is beneath her covering,
The appearance of her face,
Which is such that in her features
The benefits of courtesy of every kind
Appear there in abundance, 4155
With which her damsels are adorned.
And she is as well adorned
As they, without being set apart
From them and their beautiful array.
For they are fine enough for a king, 4160
And for a sovereign queen as well.
For these reasons I put it to you
That Happiness completely surpasses
And is of higher estate than all queens.
If I wished to describe 4165
Her crown, which is beautiful and becoming,
I would detain you too long;
For I readily see, and there can be no doubt,
That their council is drawing to a close.
And so I will spare you its description." 4170

GUILLAUME

When their council had ended,
The judge turned my way,

THE JUDGE

And said: "Guillaume, by my soul,
I will tell you this on my lady's behalf
And on behalf of Reason as well, 4175
And I am in agreement with them
That you owe three compensations,
As these have been determined and laid out,
And for these you are responsible
According to the judgment, without fail. 4180
You must—the thing is certain—
Compose a lay for the first
And agreeably, without resisting;
For the second, a song
Of three stanzas and a refrain— 4185
Listen how I qualify this—
Which begins with the refrain,
Just like the ones sung at dancing;
And for the third, a ballade.[44]
Now do not act like this makes you sick, 4190
But rather respond happily
In regard to our command,
Concerning your intentions on all these points.
I make here an end."

GUILLAUME

And because I had so grievously erred 4195
When I dared to make trouble
With a lady of such high estate
In that I attempted to dispute with her,
I, the Guillaume named above,
Who has the surname de Machaut, 4200
In order the better to acknowledge my fault,
Have composed and rhymed this little book;
And of it I will make my lady a present,
Offering her my service and
Begging her to pardon me for everything. 4205
And may God grant her peace and honor
And the great joy of Paradise
Such as I would wish for myself.
But because I do not want in any way
That my fine should remain unpaid, 4210
I wish to retire the debt without delay

By beginning work on a lay about love.[45]

Here ends *The Judgment of the King of Navarre against The Judgment of the King of Bohemia*.

Le Lay de plour (The Lay of Weeping)

I. Whoever loves well forgets but slowly,
And the heart that is slow to forget
Is like the fire that burns
And cannot easily be put out.
Also, whoever suffers an illness 5
That pleases recovers unwillingly.
In such a state, so God give me help,
Love keeps and commands me,
For Pleasure restrains me so
That the arrow of love 10
Will never be even a third or fourth withdrawn
From my heart, whatever anyone might say.
For it has so long been my companion,
There is no question of its departure,
Nor ever, by any art, 15
Will the wound it made be healed.

II. Surely a huge tree can hardly be
Uprooted, without leaving behind
  Some of its roots,
And so in a short time it is seen 20
Bearing flowers and fruit, its branches
  Growing and spreading.
Surely it is the same with love;
For when a heart is bent on
  A pure love, 25
It can hardly forget its beloved;
Rather always, through memory,
  It inclines toward that one.

III. For the water that falls down
On the root that remains 30
Makes it leaf again and flourish,
  And bear fruit.
Just the same my heart, which weeps
Bitterly all the time,
Makes my memory grow 35
  Both day and night.

        And it is this that drives me mad;
        This that covers my face in tears;
        This the reason I sigh.
           True Love 40
        Drives me to this, assaulting me,
        And Goodness who sweetens it;
        For they cannot enter in me,
           Which destroys me.

IV.   Reason and Justice, 45
        Pleasure and Nature
        By their power make
        Every creature
        Through pure will
        Incline toward greater worthiness. 50
        And I tell myself
        That for as long as I endure,
        I will never be able to see
        A love this certain,
        Goodness so well matured, 55
        Nor so much wisdom.

V.   And more, it is obvious
        That the hearts that loyally
        And without madness
        Love with a quite noble love 60
           Often think
        That in a better and nobler one
           They are lodged;
        For pleasure in its insistence
           Suggests this to them. 65
        Now, I know for certain
        That my lover without doubt
           Was the rightful flower
        Of those men with the greatest honor.
           For everyone 70
        Says over and over again,
           Including the best people,
        That he possessed every worthy quality
           In full measure.

VI.   And since there is none better, none 75
        More genteel, none fairer, more familiar with honor,
           No one,
           To judge truly,
           Should wonder

If by the shaft of love I do not wish 80
To be wounded newly by another love.
  I do not seek
  To change this,
  And I am right;
For in my heart is planted so firmly and so strongly 85
My love for him that it cannot be dislodged;
  For a heart undivided
  That could not
  Be false
Determines that I resolve completely through memory 90
Never to undertake a new love, or meet with one;
  For to take up with another
  Would do
  Me harm.

VII. Truly the beautiful memory 95
  That recalls him to me
  Makes me determined
  Never to agree
  To have another lover;
  Rather in misery, 100
  With no relief,
  With all my strength
  I intend to lament and bemoan his death,
  Saying this:
  "Lover, my comfort, 105
  My joyous pleasure,
  My peace, my refuge,
  And all my destiny of love
  Were in you.
  Oh, I shall feel pain again 110
  That tears at me on your account,
  Wounding me so terribly,
  For with you, all the good I had died
  And was buried."

VIII. Sweet love, I grieve so hard; 115
  My heart
  Mourns you so much
  Laments you so;
  So great is my grief that by my faith
  I reap all ills, 120
  Wherefor my eyes
  Are so often wet,
  My heart so anguished,

My face pale, stained by tears,
   Full of troubles 125
   And pain,
   Devoid of comfort;
   These things manifest my woe.
Sweet lover, on your bier
   Lie my laments 130
   And all my weeping;
   There I take pleasure;
In my thoughts I see you there;
   More than my custom
   I wish to be there. 135
   There lie my desires;
   There my heart remains.
I beg death to lead me there,
   For there I offer myself.
   There, I believe, 140
   I should pass over
   Death's threshold.

IX.   There sighs,
   There grows angry
My heart that suffers quite terribly, 145
   So much deadly pain,
   So much anger,
   That to tell the truth
No creature alive could even
   Describe it. 150
   There my heart grows worse
   Moment by moment.
There it can only tremble and burst.
   There it shows its grief;
   There, with no laughter, 155
   It suffers;
There it kills itself; there it desires
   That death take it soon.

X.   Sweet lover, such grief have I,
   Such terrible suffering, 160
Such great pain, such tribulation
Because I will never see you,
That sorrow stabs and wounds me
   With such a deadly spear
Through the heart that in despair 165
Over you I shall end my days.
In you was all my hope,

      And my trust as well,
    My joy, my sustenance.
    Sorrowful one! These I now have lost.
    It is readily apparent in my look
      And in my speech,
    For I possess no strength or composure,
    So much do I sorrow and grieve.

XI. With a heavy heart
    I mourn and recall
    Your great worthiness
    That I prized so much.
    It must be so;
    And I see you
    Face to face, it seems to me,
    Sweet lover,
    And always
    I remember you.
    My spirit
    And my paradise
    Were placed
    And set
    In you; so it follows
    That my heart
    Is finished and destroyed,
    For it is wretched
    And brought to nothing
    While life clings to it.

XII. Lover, I would have been quite happy
    Had you had more the coward's heart;
    This would have been worth more to me
    Than a will so hardy.
    But honor, chivalry,
    And your renown that spreads
    Throughout the world in many places
    Have separated us.
    Your death troubles me so much
    And shares out so much ill to me,
    Lover, that my heart breaks.
    But before I die, my heart humbly begs
    The True God to look upon us
    With such a loving countenance
    That in a book we will find life.

Here ends "The Lay of Weeping."

Notes

The edition on which this translation is based is Palmer, *Guillaume de Machaut: The Judgment of the King of Navarre*.

1. The opening of the *Navarre* offers a striking contrast to that of the *Behaingne*, which, utilizing a series of well-known conventions, evokes the idealized springtime of love poetry. Here Machaut refers to the cold north wind that destroys the greenery of summer, a natural indication of the world's inevitable decline into a place where, as he suggests, there is no justice or truth, only a rapacious avarice that destroys social and familial trust. The result is a constant warfare that has brought down a heavenly vengeance in the form of destructive weather. It is conventional for the disappointed or as yet unsatisfied lover to experience melancholy, but here the melancholic Guillaume can blame the state of the world for his persistent sadness. This also is a conventional element in medieval writing, the topos of *mundus senescit* (the world grows old). Throughout this opening section, which climaxes in the outbreak of the plague in northern France, Machaut gives the impression that he is following one of the numerous Latin chronicles of the period, though no specific source can be identified. The last part of his account is by far the most dramatic. God sees from his house that the world is everywhere corrupted, and so he sets Death loose on suffering humanity; Death is a beast so insatiable that he must consume heaps of corpses every day. With the abating of the epidemic, the story returns to a springtime setting and to the matters of love and romance suited to such a time. But the somber tone of the opening casts a shadow over the sometimes bitter and disturbing events of the debate between Guillaume and the lady Happiness, a contest that results in the poet's defeat and abasement.

2. Likely a reference to St. John the Silent (d. 558), who was appointed bishop of Colonia in his native Armenia at age twenty-eight. After serving in that office for nine years, he retired to a monastery where he eventually had himself walled up, there to live as a recluse. Later, for some years, he lived as a hermit in the desert.

3. The most notable of the heavenly signs, including various astrological configurations, seen as predicting the coming epidemic was the lunar eclipse on January 17, 1348.

4. This devastating earthquake occurred on January 25, 1348.

5. Machaut's point about human destructiveness is a general one, but he is also likely referring in particular to the depredations of the ongoing struggle between France and England known to modern historians as the Hundred Years' War (1337–1453).

6. By the early fourteenth century a population of Jews numbering at least 100,000 had settled in northern France, with an especially strong and vibrant community in Machaut's native Champagne. Forced to live under a series of rather onerous restrictions about where they could live and what trade they could follow, the Jews of northern France suffered a serious setback when in 1306 the French king Philip IV, influenced by rumors about Jewish attempts to desecrate the holy sacraments, ordered their expulsion from the kingdom. But Louis X allowed them to return in 1315. Further persecutions and expulsions followed the spreading of rumors that the Jews, secretly in the service of the Muslim ruler of Granada, were plotting to poison the wells and murder the Christian population. At the outbreak of the plague in 1348, these rumors of a Jewish plot were revived and credited by many in the Christian community, including educated men like Guillaume de Machaut. Persecution and murder followed, and in 1394 the Jewish community in France was again expelled, this time definitively for some centuries.

7. The flagellant movement, a distortion of a more widespread Christian practice, did

not begin, as Machaut suggests, at the time of the plague's outbreak. Originating in thirteenth-century northern Italy, this group, which amounted to a rival Christian sect with its own preachers and devotions, was officially condemned by Pope Clement VI in 1349. By that time, it had spread northward across the Alps to Germany, Bohemia, and Poland. With the outbreak of the epidemic, itinerant bands of adherents made their way from the east to northern France and traveled from town to town. In public places, they would strip down and beat themselves and each other bloody with, among other instruments, leather whips studded with small nails designed to tear the flesh. Their preachers would exhort the townspeople to repent of their sins, which, they maintained, had brought down God's wrath as punishment, a view that Machaut, like many at that time, endorsed. These devotions included the singing of hymns, as Machaut indicates.

8. Modern historians estimate that between a quarter and half of the population died from the disease in northern France. As Machaut indicates, "scientific" explanations for the epidemic ranged from the poisoning of wells to meteorological conditions (a deadly "miasma") to unusual astrological conjunctions.

9. At this point, the poem leaves behind history, with its sadness, death, and political turmoil, for the conventional setting of love poetry, as a new springtime appropriately turns the narrator's thoughts to the outdoors and, after some coaxing, to matters of love.

10. There is perhaps something of a sly double entendre in the narrator's fascination with hare hunting, since rabbits, if not hares, are conventional symbols for women.

11. The humorous interchange between the lady's messenger and a Guillaume who is none too eager to make a long journey in obedience to her command to present himself provides some evidence that her charge of his neglect of ladies and inattention to their sensitivities is perhaps not without merit.

12. Note that the gender politics of the failed-greeting motif from the *Behaingne* are reversed here. In the earlier poem, it was the lady who, lost in grief, ignored the nobleman's salute, while here it is Guillaume, preoccupied with his hunting, who does not acknowledge the lady's presence.

13. Perhaps Guillaume protests too much about his innocence of the lady's initial charge of failing to pay her proper attention. In the *Behaingne*, the lady is overcome with grief when she first crosses paths with the nobleman, but here Guillaume's excuses are weaker: preoccupation with his pursuit of the hares and the unlikeliness that he would deliberately wish to offend her.

14. Guillaume's overconfidence about his own innocence is evidenced by his admission here that he fears only the malevolence of lying gossips, not any error he might have made. Yet his failure to notice the presence of his lady suggests that the poet's monitoring of his own behavior, particularly toward women whom he should respect, might be less than reliable.

15. That is, in the *Jugement dou roy de Behaingne*, where the king's decision about who suffers more, a betrayed man or a bereaved woman, becomes the issue debated by Guillaume and the lady, later revealed as Happiness.

16. Guillaume, as it turns out, never embraces the "opposite view," as his lady puts it, but simply acknowledges that he has been defeated in the debate and, impressed by the great nobility of his erstwhile opponent, agrees to complete the assigned penance.

17. Guillaume's failure to accept correction from the lady who is to be his guide, and his somewhat arrogant defense of his public reputation, are early indications of the unreflective "maleness" that the poem humorously chides.

18. Note that Guillaume, rejecting the lady's accusation of his shortcoming, demands

that their case be presented to a man for judgment. Appropriately enough, he gets his wish when the king of Navarre agrees to decide the question. Ironically, though, the king chooses as advisors three of the lady's female courtiers, Discernment, Moderation, and Reason, who are hardly predisposed toward Guillaume's point of view.

19. Here follows a longish catalogue and "characterization" of twelve allegorical personages who make up the lady's court. The allegorical scheme is somewhat fluid, as other personifications (Moderation, Frankness) appear later.

20. Once again, Guillaume fails here to be guided by his lady's pleasure, preferring to wait until the (male) judge arrives rather than presenting his case to her female courtiers.

21. Here, as throughout the debate, the technical language of scholastic debate is invoked to describe the proceedings, creating an ironic disjunction between the formality of the language (and the intellectual procedure it is meant to control) and the often comic tone of the disputation.

22. The mini-debate between the king of Navarre and the lady is filled with no little class humor, satirizing as it does a perhaps excessive concern on the part of these noble characters with the fine points of polite behavior and distinctions in rank that hardly seem significant.

23. With the lady's formal presentation of her complaint, delivered here with considerable rhetorical flourish in the form of an extended metaphor, the debate—or perhaps trial—here begins.

24. The lady's point is that men, with more control over their lives than women, have at their disposal many courses of action to remediate romantic sorrow, including that caused by a lover's betrayal.

25. Surely Temperance is correct in pointing out that Guillaume is arrogant to claim victory, having only proven that, faced with a lover's betrayal, a man cannot better his lot by surrendering to violence, a mortal sin.

26. The "good philosopher" is likely Galen, the Greek thinker and physician (ca. 130–200) whose opinions on medicine and human physiology were rarely challenged during the Middle Ages.

27. The Middle Ages knew the tragic story of the love affair between the Trojan Aeneas and his Carthaginian beloved Dido from Virgil's epic poem, the *Aeneid*, and from the writings of Ovid. Machaut may have drawn on the long twelfth-century romance based on Virgil's epic, the *Roman d'Eneas*, but it seems likely that his main source was the monumental early-fourteenth-century French translation of Ovid's works, the *Ovide moralisé*, for the details of the story, including Dido's pregnancy (not mentioned in Virgil). After the murder of her husband Sychaeus, Dido has fled her native Phoenicia for Carthage, where, remaining faithful to the dead man, she establishes a powerful kingdom. When the shipwrecked Aeneas makes his way to her palace, Dido is seduced into loving him by the man's divine mother, the goddess Venus. This love affair shames her in the eyes of her people and neighboring rulers. Summoned by the gods to reestablish the Trojan kingdom in Italy, Aeneas abandons Dido, who commits suicide rather than face the wrath of the gods and the ignominy of this betrayal. The relevant passage from the *Ovide moralisé*, along with other medieval texts that treat the story of Dido and Aeneas, is translated in Palmer, *Medieval English and French Legends*.

28. Guillaume's defensiveness seems humorously out of proportion to the "threatening" to which he suggests he has been subjected.

29. As in the *Behaingne*, the debate here widens in scope from the agreed-upon question

of relative suffering to the more general issue of whether it is men or women who love more faithfully and deeply.

30. Like that of Dido and Aeneas, the story of Theseus was well known to the Middle Ages, especially through the writings of Ovid. Machaut's source for the legend is here again the *Ovide moralisé*. Minos, king of Crete, is married to Pasiphae, who has borne him a son, Androgeus, as well as two daughters, Ariadne and Phaedra. Because of a slight to his dignity, the god Poseidon causes the woman to develop a fatal passion for a bull; the result of their coupling is the Minotaur, a monster with the head of a bull and the body of a man. King Aegeus of Athens kills Androgeus, and Minos then imposes a deadly yearly tax on the citizens of the city of seven young men and seven maidens, who are sacrificed to the Minotaur. Theseus is chosen by lot to be one of those sacrificed, but he proves able to win the affections of Ariadne, who provides him with a ball of thread to escape from the labyrinth where the monster lives. Theseus kills the beast and escapes from Crete with Ariadne and her sister Phaedra. Stopping at the island of Naxos, he leaves Ariadne behind and makes his way to Athens with Phaedra, whom he subsequently marries. Ariadne, however, does not fail to prosper; the god Dionysus falls in love with and then marries her, and she is made an immortal by Zeus.

31. The story of Jason's pursuit of the Golden Fleece, though treated in Greek epic, was better known to the Middle Ages in the Roman poet Ovid's shortened version. Machaut's source, as for all the classic tales retold in the *Navarre*, is the *Ovide moralisé*, though he may also have known a Latin version of the Troy story in which the tale of Jason appears, the *Historia troiana* of Guido delle Colonne. Jason and his companions, the Argonauts, journey to Colchis to obtain a great treasure, the Golden Fleece. Medea, the king's daughter, falls in love with Jason and helps him obtain the fleece. After several harrowing adventures, in which Medea's command of the black arts figures importantly, the two establish themselves in Corinth, there to rule together until Jason attempts to divorce Medea so that he can marry Creusa. Medea sends the unfortunate woman a poisoned robe that delivers her to a horrible death and, to gain further vengeance on her betraying husband, murders their children, escaping the city in a chariot drawn by dragons.

32. These classical exempla, of course, also provide well-known examples of faithless, conscienceless men: Jason and Theseus.

33. The reference is to the thirteenth-century French romance *La Chatelaine de Vergy*, which traces the misery and pain that result from, first, a young wife's betrayal of her husband and, second, a jealous woman's betrayal of her husband's trust. The chatelaine's lover is approached by the duchess of Burgundy, his lord's wife, and he refuses her love, protesting that he loves another, although no one knows of their affair. The knight has promised the chatelaine never to reveal their relationship, but he is forced to break his word when the duchess complains to her husband that the man has insulted and lied to her. Only by telling the duke of his affair, its meetings arranged by the little dog the chatelaine lets into the garden to signal she is alone, does he free himself from his lord's anger and probable exile. The duke promises never to reveal the lover's secret, but he in turn breaks the promise when the duchess extorts the truth from him, though he does enjoin her on pain of death never to reveal the secret. The jealous woman does so, however, causing the deaths of the chatelaine and of her lover, who stabs himself when a servant tells him the truth. The duke exacts a terrible vengeance from his wife, killing the woman, and then he departs on a crusade. It might be pointed out that this is a particularly inapt example for Guillaume to adduce, since the story involves the betrayal of a sworn trust by two other-

wise morally irreproachable men, the lover and the duke. A translation of this work is included in Palmer, *Medieval Epic and Romance*.

34. These famed lovers were involved in tragic relationships with the wives of their sovereigns, Tristan with Iseut, the wife of King Marc, and Lancelot with Guenivere, the wife of King Arthur. As incorporated within Arthurian legend in the thirteenth century, Tristan's story ends with the young man, estranged from his beloved, dying on a battlefield of his wounds and despair. Iseut finds his body and dies herself from grief. In that same tradition, likely known to Machaut, the illicit affair between Lancelot and Guenivere leads in part to the destruction of Arthur's kingdom. "Virtuous" Lancelot and Tristan, of course, are both involved in adulterous affairs with the wives of their lords—perhaps yet another instance of Guillaume's inattention to detail in the case he makes in support of men.

35. Guillaume makes himself an unintended butt of humor by praising the power of moderation after telling the story of a lover who cuts off his own finger to demonstrate his obedience to his lady's command.

36. In the course of returning the debate to its original issue—who suffered more, the man or the woman—Guillaume manages as well to broaden it, introducing by way of defense the antifeminist view that women are more fickle and changeable than men. He thereby insures that he will lose the debate, providing strong evidence that he does harbor misogynist thoughts even if, technically speaking, he buttresses his "published" view that the betrayed nobleman is in more pain than the bereaved lady, for her "fickleness" will insure that her grief will soon end.

37. Offended by Guillaume's obstinate declaration that women are fickle and hence do not suffer long in love, the female courtiers offer a series of classical exempla to prove the persistence unto death of women in love.

38. The story of Pyramus and Thisbe has likely also been borrowed by Machaut from the *Ovide moralisé*. The two grow up as neighbors in the city of Babylon, prohibited by their parents from communicating with one another. But they find a crack in the wall that divides their two houses and, one day, make plans to meet outside the city, close to the tomb of Ninus. Thisbe arrives before the young man and, as she waits for him, is frightened by a lion. She flees in haste, dropping her veil, which the beast, its jaws bloody from a recent kill, mouths before dropping. When Pyramus arrives, he finds the bloody veil, thinks that his lover has been killed because of his negligence, and stabs himself. Thisbe returns to find him dead and, wishing to live no longer, kills herself with the same sword.

39. Also taken from the *Ovide moralisé* is the story of Hero and Leander. In Greek mythology, Hero is the priestess of Aphrodite (Venus) in Sestos, with whom Leander, who lives across the Hellespont in Abydos, falls in love. At night he swims the watery passage to visit her, but one night during a storm the light that Hero holds for him as a guide blows out. Leander loses his way and is drowned. Discovering his body the next day, Hero, despairing, throws herself into the sea and is drowned as well.

40. The point is that Guillaume offended against the dignity of the noble lady by arguing with her when she rightly upbraided him for the insults against women.

41. In addition to arguing with a lady whose views he should accept unconditionally, Guillaume is convicted for both advancing an incorrect opinion (for death is the worst of all human misfortunes) and conducting himself incompetently.

42. Guillaume, we learn, would have been made to suffer a more dire punishment had it not been for the mercy shown him by the lady, whom Guillaume, lost in his self-concern, has failed to identify properly or even inquire about. Abashed and ashamed, Guillaume now asks Reason who his benefactress is.

43. An alternative translation of the name *Bonneürté* would be Good Fortune, and indeed the lady, with her metaphysical powers and presence, partakes of some of the qualities conventionally assigned to the goddess Fortuna in the Middle Ages, following the influential portrayal in Boethius's *Consolation of Philosophy*, one of the central texts of the era and an important source for Machaut. At the same time, the lady, in her humanity and good humor, undoubtedly recalls as well Bonne ("Good") de Luxembourg, daughter of Jean de Luxembourg, king of Bohemia, and Machaut's generous patroness before her death in the plague.

44. Of the three assigned lyric penances, only a *lai* (lay) seems to have been composed, and this piece follows directly the *Navarre* itself in three early manuscripts of the poet's works, but not in the later ones that are generally regarded as more authoritative by modern scholars because the poet likely supervised their production. It may be that some years after writing the poem Machaut decided not to include the lay.

45. The lay is the most complicated of all lyric forms, composed as it is of twelve stanzas of varying length and meter, with no pattern of rhyme repeated from one stanza to the next. Confusingly, the term *lai* is also used in the Middle Ages to refer to short narrative poems, e.g. the *Lais* of Marie de France.

Geoffrey Chaucer

The Legend of Good Women

> The man hath served yow of his conning,
> And forthred wel your lawe in his making.
> Al be hit that he can nat wel endyte,
> Yet hath he maked lewed folk delyte
> To serve you, in preysing of your name.
> (lines 412–16)

Geoffrey Chaucer (ca. 1342–1400), often judged to be the greatest nondramatic poet England has produced, can be probably credited with reestablishing English as a language of cultivation suitable for polite literature. When he was a young man, the language spoken at court and used in parliamentary debate was French; by the time of his death, English held sway in official and courtly circles, and the dialect spoken in London, which was Chaucer's own, was on its way to becoming the basis for a national standard. To this important cultural development Chaucer contributed substantially by adapting, for courtiers now willing to be entertained and enlightened in English, many of the masterpieces of the French tradition, including the love poems of Guillaume de Machaut. One of Chaucer's most humorous and enigmatic works, *The Legend of Good Women*, is in part an extended homage to the French master, incorporating—if in a highly original and altered fashion—many of the important features of Machaut's judgment series.

Here too we see the development of the narrator as a fictionalized version of the author, characterized not only as a reader of old texts but as the producer of new ones, which are mentioned by name. Like the *Navarre*, the *Legend* features a complaint leveled against the narrator by an allegorical figure for his purported failure to avoid the antifeminism to which the clerkly, educated mind was then liable. Machaut's *Navarre* offers Lady Happiness and the king of Navarre as judges of the poet's (mis)conduct, and Chaucer's poem assigns a similar function to the God of Love and his beautiful consort, Queen Alceste (in Greek mythology, Alcestis). Both works offer a debate—much shortened in the *Legend*—whose resolution demands that the narrator produce further texts, this time with "correct" doctrine to manifest his conversion from an antifeminist position. Such a penance is in each instance carried out. In the *Legend*, the penance constitutes the bulk of the work, consisting of the lives of nine good women, who the narrator must demonstrate are superior to the men who disappoint and betray them.

Born into a well-off merchant family, Geoffrey Chaucer pursued a secular path to authorship, acquiring an education and an introduction to the service of his betters outside the Church. Much like Machaut, however, he began his career in a grand aristocratic household, that of Elizabeth, countess of Ulster. Obviously a man of talent, energy, and drive, he made a good marriage, to Philippa, a woman with many aristocratic connections. Most notably, she was the sister of Katherine Swynford, who became the third wife of John of Gaunt, duke of Lancaster, one of the great nobles of the realm. In various official capacities Chaucer traveled extensively abroad: to Spain, France, and, perhaps most important, Italy, where he came into contact with the superb literature of the Italian trecento, especially the works of Giovanni Boccaccio, which greatly influenced his own literary efforts. In England he held a number of offices, including important posts in the customs office and the king's works.

His literary efforts were apparently undertaken, at least in part, to advance his career as a diplomat and royal servant. Chaucer's earliest poem, *The Book of the Duchess*, memorializes the death of the duchess Blanche, wife of John of Gaunt. Like many of Machaut's works, this poem finds a fictional role for the poet's patron; the sorrowing duke appears as the man in black, who has suffered an irremediable loss and is consoled, after a fashion, by the narrator, who is a fictional version of Chaucer himself. A number of other Chaucerian pieces, notably *The Parliament of Fowls* and *The House of Fame*, show influence from Machaut and his contemporaries, but Chaucer's greatest works, *Troilus and Criseyde* and *The Canterbury Tales*, strike out in quite different directions. In *The Legend of Good Women*, however, Chaucer adapts with striking originality the love debate poem as Machaut had given it shape in his judgment series. With this work, Chaucer connects to a continental tradition that was soon also to embrace works by two of his most noted contemporaries, the French poets Christine de Pizan and Alain Chartier.

The Legend of Good Women

Chaucer's work divides into two formally distinct sections. In the prologue (1–579), the narrator describes himself as a bookish lover of flowers; he then recounts a springtime journey to a garden where, after honoring the daisies growing there and singing a hymn in honor of virtuous women from history, he falls asleep. There the narrator experiences a vision of something like lovers' heaven, where an endless throng of beautiful women pass by in stately procession. The God of Love accompanies this beatific company with his lady Alceste, spies the narrator, and, shockingly, upbraids his erstwhile servant for what he considers insults against the Order of Love and the ladies who are honored therein. The narrator protests against the injustice of this judgment, but Alceste eventually shames him from further opposition to the god and takes up the poet's defense. Reminded by Alceste that rulers should be merciful, the god is dissuaded from a harsh demonstration of displeasure, assigning a penance instead of punishment. He allows the chagrined narrator to compose the legends that, as Alceste directs, are to demonstrate his support of the "correct" opinion, namely that women can be "good" in the sense of persevering faithfully in love. The two parts of the work, then, are intricately connected, though the world of the story developed in the prologue is displaced in favor of the several literary story worlds that the protagonist, now transformed by divine fiat into a storyteller, proceeds obediently to summon into existence. The two parts of the *Legend* correspond, in a strikingly original manner, to Machaut's two judgment poems, which are linked by a radical change in structure. The narrator of the *Behaingne* finds himself becoming the main character in the *Navarre*. Chaucer's protagonist undergoes the mirror image of this change, making the passage from main character to narrator as the work progresses.

In the prologue, the narrator is forced not only to embark on a particular storytelling project. So doing, he must also demonstrate that he is innocent of the charge of holding antifeminist views—or, perhaps, provide evidence of his reformation from an antifeminist position to true, humble service of the gentler sex. His obedient carrying out of the penance imposed upon him would provide the proof of this. In any case, as the legends unfold, they do so dramatically. What is at issue in them is not only the character of the female saints but the character of the accused and harried male who must succeed in showing that the subjects whose lives he retells are good in the sense that Alceste demands that they be shown to be. Alceste's commission is not without its challenges. She requires that the narrator begin with Cleopatra, a woman quite different from Alceste herself. Cleopatra, one might say, is something of a serial killer or, at the very least, a notoriously promiscuous and self-serving woman. The legends that follow, most of which are adapted from Ovid's *Epistulae heroidum* (Letters from Heroines), a work also known as the *Heroïdes*, offer the erstwhile penitent various difficulties, sometimes related, sometimes of different kinds. These classical tales, it should be pointed out, are largely retold in the *Navarre* as well, although in much more condensed form, where they are offered as exempla in the debate between Guillaume and Happiness.

As in the *Navarre*, of central importance is the character of the narrator's performance. To put this another way, the legends in Chaucer's work are to reveal the narrator's character, establishing whether he truly believes in feminine virtue. Ironically, the poet whose devotion to proper doctrine is not beyond question in the works he has hitherto completed is required to continue composing. By virtue of the authorial task imposed upon him, the narrator becomes a performing self, a poet charged to write what his patrons require and what is, therefore, liable to either their censure or their praise. Because the legends are meant to praise the virtues of women and confirm the male narrator in his role as the servant of ladies, the *Legend* deeply engages antifeminist themes, even as it explores the rivalry between men and women for existential and textual power. The work's intricate formal structure means that antifeminism is directly at issue only in the incomplete trial to which the narrator is subjected in the prologue, which does not afford him the opportunity to prove his bona fides or, like the unfortunate

Guillaume in the *Navarre*, to reveal his underlying bias against women. Instead the narrator's views must be read out from the style and rhetoric of his retellings. The tales of famous women from antiquity are thus not simply stories meant to be read in isolation, that is, as fictions with their own, separate claims to entertainment and truth. They are to be read as the reflex of the narrator's protestations of innocence and good faith. The legends will verify his assurance that he is not an antifeminist—or, if he did in fact need to mend his ways, as the God of Love maintains, they will demonstrate that he has come to accept the correct doctrine. What matters is how these ancient stories can, in the present, be shaped into acceptable offerings to the god that testify, through the gestures of translation that re-create them, to the narrator's good intentions, his obedience to command, and his finesse.

It is a task that Chaucer, if not his embattled fictional alter ego, layers with irony. There is wry humor and irony throughout the work, beginning with the poet's eager abandonment of his books for the springtime meadows, where he indulges his desire to worship the daisy. More important, if the writing he undertakes is to be truly penitential, then the stories that the narrator is asked to translate must pose some challenge. In other words, there must be some question as to whether the women in question are truly "good." To follow the implication, perhaps one of the tasks of proper love service is to find some way to praise the virtues of women, no matter whether they merit praise or deserve some harsher judgment. Does the narrator in fact render in the prescribed fashion the authorities he must work with? At times, as with his closing comments on the fate of Thisbe, he protests too much about his desire to emphasize the virtues of women in love, even though the story he has just related focuses on a pair of lovers who are arguably equal in their virtue. In other words, the narrator has interpreted Alceste's command rather strangely, not simply as an injunction to praise virtuous women, but also either to downplay or denigrate the goodness of men. Does this misapprehension not signal a residual male chauvinism?

To take another example, what are we to make of his treatment of Dido's "decision" to act upon the passion she feels for Aeneas? In the classical tradition, her sister Anna harangues Dido about the advantages to be gained from loving the stranger; this persuasive plea removes any doubts that the queen of Carthage might still harbor about embarking on a course of moral degradation that climaxes in her ruin and suicide. Presumably an author who wished to emphasize Dido's virtue would make it clear that she was the victim not only of a divine plot but also of bad advice. Instead the narrator alters substantially the dialogue between the two women, in effect reducing Anna to a sounding board for Dido's already quite strong resolution to respond to the passion she feels. Dido becomes more the agent of her own eventual destruction, making her "goodness" certainly more problematic.

The Legend of Good Women is in many ways a tantalizingly ambiguous work, and not only in regard to the narrator's questionable conversion to what the God of Love might accept as proper service. What are we to make of the fact that the poem ends abruptly and somewhat anticlimactically with the legend of Hypermnestra? Perhaps this is its envisioned finale, but since we are never informed how many legends were planned, we cannot judge. The narrator was simply enjoined to spend in the composition of this work "the greater part of the time you have" (482). There is no return to the framing fiction, and so we are neither shown nor told of the reaction of the god and Alceste to the narrator's efforts. Did Chaucer lose interest in the poem? Or is its abandonment—if that is what the abrupt conclusion signifies—to be ascribed to the narrator? Are we to understand him as a penitent who tires of penance? Does he find himself bored by a succession of tales in which he is to develop (discover?) the same theme? Or does he find himself cured by his exertions and no longer in need of corrective labor? Chaucer provides no answers to these questions.

What is certain is this. Like other poets of the late fourteenth century, Chaucer found fascinating what we would today term *gender politics*. In this poem, following the lead of Guillaume de Machaut, he makes misogyny a central theme, accusing after a fashion (but then perhaps exculpating) his fictional alter ego of promoting a negative image of women. Both Machaut and Chaucer treat misogyny humorously, making the fictional versions of themselves somewhat ridiculous. A significant difference between the two is that Chaucer's engagement with the joys and discontents of authorship is deeper and more complex. In part *The Legend of Good Women* is a demonstration, to the court that Chaucer served, of his abilities as a translator and of the inventive and entertaining fashion in which he could make available to those of his own time the wisdom to be found in much venerated authorities.

These include not only the Roman poet Ovid, source of the legends and, more generally, of much love lore in the Middle Ages, but Chaucer's French contemporary Guillaume de Machaut, who suggested to the Englishman one way to make entertaining and playful the debate about the relative worthiness of men and women in love. For Chaucer as for Machaut, both the narrator and his subjects are, in a sense, on trial. No doubt, Chaucer's protagonist has the more difficult task set before him. To demonstrate his conformity to Happiness's version of political correctness, Guillaume must acknowledge his error (as well as his arrogance and incompetence in debate). Though their content is not specified, he must also write three lyric poems to please and mollify his erstwhile patrons. Chaucer's embattled textual alter ego, however, is challenged not only to affirm that his heart is in the right place. He must also establish that he has the skill to manage his legendary materials, which prove somewhat intractable at times. The task of translation imposed upon him, appropriately enough, is as "writerly" as it is moral, arguably a substantial improvement on Machaut's original conception. We might also observe that Guillaume must assuage the anger of an outraged female divinity, while Alceste does not attack the narrator but defends him against the charges of a male figure bent on exacting a terrible vengeance from him. In Chaucer's case, then, he has offended against love only according to a male divinity, an ironic comment perhaps on the tradition of love poetry, penned almost exclusively—with the interesting and important exception of Christine de Pizan—by men.

Chaucer's narrator escapes his books to contemplate the wonders of spring, but is returned by that contemplation, which may have its only source in his unconscious wish, to the discontents of practicing authorship. As in the two judgment poems by his French model, the author of *The Legend of Good Women* is finally only manipulating with bemused tolerance the tribulations of his fictional alter ego. In the end, like Machaut, Chaucer is merely playing a game whose rules he has himself made up.

The translation retains Chaucer's regular pentameter lines, but makes no attempt to reproduce his use of rhyming couplets.

The Legend of Good Women

A thousand times I have heard men affirm
There's joy in heaven and torment in hell,
And I agree completely that it's true.
But nonetheless I also know quite well
That there's no man living in this country 5
Who has ever been in heaven or hell,
Or otherwise knows anything of them
Save what he's heard said or found in writing.
No man can prove this by experience.
But God forbid that men should not believe 10
More than they can see with their eyes alone.
Men should not think that everything's a lie
That they do not witness or themselves do
Because, God knows, something is no less true
Just because no one can look upon it. 15
St. Bernard saw not everything, by God![1]
This means we are able to give credence
Reasonably to those books that we find,
The ones that call to mind ancient ideas
And teachings of wise men from former times; 20
These books recount the old and proven tales
Of holiness, kingdoms, victories too,
Of love, hate, and other diverse matters
That here I'm not able to summarize.
And if perchance these old books did vanish, 25
The key of memory would then be lost.
We should willingly honor and credit
Such books whenever we've no other proof.

And as for me, although I'm not too smart,
I take delight in the reading of books, 30
Put my faith in and give credence to them,
In my heart pay reverence to them all
So intently that there's no diversion
That forces me to abandon my books
Except, and this rarely, on holidays. 35
And yet when the month of May arrives,
And I can hear that the birds are singing,
And the flowers then begin to blossom,
Farewell book and my devotion to you!
Now this is also a quirk that I have, 40

That of all the flowers in the meadow
I love the best those that are white and red
Called daisies by the folk in my city.
So immense is my affection for them,
As I first said, that whenever May comes   45
No day at all dawns for me in my bed
That I'm not up and walking through the fields
To watch this flower open in the sun
As it rises early in the morning.
All my sadness this happy sight relieves,   50
So glad I am to be in its presence
And to worship it in every way
As she who is the flower of flowers,
Full of every virtue and honor too,
Always the same, pretty and fresh of hue;   55
And I love it with ever new esteem
And always shall do until my heart dies.
And this I swear, and will not lie about,
No one ever loved with greater passion.
And when evening comes, I do quickly run,   60
The moment that the sun travels westward,
To see this flower, how it goes to rest
Afraid of the night—she so hates the dark.
Her face does spread out fully in the sun's
Brightness and desires there to open.   65
Would then that I had English, verse or prose,
Good enough to rightly praise this flower!
Now help me, you with talent and power,
You lovers who can put feelings in verse!
In this case, you ought to be diligent   70
About furthering my labor somewhat
Whether your side is the leaf or flower.[2]
For well I know that before now you have
Harvested the verse and laid up the corn,
And I go after, gleaning here and there,   75
Quite happy if I happen upon an ear
Of any pretty word you've left behind.[3]
And though it does happen that I repeat
What you've said in your beautiful poems,
Forgive me, and don't be displeased by this   80
Because, you see, I do so to honor
Love, and to offer service to the flower[4]
Whose servant I'll be while mind and strength last.
She is the brilliance and true light also
That in this gloomy world guides and leads me.   85

The heart in my sorrowful breast respects,
Loves you in such great pain that you're truly
Mistress of my wit, and I am nothing.
My words, my works are so knit in your bonds
That the same as the harp obeys the hand,   90
Sounds according to the fingers it feels,
So from my heart you are able to bring
Such voice as pleases you, laughter or moans.
Be my guide and my sovereign lady!
I call on you, as on my earthly god,   95
In both this work and all of my sorrows.

But why I began to speak, to uphold
The old stories and do them reverence,
And that men should give credence to more things
Than their eyes see, or else put to the test—   100
That subject I'll treat when I see my chance.
I can't rhyme everything at the same time.
My eager spirit, always new with thirst
To see this young flower fresh in color
For which hot desire so constrains me   105
I still feel within my heart the fire,
Made me rise before the day did break—
And this was now the first morning of May—
With sober heart and willing devotion
To be present at the resurrection   110
Of this flower, when it was to open
In the sun that rose up red as a rose,
Which just then was in the breast of the beast
That once raped the daughter of Agenor.[5]
Immediately I fell to my knees   115
And, as I could, greeted this fresh flower,
Kneeling all the time until it opened
Upon the short, soft, and delightful grass,
Prettily with flowers all embroidered,
So sweet and of such agreeable scent   120
That no mention of gum, or grasses, or trees,
Or comparison to them should be made,
For other odors plainly were outdone,
As were other flowers for rich beauty.
Earth had forgotten winter's impoverished   125
Time, which had made it deathlike and naked,
So sorely grieved, too, by winter's cold sword.
Now the temperate sun has remedied all,
Clothing in green what had been bare before.

Small birds, rejoicing for the season's sake, 130
Those that had escaped the trap and snare,
Sang to show disrespect to the fowler
Who had terrified them in wintertime
And brought destruction, too, upon their brood;
They thought it good in their song to insult 135
The filthy churl who in his greediness
Had fooled them with his crafty stratagems.
This was their song: "We defy the fowler
And all his art." And some sang out loudly,
So it was a joy to hear, lays of love 140
In order to honor and praise their mates,
And also for the joyous new summer.
On the branches full of tender blossoms
They often flitted about in delight
And sang out: "Blessed be St. Valentine, 145
For on his day I choose you for my own
Without any repenting, sweetheart mine!"
And with all this their beaks began to touch
As they did honor and meek obeisance
To Love, performing all the proper rites 150
That do belong to Love and Nature too—
Construe this as you like; it's fine with me.
And those who had sinned through their unkindness,
Like the tydif in his inconstancy,[6]
Did seek out forgiveness for all their crimes 155
And humbly chanted out their repentance,
Sat on the blossoms and swore to be true
So that their mates would have mercy on them.
And in the very end they did make peace.
For a time lord Haughtiness governed them, 160
Yet Pity through his strong, gentle power
Forgave and had Mercy vanquish Justice
Through Innocence, while guiding Courtesy.
But I do not call innocence folly
Or pity a sham, for virtue's the mean, 165
As the Ethics state—this is my meaning.[7]
And so these birds, lacking any malice,
Agreed to love and did let go the vice
Of hatred, singing all in harmony:
"Welcome, summer, our governor and lord." 170

And gently did Zephyrus and Flora[8]
Lend the flowers, softly and tenderly,
Their sweet breath, making them bring forth blossoms

Like god and goddess of the flowery mead,
And there day after day I thought I might 175
Remain for the entire month of May,
Not sleeping, without any food or drink.
Quite gently I did let myself slip down,
And leaning on my elbow and my side
I made ready to spend the whole day long 180
For no other purpose—I shall not lie—
Except for gazing upon the daisy,
Which quite reasonably men may call
Either the "day's eye" or the "eye of day,"⁹
The empress and flower of all flowers. 185
I pray God that good might then befall her
And all who do love flowers for her sake!

Yet nonetheless, don't form the view my verse
Praises the flower much more than the leaf,
No more than it does the seed to spite the stalk, 190
For neither is more unwelcome or dear.
I have as yet with neither taken sides
And know not who serves the leaf or flower.
May they enjoy their service and labor!
For from another cask comes this matter, 195
From history, before that game began.

After the sun had gone west from the south
And this flower closed and went to her rest
Because of night's darkness, which she did fear,
Quite swiftly I hurried on to my house 200
To take my rest so I could rise early
To watch this flower open, as I've said,
And in a little arbor that is mine,
Well furnished with seats freshly made of sod,
I asked for the servants to make my bed 205
For the delight that I take in summer,
And had them strew all of this with flowers.
After I lay down and closed my eyes,
In an hour or two I fell asleep
And dreamed I was lying in the meadow 210
To see the flower I so love and fear.
And from far off comes walking through the field
The God of Love, holding the hand of a queen,
Who was wearing garments of royal green,
A net of gold did lie upon her hair, 215
On top of which there sat a crown in white

Of little flowers. And, I shall not lie
For all the world, just as any daisy
Has a crown that is made of white petals,
White too were the small flowers of her crown, 220
For from one fine and oriental pearl
Had her white-colored crown been created,
And, above the green, that crown colored white
Made her look exactly like a daisy looks,
Especially with the gold net on her head. 225

This mighty God of Love was dressed in clothes
Of silk, all embroidered with boughs of green
Set among a net of red rose petals,
The freshest since the world had first begun.
Crowned with a sun was then his hair so blond 230
And not with gold—too heavy that would weigh.
And thus I thought his face shone so brightly
That I could hardly look long at the man.
And in his hand it seemed I saw him hold
Two darts that were as fiery as red coals. 235
And I saw him, angel-like, spread his wings.
And although men report that he is blind,
It seemed to me that he indeed could see,
For sternly did he turn his gaze on me,
And that look sent a chill into my heart. 240
Now by the hand he held this noble queen,
Crowned with white and in green garments all clad,
So womanly, so friendly, so humble
That although men throughout this world should search,
They would not find created by nature 245
A being of even half her beauty.
And so let me recite, as I intend,
This song praising the generous lady.

Ballade

Hide, Absalom,[10] your golden hair so bright;
Esther, do away with all your meekness; 250
Hide, Jonathan, the friendly way you have;
Penelope and Cato's Marcia too,
Think not to rival her in wifeliness;
Hide your beauty, you Iseut and Helen;
Here comes my lady, to outshine you all. 255

Your lovely body, let it not appear,

Lavinia; and Lucretia of Rome,
And Polyxena, who paid love so dear,
And Cleopatra with all your passion,
Hide your loyalty in love and your fame.   260
And you too, Thisbe, who suffered for love;
Here comes my lady, to outshine them all.

Hero, Dido, Laodamia, all three,
And Phyllis, hanging for Demophoön's sake,
And Canace, by your countenance revealed,   265
Hypsipyle, whom Jason did betray,
Offer no boast, don't noise your loyalty,
Nor you, Hypermnestra, Ariadne;
Here comes my lady, to outshine them all.

This ballade may be sung appropriately,   270
As I first said, about my kind lady
Since surely even this may not suffice
To equal my lady in any way.
For as the sun will outshine the fire,
So my sovereign lady bests all others,   275
And she's so good, so fair, so debonair
I pray God only good things befall her.
For had I no comfort of her presence,
I'd have died with nothing to prevent it,
Out of fear for Love's harsh look—and words too, 280
Just as, when it's time, you shall later hear.

Behind this God of Love, across green grass,
I saw that nineteen ladies made their way
At an easy pace, in royal green all dressed.
And after came such a file of women   285
That since God had made Adam out of clay
The third or fourth portion of all mankind
Could not possibly in all this wide world
Have been as multitudinous as they.
And true in love were these women, each one.   290
Now was that a miracle? I know not,
But just as they then laid their eyes upon
This flower that I do call the daisy,
They stopped quite suddenly and together.
Then for this occasion they all kneeled down   295
And with one voice sang: "Kind fate and honor
To the faith of women and this flower
That as a symbol, praises all of us.

To this her crown of white offers witness."
And with those words, around in a circle 300
They sat themselves down quite demurely.
First sat the God of Love, and then his queen
With the white crown, who all in green was dressed,
And after, all the others in their time
According to their rank, quite courteously, 305
And not a word was spoken in that place,
Not, its length to measure, quite a furlong.

With good intent kneeling by this flower,
I waited to find out what this folk meant
And I was still as any stone until 310
This God of Love cast his eyes upon me
And said: "Who kneels there?" And I responded to
His question the moment that I had heard it,
Saying: "Sir, it is I," and drew near him
And greeted him. Said he, "What are you doing 315
So close to my flower and with such brass?
Truly, it would be better and more fitting
For a worm than you to approach my bloom."
"Sir, and why is it," I said, "you feel thus?"
"Because," he said, "you are not suitable. 320
It's my talisman, revered and pleasant,
And you my foe who wars on all my folk,
And you speak ill of my former servants
And do them harm with all your translations,
And halt people from devoting themselves 325
To my service, considering it madness
To pay Love homage. This you can't deny,
For into naked text that needs no gloss
You've translated the 'Romance of the Rose,'[11]
Which does speak heresy against my law 330
And causes the wise to abandon me.
And of Criseyde you've said what you like,[12]
And this makes men trust much less those women
Who are true as was ever any steel.[13]
Consider carefully how you answer, 335
For even though you have denied my law,
Like other wretches do many a day,
By Holy Venus, who is my mother,
If you live long enough, you'll regret it
With such pain as will be quite obvious." 340

Then this lady dressed all in green spoke up

And said: "God, do your courtesy justice
And listen to what reply he might make
To all the things that you have charged him with.
A god should not let himself feel so hurt, 345
But keep himself unmoved in his godhead.
So, therefore, be gracious and forgiving.
And if you were not a god who knows all,
Then it could be just as I will tell you.
This man may be falsely accused to you 350
So that by rights he should then be excused.
For in your court is many a liar
And cunning taleteller who does find fault,
And these drum in your ears a lot of noise
That comes right from their imagination 355
To get your notice—and out of envy.
The causes are these, and I shall not lie.
Envy always washes dirty linen,
And she does not depart by night or day
From the house of Caesar—so says Dante. 360
Yet whoever goes, she'll not lack a theme.
Moreover, this man is perhaps naive
And might do this intending no malice
But because he needs themes for his writing
And so pays no heed to what he borrows; 365
Or else he was asked to write these two works
By some personage and dared not say no,
Or perhaps he utterly regrets it.
He has not in this way gone so far wrong
To translate what ancient clerks have written 370
As he would have, had he in malice voiced
His spite to Love and written these himself.
A righteous lord should keep such things in mind
And be quite unlike the Lombard tyrants
Who only through tyranny find a reward. 375
For the man who's king or lord by nature
Should be neither tyrannous nor cruel
Like some base renter, harming what he can.
He must consider him as his liegeman
And a treasure, like gold that's in his chest. 380
This is what the philosopher's thought is:
That a king should treat his lieges justly.
There is no doubt that this is his duty.
He'll give his lords the dignity due them
Since it's right and politic they should be 385
Exalted and honored and most cherished—

For in this world they are all demigods.
Also he should do right by poor and rich
Even though their estates are not the same,
And have compassion on impoverished folk. 390
Consider the lion's gentle nature,
For when a fly bites or discomforts him,
With his tail he flicks it away, off him,
Quite gently, since in his nobility
He doesn't deign to take vengeance on a fly 395
Just as some dog or other beast might do.
Restraint should find room in a noble heart,
Which must consider all things equitably,
Always with some regard to its own rank.
For, sir, it's no achievement for a lord 400
To damn a man, not hearing his answer;
For the highborn, that's lowly behavior,
And if that person can't excuse himself
But with a sorrowing heart begs mercy
And presents himself in only his shirt 405
To attend what judgment you might render,
Then a god deliberating briefly
Should look to his honor and his error.

Because the misdeed here involves not death,
You should be more ready to show mercy. 410
Let go of your wrath, and be more pliable.
As he was able, this man has served you
And with his writing much advanced your law.
Though his talent in penning verse be small,
Still he's urged the ignorant to delight 415
In serving you through praising of your name.
He wrote the book that's called The House of Fame
As well as The Death of Blanche the Duchess[14]
And The Parliament of Fowls, so I think,
And all about Palamon and Arcite[15] 420
From Thebes, though the story is not much known;
Also many hymns for your holidays,
And these called ballades, rondels, virelays;
And to speak about other holy things,
He translated Boethius in prose 425
And wrote too the life of St. Cecilia.[16]
He also translated some time ago
Origen's book on Mary Magdalene.[17]
His penalty should be smaller therefore.
Many lays he's composed, other works too. 430

Now since you are a god and king as well,
I, your Alcestis, former queen of Thrace,[18]
I request that through your mercy you do
Never hurt him as long as he does live.
And he shall swear to you, and right smartly, 435
Not in this fashion to offend again;
But he shall compose as you will direct
A work on women ever true in love,
The ones you would choose, be they maids or wives,
And assist you as he did once speak ill, 440
Either in the Rose or in Criseyde."

At once the God of Love did answer her:
"Madam," he affirmed, "much time has now passed
Since I learned you're so generous and true,
And since the world was new I've never yet 445
Found any soul better to me than you.
If I wish to preserve my dignity,
I may not, will not refuse your request.
You decide this case; do as you think best.
With no further bother, I forgive all. 450
For he who gives a gift or does a favor,
Let him act at once—the greater his thanks.
You determine all that he is to do.
Now go thank my lady here," he ordered.

I then arose and got down on my knee, 455
And said these words: "Madam, may God above
Reward you for making the God of Love
Forgive the anger that he feels toward me,
And bestow the grace to live long enough
That I may learn the truth of who you are 460
To have helped and raised me to this estate.
However, truly I think in this case
Not to have done wrong or offended Love.
For an honest man, there is not a doubt,
Shouldn't have to partake of some thief's deed; 465
Nor should any true lover chastise me
If I mention some false lover's disgrace.
Instead, they should take the view that I do,
For what I told or wrote of Criseyde
Or of the Rose was what my author meant. 470
And yet, God knows it well, my purpose was
To further faith in love and make it dear,

And to warn of falseness and villainy
Through these examples—such was my design."
And she answered, "Give up this arguing, 475
For Love will not be so contradicted
Whether he's right or wrong; learn that from me.
You enjoy my pardon and its justice.
Now I'll state what penance you will perform
For your fault, and you should understand it: 480
You shall, as long as year by year you live,
Spend the greater part of the time you have
In the composing of a glorious legend
Of good women, maidens as well as wives,
Those who all their lives remained true in love; 485
And tell of the false men that betrayed them,
Who all their lives do nothing else but test
How many women they can bring to shame.
For in your world this is now thought a game.
And though you do not wish to be a lover, 490
Speak well of love; this is the penance I give.
And I'll say a prayer to the God of Love
To charge his servants with assisting you
In all ways and rewarding your labors.
Now go along; this penance is but slight. 495
And when you write it, give the queen this book
On my behalf, at Eltham or at Sheen."[19]

The God of Love began to smile and spoke:
"Do you know," said he, "is she wife or maid,
Queen or countess, and what might be her rank, 500
This woman who's given a small penance
To you, who've deserved to suffer more pain?
Yet pity flows quickly in noble hearts;
This you may see—she makes known what she is."

And I answered: "No, sir, may bliss be mine, 505
Nothing but that she is good, as I see."[20]

"That story is a true one, by my hood,"
Said Love, "and it's one you know well, by God,
If you will only think about it some.
Don't you have lying in your chest a book 510
That tells the great good of Queen Alcestis,[21]
Who was once transformed into a daisy:
She who for her husband's sake chose to die
And even to go in his place to hell.

And Hercules did rescue her, by God, 515
And brought her back out of hell to heaven.

And one more time I answered, saying: "Yes,
Now I know her. Is this good Alcestis,
The daisy and my heart's consolation?
Now I feel well the goodness of this wife, 520
Whose great bounty did double her renown
Both after her death and all the while she lived.
Well has she requited the affection
I feel for her flower's sake, the daisy.
No wonder Jupiter made her into a star, 525
As says Agathon, for her goodness' sake!
Of this thing her white crown does bear witness,
Because she had as many virtues
As there are tiny flowers in her crown.
In her memory, to reverence her, 530
Cybele[22] made the daisy, and crowned the flower
Entirely in white, as men may see.
And a red crown, by God, was what Mars gave
Instead of rubies, set among the white."

With this, the queen did blush somewhat for shame 535
When thus in her presence she was so praised.
Love said then: "A very great negligence
It was that time you composed in ballade
Stanzas 'Hide, Absalom, your golden hair'
And forgot to mention her in this song, 540
Because you are so greatly in her debt;
And you know well that for any woman
Who will be a lover she is the guide.
For she taught all the art of pure love,
Especially how a wife is to live 545
And all of the rules that she must observe.
Your little wit was at that time asleep.
But now upon your life I do charge you
To write in your legend about this wife
After you have completed lesser tales. 550
Now farewell! I charge you with nothing more.
Yet before I go, this much I'll tell you:
No true lover shall ever go to hell.
These other ladies sitting in a row
Are in your song if you recognize them, 555
And in your books you will find every one.
For your legend's sake, keep them all in mind,

Those, I mean, that you know something about.
For sitting here are twenty thousand more
With whom you're familiar, good women all 560
And true in love despite what might happen.
As you prefer, make poetry of them.
The sun draws west—I must travel on home
To paradise with all this company
And every day serve the daisy fresh. 565
I want you to start with Cleopatra,
And then the others, thus to gain my love.
For let us now see what man that lover
Might be who'll suffer pain as strong as she.
I know well you cannot put all in rhyme 570
What in their time such lovers accomplished.
It would be much too long to read and hear!
It will suffice me if you write this way:
To tell what's most important of their lives
From what the ancient writers chose to treat. 575
For that man with many stories to tell,
Let him be brief or he will take too long."

And with that word I seized again my books
And right then began to write my legend.

The Legend of Cleopatra

Here begins the Legend of the martyr Cleopatra, queen of Egypt.[23]

After the death of Ptolemy, the king 580
Who then held sway over all of Egypt,
His queen Cleopatra was on the throne
Until the time when it did come to pass
That a senator was sent out from Rome
To conquer kingdoms and obtain honor 585
For Rome the city, as was the custom,
So all the world would do homage to her;
And, truly, Antony was this man's name.
So it happened, when Fortune owed him shame
After his good luck had come to its end, 590
That he became a rebel against Rome.
And, what's more, with deceit he left behind
The sister of Caesar before she knew,
And would, as he could, take another wife.
And this brought him strife with Rome and Caesar. 595
Nonetheless, in truth, this same senator
Was a quite worthy, noble warrior,

And his death was such a great misfortune!
But love had driven this man so insane
And bound him ever so tight in its snare, 600
All this for the love of Cleopatra,
That the whole world he considered nothing.
He thought that no course was so right for him
As to love and to serve Cleopatra.
He cared not if, dressed for battle, he died 605
Defending her person and her rights too.
The noble queen in turn did love this knight
For his merits and for his chivalry;
And sure as he loved her, lest the books lie,
In his person and his nobility, 610
In his prowess and in his wisdom too,
He was as good as any man alive.
And she was as beautiful as a May rose.
And since short verse-making is for the best,
She became his wife, had him as she liked.[24] 615

To describe the wedding and the feasting,
For me, who's undertaken such a task
As the rhyming of so many stories—
This would be too long, for I might omit
Some theme of greater meaning and import, 620
For men can overload a ship or barge.
So to the main point I intend to skip
And let go of whatever else remains.

Octavian, furious at this deed,
Raised a host to lead against Antony, 625
To bring about his utter destruction.
With hardy Romans, all cruel as lions;
They took ship, and therefor I let them sail.
Antony knew this and wished not to fail
To encounter these Romans if he could, 630
And he made plans, and he and his wife both,
Along with all his host too, proceeded to
Take to their ships—they delayed no longer.
And it happened these two men met at sea.
The trumpet sounds, with shouts and shooting too 635
As they struggle to get the sun behind them.
Out from the ports they trundle the huge guns
And violently, at once they hurtle on,
From the upper decks huge stones flying down.
All full of barbs, the grappling hooks go in; 640

Sickles run and cut through all the rigging.
With battle-axes, men trade blows in turn,
And some of them take flight behind the mast,
Then out to drive the others overboard.
On the spear's point they impale each other.   645
Some tear the sails with hooks that are like scythes.
One offers woe's cup, bids another drink.
Peas are poured on the decks to make them slick.
They throw pots of burning lime at each other.
All the day long they spend in such a fight,   650
Till at last, just as all things find their end,
Antony's defeated and put to flight,
And his men go too, those who still best can.

With all her purple sails, the queen flees too,
Under blows that rain down as thick as hail.   655
No wonder she could not endure this.
And when Antony saw this come to pass,
"Oh woe," he said, "the day that I was born!
On this day I've forfeited my honor."
And in despair he lost all of his wits   660
And stabbed himself, thrusting right through the heart
Before he withdrew further from that place.
His wife, who couldn't find grace at Caesar's hands,
In her distress and fear fled to Egypt.
But hearken, all you who speak of kindness,   665
You men who swear falsely many an oath
That if your love is angry you will die—
Here you can witness what troth women have.
This sad Cleopatra so mourned the man
No tongue can tell what it was she felt.   670
Yet in the morning she would stay no more
And had her fine workmen build her a shrine
With all the rubies and the precious gems
She could obtain in the whole of Egypt;
And this shrine she then filled up with spices   675
And had the corpse embalmed, then had it brought,
This lifeless body, and shut in the tomb.
Next to the shrine she ordered a pit dug,
And in that deep grave put all the serpents
She could find, and afterward she declared: 680
"Now, lover, whom my mournful heart obeyed
So utterly since that blissful hour
When I swore to be yours in every way—

It is you I mean, Antony, my knight—
That never as I wake, both night and day, 685
Are you at all forgotten in my heart,
In joy or pain, in singing or dancing;
And with myself I made this bargain then
That whatever you felt, happy or sad,
So far as the power was mine to do, 690
Whatever would not besmirch my wifehood,
I would feel just the same, in life or death;
And while I draw breath, this same covenant
Will I fulfill; and it will then be clear
No queen was more loyal to her own lover." 695

And this said, naked and with a good heart,
Among the serpents in the pit she leaped,
And there she chose her burial to be.
At once these adders started striking her,
And with good courage she received her death 700
From love for Antony, so dear to her.
True history all this, no fable here.
Before I find a man this true and firm,
Who will, so loyal, receive death for love,
I pray that God let our heads never ache! 705

Here ends the Legend of the martyr Cleopatra.

The Legend of Thisbe

Here begins the Legend of the martyr Thisbe of Babylonia.[25]

Once in Babylon these things did happen.
Queen Semiramis had ditches dug[26]
Round the city, and ordered walls raised up
Very high, these made of hard-baked bricks.
In this noble city were then dwelling 710
Two lords who were of great reputation,
And on a grassy stretch so close they lived
Nothing divided them save a stone wall,
As in great towns the custom often is.
And truth to tell, the one did have a son, 715
Among the handsomest in all that land.
The other had a daughter, the fairest
Then living in the world's eastern regions.
These two came to know about each other
Through gossip of the women thereabout. 720

For still in that country this was certain:
Closely guarded were all maidens there,
Jealously too, lest some folly they do.

The name of this young man was Pyramus,
The maid was called Thisbe, so says Ovid. 725
The tales told them so boosted their repute
That as in years they grew, so did their love,
And to be sure, since they were of age,
A marriage for them could have been arranged.
But to this their fathers would not agree. 730
And with an equal pain they burned for love,
And none of their friends could cool that fire;
For privately sometimes they still did meet,
And with some tricks, to speak their desire.
Cover the coals, hotter grows the fire! 735
Forbid love, and it multiplies tenfold.

This wall that stood between the two of them
Had been split right from the top to bottom
Since the moment that it had been raised up.
And yet so small and narrow was this cleft, 740
Scarcely could any person notice it.
But is there anything love cannot see?
You lovers both, if I am not lying,
You were the first to find this narrow crack,
And with the whisper used confessing sins, 745
Through that opening they did speed their words,
Reciting as they stood close by that spot,
All their complaints of love, all their sorrow,
Whenever they did dare to do this thing.

On one side of the barrier he stood, 750
While Thisbe stood quite close to the other,
Each to receive the other's pleasant sound,
Thinking thus to deceive their guardians.
This wall they would threaten every day
And wish to God that it were beaten down. 755
Thus would they speak: "Alas, you wicked wall,
It's your envy keeps everything from us!
Why won't you split in two or tumble down?
Or at least, should you refuse to do so,
Still let us meet but one time together, 760
And at this tryst we can share kisses sweet,
And we'd recover from our chill sadness.

Yet, nonetheless, we're beholden to you
Because you are the one who lets our words
Make their way right through your stones and mortar,   765
Then should we be very well pleased with them."
And after they'd spoken these idle words,
They would kiss the cold wall of hardened brick,
Then take their leave and go forth on their way.
The evening was the best time for those two,   770
Or quite early, lest they be seen by someone.

A long time they continued in this way
Till one day, when Phoebus started shining,[27]
And Aurora with all her streaming heat[28]
Had dried all the dew from the grasses,   775
Unto this crack Pyramus made his way
And Thisbe too, just as was their custom,
And a promise that night to steal away
They plighted to each other on their troth,
To deceive their guardians, one and all,   780
By making their way forth from that city
And there, where the meadows are broad and wide,
To meet in the place at a certain time.
They did arrange that their tryst was to be
Where King Ninus beneath a tree lay tombed   785
(For ancient pagans that worshipped idols
At that time were buried there in the fields)
And close to his sepulcher was a well.
And to make this history a brief one,
Quite quickly they affirmed that covenant.   790
And the sun's light too long did last, they thought,
And under the waves would not go its way.

This Thisbe had such a great desire
To see Pyramus, such eagerness too,
That when she spied her opportunity,   795
She stole away quite carefully that night,
With her face all covered up by a shawl
Since, to keep her promise, her family all
Had she forsaken. Oh, such a pity
That a woman might ever be so true   800
As to trust a man—save she knew him better!
And at a fast pace to the tree she goes,
For in this circumstance love gave her strength,
And then close by the well she went to sit.
Alas, then there came a wild lioness   805

Out from the woods who halted at nothing,
Her mouth all bloody from killing some beast,
To drink from the well where Thisbe then sat.
And when this came to the notice of Thisbe, her heart
Full of terror, she got up at once   810
And with fearful steps ran off to a cave
That, lighted by the moon, she could see well.
And as she ran on, she let drop her shawl,
Paid it no mind, so confounded she felt,
And, too, she was so glad at her escape.   815
There she sits and hides, wonderfully still.
After this lioness had drunk her fill,
Around the well she then began to pace,
And the shawl almost at once she came on,
Then tore to pieces with her bloody mouth.   820
Having done this, no longer did she wait,
But went back down the path she'd come along.

And at last Pyramus came to that spot.
Alas, he had delayed at home too long.
The moon was shining; by it he could see.   825
As he went along quite fast on his way,
Hard to the ground he kept his eyes and gaze,
And in the sand, as he was looking down,
He saw the broad tracks that a lion made.
And in his heart he shuddered at the sight,   830
The blood ran from his face, his hair stood up.
Then he came closer and found the torn shawl.
"Alas," he said, "the day that I was born!
This single night will kill us lovers two.
How do I ask Thisbe to forgive me   835
When I'm the one who's been your death, alas!
My pleas to do this are what have killed you.
Oh, to ask that a woman come by night
To some place where such danger she might meet,
And I late! Alas, that I wasn't there   840
Some time before it happened that you came!
Now whatever lion lives in the woods,
May he tear my flesh; or whatever wild
Beast in there, let him now chew up my heart!"
And with these words, he then took up the shawl   845
And kissed it often, cried bitter tears there
And said, "Shawl, alas, only you are left,
But my blood as well you now shall feel,
Just as Thisbe's bleeding you felt before."

And with those words, into his heart he thrust. 850
Out of the wound the blood gushed quickly
Like water from a pipe that breaks in two.

Now Thisbe, who knew nothing of all this,
But, terrified, was sitting, had these thoughts:
"If it should happen that my Pyramus 855
Comes to this spot and yet cannot find me,
He may consider me unkind and false."
So she comes out and looks around for him,
Looking both with her heart and her eyes,
Thinking: "I will tell him of my terror, 860
Both at the lioness and all I did."
And at last she came upon her lover,
Still beating his heels upon the ground there
All bloody; and this sight took her aback.
And like the ocean's waves her heart did beat, 865
Pale as the boxwood tree she waxed, and soon
She found wits sufficient to see clearly
That this was Pyramus, her own dear heart.
Who could tell in words what a deathly look
Thisbe now wore, and how she tore her hair, 870
And how she began to torment herself,
And how she lay fainting upon the ground,
And how this wound she then cried full of tears,
And how she mixed his blood with her lament
And with that blood began to smear herself, 875
And how she clasped that lifeless corpse, alas;
How in this predicament Thisbe acts;
How his frosty mouth so cold she kisses!
"Who has done this? Who has been so daring
To slay my love? O speak, my Pyramus! 880
I am your Thisbe, who now calls to you."
And with these words, she raises up his head.

This woeful man, at the time not yet dead,
When he heard spoken the name of Thisbe,
He cast his heavy, death-filled eyes on her. 885
Then down they fell as he gave up the ghost.
Thisbe rose, made no noise or angry threat,
And saw her shawl and the man's empty sheath,
And the sword as well that had been his death.
Then she spoke thus: "My woeful hand," she said, 890
"Will be strong enough for a task like this
Since love shall give me the resolve and strength

To make a wound that's large enough, I think.
I'll follow in death, be a companion
In your dying, its true cause too," said she.   895
"And even though nothing save death alone
Might in truth force me to abandon you,
Not even through death will you take your leave
From me, for I will go along with you!
And now, you, our wretched jealous fathers,   900
The two of us who once were your children,
This is our prayer to you: no envy more,
But let us lie together in one grave
Since love has brought us to this piteous end.
And may righteous God send to all lovers,   905
To those who loyally love, more good fortune
Than Pyramus and Thisbe ever had!
And let no genteel woman ever think
To undergo a risk like this one was.
Yet God forbid that a woman cannot   910
Be as true and loving as any man.
And for my part, I will now make this clear."
And at this word, she quickly grasped his sword,
Still hot with the warm blood of her lover
And straight into the heart she stabbed herself.   915

Thus Thisbe and Pyramus passed away.
I find a few more only of true men
Beyond this Pyramus in all my books,
And so I've spoken in this way of him.
For it pleases us men to discover   920
A man who can be true and kind in love.[29]
See here, no matter how fine the lover,
How a woman can and dares be as good!

Here ends the Legend of Thisbe.

The Legend of Dido

Here begins the Legend of the martyr Dido, queen of Carthage.[30]

Glory and honor, Mantua's son Virgil,
To your name, and I shall, as best I can,   925
Follow your lantern as you go before,
How Aeneas swore falsely to Dido
In your *Aeneid*; from Ovid I'll take
The story's theme, versifying its gist.[31]

After Troy had been brought to destruction   930

By Greek tricks, especially those of Sinon,
With the false horse offered to Minerva,³²
By which many Trojans met their end;
And Hector, after his death, had appeared;
And a fire too fierce to be put out   935
Arose then in Ilium's noble tower,³³
Which was the chief defense of that city;
And all the land had been brought down so low,
With Priam, its king, undone and murdered;
And Aeneas was then charged by Venus   940
To flee, and he took up Ascanius,
Who was his son, in his right arm and fled,
And on his back he carried and led off
His aged father who was named Anchises;
And on the way he lost Creusa, his wife.   945
His mind was greatly overcome with woe
Before his companions in arms were found.
But at last, having found out where they were,
He made ready at a certain hour
And with full speed then hurried to the shore   950
And sailed away with all his company
Toward Italy, for Fate would have it so.
But of his adventures upon the sea,
It is not my intention to speak here,
For these do not relate to my main theme.   955
But, as I have said, my story shall be
Of him and Dido until it is done.

For long he sailed upon the briny sea
Until in Libya hardly he arrived
With seven ships in his fleet and no more,   960
And glad he was to make his way to land
Because they'd all been battered in a storm.
And after he'd come to a safe harbor,
He had a knight—Achates was his name—
And this man from all his fellows he chose   965
To go and scout the country all about.
No one else did he take along with him.
But off they went, the ships left at anchor,
His companion and himself with no guide.
A long time through the wilderness he walked   970
Until he chanced upon a huntress,
Holding in her hand a bow and arrow.
Her clothes were a bit short and showed her knees.
But she was the fairest creature by far

Whom Nature ever yet had brought to life. 975
She greeted Aeneas and Achates,
And this is what she said on meeting them:
"Did you spy," said she, "since you have walked some,
Any of my sisters walking there too,
With a savage boar or some other beast 980
That in this forest they have hunted down,
With robes tucked up and quivers arrow-filled?"

"No, madam, truly," said this Aeneas,
But to judge by your beauty, so I think,
You cannot be any earthly woman; 985
Instead, I guess you are Phoebus's sister,
And if it is that you are a goddess,
Have mercy on our troubles and our toil."

"I am no goddess, truly," then she said,
"For in this country maidens go walking 990
With bow and arrows just in this fashion.
The kingdom of Libya is where you are,
And Dido is its mistress and its queen."
And she then explained the circumstances
That had compelled Dido to this country, 995
But now those things I have no wish to rhyme.
There's no need—it would be a waste of time.
For here's the gist and point: Venus it was,
His own mother, who spoke this way to him.
She asked that he take himself to Carthage, 1000
Then vanished in a flash out of his sight.

I could well follow Virgil word for word,
But it would take me too long to do so.

This noble queen, whose own name was Dido,
Who once had been the wife of Sychaeus, 1005
And who was fairer than the sun so bright,
Had founded this noble town of Carthage,
Where in most high honor she now reigned
And was thought the true flower of all queens,
In nobility, kindness, and beauty, 1010
And lucky the man who laid eyes on her;
So desired she was by kings and lords
She inflamed the whole world with her beauty,
And greatly was by one and all esteemed.

When Aeneas had arrived at that place, 1015
Into the chief temple of all the town
Where Dido was busy with her praying,
He had made his way in total secrecy.
When he came into that spacious temple,
I cannot say if it were possible, 1020
But Venus had made him invisible—
This, with no lies, is what the book declares.
And when this Aeneas and Achates
Had meandered through and through the temple,
They found in that place painted on a wall 1025
How Troy and all that realm had been destroyed.
"Alas that I was born," said Aeneas,
"Throughout the world our shame's so widely known
That now it is depicted everywhere.
We who once enjoyed the best from Fortune 1030
Have now all been brought low, and so far down!
No longer do I care to keep living!"
And after these words he broke out weeping,
So tenderly it was quite sad to see.
This lovely lady, queen of the city, 1035
In the temple stood in her royal array,
Looking so rich, so very fair as well,
So young, so pleasant with her sparkling eyes
That if the God who made earth and heaven
Would feel a love for beauty and goodness, 1040
And womanliness, bearing, and resolve,
Whom should He love except this sweet lady?
No other woman's half so suitable.

Fortune, who over all the world holds sway,
Suddenly effected a shocking turn 1045
Much stranger than what's ever happened yet.
For all the company of Aeneas,
Who he thought had been lost at sea,
Then arrived not far off from that city,
And so some of his more important lords 1050
To that city by chance had made their way,
To the very same temple to search out
The queen to ask that she give assistance,
So widely known was she for her goodness.
And when they'd told her all their misfortunes, 1055
All about the storm and their bitter luck,
Aeneas then appeared before the queen

And openly avowed that it was he.
Who was joyful but all his companions,
Having come on their lord and governor? 1060

The queen saw how much honor they did him,
Had heard before much praise of Aeneas,
And in her heart she felt pity and pain
That a very noble man should have been
Disinherited to such a degree; 1065
And she saw the man, a true knight he seemed,
And quite well endowed in strength and person,
And he appeared a truly genteel sort,
And ably he knew how to craft his speech,
And then quite beautiful of face was he, 1070
Well put together, muscled and big boned—
For from Venus he had such handsome looks
No other might be half so fair, I guess—
And very much the lord he seemed to be.
And because he was a stranger, she liked 1075
Him even a bit more, so God help us,
For to some a new thing is often sweet.
At once her heart took pity on his woe,
And with that pity love took root as well.
And for his sadness and nobility, 1080
In his hurting he could be assisted.
To be sure, she said that she was sorry
He'd suffered through such peril and ill luck,
And in her friendly speech, she spoke to him
In just this way, saying what you may hear: 1085

"Aren't you son to Venus and Anchises?
In good faith, all the honor and respect
I may rightly pay you is yours to have.
I shall rescue your ships, your people too."
And many pleasant words she spoke to him 1090
And commanded her messengers to go forth
That same day and in no way fail to find
His ships and afterward provision them.
Many a beast she sent on to the ships
And in addition made him gifts of wine, 1095
And to her royal palace then she hurried,
And all this while took Aeneas with her.
Why do you need me to describe the feast?
He'd never before been refreshed better.
Full was the feast of dainties and rich food, 1100

With play of instruments, with song and cheer,
With loving glances and much flirtation.
This Aeneas has gone to paradise
Out of hell's pit, and therefore joyfully
He recalls the rank he once held in Troy.   1105
To dancing chambers hung with tapestries,
Furnished with rich beds and decoration,
This Aeneas is led once the meal's done.
And by the queen, after he'd had a seat
And the wine and spiced drink were cleared off,   1110
He was taken directly to his rooms,
There to be at his ease and take his rest
With all his folk, and do just what they pleased.

There was not one well-accoutered courser,
No steed very well suited to the joust,   1115
No horse gentle to ride at any time,
No bauble that was made of precious gems,
No sacks full of gold, these heavy in weight,
No ruby that was gleaming in the night,
No proud hawk for the taking of herons,   1120
No hound for hunting wild boar, deer, and harts,
No gold cup fresh carved with little flowers
That in all Libya's land could be obtained
Dido did not send on to Aeneas.
And what he spent, all that was paid for him.   1125
The noble queen in this way treats her guest,
Her generosity surpassing all.

Truly Aeneas, and this is no lie,
To the ship dispatched Achates to fetch
His son as well as valued possessions: 1130
Scepters, garments, brooches, and rings also,
Some of these to wear, others to present
To her who'd sent him all these precious goods.
And he asked that his son would bestow them,
For they should be taken to the queen.   1135
This Achates has returned from that place,
While Aeneas is quite eager, joyful
To look on Ascanius, his young son.
Yet nonetheless our author informs us
It was Cupid, who is the god of love,   1140
That, prompted by his mother there on high,
Was to assume the likeness of this child
In order to infatuate the queen

With Aeneas—as for that bit of text,
Let it be as it may, I pay no heed.[34]   1145
But this is true: the queen gave the young man
A welcome that is wonderful to hear.
And for the presents that his father sent,
With good intent, she thanked him many times.

Thus the queen takes joy as well as pleasure   1150
In all these new fair people come from Troy.
And, further, she's asked about Aeneas's
Deeds, and she has learned all the history
Of Troy; and the whole day long these two did
Busy themselves with sport and discussion,   1155
And this set such a fire to burning
Lucky Dido feels such desire now
To give herself to Aeneas, her new guest,
She has lost her color, her health as well.

Now on to the main point, the story's meat,   1160
Why I've told this tale and will tell the rest.
Thus do I begin: one night it happened
After the moon had lifted up its light,
This noble queen proceeded to her rest.
In anguish she sighs and torments herself.   1165
She lies awake, tosses, often startles
As all lovers do, so I have heard tell.
And in the end to her sister Anna
She made her complaint and spoke these words:
"Now, dearest sister mine, what might it be   1170
That terrifies me in my dream?" she said.
"This same Trojan is so much in my thoughts
Because it seems to me his shape's so fair,
And he seems to be such a likely man,
And more, so much of virtue does he know   1175
That all my love and life are in his hands.
Have you not heard him tell his adventures?
Now surely, Anna, if you advise me,
I would like to be married to the man—
That is the point. What more should I affirm?   1180
He is the one to make me live or die."

Her sister Anna knew Dido's best course,
Spoke her mind and somewhat did oppose her.[35]
But this sermonizing went on quite long,
Too long in fact for me to recount here.   1185

Yet in the end there was no withstanding—
Love will love, for no one can resist it.

Out on the ocean then rose up the dawn;
The queen, enamored, charges her people
To ready the nets, and broad, sharp spears as well. 1190
This lusty queen wishes to go hunting,
As this new and pleasant woe does urge her.
And her lusty folk have taken to horse.
To the court the hounds are then brought up,
And on coursers as swift as any thought, 1195
Her young knights gather themselves all about,
And of her women a huge press as well.
Upon a broad-backed palfrey, paper white,
Its red saddle pleasingly embroidered,
All embossed with golden bars raised up high, 1200
Sits Dido in gold, hung with precious jewels,
And she is as pretty as the bright morning
That mends the nighttime sorrows people feel.
On a courser sharp and quick as fire—
It might be turned with a gentle bridle— 1205
Sits Aeneas, looking just like Phoebus,
So handsomely was he himself arrayed.
The foam-flecked bridle with its golden bit
He controls to suit his every wish.
And this noble queen, this lady, rides forth 1210
To the hunt, with this Trojan by her side.

The herd of stags is quickly discovered,
With shouts of "Faster!" "Harder!" "Uncouple!"
"Why won't the lion come, the bear either,
So I can at once greet him with this spear?" 1215
Thus say the younger folk and move to kill
These wild stags and keep them at their mercy.

Amid all this the heavens began to rumble,
And with a gruesome noise the thunder roared;
Down came the rain, so thick with sleet and hail, 1220
With heaven's fire, that it did frighten
This noble queen, her company also,
So each and every one was glad to flee.
And quickly, to save herself from the storm,
She took flight into a little cave, 1225
And with her came this Aeneas as well.
If more were with them, this I do not know;

The author does not make mention of it.
And here the deep affection twixt these two
Began. This was the very first morning   1230
Of their joy and commencement of their woe.
For in this place Aeneas so long knelt,
To tell her all his heart, his distress too;
And quite solemnly he swore to be true,
For good or ill, never to find another;   1235
And since a feigning lover pleads so well,
This foolish Dido then pitied his pain
And took him to husband, became his wife
For evermore, as long as life might last.
And after, when the storm came to an end,   1240
Out they came and in joy they traveled home.

A wicked scandal all at once arose,
How with the queen Aeneas had gone off
To the cave; and people thought what they liked.
And when this reached the ears of King Iarbas,[36]   1245
Who all his life had been in love with her,
Vowing that he would have her for his wife,
He felt such sorrow and made such a fuss
It was a pity and a shame to hear.
But as in love it happens every day,   1250
That someone will laugh at another's pain,
Now it's Aeneas who laughs and feels more joy
With more wealth than ever he knew in Troy.

O silly women, full of innocence,
Replete with pity, loyalty, and good faith,   1255
What makes you trust men in this fashion?
Do you feel pity for their feigned pain,
Though you have such old examples before you?
Don't you see how they all betray their oaths?
Where's one who's never left his beloved,   1260
Or been unkind to her, done her some harm,
Or robbed her, or boasted of his conquest?
You can see this well and read about it.
Take heed now of this highborn gentleman,
This Trojan who knew how to please so well   1265
And pretended to be true and to obey;
So genteel and discreet in all he did,
And knew how to pay his homage ably,
At dances to attend her and at feasts,
And when she went to temple and back home,   1270

And restrain himself until he saw her,
And with her taste in mind adorn himself—
How I surely don't know—and compose songs,
Enter jousts and do many feats of arms,
Send her letters, tokens, brooches, rings— 1275
Listen now how he would serve his lady!
There when he was in danger of dying
From hunger and trouble on the ocean,
And deserted, having fled his country,
And by the storm his folk all driven off, 1280
She gave her body and her realm too
Into his hands, as if she might have been
Queen not of Carthage but some other land,
And lived in joy enough. What more to want?
This Aeneas who swore so solemnly 1285
Is weary of his game in a brief while;
His heated earnest has all blown over.[37]
And privately he readies all his ships
And makes plans to steal away in the night.

Dido was beginning to suspect this, 1290
And very much thought all had gone awry,
For in his bed at night he lies and sighs.
At once she asks what he finds displeasing:
"My dear heart, the one whom I love the most?"
Said he, "Tonight in fact my father's ghost 1295
Has quite disturbed me as I was sleeping,
And Mercury has given me the message[38]
That of necessity my fate will be
That I must sail and conquer Italy—
And this, I think, has broken all my heart." 1300
And then his feigned tears begin to flow
And in his two arms he embraces her.

"Is this the truth?" she said. "Will you do so?
Have you not sworn to have me as your wife?
God, what kind of woman will you make me? 1305
I am of gentle birth and a queen too.
From your wife you'll not flee so ignobly?
Alas, that I was born! What shall I do?"

I'll make it quick: now noble queen Dido
Here seeks out shrines and there makes sacrifice, 1310
She kneels, she cries—it's pitiful to hear.
She pleads with him and offers to become

His slave, his servant, lowest of the low.
At his feet she falls down into a faint,
Her bright and golden hair all disheveled, 1315
And says: "Have mercy! Let me go with you!
These lords who live on lands that border mine
Will destroy me only on your account.
If only you will marry me right now,
As you have sworn, then I will give you leave 1320
To slay me with your sword when evening comes.
For then it will be as your wife I'll die.
With child I am, so give my child his life!
Mercy, lord, let pity be in your thoughts!"
But all of this avails her not at all, 1325
For one night asleep he left her lying
And to his people then he stole away,
And like a traitor straightaway set sail
Toward the bounteous land of Italy.
Thus he left Dido in pain and sorrow 1330
And wed there a lady named Lavinia.

His clothes he left, and his sword standing there,
When from sleeping Dido he snuck away,
Right at her bed's head, in such haste he was
When toward his ships he proceeded in stealth. 1335
And this garment, when poor Dido awoke,
She very often kissed on his account
And said: "O cloth, when Jupiter permits,[39]
Take now my soul, release me from this care!
The course of Fortune have I all fulfilled." 1340
And thus, alas, lacking all help from him,
Twenty times she fell down in a faint.
And after she'd made to her sister Anna
A complaint—which I may not here write down,
Since putting it in verse creates such pain— 1345
And asked her attendant and her sister
To fetch at once some fire and other things,
Saying she would perform a sacrifice—
And when she could see well her chance,
Upon this sacrificial fire she leapt 1350
And with his sword thrust deep into her heart.

But, my author states, she said this more
Before she took her hurt, before she died,
In a letter she wrote, which began thus:
"Just the same," she said, "as when the white swan 1355

Begins to sing as he approaches death,
So I will make this complaint to you.
Not that I hope to get you back again,
For I know well that this is all in vain
Because the gods are all opposed to me. 1360
But since for you I lost my name," she said,
"I may well waste a word or letter on you,
Though it will better nothing, well I know.
For that wind that blew your ship away,
That same wind blew away your troth as well." 1365

But who wants to know what the letter says,
Let him read Ovid, and there he'll find it.

Here ends the Legend of the martyr Dido, queen of Carthage.

The Legend of Hypsipyle

Here begins the Legend of the martyrs Hypsipyle and Medea.[40]

Duke Jason, you chief of all false lovers,
You sly devourer and confounder
Of noble women, tender creatures, 1370
You've offered your enticements and lures
To ladies through your noble appearance,
With your words stuffed full of pleasantries,
And with your deceptive oaths and manner,
With your attentiveness and humble ways, 1375
And with your counterfeited pain and woe.
Where others betray one, you betray two!
Oh, you often swore that you would die
For love, when you suffered no malady
Save foul delight, and you called it love. 1380
If I should live, your name will be bandied
In English to make known your outlaw ways!
Now that the horn has blown, we'll have at you!
Yet truly it's a pity and a shame
That Love decides to treat false lovers thus, 1385
Giving them much more of a nice welcome
Than the man gets who has cruelly suffered,
Or endured many bloody wounds in war.
For the fox eats a capon as tender
(Though he's a trickster and betrayed the bird) 1390
As shall the goodman who has paid for one.
Though the bird is his by right and reason,
At night the wicked fox will claim his share.

In Jason's case, this wisdom is apparent
With Hypsipyle and queen Medea. 1395

In Thessaly, so Guido informs us,
There was a king whose name was Pelias,
Who had a brother, Aeson was his name.
And when for old age he could hardly walk,
He gave to Pelias the governance 1400
Of all his realm, made him its lord and king.
And this Jason was the son of Aeson,
And at the time in all his land there was
No knight his equal in gentility,
In generosity, strength, and vigor. 1405
After his father died, his bearing was such
No man was eager to become his foe,
But paid him much honor and was his friend.
And Pelias quite mightily envied this,
Thinking Jason might be in name raised up 1410
So high, his reputation so increased
By the love of the lords in that country,
He himself might be removed from his throne.
And when night came he plotted in his mind
In what way Jason best might be destroyed 1415
With no blame attaching to his scheming.
And at last he decided on this plan:
To send Jason to some faraway land
Where the man might meet with his undoing.
This was his aim, even though to Jason 1420
He made a show of affection and love,
Fearing his lords might come to notice it.

And so it befell, since rumor runs far,
The news and report became widely known
From an island with the name of Colchis, 1425
Beyond where Troy was, eastward in the sea,
That in that place was a ram men could see
With a fleece of gold that shone so brightly
There was nowhere another sight its peer.
But it was always guarded by a dragon, 1430
And by other wondrous things on each side,
And by two bulls that were all shaped of brass
And spit fire, and many things like that.
And yet this was part of the tale as well,
That whosoever wished to have this fleece, 1435
He must do two things before he'd get it:

Fight against the bulls and the dragon too.
And King Ae'tes was lord of that island.

At this time Pelias made up his mind
That he would encourage his nephew Jason 1440
To sail to that land, there to try the game,
And he said: "Nephew, if it might be
That such an honor fall to your lot
And you gain this famous treasure
And to my kingdom here bring it back, 1445
It would be for me great joy and honor.
Then I'd be held to requite your labors.
All that their trip costs I myself will pay.
Choose what people you'll take along with you.
Let's see now. Dare you make this voyage?" 1450
Jason was young and had a lusty heart,
And he agreed to take this venture on.

Argos at once began to craft his ships.
Hercules the mighty went with Jason,
And many another man that he chose. 1455
But whoever asks who traveled with him,
Let that man go read the 'Argonauticon,'[41]
For it will tell a tale that's long enough.
Philoctetes hoisted the sail as soon as
The wind blew fair, and Jason hastened 1460
From his country called Thessaly.
Upon the salty sea he sailed along
Till he arrived at the island of Lemnos—
Although Guido does not tell this part,
But in his 'Epistles,' Ovid says it's so— 1465
And of this island the lady and the queen
Was fair young Hypsipyle, so bright,
Who was the daughter of Thoas, the king.

Hypsipyle had ventured off to play
And by the seashore roamed along the cliff; 1470
Under a bank she quite soon took notice
Where Jason's ship was putting in to shore.
Virtuous, she sent quick a messenger
To learn if it was that some strange creature
Had been blown to land at night by a storm, 1475
And to give him aid, as was her custom
To help each person and provide comfort,
Being truly generous and courtly.

This messenger hastened to go down there
And found Jason and Hercules as well, 1480
Who had come to land in a tiny boat
To refresh themselves and take the air.
The morning was a temperate and fair one.
And on his path the messenger met them.
With great finesse he greeted these two lords, 1485
Delivering his message and asking
Was their ship harmed or had they bad luck,
Or some need of pilots or provisions,
For they shouldn't fail to get assistance there.
This was the queen's very firm intention. 1490

Quietly, humbly Jason then answered:
"I thank," he said, "my lady from the heart
For her goodness. Truly, we need nothing
At this time, save we are very weary
And come from the sea to refresh ourselves 1495
Till the wind favors us better on our course."

For sport this lady wanders on the cliff
With all her company along the shore,
Where she finds Jason and the others standing,
Speaking of these things as I have described. 1500
This Hercules and Jason then noticed
It was the queen and nicely greeted her
The moment they met up with the lady.
And she took heed, and knew by their manner
And by their dress, their words, their demeanor 1505
That these were gentlemen of high degree.
And to the castle then she takes with her
These strangers, and pays them great reverence,
Asks about the trials and difficulties
That they have suffered on the briny deep, 1510
So within a day, or two, or three,
She learned from the people in his ships
That they were Jason, of great renown,
And Hercules, famous from his praise,
Who sought at Colchis the adventures there; 1515
And she paid them more honor than before,
And more and more time she did spend with them,
For, and no lies, they were worthy people.
And, in fact, she spoke more with Hercules
And bared her heart to him, taking him to be 1520
Serious, wise, and loyal, careful spoken,

And without any other feelings
Either of love or villainous designs.

This Hercules has praised Jason so much
The man has been raised to the sun itself: 1525
Never was a man half so true in love
Under the vault of heaven there on high.
And he was wise, hardy, discreet, and rich—
In these next three points, no man was his peer—
And more generous and full of manly strength   1530
Than all those still alive and those then dead.
And therefore was he a great gentleman,
And likely to be king of Thessaly.
He had no fault, but he was reticent
In love and too shamefaced to speak of it.   1535
He would much rather kill himself and die
Than that men should see him act the lover.
"Were it God's will, I'd part with flesh and blood,
If only I might live to see the day,
That he should somewhere come to have a wife   1540
Fit for his rank, since such a lusty life
She should henceforth lead with this lusty knight!"
And this had all been plotted out at night
By Jason and this Hercules between them.
In this regard they did hatch a cruel scheme   1545
That should come to an innocent's doorstep,
For their plan was to enamor the queen.
As coy as any maiden is this Jason;
He looks pitiful, yet says not a word.
But to her counselors he freely gives   1550
Huge presents, to her officers as well.
I wish to God I had the time and leisure
To sketch out in verse his wooing of her.
But if there's some false lover in this house,
Just as he acts, so did Jason the same,   1555
With pretense and many a sly gesture.
No more will you get from me. Instead you'll
Read the source, which sets forth every detail.

The upshot is this: that Jason was married
To the queen and took from her possessions   1560
What he liked for provisioning his ships.
And in time he gave her two children,
Then hoisted his sail and saw her no more.

A certain letter she did send to him,
One too long to repeat or even write, 1565
And there she reproved his great treachery
And begged him to take some pity on her.
And here's what she said of his two children:
That surely in every way they were like
Jason, save they weren't able to deceive. 1570
And she prayed God, before too long a while,
That the woman who had taken his heart
Should find the man faithless to her as well;
And that woman should kill her own two children,
And the same for those who gave him his way. 1575
And true to Jason was she all her life,
And, as if still his wife, kept herself quite chaste.
Never in her heart did she feel happy,
But died, loving him, from this sorrow's pain.

The Legend of Medea

In Colchis has arrived this duke Jason, 1580
Who devours love and its dragon.
Just as matter always seeks out form,
And from one form to another may pass,
Or just like a well that has no bottom,
Just the same, false Jason can find no peace 1585
From his desire because of his urge
To take some delight with gentlewomen.
This is his pleasure and felicity.
Roaming, Jason comes upon the city
That was called Jaconitos at the time, 1590
And it was the chief town of all Colchis,
And there he recounted to Aëtes,
King of that land, why he had journeyed there,
Asking that he might be given the chance
To win the Golden Fleece, could he do so. 1595
To this request the king gives his assent
And honors the man, as it was fitting,
To the extent that his daughter and his heir,
Medea, who was so wise and pretty
That no man saw ever a fairer woman, 1600
Was bidden to be the companion of Jason
At table, and to sit by him in hall.

Now Jason was a handsome man in sum,
With a lord's manner, of mighty renown,

As regal looking as any lion, 1605
Polished in his talking and affable,
Who knew well all the craft and art of love
With no books to show him its every turn.
And since Fortune owed her a foul mischance,
She fell deeply in love with this man. 1610
"Jason," said she, "for aught I see or know
About this affair that so busies you,
You've put yourself in terrible danger.
For the man who would succeed in this trial,
He will not escape, or so I do believe, 1615
From death unless I be the one to help.
Yet nonetheless, it's my desire," she said,
"To aid you in this so you shall not die,
But go home safe and sound to Thessaly."

"My dear lady," averred this Jason then, 1620
"That you have thoughts at all about my death
Or suffering, and do me this honor—
Neither my strength nor my efforts, I know well,
Will help me merit this my whole life long.
God thank you, since I may not or cannot. 1625
I am your man and humbly beseech you
To help me in this, and I'll say no more.
But truly, though I die, I'll not give up."

Then Medea began stating to him
Point by point the dangers of this venture, 1630
And of the struggle, and in what peril
He should find himself, from which nobody
Except her alone might preserve his life.
And to proceed quite quickly to the point,
These two made an agreement between them 1635
That Jason should wed her like a true knight,
And set a time when soon at night he'd come
Up to her rooms and there swear her an oath
Upon the gods that he, for friend or foe,
Should never prove false to her, night or day, 1640
As her husband, as long as he might live,
For it was she who saved him there from death.
And so it was one night they met together,
And he swore his oath and took her to bed
And in the morning hurried on his way, 1645
For she had taught him how he should not fail
To win the fleece and finish the struggle.

And she saved his life and honor for him
And gained for him a name as conqueror
Through the cunning strength of her enchantments. 1650

Now the fleece is Jason's; he's gone home
With Medea and the great wealth he won.
But she went without her father knowing
To Thessaly with Duke Jason, her love,
Who afterward brought disaster on her. 1655
For like a traitor he went on his way
And left two young children of his with her
And, alas, falsely betrayed her—because
He was always a chief traitor of Love—
And soon thereafter some time wed a third wife, 1660
Who was the daughter of King Creon.
This is the pay, this the reward for loving
That Medea did receive from Jason,
For her faithfulness and for her kindness.
She loved him better than herself, I think, 1665
And left her father and her heritage.
And this then was Jason's greatest prowess:
That never in his own day was there found
Walking on the earth so false a lover.
And this is what she said in her letter 1670
Where first for falseness she did reproach him:
"Why did I like better looking at your
Golden hair than the power of my troth?
Why did I like your beauty and your youth,
The infinite gracefulness of your tongue? 1675
Oh, had you died when you gained your triumph,
A great falseness would there have died with you!"

Ovid can well versify her letter,
Which right now is too long for me to write.

Here ends the Legend of the martyrs Hypsipyle and Medea.

The Legend of Lucretia

Here begins the Legend of the martyr Lucretia of Rome.[42]

Now I must recount the exile of kings 1680
From Rome because of their horrible deeds,
And especially of the last king, Tarquin,
As tell Ovid and Titus Livius.[43]
Yet that's not why I relate this story,

But rather to praise and save the memory 1685
Of the true wife, truly true Lucretia,
Who for her wifeliness and her resolve
Was not only cited by these pagans;
He who's called the great Augustine[44]
In our history had compassion for 1690
Lucretia, who died in Rome the city.
About how this came to pass, I'll be brief.
And of this matter, I treat but the gist.

After Ardea had been surrounded
By Romans who were quite resolved and strong, 1695
The siege lasted long, and little happened,
So they thought themselves at least half idle.
And, as he played there, Tarquin the younger
Began to joke (for he was light of tongue)
And speak about how this life was idle 1700
Since no man there did more than did his wife:
"And let us speak about wives—that's the best.
Let each man praise his as he is pleased to,
And with this talk let us amuse ourselves."

A knight named Collatinus then stood up 1705
And thus he spoke: "No, for there's no reason
To trust the word, but trust the deed instead.
I have a wife," said he, "Who, so I trust,
Is thought good by all who ever knew her.
Let's make for Rome tonight, see for ourselves." 1710

Tarquin answered: "This is what pleases me."
Then to Rome they go and quickly travel
To Collatinus's house, and there dismount,
Tarquin and this Collatinus as well.
The husband was familiar with the house, 1715
And unannounced they go inside the place,
For there was no porter at the entrance,
And at her chamber door they halted then.
This noble wife was sitting by her bed
In dishabille, for she feared no evil; 1720
Our book relates she was spinning soft wool
To keep herself from sloth and idleness,
As she told her servants to do their tasks,
And she asked them: "What tidings do you hear?
What say folk of the siege? What will happen? 1725
I wish to God the walls had fallen down.

From this town my husband is gone too long,
And my fear about this gives me such pain
That, like a sword, it stabs me to the heart
When I think of the siege or of that place.　　　　　　　　　　1730
God save my lord! I pray him for his grace."
And with all this she then wept tenderly
And took no more notice of their labors,
But meekly she did let her eyes fall down.
And this demeanor suited her quite well,　　　　　　　　　　1735
And her tears, which were full of honesty,
Quite embellished her wifely chastity.
Her look is worthy of what's in her heart,
For deed and image—they are in accord.

And at this her husband Collatinus　　　　　　　　　　　　　1740
Entered before she was aware of him,
And he exclaimed: "Have no fear, it is I!"
And at once she rose with a happy face
And kissed him, as the custom is for wives.

Tarquin, the arrogant king's son,　　　　　　　　　　　　　　1745
Took in her beauty and her demeanor,
Her yellow hair, her manner, and her shape,
Her color, what she said in her complaint—
And no art made counterfeit her beauty—
And felt such desire for the lady　　　　　　　　　　　　　　1750
That his heart began to burn like fire,
So insanely that he lost all his wits.
For there was no way, he thought, to have her.
And the more despair he felt about it,
The more he yearned and thought her beautiful.　　　　　　　1755
His yearning was nothing except blind lust.
In the morn, when the birds started singing,
He journeyed quite secretly to the siege
And strolled by himself, deeply thinking,
His mind always renewing her image:　　　　　　　　　　　　1760
"Her hair lay so, and this fresh was her color;
This way she sat, spoke, spun; this was her look.
This is how fair she was, this her manner."
Now to heart has he taken all these thoughts.
And just as the sea is roiled by a storm　　　　　　　　　　　1765
And then, when the tempest at last has gone,
The water's full of waves a day or two,
So, although her form was absent from him,
The pleasure from that form was present still,

Or, rather, not pleasure, instead delight, 1770
Or a sinful yearning filled with malice.
"Now, in spite of her, she'll be my lover.
Fortune always favors the brave," said he.
"However I make out, it's what I'll do."
And he girt on his sword and went his way 1775
And rode till he came to Rome the city.
And, all alone, he proceeded along
Till he came straight to Collatinus's house.
Down went the sun, and the day lost its light.
And in he came to a secluded corner, 1780
And just like a thief in the night he stalked,
With all the people there gone to their rest,
And no one giving treachery a thought.
Whether by a window or other way,
At once, sword drawn, he made his way in 1785
Where she lay, this noble wife Lucretia.
And she woke feeling some weight on her bed.
"What beast is this," she said, "pressing on me?"
"It is I, the son of the king, Tarquin,"
Said he, "and if you scream or make a noise, 1790
Or wake any person in this household,
By that God in heaven who made man,
With this sword I'll stab you through the heart."
And with that he made a move for her throat
And put the sword's point right against her heart. 1795
She spoke not a word; she had not the strength.
What should she then say? She had lost her wits,
As happens when a wolf finds some lone lamb.
To whom should she complain or cry aloud?
What, should she fight with a powerful knight? 1800
Men know well that women have no strength.
What, shall she cry out and perhaps provoke
The man who grasps her throat, sword at her heart?
She asks for mercy and says all she can.
"If you aren't willing," said he, this cruel man, 1805
"So may wise Jupiter preserve my soul,
I will go and murder your stable boy
And put him in your bed, and loudly yell
That I found you in such adultery.
And so you shall be dead and lose your name 1810
To boot, for in this you've no other choice."

These Roman wives so prized reputation
Back then and were so terrified of shame

That, for fear of slander and dread of death,
She at once lost both her breath and her wits, 1815
And she lay fainted, and waxed so deathlike
One could have lopped off her arm or her head—
She felt not a thing, neither good nor bad.
Tarquin, you who are a king's heir
And should, by your right and your lineage, 1820
Act like a lord and like a true knight too,
Why have you brought disgrace to chivalry?
Why have you treated this lady basely?
Alas, you acted like a lowborn churl!

But back to my theme. In the tale I read 1825
That after he left, this ill befell him.
The lady sent for all her family,
Father, mother, husband, all together,
And her clothes a mess, with her shining hair,
Attired as women at that time were 1830
When to a friend's burial they would go,
A sorrowful sight, in her hall she sat.
Her family asked what might be the matter
And who has died; and, ever weeping, she sat.
For shame, she can't force out a single word, 1835
Nor did she dare to look them in the eye.
But in the end she told about Tarquin,
This sad event, and all the horror too.
Impossible to recount the sorrow
She and her family all feel at once. 1840
Even if people's hearts were made of stone,
This would have made them take pity on her,
So wifely was her heart, and so true.
She declared that, for her own guilt and blame,
Her husband shouldn't bear the blackened name. 1845
This she wouldn't suffer, in any way.
And upon their faith, they all did answer
That they forgave her, for it was quite just
She bear no guilt; she had had no power.
And they then told her of many an instance, 1850
But all for nothing, for quite soon she spoke.
"That well may be," said she, "but forgiveness?
I wish to be forgiven for nothing."
And secretly she then brought out a knife,
And with it thereupon she took her life. 1855
And as she tumbled down, she looked about
And still paid attention to her clothing,

Because she was worried that as she fell
Her feet or some other thing might be bared.
She so loved chastity and respect. 1860

All in the town of Rome did pity her,
And Brutus swore by her undefiled blood
Tarquin should be banished as a result,
And all his kin too; and he called the folk
And related to them all this story, 1865
And had her borne openly on a bier
Through all the town for men to see and learn
Of the horrid deed of her ravishing.
Never again was there a king in Rome
After that very day. And she was thought 1870
A saint, her day always highly honored
As was their custom. Thus Lucretia died,
This noble wife, as Livy bears witness.

I tell this for she was so true in love,
And she did not change in what she wanted, 1875
And for her heart—stable, serious, kind—
Such as men always find in these women.
Where they bestow their heart, there it remains.
For well I know that Christ himself relates
How in Israel, as big as the land is, 1880
He found in all that place no faith so great
As in a woman, and this is no lie.
And as for men, look at what tyrannies
They constantly work. Who cares to try them,
The truest of men is shaky to trust. 1885

Here ends the Legend of the martyr Lucretia of Rome.

The Legend of Ariadne

Here begins the Legend of Ariadne of Athens.[45]

Infernal judge, Minos, once king of Crete,
Your number is up—time you entered the ring.
I write this tale not for your sake alone,
But to refresh once more the memory
Of Theseus's faithlessness in love, 1890
For which the gods in heaven above
Feel wrath and have taken revenge for your sin.
Blush now for shame as I begin your life.

Minos, who was the mighty king of Crete,

Which had a hundred cities strong and great, 1895
Sent his son Androgeus off to school
In Athens. And this happened to the youth:
He was slain studying philosophy
Right in that city, just for envy's sake.
Minos the great, of whom I am speaking, 1900
Came there to avenge the death of his son.
He besieged Alcathoe long and hard,
But, as it chanced, the walls were so mighty,
And Nisus, king then of that city, was
Such a valorous man he feared nothing. 1905
He paid no mind to Minos or his host
Until on one day an incident occurred
That Nisus's daughter stood atop the wall
And surveyed the manner of all the siege.
And, so it happened, there was a skirmish 1910
And her heart was pierced by Minos the king
For his beauty's sake and his chivalry;
So sore a wound it was she thought she'd die.
To pass quickly over how this turned out,
She did help Minos to capture the place 1915
So, after, the city was at his will,
And he could save or kill them as he liked.
Yet he repaid her kindness wickedly,
Letting her drown in sorrow and distress
Until the gods took their pity on her. 1920
But, for my part, that tale's too long to tell.

This King Minos conquered Athens as well
And Alcathoe and many other towns.
Here's the result: that Minos so oppressed
Those of Athens that they were made to give 1925
Him year after year their own dear children
To be killed, as you'll learn here following.
Minos had a monster, a beast wicked
And so cruel that with no hesitation
It would eat up any man who was brought 1930
Into its presence; there was no defense.
And in every third year, beyond all doubt,
They would cast lots. And as these would then fall
On rich or poor, he had to take his son
And make a present of this child, his own, 1935
To Minos, for him to save or murder,
Or let his beast at his will devour.
And Minos did everything out of spite.

His only joy was avenging his son
And making the folk of Athens his slaves   1940
From year to year, as long as he should live.
And home he sailed when he had won the town.

This wicked custom had been long observed
When King Aegeus of Athens was obliged
To tender his very own son Theseus,   1945
Upon whom the lot had come to fall,
To be devoured—there was no respite.
And the woeful young knight was led away
To the country of King Minos the strong,
And, fettered, he was cast into prison   1950
Until such time as he was to be eaten.
Well might you weep, o woeful Theseus,
A king's son you are, yet to this condemned.
I think that you'd be deeply beholden
To who saved you from this grim disaster.   1955
And, further, should any woman help you,
You very well should become her servant
And lover true from one year to the next.
But now to return again to my theme.

The tower where this Theseus was thrown   1960
Right to the bottom, dark and wondrous low,
Had attached to its wall a privy,
And this did belong to the two daughters
Of King Minos, who in their spacious rooms
Dwelled above, facing the main street,   1965
In much celebration, joy, and comfort.
How I know not, but it happened by chance
That while Theseus cursed his lot at night,
The king's daughter, Ariadne by name,
And her sister Phaedra as well, heard all   1970
His complaining as they stood on the wall
And gazed up at the moon, which was so bright.
They did not care to go to bed so soon.
And they felt compassion for his despair.
That a king's son be in such a prison   1975
And then be eaten seemed a great pity.
Ariadne addressed her kind sister,
Saying, "Phaedra, beloved sister dear,
Can you not hear this miserable king's son,
How pitiably he cries for his family   1980
And, too, for the poor condition he's in,

And he guiltless! Surely now, it's a shame!
And if you will agree to this, I pledge
He'll be helped, however we might do it."

Phaedra answered: "Certainly, I'm as sad
For him as ever I was for a man.
And to help him—the best advice I know
Is that we secretly have the jailer
Come up here and speak with us at once,
And have this woeful man come with him too.
For if he were to defeat the monster,
Then he'd be released. There's no other way.
Let us give his heart a serious test:
That could he be provided with a weapon,
Whether he'd dare to guard and save his life,
To fight this fiend and to defend himself.
For in that prison where he must descend,
You know well that the beast is in a place
That is not dark and that has ample room
For wielding ax or sword or staff or knife.
And so I think that he would save his life.
If he is truly a man, he'll do so.
And we shall also make for him some balls
Of wax and unspun tow which he shall cast
Into the beast's gaping maw and throat
To slake his hunger and trouble his teeth.
And that same moment, when Theseus sees
The monster choking, on him he shall leap
To murder him before they come to grips.
This weapon the jailer, sometime before,
Should hide quite secretly in the prison.
And since this place is shaped haphazardly
And has many secret paths for travel—
For just like a maze was it constructed—
I've thought up something to remedy this:
That by taking along a ball of twine
He may return the same way he has gone,
Following always the string whence he came.
And after he has vanquished this monster,
Then he will be able to flee the place,
And even take the jailer with him too,
And, home in his country, raise this man high,
Since Jason's the son of so great a lord.
This is my plan, if he dare attempt it."

Why should I speak of this any longer?	2025
The jailer comes, and Theseus does too.	
And after all this had been agreed on,	
Theseus then got down upon one knee.	
"You, true lady of my life," he declared,	
I, a sorrowful man, condemned to death,	2030
Shall not part from you after this venture	
Has run its course, as long as I do live;	
Instead I shall persist in your service,	
And, just like an unknown wretch, I'll serve you	
Forever, until my heart stops at death.	2035
I will forsake my heritage at home	
And, as I said, be a page at your court	
If you will promise me that in this place	
You allow to me then the privilege	
To enjoy nothing beyond food and drink.	2040
And for my keep, I'll labor afterward	
Just as you please, so no one, not Minos—	
Since he never did lay eyes upon me—	
And no one else might come to notice me.	
So cunningly and well I'll bear myself,	2045
So well disguised, so humbly will I act,	
No man in this world will recognize me—	
All this to have my life and your presence,	
You who have done this excellence for me.	
And I shall send along to my father	2050
This worthy man who is your jailer here	
So he may be rewarded and become	
One of the greatest men in my country.	
And if I dare to say, my lady bright,	
I am a king's son and a knight as well,	2055
Thus (may God so wish!) if it might happen	
You were in my country, all three of us,	
That is, were I to accompany you,	
Then you'd see if I'm lying about this!	
And if I am humbly offering you	2060
To be your page and serve you in this place,	
I will serve you there too just as meekly,	
And pray to Mars to grant me the favor	
That a shameful death should else befall me,	
And death and poverty to all my kin,	2065
And that my spirit might travel by night	
After my dying, stalking to and fro,	
And that I might bear the name of traitor,	

For which my soul may have to bear the shame.
And should I make a claim to higher rank, 2070
Unless you agree to grant this to me,
As I have said, may I die shamefully!
And mercy, lady! I can say no more."

A handsome knight to see was Theseus,
And young also, only aged twenty-three; 2075
But whoever did look upon his face
Would have wept from pity for his sorrow.
And so Ariadne gave this answer
To his request, to his expression too:
"For a king's son and knight as well," said she, 2080
"To be my servant in such low estate—
God forbid it, for every woman's shame,
And grant that such a thing never happen,
But send you grace of heart and skill of hand
To save yourself and knightly slay your foe, 2085
And grant that I may find you afterward
Very kind to my sister and myself!
I don't repent of giving you your life!
Yet were it better I became your wife,
Since you are as gentle born as I am 2090
And possess a realm that's not far distant,
Than if I allowed you, innocent, to die
Or permitted you to serve me as a page.
This profits not a man of your lineage,
But what won't a man do out of his fear? 2095
As to my sister, since it is the truth
That she must go with me if I do go,
Or else suffer the same death that I should,
Then you must truly at your homecoming
Arrange that she be wedded to your son— 2100
This is the final part of the bargain.
Swear this here, on all that you should swear on."

"Yes, my lady," said he, "else tomorrow
May the Minotaur rip me to pieces!
My heart's blood will be yours for the lending 2105
If you wish it. Had I a knife or spear,
I would let it run and swear thereon,
For then I would know you did believe me.
By Mars, in whom I chiefly put my faith,
So that I might survive and might not fail 2110
To win the day in this fight tomorrow,

I would never seek to flee from this place
Until you should see the actual proof.
For now were I to speak the truth alone,
It's that I've loved you for many a day 2115
In my country, although you knew it not,
And above all I desired to see you
More than any living, earthly creature.
I swear upon my troth, and promise you
That these seven years I've been your servant. 2120
Now I have you, and you have me as well,
My own dearest heart, duchess of Athens."

At his resolution this lady smiles,
And at his heartfelt words, and at his look,
And she spoke this way then to her sister, 2125
Very softly: "Now, sister mine," said she,
"Now are we duchesses, both you and I,
And joined to the royalty of Athens,
And both hereafter likely to be queens.
And we have saved a king's son from his death, 2130
Just as noblewomen always are wont
To save gentlemen, as they are able,
When the cause is honest and they are right.
I think no man ought to blame us for this,
Nor, after, have for us an evil name." 2135

And to make a short job of the matter,
This Theseus then took his leave of her,
And so all the terms of his covenant
Were met just as you have heard me read them.
His weapon, his string, which I have mentioned, 2140
Were laid by of the jailer in the lair
Where the Minotaur had his dwelling place,
Quite close by the portal of the entrance.
And Theseus was led off to his death,
And proceeded forth toward the Minotaur, 2145
And using what he learned from Ariadne
He overcame the beast and was his killer.
And out again he comes using his string
Secretly, when he has slain the monster.
And from the jailer he obtains a boat 2150
That he loads up with his wife's valuables,
And takes his wife, her noble sister too,
And even the jailer, and with all three
He steals away at night from that country

And goes on to the land of Oenopia, 2155
Where he had a friend he knew rather well.
There they feasted, there they danced and sang;
And he held in his arms Ariadne,
Who kept the beast from being his killer.
And there he soon got himself a new ship 2160
And assembled many country people
And took his leave and set his sail for home.
And on an island, midst the savage sea,
Where there dwelled no creatures of any kind
Save wild beasts, and a multitude of them, 2165
He ordered that his ships should make for land.
And on that island he stayed half a day
And said he needed to rest on dry land.
His mariners did just what he asked,
And, so as to make this tale a short one, 2170
When his wife Ariadne was asleep,
Because her sister was prettier than she,
He took that one's hand and went away
By ship, just like a traitor stealing off,
While Ariadne lay sleeping right there. 2175
And to his country he quickly sails on—
May the wind drive that man to the devil!—
And finds his father there drowned in the sea.

I care to speak no more of him, by God!
These false lovers, let poison be their death! 2180
But to Ariadne I'll turn again,
Who has, from weariness, fallen asleep.
Her heart, full of misery, may awake.
Alas, for you my heart now feels pity!
And right as the day dawned she did awake 2185
And felt about her bed and there found nothing.
"Alas," she said, "that I was ever born!
I am betrayed!" and she tore out her hair
And, barefoot, went quickly down to the beach
And cried out: "Theseus, my own sweetheart, 2190
Where are you now that I cannot find you
And might therefore be done to death by beasts?"
The answer she had came from hollow rocks.
No man did she see, and yet the moon shone,
And high up on a rock she climbed at once 2195
And spied his ship, sailing on the sea.
Her heart grew cold, and she spoke then these words:
"Kinder than you, I find, are the wild beasts."

Did he not sin to beguile her in this way?
She cried: "Oh turn back, for sin and pity! 2200
That ship has not all of its crew on board."
On a stick she then did put her kerchief
In hopes that he could readily see it
And remember that she was left behind,
And turn again, and find her on the shore. 2205
But all for nothing; on his way he's gone.
And on a stone she's fallen in a faint,
And she rises and kisses feelingly
The footprints he has made along his path,
And speaks then to her bed these very words: 2210
"You bed," she said, "that once did receive two,
You shall answer for two and not for one!
Where is it that your greater part has gone?
Alas, what's to become of wretched me?
For even though some boat might come this way, 2215
Out of fear I dare not go home again.
In this fix I can't tell what to do."

What more should I tell you of her lament?
It is so long the theme's a heavy one.
In her epistle Ovid does tell all. 2220
But I'll bring my tale quickly to an end.
Out of pity, the gods assisted her,
And in the sign of Taurus men can see
The stones upon her crown there shining clear.
I wish to speak no more of this matter. 2225
But in this way the false lover beguiles
A lover true—the devil pay his time!

Here ends the Legend of Ariadne of Athens.

The Legend of Philomela

Here begins the Legend of Philomela.[46]

God is the giver of forms.

You giver of forms, You who created
This fair world, and bore it in Your mind
Eternally before You began Your work, 2230
Why then did You make it to man's disgrace?
Or, if it was not then of Your design
To make something for a purpose like this,
Why did you permit Tereus to be born,
Who was so false in love and so forsworn 2235

That from this world up to the first heaven
There's corruption when people speak his name?
And, as for me, so grisly was his deed
That when I read his disgusting story,
My eyes grow cloudy and painful as well— 2240
The poison of long ago endures still
And infects the man who will think about
The tale of Tereus, whom I brought up.
Lord of Thrace was he, and kin to Mars,
The cruel god who stands with his bloody dart. 2245
And with a pleasant demeanor he'd wed
The dear, fair daughter of King Pandion,
Whose name was Procne, flower of her land,
Though Juno cared not to be at the feast,[47]
Nor did Hymen, the god of marriages. 2250
But to attend the feast these were quite keen:
The three Furies and their deadly torches.
All night among the rafters flew the owl,
Who is the prophet of bad luck and woe.
These revels, which were filled with song and dance, 2255
Lasted for a fortnight, or somewhat less.
But now to make short work of this story—
For I have wearied of telling about him—
He and his wife lived together five years,
Till one day she began to crave deeply 2260
To see the sister she long had not seen,
So filled with desire she couldn't speak.
Yet she began to ask her husband this:
For God's love, that she might proceed right then
To see her sister and come back at once, 2265
Or if she could not make her way to her,
That he would have her sent for, she begged him.
And day after day, this was all she prayed,
With a wife's meekness in words and manner.

This Tereus had his ships made ready 2270
And by himself soon went off to Greece
To his father-in-law, whom he then begged
To consent to this: for a month or two
Philomela, his wife's sister, could have
The chance to see Procne, his wife, this once. 2275
"And she will come home again directly.
I will be with her as she comes and goes,
And guard her as if she were my heart's life."

Old Pandion, the king, began to weep
From his tender heart, thinking to allow 2280
His daughter to depart and give her leave.
In the whole world, he so loved nothing else.
But in the end she has his permission,
For Philomela's salty tears as well
Start to ask her father for the favor 2285
Of seeing the sister she so longs for.
And in her two arms she embraces him.
And then, in sum, so young and fair was she
That when Tereus did glimpse her beauty
And her appearance, unlike all others 2290
(And yet in goodness was she twice as rich),
He set his ardent heart on her so much
That he wanted her whatever might result.
And guilefully he did then kneel and pray
Until in the end Pandion said this: 2295

"Now, son," said he, "who are so dear to me,
I here entrust to you my young daughter
Who bears the key to all my heart's life.
And greet well my daughter and your wife,
And let her then sometime take such leisure 2300
That once before I die she may see me."
And truly, he feasted the man richly
As well as all the people, high and low,
Who had come with him; great gifts he gave him,
And conveyed him right through the thoroughfare 2305
Of Athens, and brought him down to the sea
And turned back home—expecting no malice.

With speed do the oars propel the vessel,
And in the end it arrives in Thrace.
And he led her up to the woodlands there 2310
And made great haste in secret to a cave.
And in this dark cave, whether she wanted
To or no, he asked her to take some rest,
At which her heart felt fear, and she spoke thus:
"Where is my sister, brother Tereus?" 2315
And after this, she wept with tenderness
And quaked for terror, pale and pitiful,
And, just like the lamb bitten by the wolf,
Or the dove who's struck down by the eagle
And has made its escape from the talons 2320

Yet still is terrified and fearful too
Lest it be seized again soon, thus she sat.
But there's no chance it might be otherwise.
Forcing her, this traitor did the deed
That deprived her of her maidenhead   2325
Despite her, using his strength and power.
Lo, here's a man's deed, and by right it's that!
"Sister!" she cries with a quite loud voice,
And "Father dear!" and "Help me, God above!"
This avails nothing; yet still this false thief   2330
Has done the lady even greater hurt
Out of fear that she might broadcast his shame
And vilify him so that all would know.
For with his sword he has carved out her tongue
And had her then put into a prison   2335
From that time forward with great secrecy,
Keeping her to use as his possession
So that she could never escape from him.
Poor dear Philomela, woe is in your heart.
May God avenge you and grant this request!   2340
Now's it's time I soon make an end of this.

This Tereus has come back to his wife
And taken up that wife in his two arms
And wept piteously, shaking his head.
And he swore that he found her sister dead,   2345
For which foolish Procne feels such sorrow
Her miserable heart nearly broke in two.
And, weeping tears, I abandon Procne
And will recount more about her sister.

This miserable woman had learned in youth   2350
How to work cloth and embroider too,
And to weave on her loom a tapestry
Such as in days gone by women did weave.
And in brief she was allowed her fill
Of meat and drink, of clothes too all she liked,   2355
And was quite able to read and compose.
But she could do no writing with a pen.
Letters she could weave, back and forth,
So that by the time a year had passed
She had woven into a large wool cloth   2360
How she had been brought by boat from Athens
And how she'd been led off into the cave.
And all the things that Tereus then did,

She wove them well and wrote this tale above,
How for love of her sister she was served. 2365
And soon she gave a ring to a servant
And, using signs, begged him to travel
Unto the queen and take that cloth to her.
And with signs she then swore many oaths
That she'd give him whatever she might get. 2370

Right away this servant went to the queen
And took her it, told all the circumstance.
And when Procne looked upon this thing,
She spoke no words, for sorrow and for rage,
But feigned proceeding on a pilgrimage 2375
To Bacchus's temple.⁴⁸ And then very soon
She discovered her mute sister sitting
And weeping in that castle all alone.
Alas, the woe, the complaining, the moans
That Procne makes about her mute sister! 2380
In their arms they enfold one another,
And thus I leave them, dwelling in their woe.
There is no point in relating the rest,
For the sum and substance is that she was
Thus served, undeserving, who'd done no wrong 2385
Against this cruel man that she knew about.
You might beware of men, if it please you.
For even though he won't, because of shame,
Do what Tereus did and lose his fame,
Or serve you as a killer or villain, 2390
The time is brief that you will find him true—
This I'd say even were he my brother—
Except when he has no other woman.

Here ends the Legend of Philomela.

The Legend of Phyllis

Here begins the Legend of Phyllis.⁴⁹

By proof as well as by authority,
That wicked fruit comes from a wicked tree 2395
Is what you may discover if you care.
But now I mention it for this purpose,
Which is to tell you of false Demophoön.
I've never heard of one more false in love,
Except perhaps his father Theseus. 2400
"May God in His grace save us from the like!"—

So may the women who hear this story pray.
Now I turn to the main theme of my tale.

The city of Troy has just been destroyed.
This Demophoön comes sailing on the sea 2405
To Athens city, to his large palace.
With him come many ships and many barges
Full of his folk, a good many of whom
Are sorely wounded, sick, and woebegone,
Having remained a long time at the siege. 2410
From behind them rises up wind and rain,
Pushing so strong the sails can't withstand it.
For all the world he'd rather be ashore,
So does this tempest hunt him to and fro.
It was so dark, he could journey nowhere, 2415
And his rudder was torn off by a wave.
And because of this the ship sprung a leak
That the carpenter could in no way fix.
Like any torch, the sea burned insanely
By night and pushed him up and down again 2420
Till Neptune then had compassion on him—
And Thetis, Thorus, Triton, all the rest—
And guided him so that he made landfall
Where Phyllis was the lady and the queen,
Lycurgus's daughter, fairer to look upon 2425
Than any flower in the bright sunlight.
And Demophoön hardly made the shore,
Weakened, tired, his people suffering
With weariness, famished by hunger too,
So he'd been driven almost to his death. 2430
His wiser men had given him counsel
To seek aid and comfort from this queen,
And see what kind of fortune he might have,
And arrange then to borrow in that place
What might keep them from woe and disaster. 2435
For sick the man was, almost dead in fact;
Scarcely could he draw a breath or speak,
And he lay up in Rodopia to rest.
When he could walk at last, he thought it best
To make at court a plea for assistance. 2440
The men knew him well and did him honor,
For he was the lord and duke of Athens,
As Theseus his father once had been,
A man of great renown in his own time.
In all his land there was no man so great, 2445

And like the father in his face and build—
And untrue in love: it was his nature.
Just as Renard, the fox's son, does,
By nature he could do what his father did
Without lessons, just as a drake can swim 2450
When it's picked up and carried to the shore.

This honorable Phyllis greets him kindly,
Well pleased with his bearing and his manner—
But, since I've had much too much before this
Of writing of those who swore false in love, 2455
And to hasten along with my legend,
Which may God send me the grace to complete,
I thus pass briefly over these events.
You've heard enough said of how Theseus
Did betray beautiful Ariadne, 2460
Who in her pity saved him from his death.
To be brief with this, Demophoön did much
The same, travelling down the very path
That his false father Theseus had trod.
For he swore to Phyllis that he would 2465
Marry her, and plighted her his troth,
And plucked from the woman everything he could
After he was healed, and sound, and rested,
And he does with Phyllis just as he likes.
And if I wanted I very well could 2470
Relate all that he did, both up and down.
He said he must sail on to his country,
For there he would make ready their wedding,
As befitted her honor and his too.
And then he quite openly took his leave 2475
And swore to her that he would not tarry,
But in a month would there return again,
And as the true lord of that country,
He had himself ordained and took their homage
Well and familiarly, readied his ships, 2480
And home he went when next he was able.
But he did not come again to Phyllis,
And she paid so bitterly with such pain
That, alas, as the story reminds us,
She took a rope and became her own slayer 2485
After she saw Demophoön betray her.
Yet first she wrote him and forcefully begged
That he'd come to deliver her from pain,
And of this I'll rehearse a word or two.

I will not labor over him at all, 2490
Or expend a single quill full of ink,
For he was false in love, like his father—
May the devil set both their souls on fire!
Yet from Phyllis's letter I'll copy
A word or two, although it's just a bit. 2495
"Your hostess," she wrote down, "O Demophoön,
Your Phyllis, who is very woebegone,
From Rodopia must complain to you
About the term established by us two,
Which you have not upheld as you promised. 2500
Your anchor, which you dropped in our harbor,
Promised us that you would no doubt return
Before the moon made a single circuit.
But four times the moon has hidden her face
Since the very day you left from this spot, 2505
And four times has lighted up all the world.
But for all that, if I may speak the truth,
No Thracian current has to this point brought
The ship from Athens. It has not arrived.
And if you would choose to reckon the date, 2510
As I or any lover true should do,
I don't complain, God knows, before my day."

But I cannot write down all her letter
Point by point, for it is too hard a task.
Her letter was quite long and rambling. 2515
But I have rhymed passages here and there,
Those where, I thought, she expressed herself well.

She said: "Your sails do not come back again,
Nor does your word own any certain faith;
But I know why you have not come," she said, 2520
"Too free was I to you with my loving.
So all those gods on whom you falsely swore,
If their vengeance should fall on you for this,
You have not the strength to bear the pain.
Too much did I trust, I can well complain, 2525
Your noble lineage and your able tongue
And all your tears, deceptively wrung out.
How could you weep so craftily?" she said.
"Can such tears as those be untrue?
Now surely, if you would remember it, 2530
But little glory should fall to your lot
To have thus betrayed a silly maiden.

To God," she said, "I pray, and often have,
That this be the greatest prize of them all,
The most honor that ever falls to you. 2535
And when of your forebears paintings are made
In which men may perceive a bit of worth,
Then, I pray God, may you be painted too
So people who are passing by may read,
'Lo, this is he who with his flattery 2540
Betrayed, treated with contempt the lady
Who in thought and deed was his own true love.'
But truly, may they read something else too,
That in this you resemble your father,
For he surely fooled Ariadne 2545
With such skill and such subtlety
As you yourself used to beguile me.
And in this regard, though it's not nice,
You're like him and are his inheritor.
But since you seduce me so sinfully, 2550
You must look upon my body quite soon,
Floating there in the harbor of Athens,
Without a burial and without a crypt,
Although you are harder than any stone."

And when anon this letter was dispatched, 2555
And she learned how false and fickle he was,
In much despair, alas, she killed herself.
She was so pained that she punished herself.
Beware, you women, of your crafty foe—
For still today examples may be seen— 2560
And trust no man in love except for me.

Here ends the Legend of Phyllis.

The Legend of Hypermnestra

Here begins the Legend of Hypermnestra.[50]

There were once in Greece two brothers,
Of whom the one was named Danaus,
Who sired from his body many sons
In the way that false lovers often do. 2565
Of all his sons there was a certain one
He loved the most from among all the rest.
And when this child was born, this Danaus
Fashioned a name and called him Lynceus.
The other brother was named Aegyptus, 2570

As false in love as ever he did like,
And begat many daughters while he lived.
And one he begat was a dear daughter
From his rightful wife, and he had her called
Hypermnestra, youngest of them all.   2575
Because of her nativity, this child
Was born to all the best of the virtues.
All the gods were pleased to bring this about:
That she should become the corn from the stalk.
The Fates, the ones whom we call Destiny,   2580
Had so fashioned the girl that she must be
Pitying, sober, wise, as true as steel,
And all this quite well suited these women.
For although Venus gave her great beauty,
So influenced she was by Jupiter too   2585
That conscience, loyalty, and fear of shame
And preservation of her wifeliness—
All seemed to her worldly felicity.
Mars the red was, at that time of year,
So feeble as to be bereft of malice;   2590
Venus has repressed his cruel power.
What with Venus and with the oppression
By other houses, Mars's spleen is so weak
That Hypermnestra dare not wield a knife
In malice, though she'd lose her life therefore.   2595
Even so, as the heavens then did turn,
She had from Saturn some bad aspects too,
And these brought about her death in prison,
Just as I shall recount here following.

Danaus and Aegyptus both,   2600
Although the two of them were full brothers
(At that time kinship did not bar a marriage),
Were quite eager to conclude a match
Between Hypermnestra and Lynceus,
And fixed upon the day that it should happen.   2605
And all this was fully agreed upon.
The arrangements are made; the time draws near.
And thus Lynceus marries the daughter
Of his father's brother, and each has each.
The torches flame up, as do the bright lamps.   2610
The sacrifices are all made ready.
Sweetly smokes the incense in the fire.
The flower, the leaf is torn from the root
To fashion garlands and high coronets.

Full is the place with the sounds of minstrelsy, 2615
With amorous songs suited to a wedding,
As in this time was the custom of all,
And this was in the palace of Aegyptus,
Who in his house was lord, just as he wished.
And thus they bring the day right to its end. 2620
Friends take their leave, and homeward they proceed.
The night has come. The bride must to her bed.
To his room Aegyptus quickly sped
And privately had his daughter summoned.
After the house was empty of them all, 2625
He faced his daughter with a happy look
And spoke to her just as you now shall hear:
"My true daughter, the treasure of my heart,
Since the first time that my shirt was tailored,
Or from the fatal sisters my doom came, 2630
So near my heart came never anything
Save you, Hypermnestra, daughter dear!
Take heed to what your father tells you here,
And then behave more wisely evermore.
For, first of all, daughter, I love you so 2635
That all the world's not half so dear to me,
Nor would I advise what is wrong for you
For all the goods here beneath the cold moon.
And what I mean shall be spoken quite soon,
With a warning I give to this effect: 2640
That if you do not do what I will say,
You shall be dead, by Him who made us all!
To be brief about this, you won't escape
At all from my palace before you die
If you don't consent and do as I say. 2645
Consider: this is a firm conclusion."

Down cast her eyes this Hypermnestra,
And quaked as the green leaf of the aspen.
Like death her color faded, seemed ashen,
And she said: "Lord and father, all your wants, 2650
As I have strength, God knows, I shall fulfill,
As long as it means not my damnation."

"I will," he said, "permit no exceptions."
And out he brought a knife, sharp as a razor,
"Hide this," he said, "so that no one sees it, 2655
And when your husband has gone off to bed,
While he lies asleep, slit his throat.

For in my dreams I have been warned of this:
That my nephew shall be my murderer,
But which one I know not, so I will be sure. 2660
Say no, and we two shall have cause to fight,
As I have said, by Him I've sworn upon."

Hypermnestra nearly lost her mind
And to depart from the place without harm
She did agree; there was no other course. 2665
And after all of this, he grabbed a flask
And said: "Let the man have a drop or two
Of this to drink when he goes to his rest,
And he will sleep as much as you would want,
The narcotic and the drug are so strong. 2670
Now be on your way, lest he think you long."

The bride comes out with a very demure face,
As the manner often is with maidens.
To the chamber she's brought with song and revel.
And, briefly, lest this tale go on too long, 2675
This Lino and she were tucked into bed,
And everyone else hurried out the door.

The night has passed, and he's fallen asleep.
Then she starts to weep very tenderly.
She rises and with fear begins to quake 2680
Like the branch that's shaken by Zephyrus,
And all in Argos city then were hushed.
As cold as any frost she now becomes,
So much does pity weigh upon her heart,
And the fear of death gives her so much woe 2685
That three times she falls down in great turmoil.
She rises again and paces here and there
And gives her hands a very hard look.
"Alas, and shall these hands of mine be bloody?
I am a young girl, and by nature's law, 2690
And by my appearance and ever my dress,
My hands are not intended for a knife,
Especially to take life from some man.
What the devil have I to do with knives?
And am I to have my throat cut as well? 2695
Then I'll bleed, alas, and come to ruin.
And it must be this thing should have an end;
Either he will lose his life or I mine.
Now surely," she said, "since I am his wife

And have my loyalty, then it's better 2700
For me to die in wifely honesty
Than to be a traitor living in shame.
Be that as it may, in game or earnest
He shall awake and rise and go his way
Out this opening before day does break." 2705
And on his face she wept quite tenderly
And began to embrace him in her arms,
Then she shakes him, and gently awakens him.

And through the window he leaps from the loft
After she has warned him and given him help. 2710
Quick this Lynceus was, light on his feet,
And he ran from his wife at a good pace.
Alas, so weak is this ill-starred woman
And helpless that before she has gone far
Her heartless father has soon captured her. 2715
Alas, Lynceus, why are you so cruel?
Why did it never cross your mind
To take her, lead her forth away with you?
For when she saw that he had gone his way
And that she could not keep up with the man 2720
Or follow him, she then did sit right down
Till she was caught and taken in fetters.
For this conclusion has the tale been told—

Notes

The translation is based on the edition of the poem in Benson, *The Riverside Chaucer*.

    1. The reference is apparently to St. Bernard of Clairvaux (1090?–1153), noted mystic, church reformer, and theologian, known popularly as the Mellifluous Doctor. He was canonized in 1174.

    2. A fashionable game of Chaucer's time, memorialized within a generation of his death in the anonymously authored *The Floure and the Leaf*, was for courtiers to divide up into the parties of the "flower" and of the "leaf"; the two would then argue the comparative merits of their devotional attachment. See also lines 188–96.

    3. Chaucer here acknowledges his indebtedness to the love poetry of his French contemporaries, including Guillaume de Machaut.

    4. The flower is the daisy.

    5. The sun is in the sign of Taurus, the bull, the shape of which Zeus assumed in order to seduce Europa, the daughter of Agenor.

    6. The tydif is a kind of bird, perhaps the titmouse, though the word is obscure.

    7. Aristotle wrote two treatises on this subject, the *Nicomachean Ethics* and the *Eudemian Ethics*, the first of which was a much venerated text in the Middle Ages.

8. After Zephyrus, the west wind, raped the nymph Chloris, she became transformed into Flora, goddess of spring.

9. The narrator's etymology is correct.

10. The three-stanza ballade apostrophizes a number of figures from mythology, classical literature, and history. Of the women named, eight have their lives told in the legends that follow the prologue: Lucretia, Cleopatra, Thisbe, Dido, Phyllis, Hypsipyle, Hypermnestra, and Ariadne. Additional references are to the Bible (Absalom, Esther, and Jonathan), Homer and the Troy legend (Penelope, wife of Odysseus; Helen, abducted by Paris; and Polyxena, daughter of Priam and Hecuba, sacrificed to the spirit of Achilles), Roman history (Marcia, wife of Cato the Younger), medieval romance (Iseut, Tristan's beloved), Roman epic (Lavinia, whom Aeneas married at the end of the *Aeneid*), and mythology (Hero; Laodamia, daughter of Bellerophon; and Canace, who committed incest with her brother).

11. Chaucer may have written the surviving fragmentary Middle English version of the famous French allegorical love vision. The *Rose* is further discussed in the general introduction.

12. Chaucer tells the story of Criseyde, who betrays her erstwhile lover to take up with another knight, in his *Troilus and Criseyde*.

13. That is, as true as any compass.

14. The work is known more generally by the title *The Book of the Duchess*.

15. The story of Palamon and Arcite, friends and deadly rivals in love, is found in the Knight's Tale, one of Chaucer's *Canterbury Tales*.

16. Saint Cecilia's life figures as the Second Nun's Tale in *The Canterbury Tales*.

17. This work, now lost, was perhaps intended as another of *The Canterbury Tales*.

18. In Greek mythology, the hand of Alcestis is won by Admetus, who is able to satisfy her father's wish that he come to receive her in a chariot pulled by a lion and a wild boar. When Admetus is doomed by the gods to die unless he provides a surrogate, Alcestis offers her life for her husband's. In one version of her story, Hercules eventually rescues her from the realm of the dead; in another, Persephone, queen of the dead, takes pity upon her and reunites the loving couple.

19. Residences at Eltham and Sheen, now parts of Greater London, were maintained by the then reigning king, Richard II.

20. Like Guillaume in the *Navarre*, who does not recognize his lady as the grand figure Happiness, Chaucer here is ignorant about the identity of the lady who has saved him from the god's wrath, even though it was she whom he praised in his ballade.

21. The transformation of Alcestis into a daisy is Chaucer's invention.

22. Cybele is the great mother goddess, of Asian origin, eventually adopted by the Greeks and Romans, in whose religion she became an important cult figure.

23. Cleopatra is the only historical figure treated in the *Legend*. After the assassination of Julius Caesar in 44 BCE, Rome was ruled by the Second Triumvirate of Octavian (later Augustus Caesar), Mark Antony, and Lepidus. Though married to Octavian's sister, Antony, who had charge of Asia and eastern portions of Roman territory, left her to live with Cleopatra, queen of Egypt, who, once married to her brother Ptolemy, had some years before been the lover of Julius Caesar. Octavian regarded Antony as a traitor, made war on his forces, and defeated them decisively at the sea battle of Actium (31 BCE). When he was misinformed of Cleopatra's death, Antony killed himself. Cleopatra subse-

quently retreated to Egypt, where she tried to come to some accommodation with Octavian. These efforts failed, however, and she committed suicide by letting a poisonous snake bite her. Chaucer's version of these events is carefully calculated to portray Cleopatra in the most flattering light.

24. Note that Cleopatra's previous incestuous marriage and her affair with Julius Caesar have been omitted from the narrator's account.

25. The story of Pyramus and Thisbe was well known to authors of the Middle Ages. Chaucer's source for the details was likely Ovid's *Metamorphoses*. For a summary of the story, see *Navarre*, note 38.

26. The mythical founder of the city of Babylon, Semiramis was thought to have vanished, after a long and successful reign, in the form of a dove; she was then worshipped as a goddess.

27. Phoebus was another name for Apollo, god of the sun in the Roman pantheon.

28. Aurora was, in Roman mythology, the goddess of the dawn.

29. The narrator's gender loyalty is made humorously obvious here.

30. Dido's tragic love affair with Aeneas, the Trojan exile destined to desert her and found the city of Rome after marrying Lavinia, is treated in the sixth book of Virgil's epic poem, the *Aeneid*, which certainly was one of Chaucer's sources. Dido is also the putative author of one of the "heroines' letters" found in Ovid's *Epistulae* (also known as the *Heroïdes*). For details of the story, see *Navarre*, note 27.

31. Of the poet's two acknowledged sources, Virgil shows the greater sympathy for Aeneas—who is the hero of his epic, after all—while Ovid, composing letters of lament for women made to suffer by powerful men, is naturally more partial to Dido. In this context, it is interesting that the narrator suggests he will "follow" Virgil, while taking his "theme" from Ovid.

32. Minerva was the Latin name for Athena, the Greek goddess of wisdom.

33. Ilium was the Latin name of Troy (in Greek, Ilion).

34. That Venus plots with Cupid to make Dido fall in love with Aeneas and thus further the collective cause of the Trojans is a key element in the *Aeneid*. The narrator puts the burden of Dido's irresponsible and self-destructive behavior more on the woman herself.

35. In the *Aeneid*, Anna incites Dido's desire for Aeneas, providing yet another strong influence that forces the queen to act against her moral instincts. In the narrator's retelling, Anna plays the opposite role, attempting to restrain her sister from improper behavior.

36. Iarbas had been one of Dido's suitors, spurned when she determined to remain unmarried.

37. Neither in the *Aeneid* nor in Ovid is there mention, as there is here, of Aeneas's wearying of Dido's company.

38. Mercury was the messenger of the gods.

39. Jupiter was chief of the Roman gods.

40. Chaucer's sources for this legend are Ovid's *Metamorphoses* and *Heroïdes*, as well as a work in Latin by a medieval author, Guido delle Colonne's *Historia troiana*. For details of the story, see *Navarre*, note 31.

41. Chaucer refers here to the *Argonautica* or *Argonauticon*, composed by the Latin poet Valerius Flaccus.

42. The source for the details of the story of Lucrece (Lucretia) is Ovid's *Fasti* (Calendar), a long poem that records notable events for the days of the year. Shakespeare's *Rape*

of Lucrece treats the same legend. Lucretia was a Roman matron, famous for her virtue, who was raped by Sextus, the son of Tarquinius Superbus. Before stabbing herself to death because of the shame she felt, she enjoined her relatives, especially her husband Lucius Tarquinius Collatinus, to exact vengeance for her violation. In a revolt of the populace, the Tarquins were driven from the city.

43. Modern scholars do not believe that Chaucer consulted the famous histories of the Roman author Livy for this legend.

44. The reference is to Augustine, bishop of Hippo (354–430), one of the Christian Church's most important theologians.

45. The sources for this legend are Ovid's *Metamorphoses* and *Heroïdes*. For details of the story of Theseus, Ariadne, and Phaedra, see *Navarre*, note 30.

46. Chaucer found this story in the *Metamorphoses* and also, it seems, consulted the *Ovide moralisé*. Philomela and Procne were daughters of King Pandion of Attica. The husband of Procne was Tereus, who ruled as king of Thrace, but he developed a desire for Philomela, seduced her, and then cut out her tongue so that she could tell no one what he had done. But she worked the tale into a cloth she embroidered and then sent to her sister, who understood the message. In revenge, Procne murdered the son she had had by Tereus, cooked the boy's flesh, and served him as a meal to her husband. The gods frustrated the attempts of Tereus to take vengeance in turn, transforming the sisters into birds.

47. Juno was the divine consort of Jupiter.

48. Bacchus was the Roman god of wine.

49. Chaucer's source here is the *Heroïdes*. Demophoön, the son of Theseus, finds himself shipwrecked on the coast of Thrace where the queen, Phyllis, soon becomes enamored of him. Pleading that he must return to Athens, he promises to make his way back to her so that they can be married. But the term for his return to Thrace expires, and Phyllis, regretting that she has shamed herself with this affair, hangs herself.

50. Chaucer's source here again is the *Heroïdes*. Danaus sired fifty daughters, while his brother Aegyptus had fifty sons; they ruled over Libya and Arabia. When their father Belus died, Danaus took flight with his daughters to Argos in Greece, where his brother, who demanded that his sons be married to his brother's daughters, pursued him. Danaus, forced to consent, ordered his daughters to murder their husbands on their wedding night. Only one of his daughters, Hypermnestra, disobeyed, arranging for her husband to escape from the city. Danaus captured her and put her to death, only to suffer death himself when Hypermnestra's husband overtook and killed him. Chaucer did not follow his source precisely, swapping the roles of the two brothers.

Christine de Pizan

Le Debat de deux amans
(*The Debate of Two Lovers*)

❧

Si vous diray
Le grant debat, ne ja n'en mentiray,
De .ii. amans que je moult remiray,
Car leur descort a ouÿr desiray
Et leur tençon
Gracïeuse.
(lines 76–81)

Christine de Pizan (ca. 1364–1430) was both unique and very much of her day. The only woman author known from the late fourteenth and early fifteenth centuries in France, she wrote a large corpus of literature including love poetry, history, devotional works, and conduct manuals for women. Born in Italy, she was a young child when her family moved to France, where her father, Tommaso di Benvenuto, from the town of Pizzano, had been invited to the French court of Charles V as the king's astrologer and doctor. Although she wrote in French, she makes mention of her ties to Italy. She was very happily married at the age of fifteen to a member of the royal chancellery, a man named Etienne de Castel. After Etienne's premature death, Christine was left to fend for herself and her extended family. She began to write, taking advantage of her contacts among the French aristocracy to offer her works to wealthy patrons. She was well known and appreciated by her contemporaries, and highly enough regarded to have been commissioned by Philippe le Hardi, duke of Burgundy, to write the biography of his brother Charles V after Charles's death. After many years in Paris, she retired to the abbey of Poissy, a short distance outside the city, where her daughter had earlier joined the Benedictine Order.

In her writings Christine presents herself as a chaste woman of learning who found great satisfaction in her studies. She oversaw the production of her manuscripts and the organization of her works into collections. Christine knew the works of her French contemporaries and predecessors, particularly Guillaume de Machaut, and drew on them as models. She also knew sacred texts and the classical authors whose work circulated in a variety of compendia. Her earliest writing was love poetry, but she quickly began to work in other genres as well. Her best-known work now is undoubtedly her *Livre de la cité des dames* (*Book of the City of Ladies*), a collection of histories of famous women who are presented as exemplars of women's abilities and virtues. They and all their virtuous sisters are invited to come live in the City of Ladies, constructed under the guidance of three allegorical goddesses, where they will be safe from scorn and harm under the benign authority of the Virgin Mary. Christine wrote a sequel of sorts to the *City of Ladies*, entitled the *Livre des trois vertus* (*Book of Three Virtues*), in which she lays out the principles of proper conduct for women of all social classes. Her works move from the practical to the theoretical, the courtly to the learned, the passionate to the intellectual. She did not hesitate to engage in moralizing about the state of the country and the responsibilities of its leaders, writing to the queen Isabeau de Bavière, for example, to remind her of her duties. One of her boldest moves was to launch an epistolary debate with some of the most learned men of her milieu concerning the moral probity of the *Roman de la rose* (*Romance of the Rose*), which she, like all the other writers of her day, both drew on and responded to in her own works. Her last known work, dating from 1429, is in praise of Joan of Arc and was written before Joan was burned at the stake. It was a fitting conjunction of two powerful female figures in the last decades of the Hundred Years' War: the outspoken writer praises the inspired heroine, finding hope in Joan's successes for a France battered and divided by a long series of defeats.

Christine produced three debate poems including *The Debate of Two Lovers*, all composed in or around 1400. The other two are the *Dit de Poissy* (*Tale of Poissy*) and the *Livre des trois jugemens* (*Book of Three Judgments*). All are written in the same form of versification, a model used earlier by Guillaume de Machaut in his *Jugement dou roy de Behaingne*. This form consists of interlocking quatrains, or four-line units, in which the first three lines, all containing ten syllables, are built on the same rhyme. The fourth line is shorter, containing only four syllables, and introduces a new rhyme for the next block of three. The resulting verse structure is versatile: fluid and easy in its pace for storytelling, it also allows for dramatic emphasis, especially when the debaters take the floor. The three poems take advantage of this flexibility, incorporating narrative and direct speech in varying proportions.

While all of the debates ponder fine points of love, their content is quite diverse. The *Dit de Poissy* describes at length a visit by a group of young noblemen and noblewomen to a Benedictine abbey. Then it records a dispute, on the return journey, between a lady and a squire, each of whom claims to be the unhappier in love. In the squire's case, he has been rejected by the lady he loves but must bear the pain of seeing her frequently. As for the lady, her knight has been imprisoned overseas and she is powerless, unable to help ransom him or give him solace. In the *Livre des trois jugemens* we find a trio of somewhat shorter case studies of thwarted love, in which pairs of men and women explain their respective complaints. In comparison, *The Debate of Two Lovers* is the most theoretical of the three: at issue is the very nature of love itself.

The Debate of Two Lovers takes a broad view, asking whether love brings more good or ill to those who experience it. In one formulation of the theme, one of the characters asks another, "Dites, ma dame, / Vo bon avis de l'amoureuse flame, / Se joye en vient u dueil a homme et fame" (412–14) [Madame, tell us / Your opinion of the amorous flame, / If it brings joy or sorrow to men and women]. Such a large question gives rise to a wide-ranging discussion, and most of the work is made up of the extensive arguments each of the two debaters brings to his side of the issue. The arguments that Christine puts in the mouths of her characters show her learning. The main speakers, a knight and a squire, evoke dozens of mythological, literary, historical, and contemporary figures in support of their points, matching example for example in a display of erudition. The rhetorical nature of the conflict is evident in that most of the examples could be brought to bear on either side of the discussion. Indeed, the story of Tristan, one of the most celebrated of medieval lovers, is used by both debaters to prove opposing points of view. Especially when drawn from mythology, each example recounted by a debater includes only those aspects of the story that uphold his point of view. Once the speeches are over, the debaters ask the narrator, a woman-poet figure easily identifiable with Christine the writer, to judge their case. She declines, but suggests they ask her patron, the duke of Orleans, and she agrees to write up the particulars and send the work to him.

Much like the question of whether knights or clerks make better lovers, the topic of whether love is a positive or negative force was a tried and true topic for medieval debate. Alain Chartier's *Debat des deux fortunés d'amours*, for example, stages a similar discussion, using characters identified as "le gros" and "le maigre," the fat and the lean, to represent the two sides of the argument. In Christine's *Debate of Two Lovers*, the primary characters are two noblemen, one a mature knight, the other a younger squire. They are never given proper names, and in their respective opinions of love they quite simply represent their types: the older, world-weary man of experience argues that to love is to follow a perilous path, whereas the young, enthusiastic lover insists that if love is true, it can only be a force for good.

Christine, however, fleshes out these stereotypes by drawing fine, individualized portraits, complete with details of demeanor, conduct, and even clothing. The framework of the debate involves a lively soirée held in the month of May at a Parisian townhouse, an event attended by an assembly of beautiful, cultivated aristocrats. We see the dancing and flirtatious behavior in which they indulge, including first and foremost the high-spirited squire. He is clearly smitten with a woman present that evening, as betrayed by his amorous glances and the emotions that cross his face. But she herself, the narrator states clearly, stays on the sidelines because she is still grieving the death of her beloved (145–61). From that vantage point, she becomes aware of the knight who also remains on the fringes. It appears evident to the narrator that he, too, is enamored of a lady there present, but he is adept at hiding it, in part beneath a long cloak that masks both the pain he feels and a lame foot that prevents him from dancing. He engages the narrator in conversation only because courtesy demands it of him. And so they talk together quietly until the squire joins them and heartily entreats them to come outside with him to discuss "s'amour preste / Plus joye ou mains / Aux vrays amans" (359–61) [whether love brings more joy or less to true lovers].

Once settled in the quiet gardens, at a remove from the hectic festivities, the debaters present their cases, drawing on personal experience as well as the compendium of exemplary lovers a sophisticated contemporary audience would recognize. In demonstrating who has fared well or poorly as a result of love, they point to figures of classical myth and literature, including Paris and Helen, Hero and Leander, and Achilles and Polixena, but also examples from medieval romance, such as the chatelaine du Vergy. They also adduce contemporary historical figures from the milieu in which the poem was composed, as in, for example, "good Boucicaut the Marshal" (1585–86) and the "valiant Constable of Sancerre" (1594–95).

The inclusion of this last group of exemplary lovers, like the vivid nature of the townhouse setting and the particularized portraits of the two protagonists, is part of the realism with which Christine overlays otherwise well-known material for her audience. The numerous noblemen named as contemporary examples of chivalry constitute a list of many of the most elevated knights associated with the French court. In most instances they are mentioned very briefly, presumably on the assumption that a contemporary audience would know their accomplishments well enough to understand and appreciate the reference. The effect of this naming of real-life heroes renders the theoretical argument much more immediate and relevant to their concerns. It would have held appeal for Christine's readers to recognize names from among their peers and ponder the nature of love as a force in their respective destinies. In that way they would be drawn much closer to the material than if it remained purely a question of ancient or mythological heroes. And it was certainly advantageous for Christine to demonstrate her own knowledge of high society and to flatter powerful figures by listing them among praiseworthy examples. The result for this author who depended on the patronage of the aristocracy was to anchor the debate in her own day and help the poem make its way into the world and find approval there.

There are other aspects of the text that also put a highly individual stamp on it. The observers who witness the debate, for example, are one unexpected element. Their inclusion is well motivated within the fiction: once the narrator has agreed to go outside with the knight and the squire to discuss their question, she suggests for reasons of propriety that they invite along two other women, a "lady who hates malicious gossip and dishonorable deeds" (386) as well as a "woman from the town" (388). Their inclusion is designed to forestall any gossip that might arise at the sight of a lady leaving for a secluded spot with two men. This provision is a small detail, but it reinforces the persona Christine cultivates for her narrator/poet in this and other works, that of a widow of irreproachable conduct who is willing to record the love stories of others but is never implicated in such entanglements herself. It is entirely reasonable, then, that the fictional Christine request chaperones.

Their role is largely silent, although the knight does take advantage of their presence to teach the squire a lesson in courtesy when he defers his speech to ask the lady if she would like to pronounce on the matter first (407–14). She declines, and the knight begins his long disquisition. Once he has finished, however, she becomes less reserved. In an address succinct in comparison with those of the knight and the squire she expresses doubt that any man, no matter how well he loves, can suffer from love as much as the knight has just explained (914–1000). Men may complain of the hardship love inflicts on them, she says, but women who believe them are unwise. She recalls the character Reason from the *Roman de la Rose* who in conversation with the young lover debunks love, telling him in no uncertain terms to avoid it (961–77). And she closes, with somewhat acerbic humor, by saying that she has yet to see the cemeteries where one might find the corpses of all the men who have died from love.

The effect of this lady's speech is twofold. First, her reference to the *Roman de la rose*, the most influential and best-known romance of the high Middle Ages, situates Christine's work in the mainstream of love literature and legitimizes her own treatment of the subject. While Christine was a major participant in the quarrel concerning the *Rose*, taking a very dim view of its representation of women and what she considered its obscene language, her own love poetry was, like that of her contemporaries, indelibly marked by its influence. She may have been opposed to the views expressed therein, but her work belonged to the same larger tradition.

Second, by choosing Reason as her reference, the lady identifies her position as antithetical to the precepts of courtly love and introduces a note of doubt concerning the validity of the whole debate. In her opinion, love is not worth the kind of earnest dispute she has interrupted with her commentary. Although presumably a lady of Christine's own class, her remarks are frankly anticourtly in their tone. She refuses to enter into the spirit of the game, calling into question whether the debate has any basis in reality. Christine the author's stratagem is subtle and clever. Her intertextual reference to the *Rose* confers on her own poem the weight and authority that come with an association with this most influential of works. At the same time, however, it gives her the opportunity to allude to her opposition to it and use an element of it to denounce the empty pretense of courtly love rhetoric.

Not surprisingly, neither of the gentlemen arguing the case engages with the scornful lady on this issue. To do so would be to risk negating the premise behind their own endeavor. What Christine hints at with the intrusion of this character is a theme expressed much more explicitly in some of her other works, namely, that love is at best a frivolous undertaking and at worst can be dangerous, especially for women. She also characterizes love literature as a light form of entertainment, not serious enough to satisfy her more scholarly interests. In the introductory passages to this debate, in the context of her address to the duke of Orleans, she suggests that the kind of poem she is sending him can bring some relief to a careworn soul. She elevates its worth with an implicit comparison between the entertainment value of her work and the music of David, who played his lyre to appease the wrath of God (33–40), making the best of an inherently trivial subject matter.

And what of a resolution to the debate? With such comprehensive and compelling proof on both sides, and with equally polished rhetoric from both speakers, there is little to choose between them. We are given no answer to the central question, only the assurance that Christine's patron will know how best to assess the opposing arguments. In the end, it appears that the purpose of the poem has little to do with determining the essential nature of love and a good deal to do with the cultivation of erudite, witty eloquence that will amuse its fictional participants and its real-life patron and audience alike.

The very end of the poem returns us to a more sober thematic register. Christine ends it with an anagram: "Mais de trouver, s'aucun au deffiner / A voulenté, / Quel est mon nom, sans le querir planté, / S'il le cerche, trouver le peut enté / En tous les lieux ou est Cristïenté" (2019–23) [But if anyone wishes, at the end, / To discover / What my name is, without seeking too far, / If he searches for it, he can find it embedded / Everywhere where one finds Christianity]. True to the chaste, serious persona Christine creates for her textual alter ego, the anagram reveals the author's name embedded in the word *Christianity*. What better way for Christine to insist that, although she writes in the best tradition of the love debate, following in the footsteps of her poetic forefather Guillaume de Machaut and leading the way for Alain Chartier, her true interests lie outside the realm of such frivolity with much more consequential fare? Like the pragmatic woman character whose interjection threatens to deflate the proceedings, Christine refuses to endorse the game even while staging for us a masterful sample of it.

Christine lived in a period when major shifts were taking place in every realm of life—political, military, intellectual, and cultural. In many ways her writings give us an unparalleled view of these transitions. She uses medieval models and modes, like fixed-form poems and allegory, but imbues them with early humanist thinking that looks ahead to the Renaissance. She was affected personally by the turbulence of the day, leaving Paris for Poissy when hostilities between Armagnac and Burgundian forces led to civil strife in the city, and that infighting among French factions as well as the larger military conflict between France and England found its way into her work as well. The combination of light and serious themes in her corpus reflects a society that indulged in entertainments and ceremony of the most lavish sort even while struggling to renovate outmoded approaches to war and redefine the lines of power connecting king, nobility, townspeople, and peasants. Taken as a whole, her body of writing shows us the thinking of a time and place that were forging the new nation of France.

Le Livre du Debat de deux amans

Here begins the Book of the Debate of Two Lovers

Royal Prince, renowned for wisdom,
Highly esteemed, powerful and of great nobility,
Schooled and learned in honor and generosity,
Most gracious   4
Duke of Orleans,[1] worthy and deserving lord,
Son of Charles, the good and charitable king—
May his soul rest forever in heaven—
My respected   8
Valiant Lord, by your great goodness
Let my little tale be heard by you,
And let it not be rejected with disdain
For lack of value;   12
May your highness not hold it in contempt
Because I have acquired but little learning
Or because I have chosen poor material,
Something unfamiliar   16
To your wisdom, which heeds only language
That is entirely virtuous and wise.
But at the same time, it does no harm
To listen to things   20
On a variety of topics, in texts or commentaries,
And even those that contain
Joyful material, be they written in verse or prose.
Listening   24
To things that by their nature bring enjoyment
Can often chase away unhappiness,
For excessive worry can often prevent
A burdened heart   28
From finding consolation when it is too wrapped up
In those matters with which it is preoccupied;
Nor can the human body, however well it is conditioned,
Live constantly   32
In a worried state. I read in a book
That when David, who wanted to follow God's law,
Wished to be relieved of his sorrow,
He played   36
Most sweetly on his lyre, and he thus often calmed
God's ire; and hearing agreeable
Matters read aloud often brings joy

To the listeners. 40
And so there is no harm in devoting time or space
To reading or listening to entertaining things.
For that reason, excellent Prince, do not be
Displeased 44
With me for wanting you to look over
A short tale that I composed
With the intent that you dispose your heart
To take comfort 48
Somewhat. Now I wish to begin
To recount to you (may God help me in this endeavor!)
A great debate that I heard hotly disputed
By two lovers, 52
For this story of mine will be all about love,
And it will be heard by Frenchmen and Germans
And all other peoples who understand the vernacular.
However, this debate 56
Needs a judgment, and so I appeal humbly
To your noble heart that it might graciously deign
To decide the affair fairly, as it will know
How to do wisely, 60
For the lovers, in whom there is nothing that could be improved,
Request it and place you in charge,
Noble gracious duke, of the whole affair.
Moreover, they will trust 64
To your decision, for they know and believe
That all the judgments that emanate from you
Are just, even those that belong
To the realm of love, 68
Which so often makes young people change their ways
For good or ill, to their joy or their displeasure;
But this stage is natural in everyone,
For as long as it lasts, 72
And no one should consider it unwholesome,
For nothing that is given by nature
Can be taken away by anyone, according to the Scriptures.[2]
Thus I will recount for you, 76
Nor will I lie about it, the great debate
Between two lovers, to which I paid close attention,
For I wanted to hear their dispute
And their elegant 80
Argument, which was never contentious.
It was in May, in the mild season,
That there assembled in a very beautiful
And elegant house 84

Located in Paris, a joyful place,
A company of young people, handsome and eager
For enjoyment; not one of them
In that assemblage wanted anything 88
But amusement, as I believe without a doubt.
The entire company was very comely,
And there were many ladies who were not the least bit disagreeable,
And many young noblewomen 92
Well dressed, for that was their intent, and
Many noble maidens; and, lest I should lie,
There were more than thirty knights
And other people, 96
Handsome and noble, adorned with silver,
High-spirited and good-looking, well and nobly turned out.
All of them, men and women, were determined
To make merry. 100
There was more than one pair of excellent minstrels,
Who made the whole house
Resound loudly. This assembly should have pleased
Everyone, 104
For festivity and joy were at such a peak
That they were a hundredfold greater than in any other,
Nor was the group troubled by discord;
Instead, it was of one accord. 108
All sadness was banished from it.
And in a space well decorated and level,
Large and wide, clean, in no way sullied,
They danced 112
Happily, on the fresh grass.
There one might have seen many a pretty turn, many a leap,[3]
Many a fancy step, and many a dart thrown
With sweet glances, 116
And retreating into secluded spots by artful means,
And everyone played his part as best he could
In that which sweet Pleasure bestows on his followers.
Thus danced 120
All the men and women, nor did they tire of it,
And while dancing they entwined their hearts
By the glances they threw at each other.
Whoever might have seen 124
The beautiful women dancing with joyful countenance—
So gaily, with polished manners,
Wearing green chaplets of flowers and columbines,
Most becoming 128
In their charm, and elegantly disposed—

Laugh, play, feign complaint,
And talk at leisure, with composure,
And seen the faces 132
Of the lovers, changing color with every turn of the dance,
And putting on many airs,
That person would have valued highly their noble comportment.[4]
And then after 136
The minstrels, who played very well,
Throughout the rooms and in the secluded corners,
One could hear singing, high and clear, in lovely phrases,
Well modulated. 140
To put it briefly, in that spot there was so much
Laughter and playing that it seemed they had sworn
To continue the festivities
Forever. 144
And I, in whom all unhappiness has been lodged
Since the day that Death served me so very harsh
A portion, because of which I will never have,
In truth, 148
Any joyous pleasure in this world; instead, I will have
Black thoughts always because of the painful remembrance
Of the man I carry in my memory
Without ever forgetting— 152
May his soul be settled in heaven—
Who left me all alone; nor is my grief
Forgotten, wherever I may be, or lessened,
In any way— 156
I was seated on a bench in that place
Without saying a word, watching the entertainments
Of the refined, noble lovers, full of charm,
So full of joy 160
That for them it was easy to find comfort.
But I, whose mind was quiet,
Was of the opinion that among all the highly worthy men
In that place, 164
There was a squire, handsome in body and face,
Who was so very attractive
That it seemed he had a larger share
Of all joy 168
Than any other man there, as God is my witness.
For my eye was always drawn to him,
Admiring the gracious manner
Of his comportment, 172
For he danced and sang so very well,
And played with such pleasure, I tell you truly,

That it seemed as if the whole world belonged to him.
So happy 176
Was he, as if he had been blessed
With all the good things that ever brought man joy,
So joyful was his gay heart,
To tell the truth, 180
That he never stopped playing and laughing,
Or singing and dancing without pause.
But no one could have criticized his games,
So well did they suit him, 184
For they made all the others rejoice
And his entertainments were so elegant
That they gave pleasure to all alike.
He never spoke 188
Without laughing, and it seemed that he was flying
When he danced; but even though he tried to hide it,
He took hardly a step in any direction
Without casting 192
A tender eye humbly, without undue pride,
At a lady there present in whom all his desire
Resided; but with such subtle discretion,
Whatever he was doing, 196
Did he throw his glance, that one could not notice
It was her, more than any other, whom he was thinking of.
I did not think that she pleased him only a little,
For it seemed evident 200
That because of her he was in an amorous state,
Even though he avoided other people
As much as he could; but the amorous condition
Is hard to hide 204
For lovers, whom Love drives mad
From loving in excess, and makes them come and go.
To put it briefly, this young man seemed thus
Overwhelmed by Love. 208
But close to the bench where I sat, on the right,
There was a knight seated beside a window,
Who, on his left hand,
Propped up 212
His bowed head, as if much troubled
And lost in thought, and he had made merry but little;
He was neither joyful nor diverted,
Nor was he enjoying himself, 216
It seemed. He was not, however,
Ugly or aged; rather he possessed more beauty
Than anyone alive and he appeared very much given

To courteous behavior 220
And honor, and blessed with
Considerable youth, handsome and not lazy.
But it seemed quite clear that he must have little happiness
And little joy, 224
For I, who was sitting on the bench at that moment,
Watched his countenance carefully
Because I saw that he was so deep in thought
And without comfort; 228
Several times I heard him say, "Alas!,"
Very softly, and he could not have been tired
Of sighing, like a man who is caught
In a snare. 232
And accordingly, his heart was so constricted
That it looked as if he had just been exhumed,
So pale was he, or that he had been stabbed
With a sharp blade. 236
And even though he went around hidden
Under a cloak that covered his knowing eyes,
So that one could not see his one lame foot
Or his misery, 240
And no matter how loyal, discreet, and wise he was,
It seems to me, he could not hide
His feelings enough to avoid frequent tears
All down his face; 244
He could not be stalwart and firm enough
To disguise the bitter coat of arms
That Love gives to those he renders weak
And sickly. 248
And so that man sat there, just as I tell you,
Mournful, lost in thought, and rejoicing but little.
Yet, may Jesus Christ grant me paradise,
It inspired in me 252
Much pity to see him so undone,
For never had anyone, however close a friend,
Touched my heart half as much
As this man 256
Did, when I saw him there, all alone,
Mournful, lost in thought, and tearful. Nor did anyone
Notice his unhappiness, I think,
But I alone, 260
For the others frolicked ever
More and more, and this man sat apart
From the crowd, more unaffected than a recluse,
Nor did he think 264

That anyone was aware of the situation
That made him sad, for everyone there was dancing
Except him and me, and for that reason he did not cease
To be pensive.   268
But the reason he was so withdrawn
Was obvious to me, for more than six times
His color changed when near him was seated
The lovely figure   272
Of a woman, one in a thousand in her beauty and gentility.
Immediately, when she was near, this man's expression changed
And he followed her with his eyes, but his glance
Was so subtle   276
That no lady or gentleman there could, by any artful means,
Perceive it, although he had eyes for no one else.
I noticed this and saw quite plainly
That the pain   280
That troubled both his heart and his head
Came from that source, I know not for what reason,
But he never stopped sighing, over and over.
And so he stayed   284
There for a long time, and thus sustained much harm.
But listen now to what happened thereafter:
When he had daydreamed for some time, he revived
A little,   288
Like a man who has quenched his great thirst
Somewhat. And I, who noticed it,
Kept watching him; but if ever I was good for anything,
It seemed to me   292
From his glance and from the look on his face
That he became aware that I could see the state he was in,
And how he sat there as if transfixed,
And it pained him   296
That I had seen it. I do not know how it came about,
But he soon got up from that place
And came toward me and took the opportunity
To speak to me;   300
And I, who wanted to go to some lengths
To cheer him up, if I could possibly manage,
On account of the pity I felt for him, because I had seen
Him in such a state,   304
I, when I saw him approach the wall
I stood up without undue haste.
But no matter whether he was the son of a king
Or a duke or a count,   308
He knew well that good breeding entails

Courtesy, which makes fine people worthier
And which teaches, instructs, leads, and conquers,
And had taught him 312
The best of intentions. For then this gentle and wise man
Had me take my seat again and, without seeking any advantage
Of rank, he sat down beside me
On the bench, 316
Humbly, without putting on airs, this man who was white
And pale of complexion, whose face showed no color or blood
As a result of loving too greatly. He put his arm
Around me 320
And then said to me pleasantly,
"What are you thinking about here all alone? For you have spoken
Not a word, and I believe that you need no entertainment here
Other than 324
Your own thoughts. Why do you not go dance?"
And I answered, "But you, sir, I see you go forth
Very little yourself and yet you should find
Endless diversion, 328
In my opinion, for in this place there are no more than four
Who are younger than you, but nevertheless I see you
Enjoying yourself very little. I do not know what so greatly
Oppresses your thoughts." 332
And he, who wished to hide from me
The pain stored up in his heart, said
In measured words, "Certainly my joy
Is but fleeting. 336
I am so awkward that I cannot dance
Nor disport myself in other ways, and yet,
I am not vexed, nor does anything trouble me;
It is my manner 340
To be pensive, I am not trying to dissemble.
God instilled in me this character;
Whether it annoys or pleases me,
It is my nature." 344
And so we talked in quiet voices
And we had already recounted many an adventure
When toward us came purposefully the man
Of whom I spoke 348
Earlier, here above. He was not heavy of heart;
On the contrary, he was joyful. Laughing, he embraced
The other man, and bantered with him
Good-naturedly, 352
And they spoke for a long time about this person and that,
But the discussion turned to love.

The squire then said happily,
"At my request, 356
Let us talk a little about love and, right away,
Let each of the three of us be quick to pronounce
His best opinion on the topic, whether love brings
More joy or less 360
To true lovers;⁵ I pray you, with hands joined,
That we discuss it, and let no one overhear. At least
We can talk about that from which many have joy.
Let us discourse upon 364
What it is to love, where it comes from, and what it avails,
This love, which seizes the heart and conquers it,
What it is good for, and whether honor or shame comes of it.
Let each of us tell 368
What he knows about it, whether it is an illness
Or great good health, and whether the lover who serves a lady
Is a beggar. Let God curse the body
Of anyone who lies 372
Regarding his opinion, and who tells less than all
He might think about the ways of love.
Now it will become obvious who expounds best on the topic.
But I suggest that 376
All three of us go outside, over the threshold
Of that door there, and go to that stand of trees
Where it is green, to sit in a secluded spot
Happily, 380
In order to talk more privately,
So that no one overhears this disquisition on love
Except the three of us." And so we got up
Quickly; 384
But on my recommendation we summoned to come with us
A lady who hates malicious gossip and dishonorable deeds;
Further, for good measure, we took with us there
A woman from the town, 388
Pretty, agreeable, elegant, and courteous;
It was done at my suggestion, for whoever silences
The rumblings and rumors of gossips
Is very wise. 392
And so we left the house, and without stopping
Entered the beautiful orchard, which was conducive
To enjoyment, more lovely than a forest
With its very beautiful trees, 396
Which produce good new fruit in season,
And where the birds amuse themselves in spring,
And in a pretty spot, make his avowals there who might,

We sat down. 400
Then the man who was the less pensive
Said to the other, who was more careworn,
"Tell us, sir, for you are more composed
And the wisest, 404
Your opinion concerning love's service,
Whether it results in profit, joy, honor, or harm."
And the other man replied, "Good friend, it is customary,
With reason, 408
That in all circumstances and at all times
A courteous gentleman does honor to the ladies;
They shall speak first, dear sir, and we will be silent.
Madame, tell us 412
Your opinion of the amorous flame,
If it brings joy or sorrow to men and women."
And the lady spoke and replied, "By my soul,
I would not know 416
What to say; in fact, as far as I am concerned, I would advise
That you speak and I will listen willingly,
For no doubt I would not speak of it properly.
Have your say, good sir, 420
For I know you will be able to speak of it better than I."
And he replied, "I must not contradict you,
Nor may it please God that ever my heart should impel me
To oppose what you say. 424
Because it pleases you, my lady, that I state
My opinion, although I may contradict others,
Concerning the facts of love and the illness
That results from loving, 428
Whether more sweetness and less bitterness comes of it,
According to what I know and what I can surmise,
From experience and from inquiry,
I will tell 432
How I feel about it, and I will not lie at all.
Even though another would speak about it better
Than I will be able to do, I will give
My entire opinion, 436
If ever I knew or saw
The ways of love, by which hearts are ravished.
It is a desire that is never satisfied,
Which by means of pleasure 440
Comes to occupy a young heart, and make it
Choose love; from this is born a longing
Of noble desire, which comes to seize the heart
In such a way 444

That it becomes loving and full of ardor
And desirous of being loved as long as it lives.
But that painful wound is so large
That it distorts 448
All reason and alters so greatly
The man who is caught that the joyful becomes glum
And the glum embraces joy;
It often happens thus. 452
It is something that causes a man to become
Completely transformed, so that he forgets
Every honor and ceases to be valiant.
Many times 456
It makes him forget customs and rights,
And he does nothing but what suits him.
It is a siren who lulls a man to sleep in order
To kill him; 460
It is venom coated in myrrh
And a state of peace that becomes ever more fractious,
A harsh bind that neither displeasure nor anger
Has any power 464
To untie. It is willpower that works hard
To harm itself, a mind primed
To desire, by good means or bad,
Easy access 468
To that in which its pleasure lies.
And when one has it, it does not suffice,
For the weary heart is always at peril
If it loves strongly. 472
For should it happen that the lover so exerts himself
That he is loved, and he is given
Comfort, still I am certain that
This joy 476
Will never be so strong that Love does not send him
A thousand troubles in return for one sole way
To have pleasure, and he will never see his heart
Secure, 480
And whether he be young or mature,
Handsome or good, never will he see himself as
So blessed that he does not proclaim himself
Most unlucky 484
Many times, if he loves perfectly.
For Fortune, which sows discord,
Will subject him to many a situation
More perilous than that 488
Of a boat propelled by oars; but the unhappy one

Will not care a bit about the perils,
As long as he loses none of his pleasures,
Bought at such great cost.   492
Ah, rightful God, how much grief is borne
To those unhappy hearts in which love has taken hold!
When I think of it, I dread
The bitter tears,   496
The harsh sobbing and the deadly lamentations
And the sighs more cutting than sharp spears.
And if I must speak of it like a cleric speaks of war,
God knows it well,   500
Of what danger and what mortal torment
The lover must endure, be he young or old,
In order to do whatever most gains him favor
With his lady,   504
If he is truly ignited by the hot flame,
Which burns and consumes the lover through desire,
Before he is loved, I believe, by my soul,
That he endures   508
Many grievous troubles. I do not know how he endures
In such torment from such lethal wounds.
Nor does he place any care or desire
Anywhere other   512
Than where his love is lodged; and thus he forfeits his share
Of all the goods Fortune distributes
In exchange for that one thing he can share in but little
With any certainty.[6]   516
Thus has the unhappy lover made his earthly paradise
From that which most beleaguers his heart,
And no matter if he be king or duke or great master,
He must take up service,   520
Whether he likes it not, and serve his lady
And true love, before he has earned happiness.
And then there is an even harsher dictum
If he is rejected: 524
Now the wretch thinks he is dead, now he curses himself;
First Hope says he will have another chance,
And then Dejection returns and denies it;
He thus has no peace.   528
In all ways this love serves him
Unpredictable fare, and will never allow any rest
For the heart in which this desire
Is settled.   532
Now suppose that Love wants to please
The lover so much that in no event has he any

Cause of pain, nor need he concern himself with anything
But happiness, 536
And that he is loved just as much as he wishes
By his mistress, who keeps her promises to him
And remains loyal; do not believe that he is not in distress
All the same, 540
For Deceitful Spying, who quickly notices
The understanding between lovers, and perceives
From their countenance the truth of their situation,
Does not refrain from revealing it; 544
Very early, with great speed, he awakens
The gossips, may God grant them an unhappy lot,
Who make Jealousy lie in wait at the pass
And erect barriers 548
And traps against the sweet pleasures of the lovers.
At that point, very often, rumors and arguments
Begin, much worse than those about land
Or possessions. 552
Dear Lord God, who could imagine
The great torment that is imposed
On the poor lover, who can have no good
Because of the talk 556
Of the gossips, who prevent him from going
To the woman he loves and wants to conceal!
Most severely do they cause the lover to suffer,
Those gossips, 560
Or the jealous one, who is very harmful to him.
Together, they take from him his gentle entertainments,
Which makes him so unhappy that he lies in bed
In despair 564
On many occasions, and he takes to bed completely,
In great danger of death, if he has no other way
To work it out, nor hope
That he might otherwise 568
See the woman on whose account his heart pains him.
There is another thing very harmful
To lovers, which causes them grief:
This is jealousy, 572
Which makes the unhappy lover forget
All courtesy, and makes him worry so greatly
That he is like a man in a frenzy,
Both far and near. 576
If he perceives that another lover is disposed
To love that lady to whom his heart is tied,
You may know for a fact that if he sees her pay him

Any attention,   580
It will alter his mind, his color and his countenance,
Nor do I believe that any other misfortune surpasses
Such a deadly anxiety, even though he pretends to be
Joyful and gay.   584
It is death and mourning, which cannot be soothed,
Nor can it find any peace,
The heart burdened with such torment.
It is a fury   588
Most bitter, which disposes the man
To do a lot of harm and damage.
Many men have lost honor and inheritance
As a result.   592
He who is jealous is up to no good.
He would be better off lying dead,
But great love has given him this reward
In recompense,   596
For excessive love makes this gift bitter
For the poor lover, who gives away his heart.
It seems to him that he stands to lose too much
If another man enjoyed   600
The possessions that he sees cost him so dearly.
But surely if the unhappy man had to die,
He would not share it even if he knew
That his lady   604
Had renounced and abandoned him, the lady in whom
He has placed his whole heart, since love conquered him
By means of a glance that originated in the lovely eye
That he prizes so highly,   608
And since he devoted himself to the lady, so well-mannered,
And since she accepted his love.
She must never be blamed for it,
It seems to him,   612
For anything in the world, but he accumulates all the troubles
In his weary heart, which trembles and sweats from anger
And often hates and then recovers its love;
It is a difficult dance   616
And a very strange life and convention,
And it all results entirely from love.
Thus within himself he has no peace or harmony,
Instead he is mad with rage,   620
The unhappy, jealous lover, when he hears tell
Or perceives that his lady is attracted
To another love, she of whom he can hear no ill spoken,
And then leaves him.   624

He is in greater servitude than a dog on its leash,
Led by the trainer, who does not let him loose;
Just so is he led by the lady who gives him little slack
In his captivity. 628
Ah, what a love is this, that one cannot dislodge
From the suffering heart, however much damage it might do!
One ought to rage in intense grief
That one is obliged 632
To love, from which bad must come, of necessity,
And that the unhappy lover remains
An obedient servant, no matter what harm he sustains,
Is a great marvel. 636
Love, O Love, there is no one who can escape your sorrow!
He who serves you rests little and is very vigilant,
And he must work hard, whether he wants to or not,
The man who is your familiar. 640
But let us still look at the luckiest,
The best loved and those who do not suffer
The wounds of the jealous who are steeped in bitterness.
Are they exempt 644
From these great ills? I do not believe so;
Instead many lost body and soul to it,
If I remember, and if I recall,
When they died 648
For such a love, in France and in Paris
And elsewhere. In such a way have many lovers
Been destroyed in former times; even Paris,[7]
Who made off with 652
Lady Helen in Greece, with considerable trouble,
Because of which Troy, which was such a splendid city,
Was then burned, destroyed, and filled with sorrow,
In which perished 656
The highest and most noble paragons of chivalry
The world has ever known, as well as such great nobility,
Even for Paris love was cruelly compensated,
And no mistake, 660
For Telamon killed him in the battle.[8]
And two other lovers, let me not forget,
Were killed, just as Ovid lays it out
In one of his books,[9] 664
By the kind of love that intoxicates foolish hearts,
For they often met to enjoy themselves
And to follow the dictates of their hearts
In a grove 668
By the name of Limaux: there, the wild beasts

Devoured the lover, which was a great shame.
And Pyramus,[10] that generous and courteous youth,
And the very lovely   672
Sweet Thisbe, the young maiden,
Did they not kill themselves by the fountain
Underneath the white mulberry tree? He died for her
And she likewise   676
Killed herself for him, which made the mulberry darken
Out of pity for the manner in which they died.
Thus did grievous death strike down the two youngsters
Because of excessive love.   680
Leander,[11] also, perished piteously
At sea, in order to protect from shame
The beautiful Hero, who wanted to claim him as her own;
In the dark of night   684
The unfortunate lover undertook this adventure,
To cross the sea in nothing but his shirt,
Until one time, by great misfortune,
He drowned there   688
In stormy weather. Behold, behold
How they are treated, the unfortunate lovers,
Who are taken and attended by Love.
What torment they have!   692
And Achilles, too, did he not die
For Polyxena, when he put his faith in
A vain promise, which quickly brought him death?[12]
Was Reason   696
Not dead and asleep in him
When he chose as his lady and lover
The woman who was his mortal enemy?
Great harm it brought him.   700
This was the work of Love, by whom many perish,
But who smiles when misfortune strikes people.
And this love took gravely by surprise
Aesacus,[13]   704
Son of the good king Priam, who was so vanquished
By excessive love that, without searching for his shield,
He jumped into the sea, for he was most enraged
That he had been refused   708
By the woman of whom he had long been dreaming;
The tales that have recounted this story
Say that when he dove he was disguised
And transformed.   712
As soon as he had plunged into the water
He was changed into that bird;

For love was he changed into that form,	
And as a result,	716
His noble body never had any other funeral bier.	
One can still see him in many rivers	
Where he demonstrates how to drown.	
The gods of that time	720
Altered his body thus as a reminder.	
But let us look at yet other lovers	
Who were destroyed and killed and exiled	
By love:	724
Iphis,[14] too, was so beset by it,	
By such a love, which had assailed him so	
That he hanged himself, like a man ill-advised,	
At the doorstep of the woman	728
Who had refused him with a cruel response	
Most harshly, and because of that event,	
The poor man killed himself; but the gods took	
Revenge on the evil woman,	732
For they turned her cruel body	
Into a statue of hard stone; and many women	
Saw it and took a lesson from it,	
As is right.	736
And in Rome, for a similar reason,	
A young man killed himself after making	
His declaration, in what season I do not know,	
To his beloved.	740
But that wicked woman, in an ill-bred manner,	
Refused him, and he, in a fit of rage,	
Pierced his flesh there before her	
With sharp knives;	744
Thus did he die. But in more recent times,	
Now let us see, regarding Tristan,[15] who was handsome,	
Courageous and valiant, loving and loyal,	
To what end	748
He came, for having loved well with a loyal, refined heart.	
Did his uncle not spy on him in order	
To kill him, and then in the end	
Cause his death?	752
But this love so counseled Iseut	
That she perished in the arms of her lover;	
By my troth, here is a pitiful end	
For two lovers.	756
And Kaherdin,[16] just as the romance tells us,	
Did he not die blacker than ink	
For such a love? And so the account of his tale	

Was full of pity. 760
Even since then, let us look at the love
Of the Chatelain de Coucy,[17] to see if he took comfort
From love. I believe that with great pleasure
He enjoyed it, 764
But the lady of Fayel, who considered him
Entirely her own, I think, paid dearly for it,
For once she knew that he was dead, she had no reason
To wish to live. 768
And then there is the very beautiful, accomplished chatelaine
De Vergy,[18] who wanted nothing
But the one to whom she had pledged
Faithful love; 772
But she and he were badly compensated
For loving greatly, for cold death was all they got.
Many have done the same, in private chambers and public rooms,
With great pain 776
Because of such love, which makes one change color
Frequently, whether it be good sense or folly,
Perspire in the cold and shiver in the heat.
But I will stop here 780
For the sake of brevity, for if I named all of them for you
It would take me, I believe, a year's time.
But there is such a huge amount of perils
That they are innumerable 784
With this kind of love, which passes like a shadow
And so constrains and burdens the unhappy heart
That it cannot count or number its misfortunes!
How many forms 788
The travails of lovers take:
Some have sought hidden ways
To find happiness, but have encountered troubles
Unexpectedly, 792
One because of denunciation, the other by a change of heart;
Another can find no relief;
Another, through not conducting himself with discretion,
Lies in a faint, 796
In many cases, and there are those who have placed
Their love too high, for which they are called
False and disloyal, and are locked in prison
Or mutilated, 800
And those who have lost their heads
In various ways, and many other misfortunes
Have come every day to those
Who are attached 804

In such a way; it is a common thing.
For such love many are carried on their biers,
Who pay too dearly for this love
In many places.   808
He who wanted to recount all such cases
That occur would have to devote a long time to it.
But it occurs very often, be it right or wrong,
Which is a pity.   812
How many rumblings are heard in marriages
Because of such love, which overcomes the foolish and the wise,
For where love takes hold, there is no heart strong enough
That love cannot change it.   816
And so, often the least likely falls in love
And abandons his home life in exchange;
It intertwines hearts in a curious fashion,
With no appeal   820
To reason, nor does it respect season,
Time or place. It is the glowing coal of love
That causes even the wisest to commit
Many a wrong.   824
It is the pitiful and unfortunate pilgrimage
That made Paris take to sea by boat,[19]
Where he kidnapped Helen of the beautiful face
Who was judged   828
Harshly by the venerated Venus
And by Cupid, her son, who has brought about
Many a love, as a result of which many have had
Their heart   832
And their entrails pierced, and not for use in divination.
Whatever the beginnings of love,
The end is always pitiable.
Flee, flee   836
This love, young men! And see
Just how ill served one is by it.
For God's sake, do not believe its promises,
For waiting on love   840
Is more costly than any other obligation.
No one embraces it without afterward repenting,
For the path of love is very dangerous,
You must know, without a doubt,   844
And it breaks faith all too easily.
It is a dark passageway, where he who undertakes it
And naively makes his way cannot see a thing,
And this is no lie.   848
So much grief comes of it, for it is an illusion,

It holds the leash tighter than that on a sparrow hawk,[20]
And harm comes of it, and most of it, I tell you,
Is proven fact.   852
Believe the man who has experienced it:
I did not, for all that, behave sensibly
In this situation; instead I was foolish and blameworthy,
That is my blunder.   856
But, by the same token, a fool can teach a wise man,
And he who has gone on a distant voyage
Can well explain how one takes shelter there
In many ways.   860
He who wants to take it as a warning, I advise him to,
For it happens this way every day.
But the foolish lover neither sees nor is mindful of
The peril;   864
He puts his life in danger,
And cannot quench the great fire and burns himself badly;
Instead this love stalks him and in its artful way
Captures the lover   868
By the pleasure he gets from loving.
It has such a hold on him that he knows not if he errs
Or if he acts correctly, and if anyone reproaches him for it,
He becomes angry   872
Rather than being grateful; the man has his ears
So full of moss and so devoid of reason
That when he hears something bitter, it seems to him
Something sweet,   876
And he mistakes his stepmother for his real mother;
Happiness seems to him to be misery,
And he is mired in misery and servitude;
Is he not asinine?   880
This is how love renders blind the foolish lover,
Who wears a sieve on his head for protection[21]
And believes he sees the sun shining when the weather
Is cloudy,   884
And thinks well of anything that pleases his eye,
That is what he is like. I wish to say what I say,
However, not because I do not have the desire
To serve love,   888
Nor to rebuke the man who wishes to enter love's service,
But only to say how to come to terms with it
For those who want to pledge their loyalty to love
With a certain heart.   892
And so, my lady, and you, fair good companion,
You can hear that the lover has far fewer

Of love's pleasures, if he is truly smitten,
Than he has joy; 896
This is known to those whom love constrains and binds
With his ties, which drives many men mad.
I should know it myself, for I suffered grievously
When I was trapped 900
In that situation; I am still not entirely
Free of it, and as a result, I have quietly suffered
Many a cruel blow beneath my cloak,
With great torment. 904
But I believe that no one derives so much good from it
That he entirely escapes this sort of pain,
As I have exhorted and said to you here;
It is not a tall tale." 908

When the courtly and amiable knight
Had finished his noteworthy speech,
Which many would believe to be true
And well told, 912
Spoken at a good pace, neither too slowly nor too fast,
The lady, who had listened to him carefully, then
Began again and said, "If I have followed
Your speech, 916
Love, by all rights, subjects lovers
To a rigorous schooling, a process neither soft nor sweet,
As I understand it, and which drives many a man mad,
With little reason. 920
But in my opinion, I believe there is hardly an abundance
Of lovers captive in such a prison,
Even though many go about
Telling their tales, 924
First here, then there, to the ladies; for all that, however,
Their heart is not in it, nor do they stay constant
In one place, even though they squander
Their words 928
At considerable length; but I do not believe that anyone
Enslaves himself to it so severely, nor ever serves
So loyally and with such unswerving thought
Both love and his lady. 932
And, saving your grace, by my soul,
I do not think that anyone is set ablaze by such a flame
That he has so much grievous suffering for a woman.
But it is 936
A common tale, told to women
To persuade them, and it does not represent

Anything real; and she who listens
To such language, 940
In the end is considered less than wise.
And as for me, I maintain that it is simply a custom
To speak thus of love, for amusement
And to pass the time, 944
And if it were true, what I hear said,
That in the old days lovers were in fact
This sincere, it must be more than a hundred years,
To my way of thinking, 948
Since this was the case; it is neither today nor yesterday
That they are thus afflicted. Rather, lovers know
How to further their cause by pleading their case
And speaking well, 952
And if, in times gone by, they languished and died
Of it, and even the happiest of them
Suffered many painful ills,
As you say, 956
I think that these days their pains are slight.
In romances they are written up
As one might wish and described properly
In long passages. 960
The *Romance of the rose* spoke of it
At great length,[22] and also comments on
That love, such as you have described it
In this place, 964
When Reason, who is very threatening,
Lectures the foolish lover who embraces such a love,
And tells him most excellently that even the greatest joy
From that kind of love 968
Is worth little and passes quickly, and shows the lover
The way to rid himself of it; and Reason says quite rightly
That it is something that misleads the lover greatly,
A harsh scourge, 972
And that it is loyal disloyalty,
And a loyalty too disloyal,
A great peril on which founder
The noble and the royal 976
And everyone who goes near it.
Thus did she explain it, but I think that very few people
Take heed; instead, all anyone wants is money
And to live the easy life. 980
And who could live thus, in the misery
You have described? I believe, by Saint Nicasius,[23]
That there is no man alive—let no one take offense—

Who could withstand 984
The ills that I hear you recount here,
However strong he might be, without dying of them.
But I have not yet heard tell where lie
The cemeteries 988
In which are buried those whom true love
Has put to death and who, on account of such a situation,
Have taken to their beds or are carried in litters
Before the saint 992
From whom this harm comes; and no matter what many people say,
I believe that no one loves except by choice.
I do not say this to contradict your speech
And your lament, 996
With all due respect, nor do I challenge
That it could be thus, but I think one must look hard
To find those who have been served so poorly
By loving greatly." 1000
Then the man who had not yet had to speak,
The squire in whom there was no hint of bitterness,
Spoke as follows, as you will hear me affirm
And recount briefly: 1004

"Fair gentle companion and friend, and dear lord,
I am astonished, nor can it satisfy me,
That you say that the worst of ills
Is the one that comes 1008
From loving lovingly; if I recall,
You said that the lover becomes completely
Doleful and pensive when this love crops up
In his thoughts, 1012
And even for the happiest, their joys are often
Ended, and sorrows amassed
Instead of laughter. And you value
Very little the joys 1016
That come to the lover in many ways,
By sweet desire, and by quiet thoughts,
And in many other situations, and nonetheless
All the pleasure, 1020
As opposed to the harm, which comes from desire
And from serving one's lady for a long time
You prize little. To anyone who hears you pronounce,
It would seem 1024
That the loyal lover who loves
With all his heart would never have any good;
He who heard you would be terrified

To love, most assuredly, 1028
If he could expect to be so rewarded for his efforts.
If it were thus, surely no one would ever love,
If such hardships were given him
And no reward. 1032
There is no man who would want to commit himself
To such a bond; he would be better off drowning
Than submitting and proffering himself
To such vexation. 1036
But concerning everything I have heard you recount,
With all due respect, I maintain just the opposite,
And that more good than harm can come from loving
Without restraint 1040
To the true lover who wants
To comport himself properly and remain loyal.
As for me, I maintain and wish to contend
That from love come 1044
All the pleasures that keep a man happy
And all the rewards that belong to the good.
They are well schooled by it and retain every honor,
Those courtly lovers 1048
Who love faithfully in order
To become more worthy and to have, in due time,
Joy and pleasure; I do not believe that in the end
They come to any harm. 1052
I agree that this love comes
From honest desire, but it should not, by rights,
Be held accountable for keeping the lover sad and doleful.
Now suppose 1056
That he is not loved, or that he is not daring enough
To declare it to the lady in whom he has placed
His whole heart, and that he never stopped
Loving without artifice, 1060
If he does right, there is no reason he should play at
Grieving. Let us assume that he is rejected:
In that case, if he behaves reasonably,
Good hope 1064
Should sustain him, wherever he is, in patience,
And he need not, on this account, flee from France
Or out of despair subject his body
To a sad death. 1068
Such unhappy adventures simply do not happen,
Saving your grace, nor is such injustice done
To a man who tries hard to love well,
As you would have it; 1072

Rather, Love pays such good wages
To his servants that their troubles
Are very small compared with the great, unparalleled joys
That he gives them in return. 1076
For when a lover surrenders himself to true love,
Which welcomes him and guarantees him protection
Against all ills, like a close relative,
It fills him 1080
With sweet thoughts that greatly enrich him,
Which remind him of the beauty he has chosen
As his lady and the sweetness that emanates from her
And all her actions. 1084
Then the lover is all replenished with joy,
When he remembers the perfect, elegant body
Of the great beauty, and that is what makes the condition
Of perfect love 1088
Bearable for him, and the hope that tutors him,
And tells him that the close bond
Will still be established, never to be undone,
Between him and her. 1092
And in this way, always hopeful, he serves the good
And comely love who frequently renews
His sweet pleasures. For if he can hear
Some bit of news 1096
That gives him hope of having what he wants,
Or if he is looked at by her more often than he is used to,
You may be certain that never does he grieve so much
That the comfort 1100
Is not still greater than all the discomfort,
Nor will desire ever prick him so strongly
That he will not have hope and sweet thoughts in good supply,
Which comfort him. 1104
This love removes all twisted thoughts
From the lover, and incites him to all good;
It takes great pains to be thus
For good and meritorious lovers. 1108
If he loves as he should, he will become
Courteous and welcoming, and well disposed toward all;
If he hates pride and is not deficient
In any way, 1112
Has no intention to play mean tricks,
Hates all vices and is properly generous,
He becomes joyous and happy, attractive,
Sincere and adept. 1116
Never will he be considered maladroit

Without something favorable then befalling him,
And so it will be said he is devoid of vice
And of vulgarity.   1120
Thus he is well schooled in every refinement
And loves honor and valor and courage
And pursues them so that his mistress
Hears good reports   1124
Of all his activities; his heart is empty of anger
And of the sin of avarice, which leads
To many misfortunes, and he dresses
In elegant clothing,   1128
And conducts himself virtuously in company,
Happy and open, and quick off the mark;
He is joyful, laughing, and gracious,
Promptly receptive   1132
To all good things, attentive and alert.
And you say that he is so troubled
By such love, which has misled him
And shackled him   1136
So that he is more enslaved than a dog on a leash,
Full of misfortune; but, my lord, saving your grace,
Instead he has arrived in a state of plenitude and grace,
Propitious   1140
To all good things, blessed and happy,
Sweet, agreeable, most pleasant and delicious.
Has it not been said of the life of love,
So gratifying, most satisfying,   1144
That loving is a pleasant, sweet, and lovely life,
For those who know how to live it
Without envy, a life that leads the true lover back
To all comforts?   1148
And it is obvious; for the tie
Never binds the lover so tightly that he can tire
Of this love; no matter how often he says, "Alas!,"
He derives so much pleasure   1152
From the loyal and secret thoughts
In his heart, which are so sweet to him,
That he would not want for anything ever to be
Cut adrift from it.   1156
It is a sweet malady; everyone should love,
Nor, if one believed me, should women be reproached,
If the world were to find out,
For it is a most attractive   1160
Pleasure, and of a happy birth
Comes this love, which rids the comely heart

Of displeasure and fills it entirely with comfort
And with delight. 1164
Dear lord God, how delightful the ardor
Provoked in the true and loving heart by a sweet glance
When it lights on the lover! Never was
A precious scent 1168
So pleasing to a man's body,
Nor any meat, however delicious.
And she should not be stingy with it
Toward her lover, 1172
The lady who nurtures the man who loves her,
For she attracts him to her love as the magnet
Attracts iron, and like the diamond
He is steadfast 1176
In his love for her, and armed with the weapons
That Love distributes to those he has enticed
To take up his service, and strengthened in his resolve.
But now let us recount 1180
What joy is received by the noble man,
The true lover, who is held prisoner
By his lady without having blundered
In any way. 1184
If it so happens that he has made such an effort
That his lady acknowledges his good intentions,
So far as to give him her love freely
As a reward, 1188
I believe that he is then much enriched,
For he has more joy, if God will pardon me,
I believe, than if he had the whole world at his disposal,
And surely even more. 1192
If he loves properly and desires her truly,
Then he has well deserved his reward,
For he cares not about his pain or his losses,
Instead, he is content. 1196
What thing could possibly perturb
The true lover, whose lady reassures him
And softly embraces and then kisses him?
What else could he want? 1200
Is he not well satisfied? Does he not have a hundred thousand
Sweet pleasures? I would consider him base
If he wanted more! He is indeed fortunate, the man who
In such a case 1204
Has had Love as his advocate;
He has no fear of being knocked flat.
Joyous is he, and he need not speak hoarsely

Or in a broken voice; 1208
The saint to whom he swears allegiance has ably cured him.
But you have said, if I do not distort your words,
That Deceitful Spying, who has found out many a man
In hiding, 1212
By whom many a big undertaking is discovered,
Does not keep silent about it; the matter is hardly concealed
By him, for, speaking heedlessly,
He exposes the lover. 1216
Thus he awakens Jealousy, who schemes
How to keep watch and denies the lover
His sweet solace. He does not take it lightly
Nor does it amuse him; 1220
Instead the unhappy lover is disconsolate,
For joy and peace have died in his heart,
And the gossips, who are back at his door,
For their part, 1224
Trouble him so greatly that he has but a small share
Of his comforts; and thus does Love
Allot him a hundred sorrows for one single portion
Of his desires. 1228
In this case, I agree that sighs engulf
The poor lover, and displeasure,
When his sweet pleasures are refused him.
But truly, 1232
When he believes and knows with certainty
That his lady loves him very faithfully,
This consolation makes him patiently
Bear his sorrow, 1236
And if, with an amiable look,
She smiles at him from afar in gracious welcome,
That is enough to give joyful desire
To the man who can do no better. 1240
He is most foolish, the lover who grieves as much
As you say, for in every case, if he wishes,
He garners enough goodness and sweetness
To rejoice in. 1244
But what wonders I can hear from you!
If it were thus, it would be better to flee
Than to let one's heart erode in such languor
And such vexation, 1248
For you tell us that the lover is jealous
If he loves well, and acts more crazed than a wolf
If he sees that someone else is after his sweet possession,
And he is suspicious 1252

Of his lady, which rankles him so much
That he cannot stay still in the street or the house,
And he reads into it many a harsh lesson,
Lacking in courtesy.   1256
It makes me unhappy to hear you ascribe
Such heresy to true love, when you attribute
Jealousy to it, which is so despised
And so reviled.   1260
You have just said to us
That despicable jealousy comes from love.
Good lord! What jealousy stems from love is surely minimal;
I cannot understand   1264
How this could be, nor can I comprehend
How one could associate suspicion and love
One with the other without insulting
Perfect love,   1268
For true love puts an end to all suspicion,
And he who has doubts certainly destroys love,
For one must believe that loyalty, which ennobles
All good hearts,   1272
Resides in the lady one loves without ceasing,
And that she would under no circumstances stoop to be false;
Any thoughts of this kind, the lover must not
In any guise   1276
Collect in his heart, for everyone believes and cherishes
That which he loves, as is commonly held,
And so it rightfully should suffice the lover,
Without further proof.   1280
And I will prove to you that it is not Love
From which springs jealousy, so reviled by everyone.
You will be able to hear my reasoning for it,
Without delay: 1284
Everyone can see, from his own experience,
That many husbands are very contrary,
Crude and hateful and belligerent,
And spiteful   1288
Toward their wives, and they are more jealous
Than worms or dogs, and always speak crossly
To them, and give them the back of their hand,
And often they beat them   1292
So hard that they knock them to their feet,
So jealous are they, but nevertheless they take pleasure
In other women, and rush into many places
Full of filth.   1296
Afterward they will say, "My wife, I love you!"

She should reply, "Go hang yourself, my lord,
You filthy brute!," but if she dare not, at least
She can think it. 1300
Then is it love that moves them in this fashion?
He who wants such love can take it;
As for me, love that causes one to grieve,
I want none of it. 1304
I reply truly to you on this point
That he who loves well and has been stung by love
Would never punch or strike a blow, I think,
Nor do any harm 1308
To himself or to another, which might debase
The love that keeps him happy and joyous
In his heart and demeanor; nor would he ever err so badly
As to be jealous 1312
Of her from whom he receives many agreeable things,
And he interprets everything in the best light,
Whatever she does. And now, if he perceives
That one or two 1316
Or many others are in love with her,
It will cause him no pain or grief;
Instead he will think that he alone is loved by her
And that he 1320
Should be happy because he has such a beloved,
In whom there is such goodness and such beauty
That everyone wants to love her for her nobility
And great worth. 1324
Thus the lover has no cause or excuse
To be jealous, or to live in pain
Because of loving well; but many in their folly
Rant with rage 1328
At love, but it is their unsound thinking
That does not know how to receive or take advantage
Of love; they are of that ilk,
And of that sort, 1332
And then they say that joy is dead in them
From loving excessively, which distresses them so much,
But it is only their twisted nature
That keeps them thus. 1336
And so without a doubt, he is much mistaken who maintains
That gentle love, to which joy appertains,
Makes the lover jealous, for never does there come
Such a malady 1340
Except from a worthless, cowardly heart, whatever one might say,
And from sad and irresolute desire,

Which leaves a person short of courage
And lacking in faith, 1344
And makes the man worry for no reason.
He thinks he is clumsier and less attractive
Than others, and when he is in sight of
Handsome, lively 1348
Young men, he is ill at ease
Because he thinks himself the ugliest of them all,
And he does not like, nor would he allow,
That they be acquainted with 1352
His love, for fear that they find more favor.
Such people are sad and hide themselves
To make sure that they are not seen.
So do not say 1356
In any way that jealousy results
From love. Instead, it comes from a heart full of fear,
In which suspicion and disdain are lodged
By ill intent 1360
Because the lover thinks himself less worthy than others,
And that is what makes the heart so heavy
In the unhappy man who concerns himself with nothing else
In his foolishness. 1364
Moreover, I must not overlook
That you said that an affair of the heart
And its difficulties caused the death
Of many valiant men 1368
In days gone by, in France and in Rome
And elsewhere; and you name many such
Who perished cruelly as a result,
As you tell it, 1372
Of such love. But listen to me a while:
I tell you truly, and do not doubt it,
That even if it is true that they were thus defeated
And placed on the bier, 1376
The blame for it should in no way
Devolve on love, for their foolish behavior
Caused them to die, and not love at all.
I ask you, 1380
Is the almond not good, sweet and appetizing?
But if he who wants and asks for it
Breaks his neck or hangs himself from the tree in the picking,
Is it worth any less? 1384
Wine is good, but if someone quaffs
So much or more that he sits in a drunken heap,
Or lies like a dead man, as if in humiliation,

Or gets a goose egg 1388
On his forehead in his silly drunkenness,
Or if he kills himself, or someone else tricks him,
I suppose one is therefore supposed to yank out the vine
That gives such fruit? 1392
With all good things, cannot one
Misuse them badly? From a good person
Can come harm for someone who goes about it poorly;
This is undoubtedly 1396
The case with love (it is not a fabrication),
For there is nothing in this world that is worth as much,
But only a fool would make use of it in such a way
That it left him worse off. 1400
It is fitting that a lover hold fast to one single love,
That he love with all his heart and always sustain
His faith and his loyalty, and uphold the truth.
But to do this 1404
He does not need to destroy and kill;
Love was created to perfect man,
And not to harm and mistreat him,
That is the truth. 1408
But because you have recounted here
Many stories that the record reveals
Of true lovers, well worth remembering,
Who suffered much 1412
From great love and who delivered themselves to death,
I wish, therefore, to tell of those who chose
The best of the game, and did so much for love
That word 1416
Of their worth spread throughout the world
Because of the valiant acts they performed
In many a great army, and so forever more
Their honorable goodness 1420
Will be spoken of widely, and nothing surpasses it,
Except a good reputation, but even after death
Praise lives on; wise is he who cultivates it.
Now, let us see 1424
If Lancelot du Lac,[24] who was so courageous
In feats of arms, received noble gifts
From such a love as we speak of now.
Was he valiant? 1428
What do you say? Did he go about exiling himself
For such love or harming his body?
I think not. Rather, even more than his possessions
Was it useful to him 1432

Above all things, and good, and profitable,
For because of it he was valiant and amiable,
And so it was neither harmful nor destructive to him,
At least so I believe.   1436
He neither killed himself nor was killed or wounded
At the hands of others; instead love filled him with joy.
There are many others as well,
And even   1440
Tristan,[25] of whom you spoke just now,
Became brave because of it, if the story does not lie.
His prowess had its good start
In love,   1444
And even though he died in great distress
Because of Fortune, who does much malicious mischief,
He did so much good for his lady and mistress
That forever more   1448
Will his great achievements be spoken of.
This was the work of Love, by which he was perfected.
And you said that nothing comes from the exploits of love
But harm;   1452
Now let us see, by God, if I remember correctly,
If everyone fares so badly with love.
In olden days Jason,[26] as the story has it,
Was saved   1456
From cruel death, which had him in its grasp
Had he not been saved from danger
By Medea, whose heart was so struck
By love for him   1460
That she protected him and brought him back from death
When he captured the golden fleece by the charm
She taught him in Colchis, after he arrived
At the port.   1464
Whoever might have died of it, this man's life was saved
By such love, but he acted improperly
When he did wrong to the woman who had preserved him
From peril.   1468
And Theseus, son of the king of Athens,[27]
When he was sent into exile in Crete,
Was saved thanks to the clever ploy
Of Ariadne,   1472
Who rescued him from harsh death; she released him
From the prison of Minos when he held fast
To his thread and cut the throat
Of the cruel monster.   1476
I am showing you that Love did no harm

To this man, for the story demonstrates
That he escaped by sea faster than the otter
Crosses a ford.   1480
And Aeneas,²⁸ after the great city of Troy
Had been burned, he who was opposed by
Fortune, who topples many a kingdom,
He sailed   1484
Across the seas, his heart sad and bitter,
And constantly invoked his gods;
But help came to him through love,
For he was welcomed   1488
And received by Dido the beautiful.
Had it not been for her, he would have been badly served,
And he did a great wrong when he failed her.
And so these three men   1492
Did not die from love; rather, they were rescued by it,
And derived many other benefits from it.
And it is true, as the stories proclaim,
That Theseus   1496
Of whom I have spoken,²⁹ who was so highly favored
That he was seen with the strong Hercules
Performing great feats, and was renowned in many parts,
As a young child   1500
Was an ugly little boy,
Hunchbacked and deformed, as says the song
That tells this story; but he changed in appearance
For the beautiful Helen,   1504
For her he became brave and undertook many trials.
You can see him in those woolen tapestries
As a golden eagle, being brought and led,
In which he was hidden   1508
Until he declared himself to the lovely woman.
Then he carried her off, which infuriated
Her relatives, and he was not allowed
To take her far.   1512
And so a man is not completely ruined
Because of that love if he learns how
To be valiant by honorable means.
Other stories   1516
Tell many true tales
Concerning faithful lovers, of which the exalted memory
Will always be considered noteworthy everywhere.
And Florimont   1520
Of Albania,³⁰ there was no one in the world
As valiant; but whence came

So many valiant deeds if not from Love, who orders
His followers   1524
To be good, and so thoroughly ennobles their hearts?
He endured many great trials
For Romadanaple, but nevertheless at great cost
He achieved   1528
Fame and honor; thus he did not waste his time
In loving well, thanks to which he attained
The accomplishments that Love provided him.
And Durmart le Gallois[31]   1532
The valiant, who was son of the good king
Of Denmark, he had such a reputation
For brave deeds that no three other men could exceed it.
I ask you,   1536
What did he lose when he fell in love with
The queen of Ireland, and submitted himself entirely
To her command? As a result he traversed many lands
In order to conquer   1540
Her kingdom for her and conducted such a great war
That he conquered it and gave her back her land,
For which he should rightfully acquire honor.
Cleomades,[32]   1544
Was he valiant because of love, and never ceased
Carrying arms? Pallamedes,[33] as well;
Do you remember the brave deeds and the
Great feats   1548
That are still told about him in all sorts of tales?
Everything he accomplished he did for Love;
So I beg you, do not let your stories
Depict him badly.   1552
And Arthur, who was duke of Brittany,[34]
For the sake of Florence, who thereafter was his companion,
Rode across both France and Germany
And many other lands   1556
And undertook many a fine contest and many a great war,
All for Love, who put him on the road
To obtaining honor; for this he undertook his adventures.
But without looking   1560
Any further, we can talk again
About our own times. We must not hide from view
The very valiant men who, without losing their sanity
Or harming themselves,   1564
Want to devote their hearts to perfect love.
I need not offer other proof,
No other document as witness, no other brief,

For most 1568
Certainly he is known, the valiant High Constable
Of France, may God find his soul worthy,
The good Bertrand du Guesclin,[35]
The brave and worthy, 1572
Who inflicted many an injury on the English,
Which earned him honor; he often sacked
Their castles, whether in the morning or at night,
And he will always 1576
Be renowned and his name invoked by good men.
He first took up arms for Love,
So he said, and the desire to be loved
Made him valiant. 1580
He was soon made so hardworking by
Love, who makes every good heart quick
To pursue honor if it desires
Praise, which is more precious 1584
Than anything else in the world. And good Boucicaut
The Marshal,[36] who was courageous, wise, and prudent,
Was valiant, generous, and handsome because of Love,
Which caused him 1588
To become thus; his two children
Wish to follow in the same path, and continue
The pursuit of arms, so as to acquire
Praise in days to come. 1592
And at the moment still lives on this earth,
May God keep him, the valiant Constable
Of Sancerre,[37] nor could one hope to find
A knight 1596
Better than he; in his day he has been made to fight
By Love, who has given him
Good counsel, for by applying himself
He has conquered so much 1600
That he has earned praise among good men;
That was the work of Love, who guided him to this.
There have been others, as I have discovered,
In this kingdom 1604
Whom Love has ruled;
The game is not over: there are still some
Who have so distinguished themselves in feats of arms
That forever more 1608
Their great and admirable deeds will be spoken of.
I do not know why I have not yet mentioned
Those who are still alive, who, by the act
Of carrying arms 1612

For the sake of loving truly, have risen in esteem.
And I could still tell tales of those who have died:
Of the good Oton de Granson[38] you have heard
Spoken at length, 1616
How he never tired of the good;
In him all virtues were amassed.
And Vermeilles Hutin[39] must not
Be omitted 1620
From among the good, may God grant him pardon.
But let us look at knights still alive,
To see if there are any who owe a great deal,
Based on their experience, 1624
To good love, men that one can find worthy,
Valiant, wise, courteous, and not greedy.
The good Châteaumorand,[40] may God save
And protect him, 1628
Who keeps armed watch over the Saracens
In the city of Constantinople, which he advises,
Helps, and protects, labors because of his faith in God;
This man deserves 1632
Esteem and honor, for he does his duty,
And those who are with him, it is true,
Gain praise, which is worth much more than possessions,
And to the French 1636
They bring great honor. And I can still think
Of many other valiant and wise men, in many places,
Whom Love has made good, courteous, and skillful,
And honorable. 1640
A good and worthy knight is l'Hermite
De la Faye,[41] and there are plenty of others
Like him, valiant and praiseworthy men,
But for the sake of brevity 1644
I will hold my tongue; but, if God grants you good health,
Now let us look to see if we can find plenty
Of younger men, who have more good than grief
And are guided 1648
By Love, who has taught them so well
That they are prepared to pursue every honor.
Courtesy and valiance are their refuge,
And that is not a lie. 1652
Concerning Monseigneur d'Albret,[42] the very worthy
Charles, who is so agreeable to everyone,
What do you say of him? Does he not seem praiseworthy to you,
His worth 1656
Such that he deserves to be remembered

In every courtyard? Is he wise and learned,
Skillful at arms? Can he be reproached
In any aspect?   1660
Anyone looking for a better man than he
Would fail, I think, for he loves reason and justice,
And Love has given him and disposed him to every good thing,
And rightly so.   1664
And now look at the Seneschal de Hainaut,⁴³
Has he been well schooled by Love?
Has he made good use of his youth?
Is he idle?   1668
Does he undertake feats of arms, is he lazy?
What do you think? Is he not anxious
To garner praise? May God grant it to him, and to those
Who resemble him;   1672
I believe many good qualities are to be found in him,
And courtesy and valor never leave him;
He is not one of those whose hearts tremble
With cowardice.   1676
And what would you have me say of Gaucourt?⁴⁴
In my opinion, he pursues feats of arms
Boldly, and there is no one who speaks badly of him,
He acquits himself so well.   1680
This is the work of Love, who opens the door of valor
For him. And in just the same way,
Love ennobles the good Charles of Savoisy⁴⁵
And makes him valiant,   1684
So that he spares neither body nor expense
To acquire praise as courageous and diligent,
Whether with a lance or a sharp sword,
In wielding arms.   1688
Castelbeart⁴⁶ and several others like him,
In whom reside goodness and valor,
They are the work of Love, who makes them do everything
In order to win praise,   1692
For there are no better knights to be found.
And Clignet de Breban,⁴⁷ too, should anyone wish
To inquire about him, is well known in France
And other lands,   1696
For he has fought in many places for the sake of Love,
For which he is and will be renowned.
These men are handsome, young, and well prepared,
And for their ladies   1700
Go valiantly bearing arms in many places,
Because of which, once their bodies are under tombstones,

Praise of them and great fame will live on
In many lands. 1704
But may they always guard against speaking ill,
For that is something that diminishes even a very noble man,
And so they will, for their good hearts lead them
Only to flee vice, 1708
And to pursue all things seemly.
Love does this, for it is his proper duty,
And he will give them recompense and benefit
If they deserve it. 1712
And so you must never say that lovers abase themselves
By loving well when they serve such a master,
One who makes them good, and if they are diligent,
You should know in truth 1716
That they will acquire, in doing their duty,
Prowess, honor, good sense, praise, and riches.
Of such men there are plenty, you may be sure of it,
Without a doubt; 1720
But should anyone wish to name the entire list
Of good and handsome lovers, the task
Would take too long, for often the listener
Of an overly long tale 1724
Gets bored; but those I have told you about
And so many others that I cannot even count
Are gracious, for there is no duke or count,
No prince or king, 1728
Who, if he loves as he should, does not hate misdeeds
And all slander, and whose condition is therefore
All the more worthy, for the disposition to love
Makes them learn. 1732
And so, fair friends, if you wish to listen carefully,
You can hear that if the lover is inclined
To have joy, Love is more tender toward him
Than harsh, 1736
If he accepts it patiently and calmly
And with hope, however much this arduous task
Is painful for him; he commits a great mistake,
The man who errs 1740
In taking the bad for himself when he sees the good.
Thus I have proved that in love one learns
Goodness and honor and devotes oneself entirely
To undertaking valiant deeds. 1744
So do not say anymore that there is such great suffering
In love, and such a lack
Of comfort, or such great travail

Or such pain." 1748

When the squire—who was wise and perceptive,
Who had spoken as truly as the Bible,
In his opinion—then fell silent,
And spoke no more, 1752
The knight began to smile a little
And looked at the squire thoughtfully, without speaking,
And then he moved toward him courteously
And said, unhurriedly, 1756
"By God, my lord, you have recounted here
Great marvels, and if anyone who came to you
To find medicine and a good draught
To relieve quickly 1760
The pains of love, you would know how to cure him of it
And to give him good advice to put a quick end
To all suffering, in order to restore the servant
To good health, 1764
If you are to be believed. But it takes little to relieve
The man who suffers little and has no discomfort;
And so you have proved your point, that is, if I keep silent,
And do not mention 1768
The big objections I could raise
Against the arguments I hear you make,
For you want to arrange exactly,
Just as you wish, 1772
The facts of love, and everyone would receive to his liking
As much or as little as he wants,
Taking the good and leaving the bad.
Neither more nor less 1776
Do you wish to control love and keep
A tight rein on it and, except in certain places,
Direct its progress, and no one would be affected by it
Except as much as he likes. 1780
It works differently, my friend: he who has such a visitor
Cannot be rid of him whenever he might choose.
Have you a heart that gives and takes away joy
As it pleases? 1784
If so, I dare say that you do not love profusely.
Neither do those who benefit
From such pleasure, as you have recounted,
Without having pain; 1788
It cannot be. It is important to know
That whoever loves from the heart, without deceit,
Perfectly, cannot avoid having

Many difficulties,	1792
Whether he likes it or not; he can never	
Set himself up so well that he can feel secure	
Or always find favor	
In his suit.	1796
Yet you speak here of a new kind of love,	
One to your liking, I do not know what it is called,	
Which you have told us about at length.	
But again I say	1800
That the lover who is true, and an obedient subject,	
Finds his heart so constrained by great love	
That it makes him jealous and aggravates	
This grievous pain so much	1804
That he cannot find rest any day of the week	
If he perceives that another lover is attempting	
To obtain the love that drives him	
In so many ways.	1808
And you think you can prove to us here in this spot	
That whosoever might be jealous is slighting love,	
But I tell you that love cannot exist, by rights,	
Without jealousy.	1812
So set your mind at ease,	
For I tell you that a loving heart	
Has greater worries and is less soothed	
In its grievous pain	1816
Than another that can easily dispense with it.	
But you speak of a love that causes little pain,	
Of which it matters little whether it be long or short,	
Or whether it passes quickly,	1820
But that allows one to say, 'Love embraces me,	
It makes me handsome, I do not tire of serving it,	
And if it gives me no wearisome thoughts,	
So much the better.'"	1824
Then the other replied and interrupted the speech,	
And said, "By God, you think you are so wise!	
It works differently than that, and noble love	
Is of another breed entirely,	1828
And we could be here until morning;	
But I tell you that true love is more	
Perfect than that and the best signs of it	
And the most certain	1832
Are when a lover who is stricken with love	
Is happy and lively and full of good cheer,	
All for the joy he derives from faithful love,	
With which he is smitten.	1836

When he is reminded of the royal
Lady he serves, all bad thoughts
Concerning his worth are chased from his heart
And he remains gay 1840
And cheerful in April and in May
And at all other times; he has no pain or dismay
From true love, which with its bright rays
Illumines him. 1844
Whatever you may say, I state again and conclude
That it is a more significant and perfect token
Of great love, both perfect and pure,
To have faith 1848
In one's love than to distrust it
Or to be jealous; I can confidently affirm
That he loves better, the man who without a care
Entrusts silver or gold 1852
Or some other big treasure
To someone else, and says to him, 'From now on,
I put my trust in you, I place in your keeping
My possessions,' 1856
Than the man who wants security,
And wants a daily accounting
Of his holdings, out of fear that the other
Wishes to deceive him. 1860
And so it is, whomever this may please or vex,
With regard to love, for he who strips himself
Of his true heart, and welcomes such an act of trust,
Giving it 1864
To someone else and granting it freely,
Without bargaining, and then no longer dwelling on it—
It is a better sign if he assumes the person
To be good, without fail, 1868
Than if he bargains in giving it away
And worries constantly that he will be cheated
Or that goodness and loyalty will fail him
In some way. 1872
For he who loves trusts wholeheartedly,
As I have said, nor could perfect love
Be otherwise, and I willingly await the true verdict
On this matter, 1876
If there is someone who might hear our two arguments
With comprehension and understand all our reasoning.
I beg you to pick a judge
Entirely to your liking, 1880
And let this case be put entirely in his hands."

The knight replied, "And without hesitation
I urge that we seek a judgment; according to your wishes,
Let a judge be chosen 1884
And elected, but let him be worthy enough
That he be valiant, courageous, wise, and learned,
Noble and well-mannered, and capable of judging
The affairs of troubled lovers. 1888
And as for me, without going on again at length,
I state and maintain that it is necessary to pay more
For the joy of love—without making light of it—
Than one gets in return, 1892
And that for every pleasure, it sends a hundred pains,
And that the man who undertakes to love
Puts himself on a very perilous path.
And what is more, 1896
I say again that the man loves more who,
Because of love, becomes downcast and reclusive,
Pensive, pale, mournful, quiet, and withdrawn
Than he who becomes 1900
Happier for it; nor is the heart as devoted
If it has allied itself with joy
Than if it is frustrated
By such love, 1904
And jealousy must reside in the lover,
On account of which one's eyes
Are often moist, lamenting frequently;
If, without reneging, 1908
He loves as he ought, he will have to endure such pain.
And you say and uphold the contrary;
Now may God grant us that we find a trustworthy judge
Without delay." 1912

And thus the two lovers finished
Their discussion, but they were greatly preoccupied
With finding a judge, someone suitable who would know
How to give them 1916
An appropriate verdict, justly, according to law.
They proposed many highly placed barons there;
Many fine, sincere, and skillful knights,
Happy and handsome, 1920
Were named by them there, and from the fleur-de-lis
They singled out some of those whose faces are pale
Beneath their hats, as a result of loving strongly,
Which does not bring them all delight, 1924
Because they do not all dare make their avowals

In matters of love, which distributes its delicacies
Variously, and makes many a good man
Grow thin   1928
In many cases. And thus with great seriousness
They selected and named the names
Of many valiant men, saying, "Let us choose this one!"
And then saying   1932
That another they named would be better.
And when I saw that they were in such a quandary
That they could not find a judge who suited them,
I then considered,   1936
Thinking hard, and decided
That I knew a good judge for their case.
As soon as I had thought of it, I said to them
What you can   1940
Hear here; I drew closer
And said to them, "If you please, listen
To my opinion on the matter and please forgive me
If I propose   1944
To resolve this dispute about love
Which you are arguing, and be sure that without a doubt
I wish to see a just pronouncement in the matter
And thus I do this   1948
With good intent; and, if you wish to delegate the case
And this debate, and if it is done
As I suggest, you will be relieved
And most happy   1952
And satisfied in your desire once and for all.
If the most noble duke of whom I am thinking
Wants to take on this case and agrees
To be the judge,   1956
You will have a good judge, valiant, wise, and expert;
It is the eminent, powerful duke of Orleans,
Of noble ancestry, may he have joy on earth
And in paradise;   1960
This man is good, wise in deeds and in words,
Just and trustworthy, and he wishes to emulate
The good men of the past, for it pleases him always
To uphold justice.   1964
He is humane, humble, gentle, and likely
In every case, and even in this capacity,
To judge correctly; nor is he so naive
That he has not learned   1968
The ways of love, notwithstanding his elevated status.
So I advise that he be chosen and selected

By you as judge, and you will have
Picked wisely, without fail, 1972
For I believe that no one else can match him;
As long as it pleases him and he puts his noble heart
To work on it until he delivers a verdict,
You cannot do better." 1976
Then the two lovers, raising their eyes,
Replied, "May God be praised for this,
You have placed us in a noble position
And found us 1980
A trustworthy judge, one whom we choose;
If it pleases him, the case will be heard,
He will decide on it as he sees fit and it will be known
If it suits him. 1984
We ask you, because you are so concerned
With our welfare, that you, who are in the habit
Of composing good and beautiful tales, which spread
Much pleasure 1988
In many places, undertake by your goodwill
To fashion a tale out of the content and the scope
Of our debate; you would thus do us a great service
And bring us great joy." 1992
Then I responded, "I am not an expert
In writing tales; nonetheless, I will not delay
In undertaking it, on account of the great nobility
Of the worthy 1996
Royal prince, who never fails
To judge fairly, to give sage advice,
And who is in all things skilled and diligent,
In order to bring joy 2000
To his noble heart, if he deigns to hear it.
Now may God grant me, in accordance with my wish,
That I can compose something that makes him rejoice
And enjoy himself." 2004
And thus, great Prince of noble deeds,
My revered Lord, to whom God give
Long life and then grant His true glory
To your soul, 2008
I have composed this poem to bring to your mind
Joy and comfort by listening to this story
Which records and recounts matters of love;
And so I beg 2012
Your highness that you deign
To receive it favorably, and not consider it foolish,
For goodwill and true desire oblige me

To exert myself 2016
To serve you, if only I know how to succeed in it.
And now it is time to finish my work;
But if anyone wishes, at the end,
To discover 2020
What my name is, without seeking too far,
If he searches for it, he can find it embedded
Everywhere where one finds Christianity.[48]

Here ends the debate of the two lovers.

Notes

The edition of the text on which this translation is based is Altmann, *Love Debate Poems of Christine de Pizan*, 84–134.

1. The duke of Orleans, Christine's patron and judge for this debate, was Louis, son of the French king Charles V.

2. If Christine has a particular biblical passage in mind, it has not been identified. The importance of the allusion is above all to invoke a highly authoritative source to justify what she writes about love.

3. The text uses technical dance terms in this description, the precise meaning of which is unclear. We are to understand that the young noblemen and noblewomen are accomplished in the art of social dancing.

4. The long sentence that runs from line 124 to 135 is a common Middle French construction describing what a hypothetical observer would have seen at these festivities. The core of the sentence can be understood as "He who could have seen [the company and their entertainments] would have valued highly [their] comportment."

5. Spoken in the squire's words, this is the first statement of the question to be decided in the debate. It will be repeated with variations several times throughout the debate, to introduce, conclude, or summarize the debaters' arguments.

6. This complicated construction means that the lover will relinquish his share of the good things Fortune can bring in exchange for "that one thing," namely his lady's favors, of which he is likely to receive very little.

7. Paris was the son of King Priam of Troy and his queen Hecuba. His abduction of Helen, wife of King Menelaus of Sparta, resulted in the Trojan War.

8. There is some confusion in this reference to Telamon. It was not Achilles' uncle Telamon but Philoctetes, another Greek warrior at Troy, who shot Paris.

9. Ovid (43 BCE–17/18 CE) is the Roman author who wrote the *Metamorphoses* and the *Heroïdes*, both of which were frequently used by medieval poets as sources for the mythological figures and stories of Greco-Roman antiquity. The following lines are full of Ovidian references.

10. Pyramus fell in love with his neighbor Thisbe (673) against the wishes of their parents. When Pyramus appeared at a tryst they had arranged at a fountain beside a white mulberry tree, he saw a lion and Thisbe's bloody veil. Assuming she had been killed, he

committed suicide. Thisbe found his body and killed herself in turn. The berries of the mulberry turned red from their blood.

11. Leander loved Hero (683), priestess of Venus, who lived in Sestus. Every night Leander swam across the Hellespont to visit his beloved. He drowned on a crossing when the light that guided him was extinguished in a storm.

12. Achilles fell in love with Polyxena (694), daughter of his enemy King Priam of Troy. Achilles tried to negotiate peace between the Greeks and Trojans in order to win the hand of Polyxena but was fatally wounded in the heel by Polyxena's brother Paris.

13. Aesacus, son of King Priam (705) and Alexirhoe, loved the nymph Hesperia. She died when, as she ran away from him, a snake bit her. In his grief Aesacus threw himself from a cliff, but he was saved by the sea goddess Tethys, who turned him into a diving seabird.

14. In Cyprus the young Iphis, a man of humble birth, hanged himself at the door of Anaxarete, the noblewoman who had rejected his suit. In revenge for her cruelty, the gods turned her to stone as she watched the funeral procession.

15. After the stories taken from mythology, the knight turns to "more recent times" (745) and chooses Tristan as the first of the medieval heroes he will use as examples of unhappy love. The tale of Tristan and Iseut was among the best-known of all medieval romances. It recounts the love of Tristan, nephew of King Marc of Cornwall, for Iseut, his uncle's wife. In one episode, Marc spies on the couple from the branches of a pine tree. At the end of the romance, the wounded Tristan dies of a broken heart when he believes that Iseut will not come to him, and Iseut takes her life when she finds him dead. Later in this debate (1440–50), the squire too makes reference to the Tristan legend, but as an example of the positive effects of love.

16. Kaherdin, brother of Iseut, plays a prominent role in the story of Tristan and Iseut as told by Thomas d'Angleterre and in the prose version of the romance.

17. The Chatelain de Coucy was Guy de Thourotte, a late-twelfth-century French poet who died during the Fourth Crusade, and the hero of a romance entitled the *Roman du castelain de Couci et de la dame de Fayel*, written at the end of the thirteenth century. In the story, he dies on crusade overseas. His beloved, the lady of Fayel (765), also dies after being tricked by her jealous husband into eating the heart of her lover.

18. A thirteenth-century romance recounts the tragic tale of the Chatelaine de Vergy, a lady at the Burgundian court who agrees to love a young knight on the condition that he keep their love an absolute secret. When he is forced to reveal the secret, the lady learns of his betrayal and dies. Her lover kills himself when he finds her and learns of the reason for her death.

19. The story of Paris and Helen is raised as an example for the second time by the knight (the first being lines 651–61). Here he includes references to the roles played by Venus, goddess of love, and her son Cupid. In a competition among goddesses, Paris had awarded the golden apple to Venus after she promised him Helen, the most beautiful woman in the world. Cupid causes his victims to fall in love by shooting them with an arrow.

20. This line is a metaphor comparing Love's command over lovers to that of a falconer keeping his sparrow hawk on a short leash. Hunting with birds of prey was a sport favored by the nobility in the Middle Ages.

21. The lover behaves preposterously and cannot trust his senses, so irrational does love make him.

22. The lady's reference to the *Romance of the Rose* is discussed in the headnote to this debate. In the *Rose* the allegorical figure Reason tries to persuade the young protagonist that love is full of contradictions and danger and that his pursuit of the rosebud is unwise, but he does not heed her advice, choosing to act unreasonably.

23. This oath refers to Saint Nicasius, a fifth-century bishop of Reims who was beheaded by barbarians while trying to save the lives of the faithful.

24. In Arthurian legend, Lancelot du Lac is the best knight of King Arthur of Britain and his Round Table. He is also the lover of Arthur's wife, Guinevere. Although their love is thwarted by circumstances, Lancelot is nonetheless inspired to great deeds by the strength of his devotion.

25. The squire takes up the story of Tristan, whom the knight has already used as an example of the dangers of love, and uses it for the opposite purpose (see note 15).

26. Jason, leader of the Argonauts, sailed to Colchis (1463) in search of the Golden Fleece. He overcame a series of seemingly impossible obstacles set for him by King Aëtes, using charms taught to him by Medea, Aëtes's daughter and a magician. Jason pledged eternal fidelity to Medea in return, but reneged on his promise when he fell in love with Glauce. Medea took revenge on Glauce and killed her own children, aspects of the story that the squire refers to in passing, saying that no matter who else died because of it, at least Jason was saved by Medea's love (1465).

27. Theseus, son of King Aegeus of Athens, was sent as part of a tribute to Crete, where he was to be devoured by the Minotaur in the labyrinth of King Minos. Minos's daughter Ariadne fell in love with Theseus and gave him a ball of thread with which he found his way out of the labyrinth. Theseus killed the Minotaur and then escaped from Crete with Ariadne, whom he abandoned on the way back to Athens.

28. Aeneas, eponymous hero of Virgil's *Aeneid*, fought valiantly on the side of Troy (1481) during the Trojan War. Once the city was defeated, he left in search of a new homeland, settling eventually in Rome. As the text tells us (1489), he was received by Dido, queen of Carthage, who provided him with help. Although Aeneas and Dido loved each other, Aeneas left Carthage, abandoning her, and Dido committed suicide. The three men referred to in line 1492 are thus Jason, Theseus, and Aeneas, all of whom were saved by the resourcefulness of the women who loved them. This passage emphasizes the redeeming force of love for the men on their respective quests, rather than their fickle behavior or the devastating consequences of that love on the women.

29. Theseus was first mentioned in line 1469 (see note 27). This second reference confuses the story of Theseus the Athenian hero with Theseus of Cologne, protagonist of a medieval romance. The allusions to Hercules and Helen belong to the first story, with which Christine takes some liberties, while the episode of the golden eagle, in which Theseus hides to reach his beloved Flore, comes from the second. Theseus of Cologne carried off Flore, who was the daughter of the Roman emperor Esmeré, after which her father laid siege to Cologne and took Theseus's father, mother, and sister to Rome as captives.

30. Florimont of Albania is the hero of the romance *Florimont*, composed in 1188 by Aimon de Varenne. Florimont married Romadanaple (line 1527), daughter of King Phillip of Macedon. They were the grandparents of Alexander the Great.

31. Durmart le Gallois is known from a mid-thirteenth-century Arthurian romance of

the same name. The queen of Ireland is the woman who inspired him to undertake the brave deeds for which he is praised.

32. Cleomades, son of the king of Spain, is the hero of a romance composed by Adenet le Roi in 1285.

33. The name *Pallamedes* provides a rhyme word in line 1546 for Cleomades, named in line 1544. Pallamedes plays a role in the romance known as the *Tristan en prose*, in which he remains loyal to Tristan despite his own love for Iseut. He also figures in a prose romance named the *Roman de Palamède*, which dates from 1240, although he is a minor character in that work.

34. Arthur of Brittany was the son of Jean, duke of Brittany, and of the daughter of the count of Lancaster. Florence (line 1554) is the noblewoman he married. The romance that tells Arthur's tale is known as *Artus de la Petite Bretagne*, but also as *Le Petit Artus de Bretagne*, or *Artus le Petit*.

35. Returning to examples of knights renowned in his own day, the squire praises Bertrand du Guesclin (1320–80). He was a military hero and advisor to King Jean II and then high constable and commander in chief of France under Charles V (1370–80).

36. Boucicaut is Jean le Meingre (d. 1367), called Boucicaut, marshal of France. The two children mentioned in line 1589 are his sons Geoffroy (d. 1429) and Jean II le Meingre, dit Boucicaut. Both were already known in the early fifteenth century for their military prowess and as examples of chivalry. In addition, Jean II was a poet and patron of the arts, and in 1399 founded a chivalric order in protection of ladies' honor known as L'Ecu Vert à la Dame Blanche.

37. Another example of a knight known for his illustrious military career, Louis de Sancerre (ca. 1342–1402) was named marshal of France in 1369.

38. Oton de Granson (b. ca. 1340–50) is one of the esteemed knights "who have died" (line 1614), to whom the squire will now make reference. A well-known poet as well as a soldier, Oton died in a judicial duel in 1397.

39. Hutin de Vermeilles (d. 1390), also on the squire's list of the recently deceased, was Charles VI's chamberlain and undertook a number of important missions for the king in that role. He married Marguerite de Bourbon, daughter of Louis I de Bourbon, count of La Marche.

40. Moving from the dead to the living, the squire starts his examples with Jean de Châteaumorand, who fought with the duke Louis II de Bourbon and, with the help of a scribe, composed a chronicle of Louis's life. He had a reputation as one of the most distinguished knights of his time and belonged to the chivalric order founded by Jean II Boucicaut (see note 36).

41. Like Châteaumorand, Guillaume de Montrevel "l'Hermite de la Faye" accompanied Louis II de Bourbon on his military adventures. In 1399, shortly before the composition of this work, he had fought with Jean II Boucicaut (see note 36) in the service of the Greek emperor.

42. Charles d'Albret, count of Dreux and nephew of Jeanne de Bourbon, wife of Charles V, was named constable of France in 1402. Like Châteaumorand, he belonged to the chivalric order begun by Jean II Boucicaut (see note 36). He died at the battle of Agincourt in 1415. Christine de Pizan dedicated a copy of this poem, the *Debat de deux amans*, to him.

43. Jean de Werchin, seneschal of Hainaut, was a poet as well as a knight. Among his writings, which have much in common with Christine's debate poems, are the *Songe de la*

barge and an exchange of poems in which a mature knight and a younger squire debate what is proper comportment in love.

44. Raoul de Gaucourt (d. 1417) was chamberlain to Charles VI. He accompanied the king on an expedition to Germany in 1388 and later was responsible for other foreign missions.

45. After the death of Raoul de Gaucourt, Charles de Savoisy was chamberlain to Charles VI from 1418 until 1420.

46. The name *Castelbeart* refers to Bernard de Castelbajac, seneschal of Bigorre and son of Arnaud-Raymond de Castelbajac and Jeanne de Barbasan.

47. Clignet de Breban was Pierre de Brebant, called Clignet (d. ca. 1430). He too was chamberlain to the king, and was named admiral of France in 1405.

48. The last few lines of the poem make up an anagram that the reader is invited to solve in order to reveal the identity of the author. We find Christine's name scrambled in the word *Christianity*—"cristïenté" in the original Middle French. She closes her other two debates poems in a similar way. The *Livre des trois jugemens* alerts the reader to decipher her name from the elements "Crist" and "fine" in the final line, while in the *Livre du dit de Poissy* it is disguised in the adjective "creintis," the last word of the text, meaning "fearful." In this practice, adopted from other late-medieval authors including Machaut, she indirectly introduces her real name at the end of the poems in which she portrays herself as a character with a writerly role.

Alain Chartier

Le Livre des quatre dames
(The Book of the Four Ladies)

❦

Haa, Destinee
Tresdure, et maudicte journee
Douloureuse, mal fortunee
Qui toute ma joie as tournee
En desconfort!
(lines 540–44)

Alain Chartier was born in Bayeux to a wealthy bourgeois family. After finishing his studies at the Université de Paris, he entered a life of service to the French royal family; he spent a decade as notary and secretary to the dauphin Charles, who would become Charles VII, and went on many missions to other countries, including Germany, Italy, and Scotland, as an emissary and diplomat. His writings reflect his dedication to the French cause. One of his best-known works, for example, the *Quadrilogue invectif* (1422), was written in the wake of the Treaty of Troyes, an agreement divesting the French royal house by which the English king Henry V was named heir presumptive to Charles VI of France, at the expense of Charles's son, the dauphin. In this poem the different estates—the People, the Aristocracy, and the Clergy, all of them children of a France in mourning—lament the plight of the country and call for collective action in support of the crown. Some of his work has a satirical edge, particularly with regard to court life. But his poetry and prose are also infused with courtly values and registers, representing the language of the nobility engaged in both entertaining and serious pursuits. He wrote in both Latin and French, and in a variety of genres.

Among his courtly works, *La Belle Dame sans merci* (1424) is the best known. In that debate poem, a knight dying of love for his chosen lady meets with nothing but resistance and indifference from her. Their verbal sparring sets one kind of discourse against another. The knight uses the vocabulary of courtly love, protesting his devotion and the dire consequences of a refusal in grandiloquent terms. He contends that the lady should take pity on him if he behaves as a good lover should. She, however, shows him no mercy: she insists that she is under no obligation to accept him and derides the sincerity of his entreaties. Her refusal can be read as a rejection of the courtly love theme, gone stale by the time Alain was writing, well into the fifteenth century. She seems to represent a model of feminine reaction and assertiveness that differs significantly from the desirable but compliant, passive, and largely silent lady of earlier texts. The portrait Alain draws of her is challenged as unflattering and unfair by the responses that his poem provoked. Whether fictional or real, an exchange of letters, retractions, and further accusations develops into a real "querelle," a cycle of responses that build on each other to perpetuate the debate. His works were printed before the end of the fifteenth century, and his influence is seen in the work of writers of a later generation, especially the poets known as the Grands Rhétoriqueurs, those who mark the transition from the Middle Ages into the French Renaissance.

Alain wrote several debate poems. Apart from the *Livre des quatre dames*, three of them are on the topic of love. One of these, *La Belle Dame sans merci*, has already been mentioned. Another is the *Debat des deux fortunés d'amours* (1425), also known as the *Debat du gras et du maigre*. It presents a corpulent knight and a thin one, who debate the relative merits of love in a poem that resembles the *Debat de deux amans* by Christine de Pizan. The larger man maintains that love is a positive force that brings out the best in the lover, while his adversary, clad in black, responds that, to the contrary, love leads to jealousy and despair. In the *Debat de reveille matin*, composed in more or less the same period, a sleepless lover wakes another man for solace and commentary on his plight. Another, the *Debat du herault, du vassault et du villain*, is one of the works in which Alain expounds on the pitiable state of France. In this poem he puts the discussion in the mouths of a wise and experienced herald, who advocates a more positive attitude and active approach than the feckless, demoralized young nobleman he encounters. The peasant named in the title breaks into their dialogue abruptly to add his viewpoint.

In Alain's *Livre des quatre dames*, composed most likely between 1415 and 1418, we find four ladies, four knights, and four unhappy endings. These are the building blocks of the poem translated here, which, at 3,531 lines, is the longest of all his poetic works. The *Quatre Dames* unfolds against the backdrop of the French defeat at Agincourt in October 1415, at which the French were crushed by an English army with overwhelmingly superior military arms and strategy. It represents a synthesis of sorts of the two major themes manifested in Alain's other debate poems and in his work as a whole, setting the conventions of a poem about the finer points of love doctrine in the context of the dire political and military situation of the country near the end of the Hundred Years' War.

Our guide through the poem is a first-person poet figure who, following the conventional model of the narrator as established by Guillaume de Machaut, is both a clerk and a lover himself. Alain plays with the double nature of the narrator by using two different poetic forms that highlight his dual roles. In the prologue, while the narrator takes the reader with him through a springtime landscape and a meditation on his own amorous affairs, revealing that he cannot bring himself to declare his feelings to the lady who has captured his heart, the text reads as lyric poetry. This opening extends for 164 lines, divided into twelve stanzas of either twelve or sixteen octosyllabic lines. Only at the very end of this passage does he see the ladies of the title, along with a shepherd and shepherdess, when he descends into a valley. The sight of them, he tells us, relieves the pain of his own unhappiness. For the reader, the mention of a bucolic setting, peopled by noble ladies and rustics, signals a transition from the narrator's personal lament to a setting traditionally associated with tales of romantic dalliance, courtship, and seduction. At this juncture the line structure changes from stanzas to continuous narrative, using relatively consistent, interlocking, four-line blocks of three octosyllabic lines on the same rhyme followed by a four-syllable line that introduces a new rhyme for the next segment. This form was already familiar from the debates by Machaut and Christine. The narrator and his own concerns step aside as the ladies take center stage, while he assumes the role of audience and scribe for their tales of woe. In the customary manner, he himself demurs when they ask him to decide the case, preferring to recommend that his lady be the judge.

The ladies' stories are much more important to the work than their individual characters. Their dispute is a familiar one: each of the four claims to be the most unhappy. But the outcome of their debate seems of little consequence, and the poem does not include an answer to their request that a judge declare which of them should win this dubious honor. The emphasis is, instead, almost exclusively on the predicaments they present, and the bulk of the text therefore consists of long passages of direct discourse in which they lay out their complaints in detail. None of the ladies is given a name. The narrator, also nameless, refers to them throughout simply as "the first lady" or "the second," and when the characters speak of each other, they use similar generic terminology. Although some attempt has been made to try to discover clues in the text to their possible identity, on the assumption that they represent historical figures well known in Alain's day, very little sets one apart from the other in terms of their rank, appearance, or conduct. When Alain first encounters them, they are all clearly consumed with grief, their eyes cast down, proceeding down the country path in single file lost in contemplation: "Si alerent les pas menuz / De leurs beaulx, blans, petis piez nuz, / Et les yeulx vers terre ont tenuz" (373–75) [They took small steps / With their lovely, white, small, bare feet, / And they kept their eyes on the ground]. While Chartier's description may surprise us with a glimpse of alluring, dainty feet, here as elsewhere the ladies are indistinguishable in their physical being, all conforming to the template of the courtly, aristocratic lady. They are uniformly dignified in comportment, beautiful in face and figure, and eloquent on the topic of love. As a result of this lack of specificity, what defines each of them is exclusively the fate of the knight she loves. Her identity and the case she presents are nothing more nor less than how her lover has fared in the war against the English.

Collectively they represent a bleak picture of the outcome of the battle of Agincourt for the French. The first lady's knight has been killed. The second lady's knight has been captured. The third knight is missing in action, his fate unknown, and the fourth is a deserter. Which lady suffers most? The first, who can never see her lover again? The second, who knows her knight to be suffering and cannot free him? The third, who must live with uncertainty? Or the fourth, who must live with shame? In this work, by virtue of its historical, real-life context, the distress of the debaters represents the very real devastation of the French aristocracy, which suffered not only the loss of many of its leading knights but also the grief, disruption of households, and social and financial consequences that inevitably resulted. Even within the playful conventions of the genre, the ladies' grief has a poignant, immediate quality that must have seemed all too familiar to Alain's readers.

The lack of resolution in this debate is a feature that Alain's debate shares with those by Christine de Pizan. In Christine's three love debate poems, just as in this one, the narrator defers the decision in the dispute at hand to the dedicatee of the poem. Such deferral is a useful literary stratagem that leaves the discussion unresolved, with no need to choose among cases each with obvious merit. It opens the possibility of further discussion as well as a reply, a device used by Machaut to make one text generate the next. It also becomes a graceful gesture of homage and humility. Christine uses it to flatter the patrons to whom she intended to send her work. In the case of the *Quatre Dames*, the gesture reinforces the fiction: it provides the narrator with another excuse to declare his devotion to his beloved. The enthusiastic agreement of the four ladies to accept the narrator's lady as their judge adds to her luster—it can only elevate her status to be asked to arbitrate a matter worthy of written record that affects women of obvious nobility, experience, and wisdom. Moreover, asking his lady to be the judge provides the narrator with a reason to write a fulsome dedication to her at the end of the poem, reminding us of his status as a lover as first revealed in the lyric stanzas at the beginning, and giving him a chance to praise her great worth again as he closes the text and directs it to her attention.

While we are given no decision as to which of the ladies is the most unhappy, there are clues in the text that sway any conclusions the reader might draw. However much the first three might grieve, the plight of the fourth—the lady whose lover ran from the battlefield—is truly the most painful. While her sisters must endure the loss of good men, she, in addition to loss, has to suffer the humiliation of having chosen a man who abandoned king and companions. Before the fourth lady lays out her case, the first has already condemned the cowards and deserters who contributed to the downfall of the whole French army. The despicable actions of the fourth man are in part responsible for the loss of the other three. In the context of the war, there is nothing worse he could have done, and the lady who loved him must share his disgrace. He is almost as false a lover as he is a knight, having failed to devote himself to the ennobling love of one worthy woman, an impetus that might have made him fight with honor. Unlike the other knights, he deserves no sympathy. And unlike the other ladies, the fourth has no consolation.

There is a decidedly feminist slant to this work, again reminiscent of Christine de Pizan, suggesting that women can rise above the factionalism, politics, and hatred of war to help each other and themselves. The second lady, whose knight has been captured, appeals to the women of England to use their influence to secure his release (1797–1823). She states, "Si pevent mont / Toutes les dames en un mont, / Et leur doulceur les y cemont" (1809–11) [They can do much, / All the ladies together, / And their sweetness calls them to it]. In her opinion, these ladies on the winning side should remember that they are as vulnerable as she was to the grief brought on by war. She suggests that nobility of character and solidarity among women transcends their allegiances to home and husband. The female character is more admirable than its male counterpart, we are told in the text. Although women are accused by men of fickleness in love, it is they, in fact, who are the more constant. The choice of the narrator's beloved lady as judge reinforces the notion that women are both proper arbiters for the lovelorn and intermediaries who can help resolve the outcome of military hostilities. The four ladies of the title are the chief claimants in this dispute, but perhaps also their own best advocates.

Alain's language in this poem is dense, elliptical, and clever. Its rhymes are rich and its language is playful. In the relatively flexible format of the poem's octosyllabic interlocking quatrains there is room for alliteration, punning, and repetition. Unfortunately, little of it comes through in translation. How can one capture in another language the force and phonetic appeal of phrases such as "Or fuÿt quant ferir falu" (3005) [Now, he fled when he should have fought]? Or the full flavor of a rich rhyme repeated at the end of four successive lines ("present" in lines 2664–67)? The tone of the poem ranges widely, from heated invective, such as the first lady's harsh censure of deserters, through the lyricism of delicious, reciprocal love, to the pathos of the despair and physical devastation the ladies are suffering.

Alain invokes many of the personified characters that commonly appear in debates of this kind, which brings to the text the linguistic economy of allegorical representation; if a character's proper name—Hope, Desire, Love—immediately conveys his or her role and attitude toward a given question, the text can avoid lengthy explanations. The reader must interpret the action on at least two levels of meaning, the literal and the abstract. That said, however, the pace of the poem is leisurely. We move methodically through several repetitions of the main arguments, and by the end the reader or listener knows the cases thoroughly. The stasis that prevails as the poem closes—with no resolution for either the four ladies or the narrator/poet in his own suit—leaves no doubt that the ultimate tone of the work is one of frustration and unhappiness. Its dramatization of contemporary affairs in France turns this literary text into social commentary as well as a classic example of the love debate genre.

Le Livre des quatre dames

To forget melancholy
And lift my spirits
I went out into the fields one mild morning.
It was the first day that Love brings 4
Hearts together and the beautiful season
Puts an end to troubles and worries.[1]
I went all alone, just as
I usually do, and I also 8
Walked on the new-grown, prickly grass
That carpeted the ground everywhere
With the marvelous colors that the
Bare winter had been missing for so long. 12

All around, birds were flying
And singing so very sweetly
That no heart could have failed to be joyful.
As they were singing, they rose in the air 16
And then they vied to surpass each other
In their rivalry, each as best it could.
The weather was not at all cloudy:
The skies were clothed in blue 20
And the beautiful sun shone brightly.
Violets grew here and there,
And all things carried out their duties just as
Nature instructed. 24

The birds gathered in the bushes.
One sang and the others added harmonies,
Giving voice from their throats to
The song that Nature had taught them; 28
And then they parted company.
None of them resembled the others;
There were so many of them that it seemed
That they would be difficult to count. 32
I halted in a grove
Of trees, pondering the excellence
Of Nature, who had undertaken
To have them make such music; 36
But I saw them overcome with joy
And in the thrall of new love,

And each one had already taken
And chosen one true mate.   40

Along this path resounding
With sweet harmonies I went,
Thinking about my unhappy fortune,
Wondering to myself   44
How Love, who is so powerful,
Can be generous with his joys except for one,
Which I cannot acquire
By any means, even though I wish   48
For no other favor from Love.
It is bad luck or misfortune;
Others commonly enjoy the benefits
While I have nothing from it but grief.   52

I looked at the trees in bloom
And the hares and rabbits running around;
Everything found pleasure in the spring.
Love seemed to govern there: 56
It seems to me that no one
Can age or die as long as he is there.
A sweet fragrance wafted from the greenery,
Which scented the calm air;   60
And babbling through the valley
A small stream ran along,
Bringing moisture to the countryside,
With its fresh water free of salt.   64

It was there that the birds drank,
After they had made their meal
Of crickets and flies
And butterflies.   68
I saw lanner falcons, goshawks, and merlins,
And stinging bees
Who built new honey houses
In regular fashion among the trees.   72
On the other side was a hedge that enclosed
A lovely meadow where Nature
Had sown in the grass flowers
Of white, yellow, red, and blue.   76
The hedge was made up of flowering trees
As white as if they were covered
With pure snow; it seemed like a painting,
There were so many different colors.   80

The stream flowed from a fresh spring
Down from bare rock,
About two yards in breadth.
It ran along the grassy bank 84
And it made a very pleasant sound
On the stones, which obstruct its flow.
I saw many a small fish, many a carp
Swimming there, reveling 88
In the water so clear, clean, and pure.
I was in no hurry to leave the place;
Instead, it grieved me greatly that
Such a fine day must come to an end. 92

Right nearby, on the downhill
Slope of the mountain,
There stood a pretty copse
That grew close along the stream, 96
And green curtains hung
From its branches down upon the bank.
Many wild birds frequent that spot—
Some fly, others bathe in the stream— 100
Ducks, wood pigeons, herons, pheasants.
Stags passed through in the shadows
And, Lord knows, those uncaged birds,
Were far from silent. 104

I was thus enjoying myself a little
As I reflected on that beauty,
And I emerged from that sadness
That I carry well concealed. 108
And then I scolded myself
And did my best to sing,
But if I enjoyed it at all
It did not last long. 112
Instead I suddenly returned
To the thought that had preoccupied
Me at first, which so cruelly,
And for so long, has plagued me. 116
The pleasure increased my torment
As I saw the happiness around me,
Since my own state was quite otherwise,
For Hope had failed me. 120

And so I said, "Oh, Love, Love,
Why do you make me live my life in tears

And spend my days in sadness
When you bring pleasure everywhere else? 124
I am sworn to your service forever,
And yet I encounter all manner of hardships,
More harshness and less help
Than those who love Deception. 128
I willingly accepted my suffering,
While awaiting the good offices
Of the beautiful one who has the power
To improve my lot;[2] 132
But I see that Duplicity advances the cause
Of those who have an abundance of favors
In which I had hoped to share, but failed.
This is not a fair distribution." 136

Thus was my heart complaining
About the great pain it felt
In that agreeable, secluded place,
Where a soft breeze was blowing, 140
So gentle that one could perceive it only
Because the grass smelled sweeter for it.
That place was the gracious dwelling
Of all the beauty and joy 144
That Nature can create in summertime.
There was nothing that could have been improved on
In all the things that could please me,
If only my lady had been there. 148

I set out to follow a long and narrow
Path, on which the tender grass
Grew thick and a little shorter
Than that all around. 152
There I was surprised by an attack
Of Desire, which overwhelmed me,
And paying no attention to where I went,
Nor thinking of my return, 156
I found myself far away, in an isolated spot.
There Desire attacked me fiercely
And I no longer knew what to do,
When, nearby, I saw a shepherdess 160
And a shepherd kissing,
And, far away, coming out of a tower,
Four ladies in noble attire;
The sight of them eased my pain. 164

When I caught sight of these ladies
To some small degree I forgot my sorrow,
Of which I have much more than I used to,
And which will cease   168
At last when it is Love's pleasure
Or when Death puts an end to it altogether;
One of those two will take it from me.
No one else can do anything   172
Except the lady who does not want my heart—
May she learn more about it than she used to know!—
Because, on her account,
The poor heart suffers   176
And feels such pain from it that
I lose both countenance and color.
But whether it be good sense or folly,
No matter what happens   180
My heart must always remain with her,
Without ever changing,
Even though it is not my lot
To have such favor   184
As to be loved by this most beautiful of ladies.
It suits me well that because of her
I suffer from the pain my heart conceals,
And that I love her   188
Only in my thoughts, within myself,
And that I name her my only lady
And call out to her in my pain,
Since I can do   192
Nothing else about it, and I dare not
Do more than think about revealing
To her the ardor I keep hidden,
For if saying it   196
Led to a rejection,
There would be nothing left to laugh about.
And so this affliction is better than something worse
And one ill is better than two.   200
Thus I remained in the fields all alone,
And among the shepherds I saw the ones
Who were in love with each other, and around them
Their lambs.   204
Their young love led them to make
Many small, gracious tokens,
And they gave each other flowers
And green garlands;   208
And then they danced across the fields

All covered with marvelous flowers,
And did many a different step.
I much desired 212
Their very pleasant life,
Which seemed overflowing with joy
And full of contentment.
And upon my soul, 216
If Love would permit that my lady,
She who so enflames my heart,
Were like a woman of humble condition,
A shepherdess in the fields, 220
I know that it would not be long before
Of my own free will I would
Be keeping sheep in the fields, leaving
Everything else behind; 224
Were that the case, I would think
No more painful thoughts, and I would more readily dare
To tell her of the malady that wearies me,
Even though I will 228
Never weary of being caught in her snares,
Even though I complain and say "Alas!"
To do her bidding means more to me than my happiness:
That is my desire, 232
Both when I rise and when I retire.
I wish for time and leisure
In which I might do something
For her pleasure, 236
And that I could accomplish it
As well as I would like,
Although not as well as I ought,
Nor as well as she deserves. 240
But even where ability is lacking,
Goodwill does not fail in the end;
If my heart has set its sights too high,
I only prize it 244
The more highly for undertaking
Such a noble enterprise.
Ultimately my lady will do with it
As she sees fit; 248
And it is of great comfort to me—
Even if I should die as a result—
That no one can say, "He is wrong
To love that lady"; 252
And I would not dare blame
Desire, who enflames me,

And from whom I have so much bitterness.
He would be 256
Heartless, the man who could consider
Her virtue, and think about her,
Without loving her willingly.
Furthermore I believe it 260
To be true, and think I know for a fact,
That many men desire to win
Her favor, and they, of whom
I am the least important, 264
Do every task that Love makes them undertake,
While I dare not expect her favor;
And never, because I fear making a mistake,
Will she know anything about it. 268
My mouth, at least, will keep quiet
And let my countenance behave in such a way
That she may perhaps see in it
A sign 272
That I feel nothing but distress.
And of all the men in France
There is not a single one whom Love assails
More cruelly. 276
But even if Hope had failed me
And I were worse off,
At least I have not failed
To choose well. 280
For my choice is to my liking
For her sweetness and good conduct.
There is nothing but complete perfection
In the beautiful lady. 284
And if I had such grace
As to be well received by her, nothing more,
Or to hear of her some
Good news, 288
Never would one see a lover
Rejoice—even if he enjoyed the ultimate favor—
Or escape all pain
Any more than I would. 292
But that cannot be:
My fortune will not have it,
Nor would the thought strike me
That it might happen 296
That she thus remember me
Or retain me as her servant,
For in no way would I be worthy of

Such a loving   300
Thought or such a gracious one,
So lofty or so happy,
Nor so rich in joy,
Seeing as I am   304
The one who brings harm to myself
By my bad luck; ever since
My childhood have I had nothing but trouble,
And in love   308
Only short-lived joy and abiding grief.
In return for loyalty I get the opposite
Of those who use deceitful means
And profit by them.   312
I must bear this unhappiness
Since everything turns out so badly for me.
In the end, if right has its reward,
A time will come   316
When Love will take great pity on me
And bestow my heart on the lady
Who, if it pleases her, will accept it.
I placed it there   320
Two months ago and renounced my claim to it,
And I promised Love
To yield it freely to her, and I surrendered
To his bidding,   324
Requesting that he transform the grief
I have suffered for more than two years,
Which is plain to see,
Because of the refusal 328
Of the lady whose servant I was,
Who put in my heart the tip and shaft
Of a loving arrow that left me
Shattered.   332
For two years I awaited her mercy:
Whatever she commanded or forbade
I did, but her intentions
Lay elsewhere;   336
Perhaps I came a bit too late
And she had set her sights on something better.
But I pray God that he keep her
And grant her such joy 340
From it that she cannot fail
To experience how Love pierces
Those for whom things do not go well,
Just as I have   344

Experienced it. Thus I proceeded,
Engrossed in the thoughts that I never leave behind,
And in a valley that I was descending
I caught sight of   348
The ladies whom I had seen earlier;
As I approached them I knew
That they had suffered much grief.
For they proceeded   352
Like women who were grieving
And wanted only to be left alone with their thoughts;
And they did not speak to each other at all;
Instead, each   356
Walked along the grassy path all alone.
They sang no songs,
Nor did they care
To gather violets;   360
Rather, each lamented her grief,
Which was constantly on her mind,
And they approached in single file, one after the other.
Their servants   364
Were quite far behind them, and they were
Gloomy in countenance and sad in their manner,
And their clothes were hardly
Extravagant.   368
I set off to meet them
Along a path that led their way,
Praising Love that such an encounter
Had happened to me;   372
They took small steps
With their lovely, white, small, bare feet,
And they kept their eyes on the ground.
So much grief   376
Were they suffering that they were not aware
Of what path they had just taken,
And they did not notice me either
Until after   380
I had come very near them,
At the edge of a green meadow
That smelled much better than cypress.
Then I said,   384
"Dear ladies, may God grant you
Joy of heart, good health of body,
And solace, better than
They appear to be!"   388
At that they raised their eyes

And one, with no smile or jest,
Said to me, "God grant that you fare better
Than we, sir, 392
And do not be vexed if we were passing by
Without greeting you, for our hearts
Are all so full of pain
And sadness, 396
Which envelops them in distress,
And are beset with such bitterness
That there is no happiness in this world
That they might receive 400
Or that they might see in any way
That would not increase their distress
And make their troubles rebel
Against pleasure; 404
For in us there is such a surfeit
Of grief and despair
That it is not in our power
To dissemble; 408
Rather, Reason has trouble restraining
Us and preventing our mouths
From crying out loudly and lamenting,
For our hearts are 412
So full of the misery they feel
That I do not know why it does not break them;
Each of them has almost dissolved
And they have all nearly cracked. 416
We wish for nothing more
Than that our bodies give up our souls
And that our lives be soon improved
By Death. 420
Death is the only remedy for them,
And so I ask her that I may die
And finish life and grief together,
For I have come to hate 424
Completely both earth and country;
Everything hurts me. My heart is assailed
By everything; Hope has betrayed it,
Which makes me lament, 428
For I am the sad and sorrowful woman
Who fails entirely in her desire.
I have lost the profit of joy,
Which sustained 432
My heart and kept it joyful,
And brought dividend enough to please me,

As was fitting;
Now it fails me."   436
Then she sighed deeply
And sat down, for her heart was failing her;
She had fainted, or nearly so.
I listened to her   440
And sorrowful as I was,
I nevertheless comforted her;
But even though I hesitated
To inquire   444
About her pain and press her about it,
I was bold enough to request
That she might grant me
The private favor   448
That it please her to tell me,
With no fear, what her problem was,
And I would conceal it well,
If need be;   452
And if she wanted to ask of me
Anything that might be appropriate,
Or if my service could be of help,
I would give to it   456
Heart and body and everything I had,
And I would do it as willingly
As I possibly could.
At that, the decorous lady   460
Turned toward me her sweet face
Which was bathed in big tears.
In her heart she bore the mark
Of terrible grief.   464
And sighing once again,
She put her two hands to her face
And said, "What pain, what misfortune!
And what great loss!   468
I will never recover from it.
Oh, Death! You have completely forsaken me
And unjustly afflicted my heart,
Which will die as a result,   472
Despite you, as soon as it can,
But not as soon as it would like.
Never will anyone be able to preserve it
From death,   476
For my sorrowful, sad life,
Which has endured too long
And which surpasses death in its harshness

And causes me such 480
Unhappiness, will rid me of it.
Wishing to follow my heart,
I will die from being sick of life.
It will happen thus, 484
For if Death continues to elude me,
My life itself will kill me
And strike me down more quickly
Than Death who is slow 488
To kill me; and I want no protection
Against her, but rather request and exhort her to come.
And Death is more generous with those
Who flee her 492
Than with those who seek refuge with her
And to whom life is a burden,
So much that they summon and pursue her;
It is unjust." 496
At that point I began to speak
And said that her despair would cost her much,
And her heart and body would be the worse for it.
And I asked her 500
On bended knee—humbling myself
Because of the pity I felt for her,
And I did not forget to say
That I, too, 504
Had troubles, so much so
That no man is as badly off as I—
That she be good enough to tell me
How it came about 508
That she should have so much pain,
And what brought her such distress;
And I would tell her what happened to me,
For in my opinion 512
Disclosing unhappy thoughts
Often lightens and diminishes the pain
They cause, whatever people say,
For Grief oppresses 516
And conceals a heart that is too constrained
When the mouth remains firmly shut.
A secret is not compromised, however,
If one reveals it 520
To a person who hears it willingly
And who is neither a gossip nor a fool,
And if not a single word of it
Is ever repeated. 524

And when the lady heard me,
She replied to me most gently:³
"I do not at all dispute
That you are 528
As discreet as you should be.
You can see the state I am in.
Since you want to listen, listen now,
For it seems to me 532
That my unhappiness is unlike any other,
And if Love is robbing you of your heart,
We can manage so much better together,
In solidarity." 536
Then she said in beautiful, pitiful language,
With tears in her bright eyes,
Which were swollen from weeping:
"Ah, cruel Destiny 540
And unhappy, ill-fated
Accursed day, it is you
Who have turned all my joy
Into suffering! 544
Alas! On that day died the man
I loved so much and so strongly
That never did lovers' hearts love each other
In such harmony 548
And with such loyalty for so long.
Now he is dead—honorably
For him, and grievously
For me. Alas! 552
Oh, heart of my most faithful lover,
I had from you and you from me
So much pleasure! Now I moan,
Since I am separated 556
From you, alone and lost,
Deprived of all pleasure.
I paid dearly for the sweetness
That I now lack. 560
Death, cruel Death, may God curse you!
How can you be so bold
As to have parted our two hearts
So capriciously 564
And separated them far from each other,
When you had nothing to do with bringing together
What formed a single entity?
Alas! A single heart 568
Cannot follow two paths;

It has but one life and one death;
And that which is but one must travel
But one journey.   572
Joy and grief, all is shared;
One death for one and for the other,
One single life for each.
You did this   576
Willfully rather than of necessity,
When, by your grievous misdeed,
You dissolved and undid
So faithful a match.   580
But—this is what distresses me—
Why did you not kill me, who am
By no means the stronger, as soon as
My dear companion?   584
How can I escape you?
Why does your arrow not come to strike me,
Why do you not attempt to catch me
Without tarrying so?   588
But the arrow's tedious delay
Will sap it of its strength
In spite of your great severity
That works   592
Against me, whom Sorrow consumes,
Which is a great misdeed.
Not to leave all or take all
Is folly.   596
He was in his prime,
And born of such a noble house;
And you took him against reason,
To my detriment,   600
Which was a foolish action on your part
And constitutes an abuse of your office,
For he was in my service
And loved me so—   604
For which no one reproached him—
And called me his lady
And made no other claim on me.
And you take him,   608
You who have nothing to do with it, which is a misdeed,
And plunge me into despair
When you fail to take with one blow
Both lady and servant.   612
Oh, why was he so eager?
Why did he lead the way

In meeting his enemies,
When out of bravery 616
He did such deeds with axe and lance
That everyone feared his strength,
By which he did great honor to France?
And if Fortune 620
Had wished that in some way
He be taken prisoner, I would be one
Of the happiest women under the moon.[4]
If people talked 624
About his honor, which would be flourishing,
And if everyone cherished him,
Then my heart would rejoice so greatly.
But it is otherwise 628
With me: I lose entirely
First this joy
And then the others likewise,
Which is why 632
I have a quarrel with Death, who with keen grief
Deprives me of a hundred thousand pleasures,
And wants me to live on, despite myself,
No matter how things are. 636
And Death takes from me what gave me
My joy, and what sustained me
With pleasure that never diminished
Even one little bit. 640
Why, therefore, does it not take me,
Why did it not take me then,
Without undoing our union
For no reason? 644
Victory or defeat,
Good health, life, death, or the grave,
Everything would have been a shared adventure;
And I would have thought 648
That I would never live on after him.
In fact, were it not for my fear of God,
I would avenge myself on Death with death.[5]
I would do it willingly, 652
And keep him company
In life and death; but I would lose
My soul for it, and take from his
The gift of grace. 656
Now I pray God that He forgive
My lover's sins and grant him mercy,
And that soon, by his will, He set free

From my body   660
The soul, which wishes to be released
And which desires nothing other
Than that we had both been killed by one blow
In this war,   664
That our bodies be together in the ground,
Both in one secure coffin,
And that we might attain paradise.
So I will double   668
My grief constantly, and remove myself
From the company of others. In this I will resemble
The turtledove: I will keep company with no one else,
For he was a man   672
Who always treated me properly,
So much did he honor and fear me,
And comfort me in my troubles.
Now he has departed,   676
Which leaves my heart pale and wan,
Afflicted with all manner of pain,
Which has already drained me of all color.
Desire remains   680
And is always present in my heart,
Which labors in vain and for nothing.
When Desire attacks, Hope fails
And takes leave   684
Of me, who have such a share of grief
That my heart very nearly deserts me
And almost breaks in two
When Memory   688
Makes me keep in my thoughts
How he used to come to me,
And his gracious manner,
And the sweet words   692
He said to me about everything;
For I can safely say that he was praised
By every noble person.
His speech   696
Became him and he regulated it well,
For he hated all types of dishonor
And honored me sweetly
Whenever he came;   700
But he did not stay away for long—
Desire often urged him to return.
Laughter and games, everything suited him.
Lord, what a loss!   704

He left me, that wise and handsome man
Of noble blood and royal lineage,
But nobler still as regards his courage,
He who by legitimate claim had 708
Acquired my love,
For which he had long begged
And sought my mercy in so gentle a manner.
But his worthiness had won me, 712
And I had tested
Him so much that I knew his heart
Was so much mine and in such a way
That I did not need to doubt him; 716
In him my desire
Was fixed and resolved,
Which Love has since confirmed.
But that miserable, wretched 720
Army
And immoderate Fortune
Can grant me nothing more
Than that my only joy last 724
Half a season.
Fortune, who is a friend of the disloyal,
Is, alas, hostile to me,
In that she could not allow me— 728
May God confound her—
A single joy in this world
That causes no harm to anyone.
And she allows many a man, in all comfort, 732
To enjoy an abundance
Of whatever gives him pleasure,
Without causing her any displeasure
And without him knowing unhappiness. 736
Such a man has not
Deserved to receive the goods
That Love shares out, for his heart
Is not bound in service but free from subjection; 740
And he should be banished
For it, since he has not feared
His lady, but rather has allied himself
With Duplicity, who has elevated him 744
To such heights
That he becomes, through hypocritical subtlety
And deception, who school him,
A thief, stealing love's treasure 748
That he has collected

From many places,
By which his joy never doubles
And many a lady is ill served. 752
But it happens
That at some point, and rightly so,
The honor of unfaithful lovers diminishes
And in the end it turns out badly for them 756
That they have
Willingly followed the wrong paths
And that they have not been constant
In love, always extending it to a third party. 760
There are numerous
Such lovers, many more than in times past,
Who have broken many promises
And cannot tire of it. 764
Often on their lips are heard
The names of many ladies, which they broadcast unfairly.
They know full well, however, that
Nature has ordained one single heart 768
For each man;
It should not be carelessly placed
Elsewhere once he has bestowed it on one lady,
Nor should he be pardoned for doing so, 772
For Love wants
To dictate, in order to reward
The virtuous, that one lady can give
As great an abundance of good as a hundred can, 776
And so wise
Is Love that he has bestowed
As much power on one lady as on six.
It pleases him more and has suited him better 780
To set one's heart
On one lady than to undertake everywhere
To serve, suffer, and submit,
To promise much and deliver little. 784
Such men cannot
Know what good is. It would be reckless
Of anyone to help such men
When they say that they would die 788
For true love, and take on
Such sad airs
And such a humble, helpful manner
In order to steal that of which they are not worthy. 792
And even if they have not, in fact,
Obtained it, they will boast,

As if rejoicing, that yes, indeed they have.
Alas, my heart has fled from so many 796
Of their speeches
And their great, foolish flatteries,
Their lying, feeble blandishments!
Greatly have I despised such frivolities. 800
But I searched until
I found a man who pleased me,
Whom I found to be good and loyal,
Whose every action I approved of. 804
There I stopped,
And prepared my heart to love him,
The heart that is about to break,
And I gave and granted it to him; 808
And in exchange
I took his, as a loving interchange.
Now I lose them both in a strange way,
And so I go, with bare feet and in rags, 812
To pray to the Virgin
Who is the true guardian of the heavens,
Offering her a lighted candle
In order to acquire mercy and forgiveness, 816
By her grace,
And that she might grant the two of us
As a gift that we not linger thus
One after the other, but rather that we preserve 820
Our love,
By her compassion, both in life and in death.
He acquitted himself well of his pledge,
And many a chronicle and tale 824
Should by now
Have been composed about him, for he dared so much
That he risked body and life,
With no cowardice or faltering, 828
Like a man of valor,
Against those who came to attack
France, and his unfailing courage
Gave them much trouble 832
To contend with.[6]
And had everyone wished to do
The same without bringing shame upon themselves,
The English would have accomplished little; 836
Instead, they would have rid us of
Our troubles and become disheartened,
And taken themselves off elsewhere,

And thereafter refrained from 840
Harming us.
The envious can drop dead:
His death increases his honor
As opposed to those who would elevate 844
Ill fame.
They have seen nothing in him but
Loyalty, whose name he bears,
For we hold as loyal those 848
Who so conduct themselves
That they fulfill their oath and duty
To their lord and support him
Unto death, and uphold 852
Their loyalty
As the need arises, as well as their fealty
Toward their lady and her beauty,
With no shameful thoughts, cruelty, 856
Or subtle tricks.
Such are the principles of the noble hearts
Whom apprentices in arms
And love should take as their example: 860
Humble, merciful,
And desirous of nothing more than honor;
Nor should they be fearful
Of anything but base deeds. 864
And such a man was he
On whom my heart was set,
Who brought me so much joy
And gently urged me 868
To keep myself
Joyful and charming, saying that his heart,
Without unseemly familiarity, was acquainted with mine,
One joy united in two hearts; 872
And he used to swear
As much to me without perjuring himself.
Why could he not have lived for me?
What made him seek adventure? 876
I would have been
So honored if my joy
Had lasted. Now I am so tearstained
I can hardly see, a lovelorn woman 880
Full of anguish
And of futile desire that vexes me,
That makes my every limb ache,
And all my senses ramble. 884

Ah, disloyal men,
Runaways, cowards and traitors,
You who love nothing but rank and jewels!⁷
You deserted all those of royal blood 888
And turned your backs
On them and went back,
Having stayed there all too briefly,
For then you abandoned them, 892
All faithless
And cowardly in your betrayal,
By which our numbers were decreased
And the hearts of the English emboldened, 896
For in throngs,
Despite the shouts and calls
Of the good men, you covered the crests
Of your helmets. May you be 900
Flayed alive
And so thoroughly beaten
That you never recover!
Such people should be swineherds 904
Or made to do
Menial work in the towns and cities,
Since they are useless in battle;
They want exorbitant taxes 908
For their presumption,
And they steal from the poor,
Deceiving all the world and cheating!
All they are good for is settling in 912
At the hearth
When their mouths are full of wine
And they have the best vintages.
Then they tell tales about their adventures, 916
The foolish braggarts;
They boast of great blows struck
And spend lavishly and incur big expenses.
And no matter who might be captured or rescued, 920
Not one of them gives it a thought;
They might be quick to spend
But they are very slow to defend.
One blasphemes against God, the other quarrels 924
In his great drunkenness,
Then sleeps until ten out of laziness,
But in battle he knows how to save
His ass fast from the crush 928
And to throw off

His helmet when the kingdom is in need.
He knows more about dice or handball;
He sleeps better in a bed than on straw. 932
Lord, what a soft bunch!
They are tender as a new bride,
Trembling like a shorn sheep.
May the quartan fever come infect 936
That pile of filth!
And may poverty never leave them
Until, sickly, they are forced to die of hunger,
Left on a bit of straw 940
And abandoned.
When they deserted you in battle,
Royal princes who provided for them,
They abased their families 944
And shamed them.
They have greatly tarnished the honor
So dear to their fathers
And for which they were called noble; 948
From such fathers came
These men who did not carry on
Those good deeds or uphold them
When they returned in disgrace. 952
It causes me so much grief
That I cannot look on any one of them
With approval, nor do I wish them well,
For they are the cause of my grief. 956
I have paid for
Their craven avarice:
Their cowardice has killed the man
Who cannot be bought back. 960
May God keep his soul!
To their great shame, their desertion is the cause
Of the defeat and of their ignominy.
Would I have acted thus, I who am a woman, 964
Or would I do so,
If it were up to me? I would rather
Die, and be the happier for it,
For I would thus maintain my honor 968
For posterity;
It is preferable by far
To die with honor as a hostage
Than to prolong one's life in disgrace. 972
Far better to destroy
The body than to have people point,

Not daring to encounter
Anyone worthy, or to enter into company. 976
And thus, in truth,
I find more pleasing the faithful service
Of the man I love without disloyalty
And can accept less well 980
That in the press
Of battle, into which he threw himself,
He found less safety
Than those who never fought there. 984
I greatly regret,
Harsh Death, that you do not more promptly sting
Those who are accustomed to worthless behavior
And who are as useful alive as dead. 988
My beloved's death,
Although honorable, is all the less agreeable because
For me his life would have been a more delightful
And valuable present. 992
Now there is nothing to be done;
That is why my life is wearisome to me
Without his, for the better his life was,
The more suitable it would be. 996
Thus I am beset
With sorrow much more than many others,
For one cannot redeem the death
Of good men, nor lament or weep for it enough. 1000
As for the wicked, however,
Who are a hindrance to others
And are worth nothing in woods or fields,
Death should come to them quickly, 1004
For their cowardly life
Is not a happy one
But rather a life squandered and of little virtue.
And so that sort of death is not regrettable. 1008
But I must weep
Because I live on after the death
Of the man who, to win my love,
Gained so much honor. 1012
And so I am committed
And devoted to Distress.
Love has given me this reward:
Hope has completely abandoned me, 1016
And my eyes no longer see
A single blessing they used to have,

For they must never see such things again.
I would lose little were they gouged out, 1020
For in all truth
I will never perceive with them
Anything that will give me joy.
Instead, I will die when I must die, 1024
Devoid of joy,
In no way beholden to Fortune
Or Love, who, all at once,
Leave me not even 1028
The smallest hope;
They leave me in a state of intense grief,
By which they greatly reduce their worth,
For since my earliest desires, they have always 1032
Nurtured me thus.
In the end, since my beloved was mortal,
I will retain as my only possession
The glory of having loved such a man. 1036
Thus my sad heart,
Which Death despises, does its duty.
So I pray God that He take from me
My miserable, accursed life 1040
That grieves me so
And that has made a truce with Death,
To the effect that Death will not overwhelm it;
And so, my life will be briefer, 1044
For I can take no more of it."
At this point she fell silent; and then
From the bottom and the depths of her heart
She gave so many sighs 1048
And so many laments,
And her eyes were so full of tears
As she made her complaint,
That I feel pity for her even now, weeping inside, 1052
Nor can I set her case
In verse without shedding tears,
Without grieving and feeling distressed.
I gave it much thought in private yesterday 1056
And I marvel,
Given the grief she assumes,
That her great, unparalleled beauty
And her fresh and rosy complexion 1060
Can endure;
Although grief makes her weep,
I never saw her face look wan;

Instead, weeping suited her better
Than laughter does many others.
Then I said to her, "My lady, I see clearly
That your laments are not feigned,
But rather forced upon you by your anguish.
Yet take heart
And learn to suffer,
For you make a very great mistake
If you wage war against yourself.
Anyone who conceals grief
Too strenuously gets twice the pain in return,
For the nature of unhappiness is such
That it decreases if one reveals it
Where appropriate;
And if one conceals it too much, it strikes
The heart and lodges within.
But the more they are shared, the less time
Sad thoughts will last.
Make an effort to think of other things
To compensate for your suffering.
And in taking care not to give offense,
Reflect on this.
Talk with these ladies
And together seek comfort.
Take my word for it and change your mind."
I spoke thus
To this lady I esteemed greatly,
Whom I addressed concerning her welfare.
And I was advising the three others
Similarly
That they should comfort her
In such a way that she might slowly
Find relief, little by little,
When one of them
Replied:[8] "Alas, I am one of those
Who feel such deadly sorrows
That no other woman has as bad.
I am therefore far
From seeing to the comfort of others,
For I am more in need of comfort
Than she and more apprehensive about
My bad fortune,
Which will not let me feel safe,
Nor do I have any way to find reassurance:
And she is not subject to the fear

And the dread
That beset me harshly,
Constrain my heart and body,
And deprive me of all joy.   1112
I will tell you
My story, and I will not lie about it,
Concerning the love that I will never
Abandon, though I have heaved many a sigh   1116
Because of it.
Sighing has brought no comfort to my heart,
Which, encouraged by true love,
Attached itself to one individual   1120
And joined with
This man who so humbled himself
That he pledged to love me truly—
And he has so many fine points!   1124
But it so happened
That before he was twenty years of age,
Many misadventures unjustly befell him
At the hands of Fortune; and it came to the point   1128
In the last ten years
That because of evil gossips,
Who falsified the truth,
Speaking ill of him and his family,   1132
His honor was
Much damaged, which was a sin,
For he is so endowed with good qualities
And devoted to everything honorable   1136
That he is praised
By all good men and said to be
Generously blessed with virtue.
But it appears that Fortune swore   1140
To do him harm—
My heart loses what it holds most dear,
As one can clearly see—
Even though he is wise and valiant.   1144
But listen
To his story: since his early childhood,
When first he could put foot into stirrup,
Fortune could wait no longer   1148
To attack him.
And since then, he is never without
Grief and Vexation, who have often
Made him tremble and served him badly.   1152
But when he overcame

One difficulty that wore him down,
Fortune immediately created
And invented a completely new misfortune, 1156
Quite unexpectedly.
I believe that God watches over good people
And keeps joy in reserve for them after sorrow,
But it delays too long and comes too slowly for me. 1160
And Fortune
Is taking too long before changing her course,
She who prevents me from seeing him,
Which leaves me pensive and mournful. 1164
And know this:
My heart is so attached to him
And my thoughts so tied to his,
The good and bad that befall us are so intertwined, 1168
That, without lying
And with no regret,
True love makes me consent
To experience the same good and bad 1172
As he does,
And because he is all mine,
I take on our good and bad
As my own, as my allotment. 1176
Nor will his
Bad Fortune ever be such a barrier
To our love that she turns
Our determination upside down, 1180
And even if she wanted
To do the worst she is capable of,
Our love would endure forever
Or each of us would die. 1184
The more Fortune tries
To harm us, the stronger our love becomes;
I see nothing good in it save this,
That Fortune has no power over love. 1188
And so I do not believe
She can bring dishonor on our love.
Fortune can never overcome
Love, who exalts the lofty hearts 1192
We so esteem.
Never has a man been so afflicted
With hardships, for, with no mistake,
The death of friends, wars and imprisonment, 1196
Vexations and losses,
The blame incurred from obvious lies,

Betrayals, and covert wicked deeds,
All these has he endured and suffered,   1200
All the while keeping his counsel
And returning good for bad,
Gently soothing his heart,
Which has never had a single happy day.   1204
But he has been
Attacked and despised by many,
Who would willingly have betrayed him,
Something that he has not deserved.   1208
He would never know
How to be anything but gentle, and he would
Never have the heart to take pleasure in something
He knew would bring displeasure to someone else;   1212
For he is reasonable,
Courteous, gentle and amiable,
Patient, charitable, and accommodating;
He wants to be agreeable to everyone,   1216
And wants no one to have the impression
That he blames, maltreats, or deceives others,
But, rather, receives everyone graciously.
And so it grieves me that anyone could harbor   1220
Blame or reproach toward him
And that Fortune so trespasses
Against the one who most touches my heart,
When never an ignoble word issues from   1224
His mouth;
Instead he gives everyone a warm welcome and reception,
Ready to grant every request,
Not hurting anyone any more than he would his own head.   1228
Nor was he ever happy
To have anyone think wicked thoughts.
Nor is he a practiced liar,
But quick to undertake any loyal agreement   1232
Of good intent.
Always aspiring to a worthy goal,
He spends his youth bettering himself.
Now he has been captured defending himself   1236
Against adversaries
Who are opposed to his prince,
After all the other incidents
And scores of misadventures   1240
That have plagued him,
From which he has not yet recovered.
My heart is so steeped

In distress that but for a little it would break 1244
When he feels
So abandoned by joy, and so overwhelmed
With sadness, which he knows so well.
Pain upon pain leads not to good health, 1248
But to grave danger.
And Fortune wants to change
Herself when she no longer knows
How to change her strange, deceitful schemes 1252
In order to remain
Harsh toward him constantly and treat
Him worse than she treats many others.⁹
I pray God that He bring him back to me 1256
By his benign
Mercy; for this reason I am journeying
As a piteous pilgrim,
Asking Him, even though I am not worthy of it, 1260
That He might
Protect him always and look after him.
Fortune is slow in giving him happiness,
Which makes it hard for him to protect himself: 1264
Her tricks occur
Suddenly, with no rhyme or reason;
They are persistently so contrary
That adversity comes to good people, 1268
Who are cast down
And vexed by Fortune,
Which saddens many hearts
When they have fallen deeply in love. 1272
And when they see
The only good thing they had in this world—
From which they had such joy,
Or realized all their dreams— 1276
Thus accompanied
And attacked by Misfortune,
It cannot but trouble and disturb them,
For a loving heart has half a share, 1280
In equal parts,
Of its one and only love,
Whether the experience be good or bad,
Laughter, tears, distress or merriment. 1284
And so it was right
That I, in my heart, be held captive
With him in a foreign, maritime land,¹⁰
Sharing his prison, 1288

Without demanding
Liberty or transgressing the laws
Of Love, who has left me starving,
Pining for what lies across the sea, 1292
There where my heart veers
Going faster than an arrow,
Without the aid of boat or other vessel.
And my body, pale as ivory, 1296
Has stayed here
For some time now, without a heart and without joy,
Which has not come to me since then,
For Fortune wounded it so badly. 1300
And so I went,
All joy destroyed,
With my heart across the salty sea;
But even though its span is wide, 1304
So much that one
Can lose one's way there without seeing land,
Never will that sea be able to separate
Our hearts, which Love brings 1308
Together and joins
In one sole will that conjoins
Them, and links them as equals,
So that there is neither greater nor smaller. 1312
Love binds
Our two hearts into one, so say I,
Like two stems on one branch.
He calls himself my true liege servant 1316
And I am his;
The only word for it is 'thine.'
If either of us is in command it is I,
By the ancient laws of Love, 1320
Who ordered it be thus
For ladies and put them
In command, which entails many a noble gift.
By this means Love rewarded them for 1324
The favors bestowed by
Their grace when they generously extend
Their mercy to those who languish
For love, which wastes away the hearts 1328
Of the most powerful.
Love makes them truly obedient,
Paying homage and acknowledging
The ladies who grant their favors 1332
As their mistresses

And most honorable princesses,
Who distribute love's riches
Sparingly or generously, 1336
As they wish,
And so, when one man sings, the others grieve.¹¹
But fools are no more used to standing still
Than mills that turn in all winds. 1340
Once they have devised
Their deceit, Love develops
Rancor toward them and punishes them,
Which makes them look downcast 1344
And they often weep.
Love takes revenge by making them fall in love
With ladies who do not take pity on them
Because of the bad rumors about them, 1348
For which they receive
As their reward that they deceive themselves
When they would be deceiving others.
And they drink exactly what they brew, 1352
Without intending to,
For sooner or later, hard or soft,
Good actions are never lost in love,
Nor does evil go unpunished 1356
No matter what one expects,
For Love, who improves hearts,
Demands a penalty for misdeeds
And gives to each his recompense 1360
Like a real judge
Who judges love debates.
But my love has never needed recourse to him
To lodge a complaint; nor have I, 1364
For we have
Two hearts completely joined in one common will,
Pierced with one and the same desire.
And may God help me in my need, 1368
For I loved him
And do love him so much that I called him
'All mine,' and he called me the same.¹²
I sang of it: now I weep, 1372
With saddened heart.
Now the joy sweet love
Had nourished is much diminished,
Without allowing me ever to sing or to laugh, 1376
Unless God takes action
And stops the pain I can barely conceal,

Provided I get him back,
For my eye does not open except with reluctance 1380
Nor will it,
Nor will it find pleasure in anything,
Until it recovers sight of him
And until God takes further action 1384
With good haste,
So that he might be relieved
Of the evils that besiege him,
Which have constantly grown worse. 1388
That tormented man,
He has experienced every misfortune except death.
He has paid Fortune's due,
And so he should be absolved of the debt, 1392
For without a doubt,
She tried so hard to reject him
That she did not know how to increase
His ills without adding death to them. 1396
But it seems to me,
Although Love joins our two hearts,
Fortune does badly in taking all my joy
By assailing both of us together. 1400
Let it suffice
That she harm me in many ways
Without overwhelming me
By taking away the sweet liberty 1404
Of seeing
The beloved who suits my heart so well
I could place it nowhere better;
I love him with undiminishing love. 1408
Weak and ill
He greeted the harsh day, his face pale,
After having composed many a ballade
In bed, where nothing seemed to him pleasing 1412
Or agreeable
Except his thoughts of love.
Even during his severe attacks of pain,
He did not stop thinking such thoughts on their account. 1416
But when the fever
Had passed from his body or stopped,
Then the other fever was on his mind
And kept his thoughts preoccupied. 1420
Nevertheless,
He could not have endured nor ever borne it
If he had not ventured onto the cruel battlefield

So that no one could spread
False rumors,
As people have done without reason.
But now all wicked men
Have ample opportunity to ponder their actions. 1428
And if they do not deign to do so,
Because of the pride they wallow in,
At least his deeds demonstrate to you
That they do wrong in wishing him ill. 1432
If only it pleased God
That my heart could replace his
As a hostage, and that no one could find
Reason to disapprove of it; 1436
Let us change places,
For then I would bear his sadness
And he would know how frightening it is
To think about that which captured 1440
His heart
And which he has not seen in a very long time.
He lives in a miserable prison
And I do not know how he bears it. 1444
I would welcome it
If it were thus or if it could happen,
For whatever became of my body,
My heart would remember my love. 1448
I would have to take on
His grief, and I would not care about
The pain that assailed me.
His well-being would count as a pleasure for me, 1452
For I am more wounded,
My heart more troubled and my body more drained,
By his great troubles, which intermingle
With mine and impede my thoughts; 1456
They harm me
More than my own troubles do,
Which makes my whole body dissolve into tears
And I sigh from the depths of my heart. 1460
More than one would think,
My pain makes place and space for his
And his is the guide for mine,
Full of grief and empty of tears. 1464
Briefly put,
My pain, should anyone want to tell of it,
Can surmount all tears,
Nor can weeping be of any worth. 1468

I have wept so much
That I have no tears left;
My heart languishes from it
And my face has lost its color   1472
And is damp.
My eyes have had no rest at night,
For in the day I dared not show
The sad heart in my ailing body,   1476
Weak and trembling.
I have made my laments secretly
And, to appear more like other people
While my heart is vexed, I keep up a joyful appearance.   1480
And if I dance,
It should not be taken as an abundance
Of joy or presumptuousness;
Instead, nowhere in all the dance   1484
(Of this I am certain)
Are there any thoughts more filled with sadness.
It used to bring me pleasure: now it brings pain.
There is no harp, no organ or dulcian,   1488
No lute nor
Other instrument that anyone might play
That I wish to hear henceforth
Since I do not have what I seek.   1492
Alas! I used to love them,
When there was nothing that
Troubled me; and I desired so much to hear them
That at the sound of them it seemed I was flying,   1496
With feathered wings
Of joy, and had I danced for a whole year
It would not have left me tired,
Spent, downcast, or weary.   1500
Love so
Encouraged and sustained me
With the joys he brought me
That my heart could bear the extra load.   1504
Everything was fine
And I was lacking nothing,
For I loved a man so worthy
That my heart did not care for anyone else.   1508
So abundant
Were my pleasures, which sprang from one man
And abounded in the same person,
That they countered all vexations.   1512
I was thus

Renewed, and steeped in happiness.
Two streams from a loving source,
Thought and Memory, set their 1516
Course toward me.
At that time they strove to please me
And brought me so many joys,
All of which came from one hand. 1520
But the misery
Of Fortune, cruel mother,
Has so troubled the clear waters of the source
That I taste in it nothing but bitterness, 1524
So much did she stir up
The streams all along their length and their breadth,
Flooding them with Melancoly
And mixing in Sadness. 1528
Oh, harsh War,
Why do you wish to triumph over me,
With no warning, so that by means of a prison
You deprive me of my paradise on earth, 1532
My happy countenance
And the joy I hold most dear,
Without reason or delay?
Toward me, Fortune is a strange 1536
And vexing archer,
And it seems that she is envious
That I ever had a happy life,
Full of delightful, sweet, 1540
And private pleasure,
Of which she deprived me unjustly
Like a wayward, wanton creature;
She takes issue with me 1544
Harshly.
Alas, Love, why do you bring to my
Weak heart a hundred severe pains
That should be enough to kill a hundred women? 1548
Nevertheless I live on,
Much worse off, in my opinion, than if I were dead.
Never in a living body have I seen such suffering.
I know not how I survive it, 1552
But I fear even more
That I am shunned and abandoned by Hope,
Who should be attentive to my needs
As the one who takes care of lovers 1556
And who should desire
That they be worthier because of him.

To decrease my suffering, Love made him
Captain of my will. 1560
Hope would leave
And absent himself often—
And Distress would agree to it—
If Regret did not hold him back. 1564
Often the door
Was opened wide for him
By Decline, overcome with ills,
But Remembrance retrieved him 1568
And brought Hope back.
In this state my poor heart
Feels tormented and pursued
On account of the one I love more than any man born, 1572
May God help me.
But I am alone and disconcerted,
For my heart, in one fell swoop,
Cursed me for loving well 1576
And abandoned me.
So now, in place of my heart, well hidden,
I carry with me Thought who is a cruel spy
And from whom I cannot be separated; 1580
So every day
Like a regular payment, Thought presents me with
His sweet semblance that represents
His person as if he were present. 1584
Then I am
Assailed by Thought who has given me
His sweet image and carved it
Into my weary thoughts 1588
And that no one
Can remove from there, nor banish,
Expel, wipe out or efface,
Without destroying body and will, 1592
For it will not
Be removed, as far as I am concerned,
Until my soul has passed on.
There will be a separation 1596
Only when one of us dies
And is no longer able to love.
The other will help the departed one in this need;
The one remaining will keep all the love 1600
For both of us,
For if he grieves and I grieve,
The last to die of the two of us

Will take on the vexations and the sorrows	1604
That the other holds now.	
That is just, because love endures.	
It belongs to the remaining partner, as next of kin,	
For the one who lives longer keeps it all.	1608
Love does not	
Make his legacies, his wills	
Or his bequests out of garlands.	
He who is unaware of that should try them.	1612
But no one	
Should waste time on love or delude himself about it	
If he wants to avoid great suffering	
Or does not know how to profit from great privilege.	1616
He who knows of it only from hearsay	
May make fun of it,	
But a bird truly caught does not fly away.	
One need not go to school	1620
To be wise	
In the ways of Love and of his powerful works.	
Learned clerks have no advantage in such things;	
Experience teaches much more than words.	1624
This I can assert:	
One's actions have much greater consequences	
Than one thinks they will beforehand.	
I speak as an expert on this matter,	1628
Not that I wish	
To say that I complain about it or suffer;	
It is enough for me that Love welcomes me	
Among his servants, no matter what pain	1632
I get in return.	
In order to take on a single servant, I serve	
Love, and, though well served myself, I enter into service,	
Which brings me worse than I deserve	1636
As recompense,[13] but	
Love, to whom I submit,	
Always serves his courtiers a helping of Pain	
As a tidbit between main courses;	1640
Otherwise, his servants	
Would gorge themselves, get drunk	
And overeat, and they would not accomplish	
Their duties and would leave his service,	1644
As I understand it,	
And find reason to quarrel with him,	
For few servants are content	
To live an easy life for too long.	1648

Love lasts
When his joys are deferred.
If lovers look back to past pleasures,
The fewer they have, the more ardent they are, 1652
For Love lures
Hearts like a falcon to the bait;[14]
Often he is led to believe
That he is being given what, in fact, is only lent. 1656
Hungry falcons are attached
To the perch to which their bonds are tied,
So that later, their hunger makes them chase
All the harder the prey they try to catch 1660
Without success.
And then, to encourage them, they are given
A bit of the prey to taste.
There is no better way to spoil the bird 1664
Than to feed him
So that he is fully satisfied:
If that happens, he flies off and leaves his master
And goes away to another place. 1668
For that reason I never
Blame Love, or any man or woman,
If after joy I am inflamed with grief;
I reproach no one but myself. 1672
But it weighs on me all the more
Because my heart is with one man, wherever he may go,
Who is such that never from French soil
Came a person more courtly than he. 1676
And may God
Grant me pardon, for I would hardly have believed
That Nature in such a small amount of space
Could have placed so much goodness and grace 1680
That in one single man
The goodness of all men could be amassed.
As to his name, who he is, what or how,
My voice keeps silent; it is my heart that names him. 1684
Desire inquires
After him, Memory asks for him,
Hope waits for him, Regret looks for him,
And Loyalty makes great demands on my heart. 1688
My glances veer
In his direction, my thoughts await him;
My ears listen for nothing
Other than to hear that his troubles abate. 1692
Everything works to the same purpose,

And even, to my surprise,
The pain that keeps me awake,
So that I can better keep vigil, itself stays 1696
On watch. And so
They all conspire to torment me,
To which my will assents,
And my heart does not regret it. 1700
I could indeed
Confess my grief,
But even though I do my penance,
I feel no repentance. 1704
The more tortured
I feel my heart, the more it is tempted
And takes pleasure in its affliction
In spite of me, by my willfulness. 1708
Thought besets
And troubles me greatly:
For he can change the lover who feels no bitterness,
Gladden and then kill him, 1712
As I myself know.
I have had long experience of both.
Since I first began to love I have not stopped,
Nor have I ever abandoned Thought, 1716
Who does not keep
His pledge, but changes it often,
Just like the weathercock in the wind;
He gives joy and then exacts a high price. 1720
But even more painful
Are the suffering and grievous thoughts
That come after short-lived joy,
Which begins but is not entirely 1724
Fulfilled or realized.
In the end, he who has complete joy
Does not know the true flavor of it,
For no good can be appreciated without a cost. 1728
Therefore I regret
All the more the very sweet charm
Of joy that Grief has made me forfeit,
Since I have endured pain because of its loss. 1732
I can see
That Love can no longer disguise himself
From me without my noticing him,
For he has revealed himself to be 1736
Just as he is described,
And he has shown me his various tricks,

Has prepared both good and ill for me,
Not in small measure but in excess. 1740
He has so exercised
His power on me, his devoted servant,
That he gave me long-awaited joy
And then made me pay for it 1744
So dearly
That my fortunes are in decline,
For Sorrow attacks me fiercely
When Hope fails me completely 1748
Without promising
To return or attending to the matter.
And then there is the sea
That comes between us, so that even a poor letter 1752
Cannot make its way,
Nor is there any news for me from him.
Since I must no longer see him,
If at least I received letters, 1756
Which brought
Comfort and lamented
The troubles that our two hearts amass,
Representing his sweet way of speaking, 1760
Humble and courteous,
At least I would recognize the hand
That has written to me, morning and night,
So many sweet words from one day to the next, 1764
And I would kiss them,
And though I would find little relief there,
And would scarcely rejoice,
In the meantime I would be somewhat soothed 1768
By looking at
His letters and keeping them safe.
This little boon is delayed by
Fortune, and I have a burning desire, 1772
No matter where I am,
That makes me want him morning and night
And pray with folded hands for
What I can least obtain. 1776
And so I lose my way,
For the more I desire him, the less I see him,
Even though in my heart I escort him
And send him my thoughts. 1780
And therefore,
Since his misfortunes were renewed,
Which removed him from my sight,

I have much less on these shores than overseas: 1784
Heart and will
Have left me, as well as anything of use;
I have my body, which is of little concern,
And the pain that makes me suffer 1788
Remains with me.
All the rest resides over there,
And what I have exhausts me;
It is a sorry remnant. 1792
Anyone who has no pity
For the condition imposed on my heart,
Which Desire keeps in distress,
Knows nothing of friendship. 1796
For that reason
I would like to ask the ladies of England
That, in order to earn praise for mercy,
They might inquire and ask about him 1800
On my behalf,
And commend his estate,
For one of them can appeal to those
Who can improve his lot. 1804
Truly, it is unlikely
That such worthy nobility
Not inspire many honorable thoughts
In an agreeable lady who commands respect. 1808
They can do much,
All the ladies together,
And their sweetness calls them to it.
What they have seen happen to me 1812
As a result of the fighting
Could happen to them if the war
Does not end shortly, striking them down—
And the higher one stands, the further one falls— 1816
If it turned out
That their situation worsened
And other events served them ill,
And that is equally true if it happened that we 1820
Gained the upper hand.
I know of no recourse
That could help me more than they.
I am between life and death, 1824
Sad and weeping,
Dying as I desire death,
Which is a long time in coming
When I have nothing else remaining 1828

Of Love, who defeats me
With no opposition on my part,
For it is not right that I fight him
And it does no good if I flatter him. 1832
These pressing ills
Were created by Fortune for me to endure,
And Desire takes in tribute
My entire will, which is crushed, 1836
On which he takes revenge.
When Hope aligns himself with Desire
The mix is all the more cruel for it
Than when Hope is lacking; it seems so to me, 1840
And thus I can say
That my suffering is longer and worse.
Desire hunts me down, Hope takes aim at me;
I cannot vanquish the one or flee the other. 1844
I am in this position
Because of Fortune who bears the blame for this,
Nor ever did a woman with more reason call herself
The saddest one who ever loved." 1848
Then she fell silent,
The lady with the sorrowful heart,
So as to recall it well,
But then she could speak no more. 1852
Instead, tongue and voice
Failed her, for from her heart sprang
Grievous sighs that so assailed her
That her heart and body trembled from it. 1856
So hard did her afflictions
Hit her that they stopped up her mouth,
And the sighs that racked her
Interrupted her gentle speech. 1860
Wringing her hands,
Shaking her head back and forth,
She was in such despair
That I never saw distress as great 1864
As she was suffering.
Her heart was so cruelly agitated
And her body labored so hard
That she then fell into a faint. 1868
Her gracious, lively face
Was pale and thin,
So harsh was the effect of the fainting spell.
Now, I had no smelling salts or vinegar; 1872
So then

I looked up and down a path,
And picked a branch of wild rose
And put all of it close to her nose,   1876
Right up against it.
And when the odor began to penetrate
To her heart, she grasped
The branch, so scented and prickly,   1880
And arose
From her swoon,
Like a man dazed, quite confused.
Then I recalled and said   1884
To all the ladies,
Exactly as the words came to me
Because of what had just happened
With the wild rose, which had revived her,   1888
That it is right that
There be joy and hardship in love,
For neither Reason nor Nature ever
Made anything sweet without a sting,   1892
As everyone can see:[15]
"Rosebushes that put forth roses
Have thorns, and always have had,
Which prevents us from picking them   1896
Without injury.
When picking, the hand is not steady,
For uncertainty frightens us,
Whether it be medlar or ripe chestnut.   1900
Love molds
His servants in a way similar
To that of the bee, which makes honey
In the hollow of an oak or an elm.   1904
There concealed
And hidden lies the great sweetness,
Packed tightly in the hive of sweet honey.
But it is dangerous to extract it   1908
Because of the hidden recesses
And the impenetrability of the tight spaces.
One must try three times and more
Before obtaining all the gifts there.   1912
And if someone
Comes and hastens to collect honey,
The bee comes to greet him
And he cannot retreat   1916
Or withdraw,
For the bee will rush at him,

And leave its sting in him,
Something he will not be guarding against.   1920
Then will he receive
The sharp point that he does not notice.
Not knowing, he will deceive himself about it
Until he is forced to suffer from it.   1924
When he takes his share
He will be struck quickly
With the sting secretly
That he will later see openly.   1928
For so worthy
Is Nature that sting and salve,
Gentle and harsh, all are born
Of one expression, or all of one root.   1932
One accompanies
The other so as better to take hold
Of hearts, and better to surprise them:
One soothes, the other wounds.   1936
And in short:
Pleasure is sweet, but timid;
The sting that pricks sharply,
That is Desire, who shoots skillfully.   1940
Love allows
That he who experiences some of his pleasures
And who is willing to serve him
Should have a hundred good and bad things together.   1944
To attract hearts,
Love gives some sweetness and then the opposite
Through Desire, which he deploys with skill,
So as to prevent them from withdrawing   1948
From his service,
For Love, by his rightful custom,
Is the prison of Free Heart,
Where Goodwill keeps him for security   1952
So that he will not try to escape.
And Sergeant
Pleasure gives them lodging there,
But Loyalty undertakes to have Free Heart   1956
Set free, and stands bail.
This prison
Is guarded by Desire who speaks little
Even though at heart he is of warm disposition.   1960
He breaks the heart and drives it mad,
And does not allow it
To leave, neither for gift nor for promise,

For Desire keeps Heart tied up on the leash 1964
Of Gaze, with hardly a pause,
And torments him,
Day after day, week after week,
Until Desire holds Heart under his dominion. 1968
And then he brings him before Fear
Who has the task
Of upholding justice in matters of Love.
Fear governs the administration 1972
Of Love, as the one best suited to the task.
There, the obstinate one
Is tormented at great length
And examined in front of Fear 1976
For what he has never stopped thinking;
There Heart must tell
At great length about his illness,
But even though he does his best to speak, 1980
He has no flesh on him so brave
It does not tremble.
It is proper that Heart fear the judge,
And he does not have it in him to speak properly 1984
Without straying from the topic a hundred times,
Even though on the ledger
Of Memory, he records everything.
But when the eye administers joy, 1988
The joy by entering prevents from departing
What resides
In sad and mournful thought.
It cannot leave, for their steps are taken 1992
All together; so it returns
Toward the heart
Where it stays, midway through the voyage,
Without delivering its message, 1996
Which thereafter leaves it enraged with grief.
We will be thus
As long as we love lovingly,
For we will not escape from Desire. 2000
Desire is the amorous goad
Who spurs the lover
At top speed toward the favors he seeks,
And causes him to pursue his quest, 2004
Which wearies him less the further he goes.
So it is with me,
For I have not ceased nor do I stop
Pursuing what pleases me, 2008

Which I am ill prepared to have,
And poorly versed
In how to handle misfortune.
But whoever loves truly 2012
Must have a strong and patient heart;
You must aspire to that."
Then the third lady said,[16] "Now listen to me.
You claim to be the most afflicted 2016
And you defend your cases well.
I do not complain
About that, nor do I hold your problems in disdain.
Every wounded person laments his injury 2020
And knows his case and his symptoms.
But of another's case
He knows neither the gravity nor the burden,
Nor can he assess it as well 2024
As the person who has experienced it.
You may speak
Very well, whether you say good or ill,
Of the hurt you claim as your own. 2028
But do not amuse yourself at another's expense.
You suffer
Your own troubles; mine you do not comprehend,
And therefore you should not compare them. 2032
You injure me by doing so.
But since we are
Engaged in comparing the harsh burdens
That make us lose rest and sleep 2036
For the sake of four lovers and four men,
I will not
Refuse; and it is not right for me to avoid
Recounting the pain that wearies 2040
My heart, which is abused by Vain Hope,
And in which dwell
More than ten score displeasures,
While not one single good appears there. 2044
Since we are comparing one misfortune with another,
From now on
I dare say, while upholding
My case and proceeding with reason, 2048
That the misfortune that has me in its grip
And is but a single one
Is itself the equivalent of your two,
Worse than either one or both of them. 2052
I have all of yours, not just a single one.

And so I boast,
If it is boasting to be unfortunate,
That my sadness is a heavier burden   2056
And that I am an unhappier lover
By far than any
Of you. One laments her dead lover;
The other, the capture and bad fortune   2060
Of hers, whom Adversity plagues
Unjustifiably.
The first deplores the loss
Of Hope, as if forsaken by him forever.   2064
The other says, 'Desire has ravaged
And exhausted me,
Not to mention untrustworthy Despair.
The more my desire drove me to believe it,   2068
The more my fear and pain increased.'
At great leisure
One lady laments past pleasures.
The other feels only displeasure,   2072
And thereafter she is assailed by desires
In many an attack.
Although one lady has grievous hardships,
All her ills befell her at once;   2076
The other still suffers new ones.
But the first
Says that she has more to lament
For she loses hope entirely   2080
And she is not so flighty
That she could
Love another man, no matter what good might be in him,
For she has never known what it is   2084
To transfer her affections, nor would it please her.
Though her heart
May be pensive, harboring Distress
And forging her worries,   2088
At least it is not fickle.
Now it is not possible
Or more sensible for her to do otherwise:
A change of heart is impossible;   2092
To go against her heart is not advisable.
She is obliged to love,
Though she no longer has her beloved
And she has no lover, nor anyone who equals him,   2096
For she cares for no one else.
The other lady argues

That she is sadder and more disadvantaged,
For Doubt and Fear assail her 2100
And Desire invades her.
Hope, above all,
Is harmful and painful to her;
It is the gleaming whetstone 2104
On which Desire hones his edge.
Hope urgently
Sharpens and urges on Desire,
Who prods and pricks her keenly. 2108
And Desire wears down and devastates Hope
In the long run,
Leaving nothing that can be salvaged,
Until it has consumed it entirely; 2112
It is a hard morsel to swallow.
Which tower is
In a worse state and the more fully vanquished?
The one that was taken some time ago, 2116
Or the other, under siege on all sides
And under attack,
Which no one rushes to defend,
And where there is no soldier or vassal 2120
Who can find a means of escape?
There is groaning,
Shouting, weeping, bristling of hair
And cruel weakening 2124
Of the heart; think about whether I am lying.
The other tower has
Finished suffering these alarming fears,
Even though its doors have been breached; 2128
It no longer needs watchmen or spies.
'Thus, by my soul,'
Said the second lady, 'is the case of the lady
Whose lover lies dead under the gravestone, 2132
May God grant him pardon for his soul!'
Although she has amassed
And stored up great grief
On account of her love, who passed on some time ago, 2136
The sorrow of it is soon gone.
My destiny
Is different and less certain.
I am like the undermined tower 2140
That has not been completely captured
Even after a long time;
One fears that it will fall

Or that things will turn out badly for those within; 2144
I fear that everything will crumble.
But all the more harsh,
Vexing, sharp, and bitter
Are my long and dark trials for me, 2148
For my suffering comes from cruel blows,
Not all contained
In one. And by God who made us all,
I have a hundred of them, and each is enough 2152
To defeat a strong heart.
Those two
Go along conversing, disagreeing with each other
And reflecting on their sorrow; 2156
Each maintains she is telling the truth.
But once they have finished
Claiming their rights and scrutinizing them,
My heart is still more marked by grief than theirs, 2160
Wounded more badly and pierced through.
And with no debate,
To put an end to all their arguments,
Wounds come to settle in my heart, 2164
And I have four for every one of theirs.
Alas! I do not know
If my love and fiancé
Is dead, captured, or held for ransom. 2168
And so I vacillate between
Hope and despair,
Full of fears, like a woman
Who feels pain but knows not what sort. 2172
I do not know which name to use:
Whether love's widow
Or prisoner. And I can find
No witness or proof concerning the one I love, 2176
Whether he is alive or not; this is new pain.
How I worried,
Talked to myself about my suffering,
When it was the battle I feared: 2180
Now I am less sure even than I was,
And less certain!
If I have any hope, it is in vain,
And I cannot lose hope without pain, 2184
Nor do I know what I am grieving.
Often I imagine
His death, which gnaws at my heart with grief,
And then I envision the prison instead, 2188

And do not know which of the two is the lie.
Whatever detains him
Is either death or harsh imprisonment;
This I know well, one of the two has befallen him. 2192
But it grieves me that I do not make haste,
Without further delay,
Plagued by enough troubles to kill me,
To reach the truth quickly 2196
Concerning what I should lament the more
And in large measure,
For obtaining reliable information
About his troubles would cut short 2200
My sorrows and bring relief.
No one would know,
Even though he might want to, how to comfort
Someone who did not know what he had, 2204
If it was clear to him only
That Grief was breaking
The heart that anticipated
Its pain and understood all too well 2208
That it would not get better.
Even after having walked
A fair distance and having sought to inquire
Where one will be relieved of such a burden, 2212
I cannot hope to get off lightly;
Rather, powerful love,
Which does not wish me to remain in this state,
Makes me inquire without delay 2216
What I am afraid to know.
To test
Hearts in which there is nothing to reproach,
Love makes them search and ask for 2220
What they would rather not find.
My thoughts
Are completely stalled in that fear.
I lament his death; I fear he is imprisoned. 2224
If I flee from one, the other drives me away.
So constricted
Is my heart, pierced by two darts,
Trapped between two misfortunes 2228
That it would be better off buried;
And so I contend
That I am the unhappiest and I stand by it.
And if someone should say, 'What is your complaint?' 2232
I submit both: death and imprisonment.

Adversity
Is such that by necessity
I have one of those misfortunes in reality 2236
And the other in fear and anxiety.
I suspect both;
Neither of them is to my advantage.
My suspicions run wild; 2240
That is a danger for anyone.
And so vie
Two misfortunes that battle within me
And struggle for control of my heart, 2244
With the intent of thwarting one another
Like brigands,
Pillagers and adversaries of joy,
And commissioners of my death. 2248
But they are not both false:
When I am able,
I will rescue my heart from one of them.
Nevertheless I will stay with the other, 2252
And live in sadness and die
Far away, in the shadow
Of Hope, of which I have little.
But the heart encumbered by Ardent Desire 2256
Counts time in days, nights, and hours.
The nights are so long
For me, interspersed with worry,
Ever since our voices were sealed 2260
With kissing and our tears mingled
When he took his leave,
The man I have since dreamed of so much,
Whom I love, before God, as much as myself. 2264
Now he is dead, or very far away.
Alas! who would have thought
That he would thus ask leave to depart,
And that he would take his leave, 2268
Without ever making it up to me,
Thereby diminishing
Our joys? The heart never realizes
That Love is so powerful 2272
As when troubles are vexing it.
Now I recognize
Love; no longer do I mistake him,
For he holds his tourneys in my heart 2276
And teaches me what worries are.
I have felt

Love's armed assaults ever since I consented
And agreed to enter his service, 2280
But I have never been disloyal.
Whoever holds a fief
From such an overlord, that bond is no game.
I hold from him but one heart; and by God, 2284
That heart, too, rests in only one place,
Nor will I place it elsewhere.
No longer will I concern myself with this;
Rather, I will submit to Love in such matters. 2288
I have promised; I will promise no more.
Thus I am tied
And bound by the bonds of Love,
And I do not feel overlooked 2292
If Death has not yet claimed me.
Love ravages
Hearts, and never has its fill.
It is a bird that lives on hearts; 2296
No one ever saw such a bird.
But it is
All the more honorable for acquiring
As its prey and its conquest 2300
The most noble of beasts,
Wherever it lies.
Love is similar to the guest
That one houses out of generosity, 2304
Who subsequently wants to take over
The house and the compound
Once he has moved in;
And he holds his host in greater subjugation 2308
While he is lodging there
Than if the man were in irons or bonds,
Making his lament.
For love is a pleasing pain 2312
And a great, hurtful comfort;[17]
It is a war that appeases,
A shield to take aim
Against, and it retreats to attract. 2316
Love obscures in order to display.
It is an ill that seeks its contrary:
A sweet harshness,
A gracious domination, a wholesome languor, 2320
A fatal pleasure, a frail vigor.
It is a generosity of heart,
A brave fear,

A most resolute cowardice 2324
An assurance that makes bold to fear,
An ambush that emboldens the heart
And that uncovers
And strikes the heart, and then recovers 2328
And closes it, and afterwards reopens it;
Love is the rightful master of the game.
And if anyone has pondered
Love's nature, which is not very thoughtful, 2332
It is an illness of the mind,
In which all joy is expended
In desire.
It is the illness that gets worse 2336
The more it gets better.
It is recognized from the sighs of the afflicted,
Not from the pulse,
As in all other illnesses. 2340
Joy and grief are its end points,
But grief is its final result,
For love ends
In grief when it has run its course; 2344
Other illnesses give way
To joy when they are over.
If Love heats
A heart in its great, smoky fire, 2348
He forges it into the shape and size
He chooses, like a blacksmith on the anvil,
Who, using fire,
Transforms a sword into a ploughshare 2352
And changes its nature;
The ploughshare nourishes, the sword slays.
And thus does Love
Mold hearts in the shape of his mold: 2356
He changes, transforms, and shakes them up,
Once he has enlisted them.
But he gives himself
More fully to hearts that are disposed 2360
To be well mannered
And devoted to noble pursuits,
Where there is courage
Or clear-minded understanding, 2364
And lovers are improved thereby;
Anyone who believes the contrary is lying.
Love wishes
To reside in a noble dwelling, 2368

Whether in a happy guise or sad;
He could not stay elsewhere.
He makes so bold
That he hurries the tardy, 2372
Emboldens the cowardly
And makes the valiant even braver
If they are such
As wish to distinguish themselves in the right places 2376
And take pains to become more worthy
So as to please the beautiful lady with beautiful eyes.
Without wavering,
They intend to be upstanding 2380
And oppose dishonor
In order to become her equal
And in an appropriate manner,
For it was the custom, in matters of love, 2384
That he who wanted to love a shepherdess
Would carry a shepherd's satchel
And dance to the sound
Of the flageolet.[18] Everything would be pleasing to him: 2388
Whatever she wanted, he would like;
Whatever she avoided, he would forgo.
Love is a thief
Of hearts, or at least knows how to alter them, 2392
Good to the good, and tricky with the tricksters.
Love is the golden fetter, inlaid with precious stones;
Whosoever trusts to it
Is caught but has no desire to escape. 2396
Love is beautiful sunshine, followed by rain;
At times it brings pleasure and at others is vexing.
Love fashions
His steps like a 'dance basse':[19] 2400
First he moves forward and then doubles back,
Then he turns, and then moves aside.
Thus engaged,
With all its resources committed, 2404
The will is driven mad,
Having sorrow and joy all combined;
So it declares itself
To be what others feel, see, or smell of it, 2408
And takes its example from the flame,
Which makes itself seen and sheds light,
But not without smoke,
For a blazing fire, 2412
Fanned and thickened by ardor,

Always emits either flame or smoke.
The lover betrays his feelings
When he sees his lady at a party or event, 2416
For either his heart must break
Or his composure crumble.
Great love demands
The entirety of the hearts it has struck; 2420
Every expression, every thought to be found
In a lover flow together into one,
Following the same path,
For small and larger streams 2424
Flow to the sea by different routes,
All descending there
In their own fashion:
The lover's thoughts thus come back 2428
Together; they pass through plenty of detours
And some amazing trials.
A trembling heart
Where sorrows gather portions out some of them 2432
To its conduct, actions, and appearance,
Or else they completely seize it.
Whereas it flees
From them when Desire has the upper hand, 2436
If he is the one in charge of the situation,
For the tone of the household is set by its master:
Thus do lovers
Pursue and strive for what they wish, 2440
Following Desire more than Reason;
And even their appearance conforms in this,
Accompanying them
As they stray from a direct path, 2444
Paying no heed to Danger.
Desire looks only straight ahead:
He looks neither behind nor to the right,
And thus the lover does not know the state he is in, 2448
For whoever is not master of his own heart
Cannot be master of his conduct.
And so my heart
Is enclosed in the loving enclosure 2452
All closed off with thorny hedges,
Which prevents me from leaving.
It is because of the sting
Of Desire, by whom I am so badly stung, 2456
And if I prepare myself to remain there,
I am a stranger to all comfort.

To leave
Is painful for me; to separate myself from it is hard. 2460
My heart has no one who can share
Its hardships; it is a solitary martyr.
So I am pulled
And martyred by two kinds of suffering, 2464
When the joy that I have desired
The most is completely ruined for me
By fear, so very
Strong that I do not know what to think: 2468
Whether I should fear or have hope.
Dead or alive, he is in my thoughts;
He has sustained
Them all. This is what has happened to me: 2472
I have retained nothing but the afflictions;
I do not know what has become of all the rest.
I have described
The hidden hardships of Love; 2476
But whoever else has examined them,
I know them to be harsh and stinging.
And so
You have heard me speak, sapped by grief. 2480
Am I then the least happy
Of all the ladies? Say, 'Yes!'"
I was a bit slow
To respond to her violent tale, 2484
But I wanted very much to say
That I was not the only unhappy one.
In this dispute
They were agreed, among other things, 2488
That I should record their arguments.
I do not remember everything they said:
Together they told
All the evidence that supported their respective sides, 2492
And they put forward so many arguments
That I do not know where they found so many
To such good effect,
Except perhaps that Love had filled 2496
Their hearts so completely with his art
That the mouth talks about it at such great length
And laments,
For just as the heart bewails its state, 2500
The mouth of a lover talks about
What the heart must feel;
When Love forges

His arrows in the heart, as he would do in his forge,	2504
The burning smoke that spews forth	
Issues from the mouth and is disgorged.	
Then I began	
To reflect on their case, for it is wrong—	2508
Lacking in good sense and frivolous in intent—	
To listen too late and judge too early;	
He is truly a coward,	
The judge who tires too quickly	2512
And swallows without having chewed	
When he renders judgment on cases all lumped together,	
Without pausing	
To listen to every argument	2516
That anyone wishes to make, and how one understands	
The rights of the parties, and the question at issue.	
For fear of doing so,	
I kept silent as I listened to them,	2520
Accumulating their arguments	
As they continued recounting their tales;	
And I concerned myself	
Only with thinking what I should say.	2524
I expected to hear nothing further,	
But the line of thought I was pursuing	
Ended, for the	
Fourth of these ladies spoke	2528
And interrupted my thinking at that point.	
The quarrel that had been discussed at such length	
Began anew,	
For the fourth lady thereupon	2532
Began a new lament.	
In gentle words, she challenged the others,	
And wept	
So much that her lovely eyes were bathed	2536
In tears to the point that she could hardly see.	
But she was ashamed at becoming so distressed.	
What troubled her	
Was Shame, which doubled her pain;	2540
And her sorrow was redoubled because	
In telling about her shame, she doubled it,	
Saying to them,[20]	
"My ladies, what are you talking about?	2544
I disagree with what you say,	
Not in order to be dismissive	
Or to anger	
Your hearts, which I hold more than a little dear;	2548

But concerning what applies to me
And what I hear myself reproached for here,
I must respond.
Great grief comes to exhort me 2552
To expound upon my most shameful case,
Which makes me completely dissolve in tears;
And I worry less
About the sorrow than the shame. 2556
I hear one of you who says
That because of me, her grief is greater,
Or because of him
Whom I thought better than he was 2560
And whom I loved more than anyone.
You did not speak of such a man today.
Now, he fled
Like a coward and ran away 2564
And so has forsaken honor.
And people say, 'Why was he there,
He and those like him,
When their harmful cowardice 2568
And their dishonorable flight
Caused the death of so many worthy men—
Thousands of them—
And caused the loss of the knights 2572
Who were the pillars of France,
Led away like oxen in a yoke
To perilous prisons
Where there are nothing but lice and nits?' 2576
Their laggardly, cowardly behavior
Has made so many ladies sorrowful
And tearful;
So many tears have been shed 2580
By many great ladies held in high esteem
Who are left alone because of it,
Just as you say.
And therefore all together you curse 2584
The fugitives for their failings,
From which they will never be absolved,
Since they angered
The good men, as has been said, 2588
And on account of which I have a heavy heart,
For I can be reproached
For having loved
A cowardly fugitive, vilified 2592
And accused of such dishonorable acts,

Who besmirched his good name so badly
As to flee
In such a situation and to harm others, 2596
Polishing his basinet
And putting on his armor just to run away!
Oh! What a day!
Foolish me, poorly endowed with sense, 2600
Why was I ever possessed to love him?
And why was I ever born that fateful day
Into such error?
The eyes that caused me the sadness 2604
Bear the pain and the tears of it.
Alas! How did I come by the cowardly heart
That pulled me in that direction?
I would have thought that, to hold back 2608
Or to flee or to attract,
A heart would have considered what good or harm
Would come to it before
It made its choice and took its pick; 2612
But I now perceive quite the opposite
When it is I who fail myself.
Love made me
Choose what was the worst for me: 2616
A man who grows worse from receiving favors
And brings about my martyrdom as a reward.
I will pay him back,
Even though my heart feels tender toward him; 2620
To all appearances, I will not concern myself with it.
Alas! To whom, then, should I complain
Except myself,
Since it was my heart that made my mouth say 2624
What I must now suffer for,
Carrying a burden heavier than a millstone?
That is just,
For I sought my own misadventure; 2628
So I do not blame inscrutable Fortune for it,
Or death, or the dire battle.
And I bear no hate
Except toward the heart that alone prompts 2632
My deceptive, empty thoughts
To seek pleasure and find pain.
I trusted in
False Seeming in league with 2636
Pretense, which strikes without
Warning, and then causes one to forget

Just like before.
Oh! Deceptive False Speaking! 2640
Now I am well aware
That your sweetness is more harmful
Than the beauty of a sunrise when it is
Accompanied by wind.[21] 2644
I knew nothing of your treachery
Nor that you would set forth,
Except when the heart prompts you to it
On rare occasions.[22] 2648
Who would have guessed that you would ever dare
Issue from the mouth through which you pass
Without providing a written safe-conduct
For the heart? 2652
The speech of a lover, by Jesus Christ,
Is the copy, in unwritten form,
Of what is inscribed in the heart
By passion, 2656
Which is solemnly examined
And collated by Truth
And related by the mouth
In the presence 2660
Of the lady who holds power in this matter;
And there should be no difference
Between what he says and what he thinks,
But nowadays 2664
Many make a present of words,
Saying, 'I present you with my heart,'
Without the heart being present there.
And thus they enchant 2668
Whoever believes them; they sing without joy,
And if they have no ladies, they brag of it anyway;
If they do have, they abandon them without cause,
Or invent a reason 2672
To blame them, without having any proof.
And there is the kind of man, wherever he may be,
Who takes a new lady every day;
I know it to be so. 2676
They know how to lie, how to make pledges fittingly,
And they vouch for one another.
But such a love is like snow,
Quickly spread, 2680
Or like the ice that forms at night
That breaks in half all of a sudden;
It is nothing but folly to rely on it.

And in truth, 2684
Even though they dress in cheerful raiment,
Keeping company with them and seeing them
Brings nothing but nonsense in return.
And they delight 2688
In relaying the biggest secrets
About the places they frequent and where they live.
They unburden their throats at will;
They are never 2692
Satisfied until they have insulted
With evil remarks the ladies
Who are all too easily duped.
They strive until 2696
They have stripped the ladies of their honor;
And so they are the same as those who kill,
For they never restore
The honor they take away 2700
With the words that fly out of their mouths,
When they chatter together thus
About their deeds and make merry together.
May God protect me 2704
From hearing this kind of talk from good men!
But as for the bad ones, may God mend their ways
Or else give them back their due!
For they desire 2708
That others who are inclined to the same sort of thing
Recount in their hearing that they saw them,
Where they went and what they did;
Then they are overjoyed, 2712
Telling them that they are mistaken,
And then they themselves spread it about so much
In other places that everyone must learn of it.
Such is their style 2716
That they name the street and the town
Or drop a thousand little hints,
Whereby everyone everywhere knows
All about the affair, 2720
Which makes the teller of the tale very happy;
For however much he dissembles or bides his time,
This is the result he is striving for.
Alas, alas! 2724
The person who leaves his reputation to be betrayed
In the hands of people such as these
Has begun to hate his good name!
But what bravery 2728

Will a man show in deadly combat
If he does not have the constancy
To keep his tongue quiet?
He could hardly prevent himself 2732
From fleeing from any danger
If he could not even hold his tongue
Concerning the good that came to him,
So as not to talk about it, 2736
And not allow to fly from his beak
What by all rights he should keep secret
Or be called a traitor.
Now let us notice 2740
The way in which one treachery
Attracts another, to put it thus.
If we pick out the deserters correctly,
Soon their deeds 2744
Will be proven blameworth
And they will be found to be fugitives
Who have proved to be false lovers,
Whose misdeeds, 2748
Whose immoderate misconduct—
Their sorry hearts concealed by arrogant conduct—
Have betrayed both ladies and kings.
And their transgressions, 2752
Which have left them so tainted
And drawn to indulgence,
Have prevented them from doing good,
For the indulgence, 2756
The great excesses and the vices
That sustain them, dolts that they are,
Hold them back from those noble deeds
That embolden. 2760
They become too soft from the easy life,
Which makes their hearts cowardly
And saps their integrity.
They no longer bother 2764
To travel nor to keep the company
Of good men, but rather backslide
From idleness, which makes their exploits come to grief.
So I say again 2768
That their vile and ignoble flight
Gives the victory to their enemies
More than the bravery and distinction
Of their betters. 2772
The good fighters of former days,

Were they soft and slothful, disloyal,
Did they slander and pillage?
Certainly not! 2776
They were all equally good;
But the world is dishonored—
And will be still—because these cowards did not
Bring help, 2780
For Honor has not been much in fashion
And no one has sustained it
Since the good Bertran died.[23]
They have dodged blows 2784
And stepped aside.
Profit has taken precedence over Honor;
Good men have enjoyed no advancement.
Instead, Self-Indulgence, 2788
Flattery, Recklessness, Duplicity,
Ignoble Heart, elegantly turned out,
Have ruled the day with Covetousness
Who led the way, 2792
On account of which everything came undone
And the public good was damaged.
No one followed the example of
Their ancestors, 2796
Who were wise and knowledgeable,
Strong, courageous, and patient,
Prepared for misfortune.
Everyone dresses up 2800
And wants to make merry;
They look like herons in a pool
Who are waiting to be told, "Watch out!"
And to be caught 2804
Without warning that others intend
To hurt them, and are learning
The tricks that take them by surprise,
Binding their wings. 2808
Many of them play the grasshopper
And in order to win large sums
They defend false causes
And devote themselves 2812
To the service of those who give them the most
And who intend to do no good;
And then the princes pardon them
And they are received 2816
Better than those who remained
Loyal, and always upheld

The rights they have defended so well.
And so Fortune rules, 2820
Following no route or path;
First it veers one way, then the other;
There is little one can count on in such actions.
Alas! Fleur-de-lis,[24] 2824
In which God long ago delighted,
Just as I read it in writing,
Your name is not shrouded
Nor are you defeated 2828
Or deformed by Dishonor,
For those of your house have done you
Honor by their perfect valor,
Some of whom 2832
Are now no more than dust. Those whom you engendered,
The charitable and kindhearted noble princes,
Comported themselves better there than lesser men,
For they were all run through, 2836
Wounded, beaten, and unhorsed,
Covered and crowded by the dead,
All either captured or buried.
Each man 2840
Took up his axe and struck about him,
But Fortune caught them:
Of the royals, none escaped,
For without turning 2844
Their backs in order to retreat
They all preferred to stay there
In order to endow their heirs with honor.
They encountered 2848
Such misfortune that they ended their lives there.
Oh, deserters! They showed themselves
To be so good that they pointed up your shame!
Now blush 2852
With shame and do not venture out in daylight,
For certainly, if you were worth anything at all,
You would not have abandoned such good princes
Who defended 2856
The field and sold their lives dear;
But the weak cowards split
The ranks when they took flight
To leave the place 2860
Without ever drawing a sword there.
There was no one who could
Pursue them at swordpoint,

So they 2864
Broke ranks and slipped away;
They left their honor behind them
And debased their lineages.
What would their ancestors 2868
Have done to them, what insults would they have
Hurled at them if they had seen them
Flee in that way? Their notable grandfathers
And fathers, 2872
Whose brave deeds are so illustrious, would have
Detested them and wished them an inglorious death.
These worthless men are nothing but old gossips.
We do not believe 2876
Until we see with our own eyes,[25]
But I doubt that we will have good fortune
As long as we are rife with sin.
Reason is shattered 2880
So much by corrupt living
That a man in tattered clothing,
Even if he is good, appears to stink
In company, 2884
Whether they be counselors or rulers,
All of whom are less diligent
In acquiring virtue than elegant apparel.
Thus a man 2888
Spends much more than is appropriate
On clothing and accessories.
He goes into debt and then repents of it.
The trick is this: 2892
If he has a rich lady, he plunders her wealth
And makes her outfit and clothe him;
He laughs at her and she ruins herself.
I know men like that 2896
Who have ladies in many houses,
Whose large assets they draw on
And are their mortal enemies,
In that they do not 2900
Maintain their loyalty nor all the rest.
They are today's sort of lover,
Much more idle talk than action.
In the street 2904
They ride along the paved path,
Each casting his eye at every woman.
Together they make a badly
Harnessed plough 2908

And they go about all scatterbrained.
They call every woman a shrew;
Nothing will ever be kept confidential.
If they rode 2912
Through a hundred streets, they would ogle every woman;
And the ladies who do not hate them
Cannot believe that these men give them less than
Their whole hearts, 2916
Of which the ladies all together have not a quarter.
Alas, the honorable profession
Of arms has no need of such men,
For anyone censured 2920
Has never thereafter been exalted
Or glorified or had a following in France.
How false these wastrels have been
In matters of love, 2924
For if stories are not mistaken,
True love makes hearts valiant,
Enterprising, and ready to attack
As well! 2928
If they love honorably
They live a life of integrity,
Which is congenial to everyone.
He gains much 2932
Who obtains from love what honor requires.
But those who, in serving love,
Impose dishonor on it, strike it with
Too quick a club. 2936
That is serving with disservice,
And it seems to me that such a servant
Deserves to lose everything
If he wants 2940
To impugn his lady's honor and betray it.
That seems much less like loving than hating;
It is not love, but rather hatred.
Alas, it is used 2944
Today as if it were a joke.
I see few men who fall in love or toy with it
Unless they have nothing to do or are killing time.
However things go, 2948
All they want is to love at their leisure
And that everyone does what gives them pleasure;
And let whoever wants to, bear the displeasure.
But if they understand well 2952
What love is when they are drawn to it,

The agreeable troubles that love renders
They fortify and improve their hearts.
He who fixes his heart 2956
On love tempers and strengthens it
And prepares it to withstand suffering,
Which makes him in every way more sound
And more assured, 2960
Solid in his values and more mature,
Neither too bold nor too timid,
And fortunate in battle.
And he who knows 2964
How to try to govern his conduct by love
Will know much better how to succeed
In managing his duties well.
He who strives hard 2968
To love must conceal his pursuit;
He must know how to behave and speak;
In this way he cannot fail to perfect himself,
And so, those who do 2972
Must be well loved and well renowned,
Named the true representatives of honor,
They who are so scarce these days.
Now, I believed 2976
That Love had guided my heart well
Toward a good man, not an arrogant one;
And he is entirely devoid of honor.
Would my heart 2980
Not have affirmed that it would always love him?
Now, no matter who might speak well of him, he is
The falsest man God ever made.
He sighed deeply 2984
At his departure, and put his hand
In mine, and promised me
That he was surrendering his heart
And he would do 2988
For me so much that there would be news of it
To his credit, much more than one would think,
Or he would never stop pursuing this goal.
And he told me 2992
That he wanted nothing other
Than to please me, and that he valued me so greatly
That he chose me as the guardian of his heart.
Then he embraced me, 2996
But the pain of love hardly wounded
His heart, which flew far away.

He thus made fun of me
Because I was   3000
Afraid for him, sad and frightened,
Full of fear, bewildered;
And even had he seen me drowning,
He would not have cared.   3004
Now, he fled when he should have fought;
His love for me was worth nothing to him
And his honor was neglected.
Safe and sound, unwounded,   3008
He returned from there, which makes me feel
Distaste and makes me hate more strongly
The man I loved more than anyone else.
And since then   3012
I have seen him often, which intensifies my pain,
For distance soothes the heart
While seeing him is aggravation.
So I say fie   3016
Upon my heart and no longer rely on it,
And I challenge it to fight to the death,
Since because of it I committed such a folly
As to fall in love with him   3020
First, two years ago in May.
Since then, I have undertaken to love,
For never have I called anyone else my lover.
Now it has come about   3024
That everything went wrong from the beginning,
And so, Love, who disappointed me so badly,
Will never again hold my relapsed heart
In order to damage it worse   3028
And to make it sigh like this,
If I can ever free it from him.
I can take a lesson from my own case:
He who, to have a beloved,   3032
Makes his heart the property of someone else
Must know what he is doing;
The hard part is reclaiming
A heart that has been promised.   3036
Why did I thus reveal it
Only for it to be so misguided
When I failed to put it to better use?
I am trying hard   3040
To forget it all, in order to recover,
But I cannot, at any price,
Get rid of either the love or the hate.

The love has been 3044
Settled there for a long time, and very strong;
His misdeed put the hatred there:
The difficult task is to remove them.
If a lover departs 3048
Or if he dies on some worthy mission,
The honorable action proves his loyalty.
But I have lost mine dishonorably,
Shamefully, 3052
In hideous infamy.
The others were pitiably
Captured, or died virtuously
For the crown; 3056
And whatever happened to the person,
There remains, at least, the good name,
Which resounds for life.
But more painful 3060
Is the injury that I am made to suffer:
I lose my servant who is alive and well,
And his honor, too, which predeceases him,
For in his actions 3064
He reveals his dishonor
By acting the coward.
I lose him by getting him back:
His shameful 3068
Return sets me free from him;
Getting him back is my separation from him,
And thus I am released from my promise.
Therefore Death 3072
Bears no blame for my grief—I absolve her of it.
Prison does not block my path from going
To see him. So there is no one to blame
But my own sorry self, 3076
Who would rather see death
Than have to blame my lover thus;
But one must drink one's own brew.
So I hate myself 3080
And all the words we ever spoke
At the place where we first saw each other
And the hearts that we gave over to Love,
The memories, 3084
The thoughts and the promises,
The looks and the expressions,
For which I bear grievous penance,
If I dare say so, 3088

For since the time I first loved him,
There has been for me no part or share
Of honor, joy, or praise.
Where there is no treachery, 3092
The honor, the goodness, and the dignity
That remain overcome the sadness
For a lady who loses her suitor on the battlefield.
But I, now, have no comfort; 3096
Instead his loss is even worse than if he had died;
And so I say that my pain is the greatest
And I wish to hear a judgment to know if I am wrong."
"So judge the case," 3100
The third lady said to me, "and summarize
The debate, and see to it;
But make sure you include
The claims of every lady, 3104
And say which of them is in the greatest quandary,
Which one sweats the biggest drops of blood,
When all avenues are blocked to her.
When spring returns, 3108
After a year's worth of masses, the first lady
Can properly find a new lover
In order to regain some joy and pleasure.[26]
The fourth can 3112
Do it as soon as she likes.
And if the second is grieving,
She finds her real grief in hope.
But poor weary me, 3116
My poor heart pines whether he is alive or dead,
Which means that perhaps I love alone,
And yet it is not right I give my heart elsewhere.
Without hiding anything, 3120
I can neither, to be brief,
Describe myself as having a lover
Nor change my affections and find a new one.
Think about that." 3124
Then the first lady called to me
And restated her arguments,
Concerning her lack of hope that she
Could ever have 3128
Joy, pleasure, contentment, or peace,
For she would never be able to find a man
As true, as noble, as perfect as the one
That Death deprives her of, 3132
Leaving her to take in Despair as a guest;

The others have Hope at their sides.
And then she asked me to take note,
Before delivering 3136
Judgment, that there is no reproach,
No prison, no loss so savage
That death cannot outdo it in causing grief;
It is nonsense 3140
To compare it to other trials
In which one has counsel or respite,
For Death has neither remedy nor dispensation
Anywhere. 3144
"For God's sake," said she, "judge rightly
And may your verdict be so just
That my rights are upheld in it."
Thus I had 3148
So much to hear, from so many sides,
That I did not know what I should do,
Nor did I know whom to listen to.
One lady spoke, 3152
Another lamented and grieved;
Many a tear ran from her eyes.
Each of them wanted to respond:
They explained their cases 3156
And cursed the battle
Each and every one; they heaped scorn on the deserters,
Praising those who lay dead
Or captive 3160
In the prisons where they are alive in bondage,
By whom the king was well served.
Those men have merited great reward
But do not reap it. 3164
They said so much that, had the deserters heard,
They would not at all have rejoiced;
And I believe that they would never have fled,
But rather would have asked 3168
For pardon, and marshaled their powers
Enough so that they mended their ways
And commended themselves to good men.
They were criticized there, 3172
And their actions made public,
As if they were men cast out
Or sent to the scaffold.
And if one of them 3176
Had been hidden nearby, well concealed,
Not even for a dukedom would he have wanted

Anyone to spot him or call to him.
Rather, you may believe 3180
That on account of his shame in this war,
If he was not able to leave in haste,
He would happily have gone to ground,
For one lady said of them 3184
That it would be a good thing if they were hanged,
And another said that no one should listen
To them, and that they should be barred
From upstanding society, 3188
From courts, jousts, and celebrations,
And that ladies should never
Be prepared to listen to their entreaties,
But instead 3192
They should be shunned with no refuge,
And everyone should flee those
Who fled from the field of battle
Like shirkers; 3196
And they have, like outcasts,
Damaged the honor and taken the money
Of the reigning king of France.
Then suddenly 3200
The second lady tugged at me, saying, "Fair sir,
Listen to what I want to tell you.
I think that you and I
Desire the same thing, 3204
And that my aims are also yours.
If you pronounce a verdict in my favor,
You can be sure that you will not be lying.
You know well 3208
For what reason and for how long
We have had no good fortune in France.
Everyone knows what this comes from, even though
People dissemble 3212
And avoid the truth and back away.
But we will never have joy, neither man nor woman,
As long as France lacks belief
And until people see things 3216
The way they should have from the beginning.
If one would only realize it, people believe
In lies more than in what they can see;
They thus banish 3220
The truth, and do not fear justice.
They listen to those who invent falsehoods
And lure them into sedition.

Then the simple 3224
Are amused and abused
By people skilled in evil deeds,
And, for their illicit pleasures,
They give them 3228
The chance, through deception
And false machinations,
To seek their own destruction
And to insult 3232
The man who is in danger for doing good,
Whose heart they would want to eat
In order to revenge themselves unjustly,
Thereby destroying 3236
The innocent man of splendid virtue,
Resplendent in his honor,
Who never did harm to anyone;
But he has been 3240
Attacked by the truly deceitful
Or by rustic officials of the judiciary,
Unfairly abused and then detested.
And there he was placed 3244
By Fortune, to whom he is subjected,
For he was not able to live with his friends.
Now he is captured by his enemies;
It would appear 3248
That earth and sky hate him
And that Fortune seeks his death,
When she does not let him live in peace.
Never did he know 3252
What joy was, nor did he have any;
And if he wanted to have it, he could not,
Because of the new troubles he endured
And endures still. 3256
His troubles are apparent to everyone,
Which causes my heart to suffer just as many;
Whoever says he has it worse is deceiving himself.
Death has hurt us. 3260
The matter is well known;
It cannot be concealed.
Never has there been such a case in France.
His other sufferings include 3264
Disloyalty, failure to respect homage,
The loss of friends and inheritances,
Insults, false statements,
And fabricated charges 3268

That have been leveled at him most unjustly.
Now, on top of it all, he is in prison,
From which he has not yet emerged.
So remember   3272
My claim, and there is no need to discuss the matter
Further, for whatever anyone might say,
I am in the right, and so the judgment must be for me."
I was well aware   3276
Of her great anger and I reflected on it,
But I held in high esteem the great love
That I saw in that lady.
She was so loyal   3280
That Fortune, however harsh and base,
Cannot diminish the dedication of her wan heart
Toward her very special love.
And so they lie,   3284
Those people who say and concur
That no matter what kind of love ladies feel,
They always desire to change their minds.
Such nonsense   3288
Is invented as mockery,
For—it is no falsehood—love is
More often destroyed by men,
And they are less reliable   3292
In these matters. Men maintain the fiction
That women are changeable,
But they have shown themselves to be much more
Inconstant than ladies,   3296
In matters of both the conscience and the soul,
For ten years now, during which they have been ignoble
And have proved to be less steadfast than women
In doing their duty.[27]   3300
This has become known in France;
They have returned with wealth
And they have not upheld the truth.
Then in battle   3304
They have fled like poltroons,
Showing that they care nothing for honor
And that they are lacking in loyalty.
Now, if they were to hold their tongues   3308
And stop assigning blame to women
For matters in which they do not deserve it,
If they were to recognize their wrongdoings
And their flighty   3312
Hearts, which spend their time acting shamefully,

Then with honor and good courage
Women could certainly seize
The advantage.   3316
I wanted to comfort this lady
In order to ease her vexation,
Nor could I give up on the idea.
I felt pity   3320
For the way Fortune thus overwhelmed
The man who had perfected all good qualities
And never caused harm to anyone.
So I said,   3324
"Take hope, and do not despair.
Do not yet despise Fortune too much
And do not be afraid of anything.
Do not think   3328
That Fortune will always be this way.
And if at the moment she stings you,
She will put everything back in good order.
And likewise   3332
I maintain, based on experience,
That an unhappy beginning
Gives promise of fulfillment;
Great sorrow or loss   3336
Without cause are a path that leads to good.
God does not cause us to suffer any unwarranted
Pain that is not later compensated.
He would not delay   3340
So long hold back your lover's joy
If He were not concerned with his eventual good
And if He were not saving a big reward for him."
Then, while I was   3344
Telling about these things,
And comforting the most excellent lady,
The fourth lady was deploring her case
Most bitterly   3348
And said, "I seek a pronouncement
That their contentions and their arguments
Do not work to my detriment.
All three say   3352
That the deserters, whom they curse so sharply
And whom they criticize quite rightly,
Are the reason why they are bereft, with suffering
That is endlessly renewed.   3356
So if their mortal suffering
Is the result of the action of the deserters,

I am much more affected by it than they are."
And so I saw 3360
And realized at that moment
That I could not succeed
In judging this case, and would do it reluctantly.
Then I seized 3364
A favorable moment, during which I reconciled them.
I detached myself from their debate
And made known to them another judge
And said out loud: 3368
"You don't need to hear my opinion,
For my knowledge is of very little worth;
But I will find you the kind of judge
You need, 3372
And then, moreover, I will inquire of that judge
So as to secure your favor,
And I will request a judgment for your case.
Everyone would agree 3376
That in matters pertaining to ladies,
A lady, for her part,
Would render a much better judgment
Than a man, surely, 3380
And would better understand the what and how.
I name my lady as your judge,
She who has no equal between here and Rome;
And she will know 3384
Which one of you is right
And she will not keep the truth silent.
I ask if what I propose will suit you."
They agreed 3388
And accepted my lady as judge
Once they had heard me say such good things about her.
And from my words they understood
That because of the good sense 3392
And the goodness I sense in her,
I consent to be all hers.
But I do not assent to tell her so,
And it will soon be 3396
A whole year since Love wounded me in this way.
He worked hard on my heart,
Which has not recovered its good health since,
But aggravated 3400
My suffering, which, since then, has not eased,
And beset me with every possible pain.
Alas, God, will I ever dare

Tell her? Dare? 3404
It would be better for me to keep my counsel
Than to propose such foolishness,
For I can suppose with great certainty
That she would 3408
Kill me by refusing.
Her exalted heart would never be mine,
For she would have to stoop too low.
I would not mind 3412
If only she knew; that would be worth much to me,
Whether she gave me her love or withheld it;
And she would not love me if she did not wish to.
I have often been 3416
Close to her, both winter and summer,
But one day I was urged to speak
And I told her, very willingly,
In private, without dissembling, 3420
That a lover must remain apprehensive for a year
Without daring to reveal the complaint
That belabors his thoughts.
She remembers 3424
Those words well, perhaps;
But if the memory of them comes back to her,
She knows that the end of the year is approaching.
Now may God grant me 3428
That eventually I find enough favor in her eyes
That her intentions toward me be such
That I may be forever better off.
Now she is the arbiter 3432
Of this debate that I am recording
And that I will provide for her to judge.
God grant that she acquit herself therein with honor.
The ladies strove so hard 3436
And paid such honor to my lady
That they left it to her judgment.
They wept as they left me
And gave me 3440
Their hands, and ordered me to say
That they commended themselves
To her and asked for her findings.
We traveled a long way 3444
Until we came to a crossroads
And at that spot we parted,
For we no longer followed the same path.
Then I turned away 3448

From there and stayed no longer.
I returned toward Paris,
For I am not happy unless I am there.
For that reason, 3452
In order to discharge my duty,
I transmit and deliver this book to my lady,
By whom I can live or die.
She will read it 3456
And will not refuse them
And then she will pronounce her opinion;
Thus we will know how things turn out.
But to make an inquiry 3460
About the matter into which I inquire
And find the most honorable means,
I send her this request
That I have written:[28] 3464
"To the most beautiful lady I see,
In whom I have placed for safekeeping my joy
And my heart, wherever I may be,
I wish happiness evermore, 3468
Good health, and long-lasting youth;
And that she may demonstrate to me her generosity
And her desire to relieve me of my distress
So harsh and great. 3472
And so in this I commend myself to you
Since I do not dare make any other request.
I have been commissioned to ask
Your opinion, Beautiful One, 3476
On a very novel question,
And I have put the debate about it
In this book, in rhyme, just as it took place,
Written out fully; 3480
And if I do not recount it as well
As it was told to me,
I plead ignorance as an excuse.
Now read it, 3484
If you please, in order to pronounce
From your own lips, or at least write out,
Which you choose as the saddest
Of these four loving women, 3488
Beautiful ladies all, good, and wise,
Who are sad and woeful
And who seek your verdict
On their debate. 3492
And you have considerable knowledge;

For this reason they have subjected themselves
In this matter entirely to your conscience.
This presumption   3496
I undertook at their request,
For they beseeched me strongly to do so,
Which I take as a command
And am thus   3500
Obliged to obey; I agreed to it.
This messenger came to me
And I consented willingly to the request.
It is the retreat   3504
In which I seek joy for a long duration
And when the heart moves there,
It draws the other limbs along.
Good will come to me of it,   3508
For when your hand holds
This book and when it suits you to read in it,
You will be reminded of the messenger
Who no longer has anything,   3512
Apart from his suffering, that is his.
And yet he desires truly
That for his great good, you might often
Be able to look at   3516
This book, and that you might read as well
Into his heart, and thus come to know
What power you have over him,
Acquired by right,   3520
For your sweetness won me over
And I did not seek a remedy for it;
Love was well aware and inquired into it.
May this little book   3524
Undertaken for your sake be well received,
For if there is anything of value in it,
It comes from the love with which I am smitten;
And if I have undertaken   3528
Too lofty or too foolish an enterprise
By putting myself in your service,
Do what you will with what is yours."

Here ends the tale.

Notes

The edition of the text on which this translation is based is Laidlaw, *Poetical Works of Alain Chartier*, 198–304.

1. This traditional springtime opening immediately sets the scene for a meditation on love. In the following strophes, the standard elements will be mentioned, including sunshine, tender grass, flowers of all colors, fresh running water, a sweet-smelling breeze, and a multitude of birds who have chosen their mates and whose singing and chatter represent the sound of love poetry as much as the new season. Nature is the force responsible for this renewal and affirmation of love and life. In contrast to the natural elements that surround him with happy regeneration, the lover-narrator himself will give vent to his despair, caused by unrequited love.

2. The lady to whom the narrator has lost his heart is never identified in anything but the most generic of terms. Having expounded on his melancholy here at the beginning of the debate, he comes back to the lady at the end, renewing his declaration of devotion and asking her to judge the cases of the four ladies.

3. After two short exchanges with the narrator, the first lady begins here her long exposition of unhappiness resulting from the death of her lover.

4. The first lady expresses the opinion that she would be far happier if her knight had been taken prisoner rather than dying on the battlefield. The speech of the second lady, directly following, will contradict her point of view.

5. The lady says she would commit suicide if it were not a sin in the eyes of God.

6. Once again, as in line 619, the first lady tells us that her knight died in service to France. Here she adds that the conflict was against the English. These details and others allow us to assume that the conflict in which all four of the ladies' lovers came to a bad end was the battle of Agincourt, which took place in 1415.

7. Throughout her speech, the first lady has praised loyalty as a knight's most important virtue, including loyalty to his lady and his country. Here she begins to lambaste, in strong language, those soldiers who deserted the French forces at Agincourt and thus put their comrades at risk. This passage bears directly on the plight of the fourth lady, below.

8. Here begins the speech of the second lady, whose knight was taken prisoner in the battle. Her argument for insisting that she suffers more than the first is that she is full of fear and dread as to the fate of her lover, whereas the first lady, knowing that her knight has died, need no long worry about his suffering and whether she will see him again. The second lady explains that her lover has been a victim of bad Fortune since his youth.

9. The gist of this difficult sentence seems to be that Fortune, when she has exhausted her usual tricks, prefers to change herself, in order to come up with new ideas, rather than give up her harsh treatment of this particular knight. Her tricks are described at greater length starting at line 1265.

10. We can assume that the "foreign, maritime land" of line 1288 ("terre estrange et maronniere") where the lady's knight is imprisoned is England. On the basis of details mentioned in the second lady's speeches, Laidlaw posits that the knight in question here might be Charles d'Orléans, who was taken prisoner at Agincourt. The lady says expressly that she will not identify him—"As to his name, who he is, what or how, / My voice keeps silent; it is my heart that names him" (1683–84)—but the emphasis she puts on the bad fortune her knight experienced before his capture certainly fits with Charles's experience. As a youth he lost his father (Louis d'Orléans), mother (Valentina Visconti), and first wife

(Isabelle of France, daughter of Charles VI). If this knight were Charles d'Orléans, the lady might be his second wife, Bonne, daughter of the count of Armagnac. For details of this hypothetical identification, see Laidlaw, *Poetical Works*, 35–36. Lines 1474–80 might undermine the argument; if the second lady were her lover's wife, she could and should show her grief openly.

11. The one man who sings is the one on whom the lady has distributed "love's riches" (1335). The others grieve because they were not favored by her.

12. This provides a good example of what is lost in translation. The original passage reads ". . . tant l'amoie / Et aime que je le nommoie / 'Tout mien,' et lui moy 'toute moie'" (1369–71). There is, of course, the matter of gender: English lacks a masculine form of "all mine" for the term of endearment the lady used for the knight and a feminine form for what he called her. Moreover, Middle French had two forms for the first-person-singular possessive pronoun, represented here by "mien" and "moie." The variety of morphological forms is reduced in standard modern English to the term *mine*.

13. The passage that ends here is notable for its dense repetition of words, both nouns and verbs, with the root *to serve*. In the original there are six of them in the four lines 1633–36. There is a similar passage at lines 2936–39.

14. The heart of the lover is compared here and in the following lines to a bird of prey like the falcon, trained to hunt by being given no more than a small taste of what it catches. Hunting metaphors like this one are common in descriptions of the yearning and hunger experienced by the lover and the tight control Love exercises over him.

15. The narrator intervenes here, inspired by the roses with which he has revived the second lady from her faint. He develops, first, a long metaphor that compares Love to a bee, which provides sweetness but also stings. He then launches an allegorical description of Love as the prison of Free Heart. He ends with a brief reference to his own troubles in love (lines 2006–11) before the third lady begins to speak.

16. The third lady begins to make her case here. Without acknowledging the narrator's intervention, she addresses the two other women who have spoken, maintaining that her suffering is worse than theirs because she has all of their pain combined (see lines 2045–52). She suffers from Vain Hope (line 2041) as well as from her uncertainty regarding the fate of her knight, having to imagine him both in prison and dead. Before giving the details of her own situation, she summarizes the arguments of the first two speakers.

17. The third lady elaborates here on a standard description of love as the paradoxical "golden fetter" (2394) that brings both pleasure and pain.

18. The flageolet is a small flute of the sort that shepherds might carry with them to make music in the pastures.

19. Laidlaw glosses Chartier's term *dance basse* as a "slow and rather stately dance" (*Poetical Works*, 456 n. 2400). For the definition he cites E. Huguet, *Dictionnaire de la langue française du XVIe siècle* (Paris: Champion, Didier, 1925–67). The lady's description of the steps involved is not precise enough to identify it further. The point of this dance metaphor is that love choreographs affairs of the heart, putting the lover through complicated paces.

20. The fourth and last lady begins her speech here. Although she, like the others, is full of sorrow, her greatest affliction is shame because she loved a man who proved to be a deserter. She laments not only her own pain but the lack of good knights in comparison with former days.

21. This comparison may be a nautical reference. A sunrise that promises good weather can be treacherous to the sailor if accompanied by a stiff wind.

22. My rendering of lines 2645–48 is inspired by Laidlaw, who translates this difficult passage as "I did not realise your treachery or that you would set out except when the heart leads you to do so at long intervals" (*Poetical Works*, 457). The metaphor, according to Laidlaw, is that of False Speaking undertaking a journey. The lady is used to hearing a lover speak of love only occasionally, when his heart prompts him to overcome his customary fear of declaring his feelings.

23. Laidlaw, *Poetical Works*, 458 n. 2783, identifies "Bertran" as Bertran du Guesclin (1320–80), who was Constable of France for the last decade of his life under Charles V. Christine de Pizan also uses him in the *Debat de deux amans*, lines 1569–85, as an example of a knight renowned for chivalry.

24. The fleur-de-lis represents, of course, the royal house of France. The lady is saying that the kings and princes of the realm acted honorably; they suffered heavy losses and are not to blame for the defeat of the French forces.

25. Laidlaw, *Poetical Works*, 458 n. 2876–77, identifies this as a biblical reference, alluding to John 20. See verses 25–29, in which Thomas will not believe that the other disciples have seen Jesus until he has seen Him with his own eyes.

26. The first lady can legitimately take a new lover after mourning her dead knight by saying the necessary prayers for a year.

27. Laidlaw sees the allusion in lines 3295–3300 to the inconstant behavior of men in France for the last ten years—"Puis dix ans" (3298)—as a reference to the civil war that started in 1405 between the Burgundian and Orleanist factions (*Poetical Works*, 35). In this passage of his introduction, Laidlaw puts these words into the mouth of the second lady; his punctuation of the text, however, attributes them to the narrator's unexpressed thoughts, with which I agree. The narrator is not only blaming the factional comportment of French noblemen but also praising women for their constant nature.

28. What follows is the text of the request the narrator says he composed to accompany the debate that he is sending to his lady. The opening uses the standard format for a formal letter. Sending her the debate he has recorded and asking her to judge it gives him an opportunity to try to further his own suit with her. The book he sends her will remind her of him and stand as a token of his love.

Bibliography

Alain Chartier

Primary Sources

Laidlaw, J. C., ed. *The Poetical Works of Alain Chartier*. Cambridge: Cambridge University Press, 1974.

Secondary Sources

Blumenfeld-Kosinski, Renate. "Two Responses to Agincourt: Alain Chartier's *Livre des quatre dames* and Christine de Pizan's *Epistre de la prison de vie humaine*." In *Contexts and Continuities: Proceedings of the IVth International Colloquium on Christine de Pizan (Glasgow 21–27 July 2000), Published in Honour of Liliane Dulac*, edited by Angus J. Kennedy, with Rosalind Brown-Grant, James C. Laidlaw, and Catherine M. Muller, 1:75–85. Glasgow: University of Glasgow Press, 2002.

Cayley, Emma J. "Drawing Conclusions: The Poetics of Closure in Alain Chartier's Verse." *Fifteenth-Century Studies* 28 (2003): 51–64.

Hirschel, Grete. *Le livre des quatre dames von Alain Chartier: Studien zur französischen Minnekasuistik des Mittelalters*. Wertheim a.M.: E. Bechstein, 1930.

Hoffman, Edward Joseph. *Alain Chartier, His Work and Reputation*. New York: Wittes, 1942. Reprint, Geneva: Slatkine, 1975.

Meyenberg, Regula. *Alain Chartier, prosateur et l'art de la parole au XVe siècle: Etudes littéraires et rhétoriques*. Bern: Francke, 1992.

Geoffrey Chaucer

Primary Sources

Benson, Larry D., ed. *The Riverside Chaucer*. 3rd ed. Boston: Houghton Mifflin, 1987.

Secondary Sources

Blamires, Alcuin. *The Case for Women in Medieval Culture*. Oxford: Clarendon Press, 1997.

Delany, Sheila. *The Naked Text: Chaucer's Legend of Good Women*. Berkeley and Los Angeles: University of California Press, 1994.

Frank, Robert Worth, Jr. *Chaucer and the Legend of Good Women*. Cambridge, Mass.: Harvard University Press, 1972.

Fyler, John M. *Chaucer and Ovid*. New Haven, Conn.: Yale University Press, 1979.

Green, Richard Firth. *Poets and Princepleasers: Literature and the English Court in the Late Middle Ages*. Toronto: University of Toronto Press, 1980.

Kiser, Lisa J. *Telling Classical Tales: Chaucer and the Legend of Good Women*. Ithaca, N.Y.: Cornell University Press, 1983.

Payne, Robert O. *The Key of Remembrance: A Study of Chaucer's Poetics.* New Haven, Conn.: Yale University Press, 1963.

Percival, Florence. *Chaucer's Legendary Good Women.* Cambridge: Cambridge University Press, 1998.

Guillaume de Machaut

Primary Sources

Palmer, R. Barton, ed. and trans. *Guillaume de Machaut: The Judgment of the King of Bohemia/Le Jugement dou Roy de Behaingne.* New York: Garland, 1984.

———, ed. and trans. *Guillaume de Machaut: The Judgment of the King of Navarre.* New York: Garland, 1988.

Secondary Sources

Calin, William. *A Poet at the Fountain: Essays on the Narrative Verse of Guillaume de Machaut.* Lexington: University of Kentucky Press, 1974.

Cosman, Madeleine Pelner, and Bruce Chandler, eds. *Machaut's World: Science and Art in the Fourteenth Century.* New York: New York Academy of Sciences, 1978.

Earp, Lawrence. *Guillaume de Machaut: A Guide to Research.* New York: Garland, 1995.

Palmer, R. Barton, ed. *Chaucer's French Contemporaries: The Poetry/Poetics of Self and Tradition.* New York: AMS Press, 1999.

Wimsatt, James I. *Chaucer and His French Contemporaries: Natural Music in the Fourteenth Century.* Toronto: University of Toronto Press, 1991.

Christine de Pizan

Primary Sources

Altmann, Barbara K., ed. *The Love Debate Poems of Christine de Pizan.* Gainesville: University Press of Florida, 1998.

Blumenfeld-Kosinski, Renate, ed. and trans., and Kevin Brownlee, trans. *The Selected Writings of Christine de Pizan: New Translations, Criticism.* New York: W. W. Norton, 1997.

Roy, Maurice, ed. *Œuvres poétiques de Christine de Pisan.* 3 vols. SATF. Paris: Firmin Didot, 1886–96.

Willard, Charity Cannon, ed. *The Writings of Christine de Pizan.* New York: Persea, 1993.

Secondary Sources

Altmann, Barbara K. "Reopening the Case: Machaut's *Jugement* Poems as a Source in Christine de Pizan." In *Reinterpreting Christine de Pizan,* edited by Earl Jeffrey Richards, Joan Williamson, Nadia Margolis, and Christine Reno, 137–56. Athens: University of Georgia Press, 1992.

Altmann, Barbara K., and Deborah L. McGrady, eds. *Christine de Pizan: A Casebook.* New York: Routledge, 2002.

Hicks, Eric. *Le Débat sur le "Roman de la rose."* Paris: Champion, 1977.

McLeod, Enid. *The Order of the Rose: The Life and Ideas of Christine de Pizan.* London: Chatto and Windus, 1976.

Willard, Charity Cannon. *Christine de Pizan: Her Life and Works.* New York: Persea, 1984.

———. "Lovers' Dialogues in Christine de Pizan's Lyric Poetry from the *Cent Ballades* to the *Cent ballades d'amant et de dame.*" *Fifteenth-Century Studies* 4 (1981): 167–80.

General

Armstrong, Adrian. "The Deferred Verdict: A Topos in Late-Medieval Poetic Debates?" *French Studies Bulletin* 64 (1997): 12–14.

Badel, Pierre-Yves. "Le Débat." In *La Littérature française aux XIVe et XVe siècles,* edited by Jean Frappier, Daniel Poirion, and Aurelio Roncaglia, 95–110. Grundriss der romanischen Literaturen des Mittelalters 8.1. Heidelberg: Carl Winter, 1988.

Baird, Joseph L., and John R. Kane, eds. *La Querelle de la Rose: Letters and Documents.* Chapel Hill: University of North Carolina Press, 1978.

Boase, Roger. *The Origin and Meaning of Courtly Love: A Critical Study of European Scholarship.* Manchester: Manchester University Press, 1977.

Bossy, Michel-André, ed. and trans. *Medieval Debate Poetry: Vernacular Works.* New York: Garland, 1987.

Calin, William. *The French Tradition and the Literature of Medieval England.* Toronto: University of Toronto Press, 1994.

Cerquiglini-Toulet, Jacqueline. *The Color of Melancholy: The Uses of Books in the Fourteenth Century.* Trans. Lydia G. Cochrane. Baltimore: Johns Hopkins University Press, 1997.

Champion, Pierre. *Histoire poétique du quinzième siècle.* Paris: Champion, 1923.

Hult, David F., and Joan E. McRae, eds. *Le Cycle de "La Belle Dame sans Mercy": Une Anthologie poétique du XVe siècle.* Paris: Champion, 2003.

Kelly, Douglas. *Medieval Imagination: Rhetoric and the Poetry of Courtly Love.* Madison: University of Wisconsin Press, 1978.

Kibler, William W., trans. *Chrétien de Troyes: Arthurian Romances.* Harmondsworth: Penguin, 1991.

Oulmont, Charles. *Les Débats du clerc et du chevalier dans la littérature poétique du Moyen-Age.* Paris: Champion, 1911. Reprint, Geneva: Slatkine, 1974.

Palmer, R. Barton. *Medieval English and French Legends: An Anthology of Religious and Secular Narrative.* Glen Allen, Md.: College Publishing, 2006.

———. *Medieval Epic and Romance: An Anthology of English and French Narrative.* Glen Allen, Md.: College Publishing, 2006.

Poirion, Daniel. *Le Poète et le prince: L'Evolution du lyrisme courtois de Guillaume de Machaut à Charles d'Orléans.* Paris: Presses Universitaires de France, 1965.

Walsh, P. G., ed. and trans. *Andreas Capellanus on Love.* London: Duckworth, 1982.

Zink, Michel. *Medieval French Literature: An Introduction.* Translated by Jeff Rider. Binghamton, N.Y.: Medieval and Renaissance Texts and Studies, 1995.

www.ingramcontent.com/pod-product-compliance
Lightning Source LLC
Chambersburg PA
CBHW021333230426
43666CB00006B/282